The Guy Liddell Diaries, Vol. I: 1939–1942

WALLFLOWERS is the codename given to one of the Security Service's most treasured possessions, the daily journal dictated from August 1939 to June 1945 by MI5's Director of Counter-Espionage, Guy Liddell, to his secretary, Margo Huggins. The document was considered so highly classified that it was retained in the safe of successive Directors-General, and special permission was required to read it.

Liddell was one of three brothers who all won the Military Cross during World War I and subsequently joined MI5. He initially served with the Metropolitan Police Special Branch at Scotland Yard, dealing primarily with cases of Soviet espionage, until he was transferred to MI5 in 1931. His social connections proved important: in 1940 he employed Anthony Blunt as his personal assistant and he became a close friend of both Guy Burgess and Victor Rothschild, and was acquainted with Kim Philby. Despite these links, when Liddell retired from the Security Service in 1952 he was appointed security adviser to the Atomic Energy Commission, an extremely sensitive post following the conviction of the physicist Klaus Fuchs two years earlier.

No other member of the Security Service is known to have maintained a diary and the twelve volumes of this journal represents a unique record of the events and personalities of the period, a veritable *tour d'horizon* of the entire subject. As Director, B Division, Liddell supervised all the major pre-war and wartime espionage investigations, maintained a watch on suspected pro-Nazis and laid the foundations of the famous 'double cross system' of enemy double agents. He was unquestionably one of the most reclusive and remarkable men of his generation, and a legend within his own organisation.

Nigel West is a military historian specialising in security and intelligence topics. He lectures at the Center for Counterintelligence and Security Studies in Washington DC and is the European editor of the *World Intelligence Review*. In 1989 he was elected 'the Expert's Expert' by the *Observer* and in 2003 he was the recipient of the US Association of Former Intelligence Officer's Lifetime Literature Achievement Award.

THE
GUY LIDDELL DIARIES

VOLUME I: 1939–1942

MI5's Director of Counter-Espionage
in World War II

Edited by Nigel West

Routledge
Taylor & Francis Group

LONDON AND NEW YORK

First published 2005
by Routledge
2 Park Square, Milton Park
Abingdon, Oxfordshire
OX14 4RN

Simultaneously published in the USA and Canada
by Routledge
270 Madison Ave,
New York
NY 10016

Routledge is an imprint of Taylor & Francis Group

© 2005 Westintel

Typeset in Bembo by GreenGate Publishing Services, Tonbridge

Printed and bound in Great Britain by MPG Books Ltd, Bodmin

British Library Cataloguing in Publication Data
A catalogue record for this book is available from the British Library

Library of Congress Cataloging in Publication Data
Liddell, Guy Maynard, 1892-1958.
The Guy Liddell diaries : MI5's director of counter-espionage in World War II / Nigel West.
p. cm.
Includes bibliographical references and index.
ISBN 0-415-35213-4 (hardback) – ISBN 0-415-35214-2 (pbk.)
1. Liddell, Guy Maynard, 1892-1958–Diaries. 2. Great Britain. MI5–History–20th century.
3. World War, 1939-1945–Secret service–Great Britain. 4. Espionage–Great Britain–History–
20th century. 5. Spies–Great Britain–Diaries. I. West, Nigel. II. Title.

D810.S8L554 2005
940.54'8641'092–dc22
2004017333

ISBN 0-415-35213-4

CONTENTS

EDITOR'S NOTE

The original diaries were written in twelve volumes, each with a separate index, and contain many acronyms, abbreviations and references to people and organisations that are not immediately identifiable. Accordingly, the editor has interpolated to clarify and explain. Where possible, names have been given in full, but the diaries have been redacted by the Security Service so some individuals and passages remain obscure. There are, however, several lapses in the redactions, so it is perfectly possible to identify Rex Howard, Cuthbert Bowlby, Walter Bell, Tim Milne and Phillip Johns as SIS officers whose names have not been obliterated entirely.

In addition, some codenames have been altered to avoid confusion. For example, the double agent Sam McCarthy is referred to in Liddell's early diaries by the codename MAC, whereas this was later changed, probably as a security precaution, to BISCUIT.

The additional information added is based on the editor's personal knowledge of BALLOON, BRONX, BRUTUS, COBWEB, DREADNOUGHT, FREAK, GARBO, GIRAFFE, JEFF, METEOR, MUTT, TATE, TRICYCLE, and ZIGZAG, and interviews conducted with many wartime MI5 officers, among them T.A. Robertson, Michael Ryde, Rupert Speir, Gerald Glover, Peter Ramsbotham, Peter Hope, John Gwyer, Leonard Burt, John Maude, Billy Luke, Cyril Mills, Hugh Astor, Herbert Hart, Christopher Harmer and Russell Lee. From SIS he was able to discuss wartime operations with Hugh Trevor Roper, Felix Cowgill, Phillip Johns and John Codrington, all of whom are mentioned repeatedly in the diaries.

ACKNOWLEDGMENTS

The editor owes a debt of gratitude to Thomas Cheplick, who toiled in the National Archive at Kew in the preparation of this volume. Also to Hayden Peake, Ray Batvinis, Dan Mulvenna and Glenmore Trenear-Harvey who gave generously of their specialist knowledge of this field. The project could not have been completed without them.

Among the members of the Liddell family who assisted my research were Sir Sandy Reid, Leonard Ingrams, Georgina Rowse, Joan Booth and Theresa Booth.

PERSONALITIES

Goesta Caroli	MI5's double agent codenamed SUMMER
Tony Caulfield	MI5 officer
Bill Cavendish-Bentinck	Chairman of the Joint Intelligence Committee
CELERY	MI5 codename for Walter Dicketts
Edwin Clayton	Assistant DPP
Hugh Clegg	FBI official
COBWEB	Ib Riis, SIS double agent in Iceland
John Codrington	SIS Head of Station in Gibraltar
William Codrington	Head of the Foreign Office's Security Department
COLOMBINE	SS defector Zech-Nantwich
Patrick Cooper	Ministry of Supply
COSTAR	Double agent at the British Legation in Lisbon
Felix Cowgill	Deputy Head of SIS's Section V
William Charles Crocker	Member of the Security Executive
Malcolm Cumming	MI5 officer
Edward Cussen	MI5 officer
Edouard Daladier	French Prime Minister
Claude Dansey	Assistant Chief, SIS
Captain Daru	French intelligence officer
General Francis Davidson	Director of Military Intelligence
Dawkes	MI5 agent
Dr Harold Dearden	MI5 psychiatrist and Camp 020 medical officer
Alastair Denniston	Director of Government Code & Cipher School
Walter Dicketts	MI5 double agent codenamed CELERY
Deputy Director-General	Sir Eric Holt-Wilson
Director-General	Major-General Sir Vernon Kell
Richard Dixon	Regional Security Liaison Officer
DRAGONFLY	MI5 double agent named Hans George
DUCK	MI5 agent in the Spanish Embassy in London
John Dulanty	High Commissioner for Ireland in London
Bertram Ede	Defence Security Officer, Malta
Dick Ellis	SIS officer attached to BSC in New York
FATHER	MI5 codename for a Belgian pilot and double agent
Donald Fish	Scotland Yard detective seconded to MI5
David Footman	SIS officer, Head of Section I
Major Foulkes	MI5 officer seconded to SOE
FRANK	MI5 agent
Malcolm Frost	MI5 officer seconded from the BBC
Roger Fulford	MI5 officer
Friedle Gaertner	MI5 double agent codenamed GELATINE
Richard Gambier-Parry	Head of SIS's Section VIII and the RSS
GANDER	Carl Grosse
GELATINE	MI5 codename for Friedle Gaertner
Hans George	MI5 double agent codenamed DRAGONFLY

E.W. Gill	MI5 wireless expert
Tony Gillson	MI5 officer
GIRAFFE	MI5 double agent named Georges de Graaf
Gerald Glover	RSLO in Kent
Admiral John Godfrey	Director of Naval Intelligence
GOOSE	Kurt Grosse
Georges de Graaf	MI5 double agent codenamed GIRAFFE
Laurence Grand	Head of SIS's Section D
Kurt Grosse	MI5's double agent codenamed GOOSE
Lord Halifax	Foreign Secretary
Jasper Harker	Director, B Division
Christopher Harmer	MI5 case officer
Tommy Harris	MI5 case officer in the Spanish Section
Herbert Hart	MI5 officer and analyst
HATCHET	MI5 double agent Albert de Jaeger
Ronnie Haylor	MI5 officer
Edwin Herbert	Director of Postal Censorship
Clarence Hince	FBI official
Edward Hinchley-Cooke	MI5 interrogator
Sir Sam Hoare	British Ambassador in Madrid
Roger Hollis	MI5's expert on the CPGB
Jack Hooper	SIS officer
Henry Hopkinson	Sir Alexander Cadogan's private secretary
Reg Horrocks	MI5's management efficiency expert
Commandant Howard	French BCRA intelligence officer
Rex Howard	SIS officer
Harry Hunter	Head of MI5's Watcher Service
Gladwyn Jebb	Deputy Secretary, Foreign Office
JEFF	MI5 double agent Tor Glad
Herschel Johnson	First Secretary, US Embassy in London
Alex Kellar	MI5 officer
Sir Norman Kendal	Assistant Commissioner (Crime), Scotland Yard
Thomas Kendrick	SIS officer, formerly Passport Control Officer in Vienna
Joseph Kennedy	US Ambassador in London
Eric Kessler	Swiss press attaché, codenamed ORANGE
Bernie Kiener	MI5 double agent codenamed RAINBOW
John King	Soviet spy in the Foreign Office
Klop	Klop Ustinov, MI5 agent
Max Knight	MI5 agent-handler
Walter Krivitsky	Soviet defector
LAND SPIDER	SIS double agent Ib Riis
Joseph Lenihan	MI5 double agent codenamed BASKET
Isaac Don Levine	American journalist

Cecil Liddell	Head of MI5's Irish Section
Billy Luke	MI5 B1(a) case officer
Sam McCarthy	MI5's double agent codenamed BISCUIT
Mr Machell	MI5 officer
Alan MacIver	MI5 officer in charge of the RSLOs
Kenneth Maidment	RSS cryptographer
Ivan Maisky	Soviet Ambassador to London
John Marriott	MI5 officer and Secretary of the XX Committee
Noel Mason Macfarlane	Former British military attaché in Berlin
J.C. Masterman	MI5 officer and Chairman of the XX Committee
John Maude	MI5 officer
Raymund Maunsell	Head of Security Intelligence in the Middle East
Sir Alexander Maxwell	Permanent Under-Secretary, Home Office
Charles Medhurst	Director of Air Intelligence
Tito Medlam	DSO Gibraltar
Edward Merrett	DNI's private secretary
Dickie Metcalfe	MI5 double agent codenamed BALLOON
Cyril Mills	MI5 case officer, later DSO in Ottawa
Helenus ('Buster') Milmo	MI5 officer
Desmond Morton	Winston Churchill's intelligence adviser
Eric Mockler-Ferryman	War Office, Home Forces
Ewen Montagu	NID representative on the XX Committee
Herbert Morrison	Home Secretary in the War Coalition Government
Sir Oswald Mosley	Leader of the British Union of Fascists
MUTT	MI5 double agent John Moe
M/Y	MI5 agent
ORANGE	MI5 source in the Swiss Embassy, Eric Kessler
Arthur Owens	MI5's double agent codenamed SNOW
The Oxford Don	John Masterman
P	Wolfgang zu Putlitz
Sir James Paget	Passport Control Officer, New York
Charles Peake	Ministry of Information
PEG	Saboteur in Gibraltar
PEPPERMINT	MI5 double agent José Brugada
Peters	MI5 double agent
Toby Pilcher	MI5 officer in the legal section
Pilkington	MI5 officer and head of F2(c)
POGO	Spanish journalist named Del Pozo
Harry Pollitt	Secretary-General of the CPGB
Dusan Popov	MI5 double agent codenamed SKOOT, then TRICYCLE
Peter Quennell	SOE, Gibraltar
RAINBOW	MI5 double agent named Bernie Kiener

Peter Ramsbotham	MI5 officer in the American section
RATS	José Estella Key
Ronnie Reed	MI5 radio operator
Ned Reid	MI5's financial expert and Guy Liddell's cousin
T.A. Robertson	Head of MI5's B1(a)
Wulf Schmidt	MI5's double agent codenamed TATE
Alexander Scotland	MI9 interrogator
John Senter	MI5 officer seconded to SOE as security officer
Hugh Shillito	MI5 officer
Derek Sinclair	MI5 officer and son of C, Sir Hugh Sinclair.
SKOOT	MI5 double agent Dusan Popov, later TRICYCLE
SNOW	Arthur Owens
SOSO	Double agent at the British Legation in Lisbon
Reg Spooner	Scotland Yard detective seconded to MI5
SPRINGBOK	MI5 double agent Hans von Kotze
Lord Stanhope	Leader of the House of Lords
Oliver Stanley	Deception Coordinator
Robin 'Tin-Eye' Stephens	Commandant of Camp 020
William Stephenson	Director of British Security Co-ordination in New York
Major Richard Stevens	PCO in The Hague
Harry Stone	MI5 officer
Richman Stopford	MI5 officer
STORK	MI5 agent
Kenneth Strong	Former British assistant military attaché in Berlin
SUMMER	MI5's codename for Goesta Caroli
SUNDAE	Spanish double agent in Algeciras
SWEET WILLIAM	MI5 double agent
Lord Swinton	Chairman of the Security Executive
Derek Tangye	MI5's press liaison officer
TATE	MI5's codename for Wulf Schmidt
Edward Travis	Director of GC&CS
Hugh Trevor Roper	SIS's expert on ISOS
TRICYCLE	MI5 codename for Dusan Popov
Theo Turner	MI5 officer
Klop Ustinov	MI5 agent codenamed Klop
Sir Robert Vansittart	Chief Diplomatic Adviser at the Foreign Office
VCIGS	General Sir John Dill
Sir Philip Vickery	Director of Indian Political Intelligence
Alf Wall	Member of the Security Executive
WEASEL	MI5 double agent
Dick White	MI5 officer and future Director-General
Jock Whyte	MI5 officer

Sir Horace Wilson	Permanent Under-Secretary at the Treasury
Ian Wilson	MI5 B1(a) case officer
Malcolm Woolcombe	MI5 officer
Courtney Young	MI5's Japanese expert
ZOR	A White Russian contact

EXECUTIONS

George Armstrong	Having offered his services as a spy to the German Consul in Boston by mail, the 39-year-old seaman was returned to England for trial. He was convicted in May 1941 and hanged at Wandsworth in July 1941.
François de Deeker	Arrested in September 1941 in Scotland after he had landed from a flying-boat, de Deeker was tried in June 1941 and hanged at Wandsworth in August 1941.
José Estella	A Spanish saboteur, Estella was arrested in Gibraltar in February 1942, tried in London in May and hanged at Wandsworth in July 1942.
Josef Jakobs	A parachute agent who landed in Huntingdonshire in February 1941, the 43-year-old German dentist broke both his ankles on landing. He was court-martialled in August 1941 and shot at the Tower of London 10 days later.
Charles van den Kieboom	A 26-year-old Dutchman, he was landed by boat at Dymchurch, Kent, in September 1940. He was tried in November and hanged at Pentonville in December.
Carl Meier	A 24-year-old Dutchman from Coblenz, he was landed by boat at Lydd, Kent, in September 1940. He was tried in November and hanged at Pentonville in December.
Karel Richter	A Sudeten German, Karel Richter had worked on the Hamburg–Amerika Line before the war and was parachuted into Hertfordshire in May 1941.
Alphons Timmerman	A Belgian seaman, Timmerman was arrested at the Royal Victoria Patriotic School, tried and executed.
Jose Waldberg	A 25-year-old German from Mainz, he was landed by boat at Dungeness, Kent, in September 1940, tried in November and hanged at Pentonville in December.

BRITISH INTELLIGENCE ESTABLISHMENTS

Barnet	Headquarters of the Radio Security Service
Blenheim Palace	MI5 wartime headquarters in Oxfordshire from 1940
Broadway	54 Broadway, SIS headquarters in London
Camp 020	Latchmere House, Ham Common
Camp 020R	Reserve detention centre at Huntercombe Place, Oxon
Camp WX	Isle of Man
Camp Z	Mytchett Place, Aldershot
Cockfosters	Air Intelligence interrogation centre at Trent Park
Dollis Hill	Post Office Research Station
Glenalmond	SIS Section V headquarters in St Albans
Hendon	MI5 safe-house in Crespigny Road, NW4
Kinnaird House	Headquarters of the Security Executive in Pall Mall
The Old Parsonage	Safe-house at Hinxton, Cambridgeshire, called 'The Home for Incurables'
Praewood	Headquarters of SIS's Section V in St Albans
Room 055	MI5's interview room in the War Office
Royal Victoria Patriotic School	MI5's refugee screening centre on Wandsworth Common, south London
St James's Street	MI5's headquarters in London from 1941
Tring	Home Farm, Lord Rothschild's estate house in Hertfordshire
Whaddon	SIS's communications headquarters
Wormwood Scrubs	MI5's emergency headquarters in London, evacuated in 1940

GLOSSARY

AID	Army Ordnance Inspection Department
B1(a)	MI5's German double agent section
B1(g)	MI5's Irish section
B2	MI5's Agent Section
B5(b)	Max Knight's section
B6	MI5's Watcher Service
BCRA	French intelligence service
BGSI	Brigadier General Staff (Intelligence)
BJ	Diplomatic intercept
BSC	British Security Co-ordination
C	Chief of the Secret Intelligence Service
CID	Committee of Imperial Defence
CID	Criminal Investigation Department
CIGS	Chief of the Imperial General Staff
CPGB	Communist Party of Great Britain
CPUSA	Communist Party of the United States of America
CWS	Central War Security
DF	Direction-Finding
DMO&I	Director of Military Operations & Intelligence
DNI	Director of Naval Intelligence
DPP	Director of Public Prosecutions
DUFF	Microdot
F2(c)	MI5 section dealing with Russian intelligence
FBI	Federal Bureau of Investigation (United States)
FFF	Free French Forces
FSP	Field Security Police
4th Department	Soviet military intelligence service
GC&CS	Government Code & Cipher School
Group 1	Wireless intercepts of Abwehr hand ciphers
Group 10	Wireless intercepts of Abwehr machine ciphers
IPI	Indian Political Intelligence
IRA	Irish Republican Army

ISBA	Intelligence Service/British Agents
ISK	Decrypted Abwehr machine cipher wireless traffic
ISOS	Decrypted Abwehr hand cipher wireless traffic
ISSB	Inter-Services Security Board
JIC	Joint Intelligence Committee
MAP	Ministry of Aircraft Production
MI7	War Office propaganda branch
MI8	Radio Security Service
MSS	Most Secret Source
NID	Naval Intelligence Division
NSDAP	Nazi Party
OGPU	Soviet intelligence service
OSS	Office of Strategic Services
PCO	Passport Control Officer
PID	Political Intelligence Department
PPU	Peace Pledge Union
PWE	Political Warfare Executive
RCMP	Royal Canadian Mounted Police
ROF	Royal Ordnance Factory
RSLO	Regional Security Liaison Officer
RSS	Radio Security Service
SB	Special Branch
SCO	Security Control Officer
SIC	Security Intelligence Centre
SIS	Secret Intelligence Service
SO2	Special Operations 2
SOE	Special Operation Executive
Special Material	Intercepted diplomatic telephone conversations
VCIGS	Vice Chief of the Imperial General Staff
ZPT	Intercepted enemy naval wireless traffic

INTRODUCTION

Guy Liddell was an exceptional intelligence officer in every way, as his extraordinary wartime diaries demonstrate. During World War I he won the Military Cross, like his two brothers David and Cecil, all three having joined the Royal Artillery as private soldiers and then received commissions. They had been educated at the University of Angers and all three spoke French fluently. David became a gifted painter, and trained in Paris, while Cecil, who qualified in law, never practised as a lawyer. In 1919 Guy joined Scotland Yard as a civilian counter-intelligence officer working for Sir Basil Thomson's Directorate of Intelligence.

The ambitious and colourful Thomson, a former prime minister of Tonga and governor of Dartmoor Prison, had intended to develop a domestic intelligence organisation that would encompass Special Branch and MI5, but his plans were to be thwarted by powerful influences in Whitehall and intensive lobbying by Vernon Kell of MI5. When Thomson was forced to resign from Scotland Yard in 1921 by the Commissioner of the Metropolis, supposedly because of a breach of security at Chequers, in which Irish republicans had daubed slogans on the walls of the prime minister's country home, his scheme was abandoned. Liddell and his small team of analysts, Hugh Miller, Bunty Saunders and Miss McCulloch, remained on the staff of Special Branch until 1931 when, following the Treaty of Westminster, they were all transferred to MI5 where Liddell acted as deputy to the director of the counter-espionage branch, Brigadier Jasper Harker.

Although MI5 operated in conditions of great secrecy, most of Liddell's very extensive social circle knew where he worked. Before his marriage he shared a flat with his brother Cecil in Ashley Gardens. His eccentric, wealthy wife, the Hon. Calypso Baring, was the daughter of the Irish peer Lord Revelstoke, and they did a lot of entertaining at their Lutyens-designed home in Cheyne Walk, one of London's most desirable addresses, overlooking the Thames in Chelsea. Visitors invariably commented on Calypso's avant-garde style, and her unusual choice of wallpaper, *The Times* newspaper, in the entrance hall. A great mimic, Guy was always popular at dinner parties, usually accompanied by one of his brothers. He danced beautifully, occasionally volunteering to teach an Irish jig, and was very musical.

Separated from Calypso, who suddenly went to live in California with her half-brother Lorrilard (Larry) Tailer, and isolated from his children, Peter, Gay, Lucy and

Juno, Liddell was a lonely figure, who was absorbed in his work. He occasionally found solace in the cello, at which he excelled, being one of the country's most gifted amateur players. For much of his life he played in a quartet in Bromley, and he often told friends about how he had owned three cellos duing the Great War, each strategically located in the event of an advance, retreat or other eventuality. Alone in London, he moved into a flat in Richmond Court, Sloane Street, reliant on his network of family friends, such as the Jebbs, Meinertzhagens and Bellocs, to supply information and develop contacts.

For the first year of the war Liddell's daughters lived with his widowed cousin Mary Wollaston in Winchester, and Peter at his prep school in Surrey, and then they moved to live with their mother in California. Meanwhile, Liddell became increasingly absorbed in his work and drew on his family and friends to help MI5. Both his brothers were to join him, with Cecil heading the Irish section, as was his cousin, Sir Edward Reid, the banker.

Under Liddell's supervision B Division undertook several important investigations into German and Soviet espionage before World War II. His study of the MASK decrypts, intercepted Comintern wireless traffic exchanged with the Communist Party of Great Britain's clandestine wireless station in Wimbledon, convinced him of the threat from Russia, and the arrest of Percy Glading, the CPGB's National Organiser, in February 1938, proved that the Party was engaged in espionage directed by the Kremlin. Although Liddell's ill-advised friendships with Guy Burgess and Anthony Blunt were to compromise his MI5 career, and prompt concerns as to his loyalty, nobody reading these diaries could doubt his deep commitment to his country and its traditions. Together, MASK and the Woolwich Arsenal case proved to Liddell that the Soviets posed a potent threat to Britain and his concerns about Soviet officials visiting the country are clearly reflected in the pages that follow.

As well as expressing anxiety about the Soviets, Liddell was equally suspicious of German intentions, and during the investigation conducted into the copious correspondence of Mrs Jessie Jordan in 1938 he took the opportunity to alert the American and Canadian authorities to the scale of Nazi intrigues in North America. His visit to J. Edgar Hoover in Washington DC to brief the FBI Director on the contacts the Dundee hairdresser had in the United States formed the basis of the FBI's first German counter-espionage case, that of Sergeant Gunther Rumrich. Characteristically, Hoover took all the public credit for a successful investigation, although his leads had been supplied by Liddell.

At that time the FBI had very little experience of espionage, and the United States had no central intelligence organisation. The Office of Strategic Services would not be formed until 1942, and the CIA did not come into existence until after the war, in 1947. Accordingly, Liddell's main contact with the Americans was through Herschel Johnson, a First Secretary at the US Embassy in Grosvenor Square, who acted as a conduit for the exchange of intelligence.

During his trip to America, Liddell took the opportunity to visit Ottawa to encourage the Royal Canadian Mounted Police to devote more resources to dealing with the threat posed by Russian and German espionage. The collaboration he fostered proved to be the foundation of a long, fruitful era of co-operation between the Canadian authorities and the Security Service, which lasts to this day.

In 1940 Liddell succeeded Jasper Harker as Director, B Division, and in 1945 was appointed Deputy Director-General, a post he held until 1953 when he retired to become security adviser to the Atomic Energy Authority.

Unquestionably, Liddell was the pre-eminent counter-intelligence officer of his generation, respected by his adversaries and admired by his subordinates. He had an unrivalled reputation for discretion and an intuitive talent for handling the most difficult cases in a highly politically-charged atmosphere with constant interference from Whitehall officials and interventions from senior politicians. That Liddell was able to guide Britain's counter-intelligence agency through these minefields without scandal and controversy, during a war which lasted nearly six years, is eloquent testimony to his remarkable abilities. But beyond offering a unique glimpse into how Whitehall wrestled with the challenges of alien internment, foreign visitors, diplomatic spies, enemy parachutists and leakages of military information, the diaries shed important new light on events that hitherto have been shrouded in an almost comprehensive cloak of official secrecy. Not a single MI5 officer ever published an account of his war work, and those who sought permission to do so were discouraged and even threatened. A very few wartime officers were allowed to make veiled references to their temporary employment by the Security Service, such as Derek Tangye, Stephen Watts and Victor Rothschild. When John Bingham's widow attempted to publish his biography she was prevented from doing so, and as Madeleine herself had worked in B Division the advice she received from the Treasury Solicitor was potent. Even Sir Vernon Kell's widow was unable to obtain permission to release an entirely innocuous volume of memoirs about her husband, the organisation's first Director-General. Later her son, John Kell, was to pass the manuscript to the journalist John Bulloch, who made a pioneering attempt to write about a taboo subject. He too came under considerable pressure to exercise discretion in recounting a few episodes of MI5's history, much of which was anyway in the public domain, and not to disclose the identity of any of the personnel. The extent of Whitehall's determination to keep the activities of the Security Service secret in the latter half of the twentieth century is hard to exaggerate. When Roger Hesketh tried to publish his history of Operation FORTITUDE, the deception campaign he helped devise to ensure the success of D-Day, he met with obstruction and procrastination, followed by comprehensive redactions. Even an innocuous foreword penned by Tommy Robertson for a wartime history of MI5 was banned on the basis that his contribution would set a precedent and enhance the status and credibility of a book that did not have official approval.

The first peek under the skirts came from the unlikely source of Sir John Masterman, the Oxford don, Provost of Worcester College and a novelist of some note. When he approached the government for sanction to release his account of the XX Committee, which he had chaired from its inception in January 1941, he had the advantage of having taught both the Foreign Secretary, Sir Alec Douglas-Home and the Prime Minister, Ted Heath. Although the Intelligence Coordinator to the Cabinet, Sir Dick White (himself a former D-G of MI5 and Chief of SIS), was thoroughly opposed to the project, Masterman played a trump card. He had been commissioned by Sir David Petrie to write an internal history of the XX Committee at the end of the war, and he had retained an illicit copy of the completed document. He now proposed to publish it in the United States with the help of his old OSS friend Professor Norman Holmes Pearson, who had persuaded the Yale University Press to print it. Faced with this force majeure, and the embarrassment of a very public scrap with a revered academic, the government reluctantly agreed to a sanitised version of the manuscript, with references to the 'most secret source' provided by Bletchley Park removed, and certain other passages redacted. Masterman himself later claimed in his autobiography, *On The Chariot Wheel*, that his argument for the need to generate MI5 some good publicity to outweigh the many security lapses of recent years, while it had prevailed, was actually quite spurious. MI5 and Whitehall were infuriated by his behaviour, but his cause had been strengthened by the retention of a former MI5 case officer, Christopher Harmer, as his solicitor. Masterman published *The Double Cross System of the War of 1939–1945* in 1972, much to the irritation of the mandarins and the book served to reveal how the Security Service had taken control of the enemy's entire spy organisation in England. Coincidentally, the book saved another author, Ladislas Farago, from considerable anguish as he had been planning to release *Game of the Foxes*, his analysis of German wartime espionage, based on his lengthy study of the Abwehr's records. Only in the nick of time did he acquire an advance copy of Masterman's astonishing story and change his own text to recognise that the masterspies in England during World War II were all operating under the control of Liddell's ingeniously manipulative case officers.

Whitehall's efforts to suppress Masterman's references to ULTRA were to be frustrated in 1974 when Anthony Cave Brown and Fred Winterbotham disclosed how the Anglo-American cryptographers had succeeded in beating the enemy's Enigma cipher machine (and its derivatives). Cave Brown's *Bodyguard of Lies* and Winterbotham's *The Ultra Secret* opened the floodgates and in 1976 prompted the Foreign Secretary, Dr David Owen, to announce a new policy regarding Bletchley Park: wartime cryptographers were allowed to disclose their work and discuss the impact of their achievements on the war, but not to reveal the technical methods adopted to retrieve the Enigma cipher keys. Even this prohibition was broken by Gordon Welchman with *The Hut Six Story*, and eventually the government relented and commissioned an official history from a team of historians led by Professor Sir Harry Hinsley. *British Intelligence in the Second World War* was released in five volumes, one of which dealt with security and counter-intelligence, authored by a former MI5 deputy director-general, Anthony Simkins. However, conforming to the style prescribed by the Cabinet Office, neither this nor its companion volumes mentioned by name any of the fascinating personalities, and Simkins only identified in passing Guy Liddell as the Director of B Division, the man responsible for much of MI5's astonishing contribution to the final victory.

The objective behind the political decision to prepare an official history of British Intelligence was to staunch the growing demand for the disclosure of the original decrypts which so influenced the tactics adopted by the Allied military commanders. Prior to the reluctant admission that the Allies had been reading much of the enemy's most important wireless traffic, the ULTRA secret had been carefully guarded. Even Kim Philby's memoirs, *My Silent War*, written by the defector in Moscow, safe from the reach of the Official Secrets Act, made no reference to the brilliant coup pulled off at Bletchley Park, a signals intelligence operation in which Philby himself had been intimately engaged. The SIS branch in which he had worked throughout his wartime service, from September 1941 onwards, had been dedicated to the study of intercepted Abwehr wireless traffic, yet the traitor was more interested in regaling his readers with gossip about his colleagues than explaining the historic implications of the decryption success which had saved many thousands of lives in the U-boat war of the north Atlantic, turned the tide of the Afrika Korps in the Libyan desert, helped trap the Kriegsmarine's feared surface raiders and ensured the invaders prevailed on D-Day.

While Philby may have been reluctant to apportion praise to the denizens of the secret world, plenty of other participants wrote of their individual contributions. Peter Calvocoressi recalled his experiences at Bletchley, while Ralph Bennett analysed the way ULTRA had been exploited in the field. Revisionists reinterpreted the war at sea, and new light was shed on the Naval Intelligence Division by Patrick Beesley. Suddenly the world understood what Winston Churchill had cryptically acknowledged as his 'most secret sources'.

If one of the motives for allowing greater freedom to study Bletchley Park's original intercepts had been to quench a thirst for greater knowledge about Britain's secret history, it was unsuccessful, for in the early 1980s numerous authors, biographers and historians turned their attention to a neglected field, The startling announcement by Prime Minister Margaret Thatcher in November 1979 that Professor Sir Anthony Blunt had been a lifelong Soviet mole who had accepted an immunity from prosecution in April 1964 prompted more research into an area of study that hitherto had been avoided and actively discouraged. Blunt, of course, had served in the Security Service from June 1940 until September 1945, and had confessed to having haemorrhaged to the NKVD every secret that had passed his desk. This news came as a devastating blow to his friends, his family, his surviving wartime colleagues and to an intelligence establishment that had attempted to salvage a reputation tarnished by the defections in 1951 of Guy Burgess and Donald Maclean.

Although Liddell was not alive to endure the pain of Blunt's public exposure, having died unnoticed in 1958, he was to become the focus of intense speculation and criticism. He had known Guy Burgess, who had worked secretly for MI5 in 1940 running, among several other agents in his homosexual *galère*, Eric Kessler, the Swiss journalist and diplomat codenamed ORANGE. Naturally Burgess's covert role for the Security Service had been hushed up at the time of his disappearance, when he had been described as a mere junior diplomat, and the official White Paper on the defection had not even hinted at his wartime links with SIS's Section D and

MI5. Liddell's friendship with Burgess had been embarrassment enough, but he had actually employed Anthony Blunt as his personal assistant, and had entrusted him to conduct the most sensitive inquiries on his behalf. For example, when Blunt first joined Liddell's personal staff he was assigned the task of reviewing the performance of Harry Hunter's embryonic and ineffective Watcher Service, thus enabling him to give his Soviet contacts an authoritative assurance that their *rezidentura* in London had nothing to fear from MI5 surveillance, which was fully occupied in keeping suspected fifth columnists under observation. Checks in MI5's registry showed that Blunt had also completed a lengthy study of TRIPLEX, the highly secret operation in which the diplomatic bags of target neutral embassies were routinely diverted and opened. Worst of all, Blunt had been authorised by Liddell to identify, and report on, MI5's entire stable of agents inside foreign embassies in London. Naturally, Blunt's conclusions were devoured in Moscow almost as quickly as they were read in St James's Street.

The discomfort of Liddell's many friends and admirers turned to anger when his loyalties were questioned. The first to reinterpret some of Liddell's greatest successes as dubious triumphs was Richard Deacon, the author of *The Greatest Treason* (1989), in which he suggested that although the Woolwich Arsenal case had resulted in the conviction of Percy Glading and two other members of his network, the big fish had been allowed to escape. There was some truth to this allegation, in that the Soviet illegals who had controlled the spy-ring had evaded MI5 surveillance and avoided both arrest and identification. Deacon suggested this was a consequence of treason at a high level inside MI5, and not sheer ill-fortune, and he roundly denounced Liddell as 'the fifth man'.

As Anthony Blunt had not joined MI5 until 1940, more than two and a half years after Glading's arrest, Deacon's candidate for the traitor was Liddell. The allegation had stirred Dick White to protest his mentor's innocence, but the scent had been laid eight years earlier by David Mure in *Master of Deception*, in which he drew a scenario with Liddell masterminding one intelligence failure after another, a veritable genius of duplicity helping other moles to burrow deep into the British establishment. Mure's unsubstantiated charges were all the more grave because although Deacon, the pen-name of Donald McCormick, a former foreign editor of the *Sunday Times* and a wartime naval officer, had not served in intelligence, Mure had been based in Cairo during World War II and had been engaged in deception operations across the Middle East. While Deacon's book could be dismissed as journalistic speculation, Mure knew what he was talking about and had been involved in the CHEESE double agent case. Mure's theory was enhanced by the Cambridge historian John Costello who, in his impressive biography of Blunt, *Mask of Deception*, named Liddell as a Soviet spy, but only on the basis that there was no other rational explanation for Blunt's prolonged treachery. Once again, the allegation caused dismay among Liddell's former colleagues, especially when Peter Wright revealed that several mole-hunts had been conducted in the 1960s on the assumption that the Security Service had suffered high-level penetration. Prompted by Mrs Thatcher's inaccurate statement to the Commons in November 1979, drafted for her by MI5, that all the incidents of penetration could be attributed to Anthony Blunt, Wright revealed to his co-author Chapman Pincher in *Their Trade is Treachery* that the Deputy D-G, Graham Mitchell, had been a suspected mole before his retirement in September 1963 and, most explosively, that the Director-General himself, Sir Roger Hollis, had also been investigated as a possible spy. Wright was to go into further detail in a subsequent book, *SpyCatcher*, co-authored with the television producer Paul Greengrass, in which he remarked that anybody who read the Liddell diaries could not remotely suspect him of having betrayed his country.

We can now say, based on what has been released from the Soviet archives, and on evidence from the KGB defectors Oleg Gordievsky and Vasili Mitrokhin, that there is nothing to support the assertion that Guy Liddell did anything other than serve the Crown faithfully, and his diaries show a humanity and commitment to democratic ideals which might seem an anathema to most secret policemen.

Hinsley's magisterial oeuvre was followed by an extraordinary development which occurred as a result of the collapse of the Soviet Bloc. The KGB archive, opened to a group of Western historians, was found to include a vast collection of secret documents removed from MI5's registry during the war by Anthony Blunt. Among the papers was an early draft of Jack Curry's internal history of MI5, written in 1945 and covering the period from 1909. When this was declassified in Moscow, the Director-General, Dr Stephen Lander, himself a Cambridge-educated historian, approved the release of the final version to the Public Record Office at Kew. Curry's history was to be published, but it had been redacted and gave a very partial view of MI5's performance, skating over the difficulties experienced by Liddell, who was scarcely mentioned. Also released was Colonel Robin ('Tin-Eye') Stephens' postwar account of Camp 020, MI5's secret interrogation centre at Ham Common. Stephens had been the camp's controversial commandant and, as might be expected, his views were colourful and robust. However, although the author gave individual pen-portraits of some of the inmates, he was unaware of the wider counter-intelligence scene so his section's history gave a less than comprehensive picture, and of course omitted any references to Liddell.

Liddell's own diaries were never intended for publication, and were read only by selected MI5 officers as a training aid to give an idea of how the Security Service had risen to the challenge of a world war with the Axis powers. Dictated to his secretary Margo Huggins each evening, they act as a war diary for an agency which kept meticulous personal and subject files on suspect spies, subversives and organisations. Throughout the Cold War they were considered so sensitive that they were codenamed WALLFLOWER and retained in the Director-General's personal safe, to be shared with, among others, Peter Wright.

So what makes the *Liddell Diaries* so important? First, there is the information that can be found nowhere else. When referring to 'special material' Liddell inadvertently reveals the countries, including France, Eire, Persia, Finland, Sweden and the Soviet Union, which were the subject of regular telephone monitoring. Hinsley exercised considerable, understandable discretion over diplomatic targets, and doubtless was under an obligation to avoid identifying the countries monitored regularly and successfully. Yet Liddell's comments prove that at least the telephone communications of certain embassies were recorded on a regular basis and circulated to senior intelligence officers. They are also an extraordinary daily commentary on what was truly happening behind even the most *sub rosa* of scenes. For example, on one occasion an SIS officer asked Liddell to record in his diary a prediction, to see if it would come to pass, and on another Liddell noted a request for a particular issue to be omitted from the official minutes of the meeting.

As well as describing investigations conducted by MI5 not mentioned elsewhere, Liddell also gave an insider's account of the tensions that existed between the government, Whitehall and other agencies. Whereas Liddell's Director, Jasper Harker, evidently worked well with the Permanent Under-Secretary at the Home Office, Sir Alexander Maxwell, he found the creation of the Home Defence Security Executive in June 1940 a major irritant. The Security Executive was established because of what Churchill perceived as chaos in MI5's management when he dismissed the Director-General, Sir Vernon Kell. The exact constitutional role of the Security Executive was never fully established and Liddell certainly resented the interference of (Sir) William Charles Crocker, an influential City solicitor who had little idea of MI5's work and disastrously transferred a group of Scotland Yard detectives into B Divison, much to the irritation of Special Branch. Crocker had been imposed on MI5 to shake up the organisation, but his activities, combined with the interference of another outsider, Malcolm Frost from the BBC, were to cause lasting resentment within the Security Service.

Liddell makes no attempt to conceal the internal rivalries and friction that at times threatened to paralyse the entire organisation. Miss Paton-Smith's all-important Registry seethed with discontent and the imposition of a Wireless Branch to supervise illicit communication with the enemy proved a short-lived and wasteful experiment, a classic example of duplication and bureaucratic ineptitude. The arrival of Reg Horrocks, a management expert, and his assistant, Mr Potter, to advise on improvements, did little to alleviate the tensions that developed inside the organisation, as well as with SIS, RSS, SOE and PWE, all clandestine departments that were occasionally viewed as adversaries.

The Guy Liddell Diaries are of enormous significance for two reasons. First, very few people were in a position to take a broad overview of the conduct of the war from a vantage point that included access to all the most secret information available. Churchill, of course, saw plenty of ULTRA decrypts and enjoyed poring over the original Enigma intercepts that Stewart Menzies selected for his inspection each morning, but few other members of his War Cabinet were privy to the source of his sometimes eerily prescient knowledge of the enemy's intentions. None of the other published war diaries, including those of the CIGS, General Sir Alan Brooke, referred to golden eggs laid at Bletchley, so on the basis of a global perspective, the *Liddell Diaries* are important historical documents. The second reason, already mentioned, is the paucity of material available from inside the Security Service. Whereas four of the wartime double agents wrote about their adventures – Lilly Sergueiev (codenamed TREASURE), John Moe (MUTT), Dusan Popov (TRICYCLE) and Eddie Chapman

(ZIGZAG) – none of their case officers broke their silence. The lacuna is all the more remarkable given the number of authors who worked in the Security Service. Max Knight, John Bingham, William Younger, Gerald Glover and Derek Tangye were all to write books, and although some of them published spy novels, none gave non-fiction accounts of the cases they had run, or even disclosed the true nature of their employment. The single exception was Joan Miller, one of Max Knight's secretaries, who was used to penetrate a group of suspected fifth columnists in 1940, and later gave a brief version of her experiences in *One Girl's War*, an innocuous memoir eventually published in Ireland after legal injunctions prevented it from being released in England.

Within the diaries Liddell inserted a couple of items, one being a summary of enemy agents compiled by Helenus Milmo, that has been added to these pages as appendices. The other, no less instructional, is a memorandum written by Lord Rothschild to Liddell at the end of March 1942, remarking on a description of an unidentified British counter-intelligence officer given by W. Somerset Maugham, the author of *Ashenden* and himself an SIS officer during World War I. In fact Liddell's diaries reveal that he had lunched with Maugham in August 1940, to help him with a series of articles he had been commissioned to write about fifth columnists, but as this social occasion had occurred before Rothschild had joined MI5, he perhaps had been unaware of its full significance. Rothschild writes:

> Taking into consideration the disguises you habitually put on when out of the office I think that the following extract from a recent book by Somerset Maugham might be of interest to you:
>
>> I examined a number of secret reports dealing with the Fifth Column and I was fortunate enough to meet some of the men whose job it is to watch its activities in Britain and to take the necessary steps to counter them. I cannot tell their names; I can only say that in appearance they do not at all resemble the secret agents of fiction. If you met them you would never dream they have anything to do with the occupation they follow. Another was a plump man with grey hair and a grey moon face, in rather shabby grey clothes. He had an ingratiating way with him, a pleasant laugh and a soft voice. I do not know what you would have taken him for but if you had found him standing in a doorway where you had sought refuge from a sudden shower – a motor salesman perhaps, or a retired tea planter.

From amusing anecdotes to deadly serious issues of life and execution, Liddell takes us through the matters that preoccupied him while he fulfilled one of the most demanding roles in Britain's most secret wartime world. In short, until now there has never been any authoritative insider's account of what it was like to work in the wartime Security Service, nor any candid commentary on the counter-intelligence conflict fought by MI5 against both the Axis and the Soviets.

Nigel West

1939

We reviewed the position generally regarding measures that could be taken now in order to speed up the arrest of cases under Defence of the Realm Act, Clause 24(c), on the outbreak of war. I suggested to Jasper Harker that he should see Home Office and find out whether they approved all the cases we have put before them. If so, do they agree to our giving the names of these people to chief constables, and asking them to keep the individuals more or less under observation from now onwards.

We can I think assume that nearly all Germans featuring on our Suspect Index will have gone prior to a declaration of war. The only possible exceptions are Fräuleins Ahleldt and Binzer, both of whom are remaining, it is thought only because they expect that as women they will be repatriated. Discussed whether it was worthwhile getting a Deportation Order against them. It was generally agreed that this would serve no very useful purpose.

The case of Kuchenmeister was also discussed, but we felt that the chances were that he had already gone and that there was very little that he could pass on to the Germans that he has not given them already. The only thing he could possibly report would be increased activity which on the whole might be a good thing. He must already know the location of all our armament factories.

SIS telephoned to say that from an intercepted conversation between Herr Kling of the German Embassy and Lord Brockett, the latter was meeting Kling at a picture-shop halfway down St. James's Street. Brockett said "The owner is a great friend of mine. This is confidential. I will be there and bring my wife. It will not be so suspicious then. The owner does not know who I am supposed to be meeting. 30 St. James's Street is the number."

We ascertained that this was Leggatt's the print shop but did not see however that any useful purpose would be served by observation, unless general suspicion attaches to the activities of Lord Brockett. It seemed possible that Downing Street might be making use of him so I suggested therefore to Harker that he should find out from Sir Joe Ball if this were so.

29 August

We informed the Director of Naval Intelligence a short time ago that as a result of a speech of Lord Stanhope's mentioning the efficiency of our submarine detectors, the German intelligence service had become very interested in this matter, as they themselves had nothing of the kind. Enquiries made by a naval officer show that Asdic is being fitted to trawlers in a number of ports by naval ratings. The firms undertaking this work and local police have been warned, but the surface of leakage is bound to be considerable. The Admiralty suggested that an MI5 officer should be sent down to each port with a view to ascertaining that undesirable people do not have access to the trawlers in questions. I discussed this matter with Jasper Harker but it seems that no useful purpose can be served by the presence of an MI5 officer and that all that can be done in the circumstances has already been done.

30 August

Klop has sent in a report which indicates that the Germans have got the jitters. It is rather a case of order, counter-order, disorder. There have been recriminations between Nazi Party and non-Party men. Non-Party men are saying: "We always told you that you get us into this mess, and you will be the first people to suffer for it." P has the impression that we have Hitler on the run and that nothing should be done to provide him with a golden bridge to make his getaway.

'P' was Wolfgang zu Putlitz, a German diplomat and formerly the press attaché at the German Embassy in London who had been run by Klop and Dick White for several years.

I discussed this morning with Eric Holt-Wilson and Patrick Cooper (of the Ministry of Supply) the Home Secretary's suggestion that tribunals should set up to deal with enemy aliens. My personal feeling is that enemy aliens should be interned and that they should be called upon to show cause why they should be released. The present suggestion, which envisages a tribunal in each police district, will not in my view be able to deal with all the cases for at least eight months. In the meantime the Germans will have an opportunity of working on enemy aliens in this country and organising them into some sort of intelligence service. From an MI5 point of view, it would be far preferable to have them put away. I was told however that it had already been decided by the Committee of Imperial Defence that internment of all enemy aliens was impossible and undesirable and that there was nothing further to be done.

31 August

I discussed with Dick White the question of searching the German Travel Bureau and steamship line offices in time of emergency. We agreed that this would be desirable, and he is getting out the necessary particulars for the Special Branch.

Klop has sent in another report emphasising the previous one. He seems very confident that disintegration has set in and even suggests that if the order were now given it is doubtful whether the Germans would march. It is difficult to estimate how much his views are based on documents or on gossip in diplomatic circles. It is also difficult to assess the significance of the new War Council from which Goebbels, Himmler and Ribbentrop are all excluded. It may be one further move in the general game of bluff, or it may indicate that there has been some sort of serious internal dissension.

1 September

I attended a meeting at C's office at 9. 30 to discuss with Captain Daru of the *Deuxième Bureau* the setting up of an Anglo-French Bureau in this country. The purpose of the Bureau is to obtain information from existing French agents operating through Scandinavian countries and to recruit such agents from neutral seamen and others who may be thought suitable. For this purpose it is necessary for them to have a close liaison with ourselves and have the necessary facilities at ports through our security officers and the immigration authorities. We shall also be able to give them other facilities, although their main purpose is espionage and not counter-espionage. Major Thornton of SIS will be a permanent representative on the Bureau and act as liaison officer between the French and ourselves. The French Bureau will consist of Captain Daru and two other officers, and a staff of about nine secretaries and orderlies. The Director-General has approved of this arrangement.

After this meeting I went on with Felix Cowgill to Transport House where we saw Tollerton. We have arranged with him to obtain a document which will fill the requirements of our double-cross agent Peters. The Ministry of Transport has a very elaborate and efficient scheme for the diversion of shipping which is already in operation. A questionnaire to ports was sent out some time ago in order to enable the Ministry of Transport to work out this system. We are letting Peters have a copy of this questionnaire which he could quite easily have obtained since it has been in the hands of port authorities.

At the request of the Home Office, the Director-General and Harker agreed that nobody on our lists of Nazi Party members or suspects should be stopped at ports unless we had any very special reasons for holding them.

2 September

The Director-General suggested to the Commissioner of the Metropolis that he might consider having up Sir Oswald Mosley and Harry Pollitt and asking them what their attitude is and that of their party in the present situation. It was thought that in this way one might get some public declaration of policy from them which would help us and the police dealing with the Fascist and Communist problem.

The Commissioner thanked the Director-General for the suggestion but was actually at the time considering what course of action he should take with regard to both parties. He had come to the conclusion that for the time being it would be better to wait and see whether they infringed the law in any way. If they did, he would act immediately.

Francis Aiken-Sneath says that until 31 August the Fascists were taking a definitely pro-German attitude, but that there had not been any time to estimate whether a change had taken place in the last two days.

Roger Hollis says that the Communist Party shows strong signs of supporting the war on grounds of Germany's aggressive action to deprive the Poles of their independence.

3 September

Present reports show that out of a total of 826 Germans, 349 have left voluntarily and 69 have been arrested. This leaves a total of 408 unaccounted for.

The Germans have also protested about the arrest of Graf the baker. We have given orders that he is to be held, as we wish to interrogate him.

At present, with the exception of sixteen individuals specially selected by us as technicians, all Germans are being allowed to leave. Other aliens can also leave without permission for a period of about seven days when the Permit Office will be set up. The same applies to British subjects.

The Oxford Don took matters into his own hands yesterday and objected on security grounds to the internment of two Germans who had been resident here since 1926. The Home Office got into a flat spin and the decision had to be reversed.

4 September

[Deleted] of SIS rang up to say that he thought that they might usefully recruit some agents from our interned suspects before they were sent back to Germany so I arranged with Dick White to look out for any likely cases.

Special Material of 2 September showed that at 9.20pm von Hessen was trying to establish contact with Sir Horace Wilson through George Steward of the Downing Street press office. From a conversation that von Hessen had had at 9pm with Dr Paul Schmidt, the interpreter in Berlin, it was clear that Schmidt, who was apparently acting more or less on his own, was anxious to get Sir Horace Wilson over to Berlin on a confidential mission which should not be disclosed either by the Germans or ourselves. The impression given was that Schmidt was genuinely working for an eleventh-hour settlement behind the backs of his chiefs.

The Americans, through our embassy in Washington DC, have informed us through Isaac Don Levine, a journalist who was closely associated with Walter Krivitsky, the Soviet agent, that a coding expert named King of the Foreign Office has for a long time been handing out information to the Soviet authorities. They also have another agent (unidentified) in the Cabinet Secretariat. King appears likely to be John H. King. Sir Alexander Cadogan is prepared to let him run for forty-eight hours on the chance of our procuring evidence, but he is then to be arrested. Jasper Harker is consulting Sir Horace Wilson about the man in the Cabinet Secretariat.

John King was arrested and confessed to espionage. The unidentified spy in the Cabinet Secretariat was John Cairncross, who would continue to spy until 1951.

5 September

We have an interesting report from Special Branch about the attitude of the Communist Party. They have decided to liquidate their branch offices and to adjust their press to conform with the war policy. They also intend to join the army and show that they are able fighters in the cause of anti-Fascism. While they realise that they may lose 75% of their membership they think that after hostilities cease they will have made a strong nucleus on which to build in the remaining 25%.

We are prepared to let Communists into the army rank and file but it is not our intention that they should obtain posts where they have access to confidential information. Tom Wintringham has just applied for such a post under the War Office, with the Transport, Mechanical Section, which is anxious to employ him. We are intending to oppose his employment in a confidential capacity.

Tom Wintringham, a veteran of the Spanish Civil War, was a leading CPGB member and assistant editor of Workers' Weekly.

John Dulanty, the High Commissioner for Ireland, rang up today to know if we would allow thirty Germans to pass through this country in transit. He said they were all decent people who wanted to return to their own country. He is going to give us their names. He complained that Dublin was unable to get into telephonic communication with their legation in Paris, but he is going to tackle the Dominions Office about this.

Special Branch has informed us that 139 Germans have been arrested and 12 British subjects, leaving 260 still unaccounted for, probably because the search of the Travel Index is not yet complete.

A man calling himself William Muller, alias Knigge, went to the police today offering information. He said that on the advice of the British Consul in Cologne he had returned here on 2 September, that he had been working on various fortifications on the western front and could offer information of value. He was detained at Rochester Row police station pending examination by Edward Hinchley-Cooke who tells me that he is a thoroughly unsatisfactory person. His passport bears no outward stamp by the German authorities although he says the train was held up at the frontier. The fact that he comes from Cologne is also suspicious. We are proposing to hold indefinitely or at any rate until we can make further enquiries.

A Jew called Rosenstein turned up at the Home Office saying he had a lot of information about fortifications on the Rhine. It appears that he had been to several other offices but everybody was too busy to talk to him but he had been seen by Francis Aitken-Sneath. Max Knight has got an agent who is to be in charge of Mosley's secret headquarters. The British Union of Fascists have already gone very near to infringement of the Defence of the Realm regulations on an instruction that they have issued to their members in the forces.

Our agent Dawkes has received £20 from the Germans through a bank in Oslo, and has enquired regarding ways and means of communication in the future in view of censorship.

6 September

There is a question tabled in the House of Commons to ask what steps have been taken to liquidate the Link and the Anglo-German Fellowship. Coka Carroll of the Link [*and editor of the* Anglo-German Review] has already handed in a complete list of his members to the police and offered to give them facilities to search his papers. By now he has probably destroyed anything of an incriminating nature. As regards the Anglo-German Fellowship, this organisation has been moribund for some time.

T.A. Robertson's section reports that warning signals were intercepted before the raid on Kiel somewhere in the vicinity of Driffield aerodrome from which the raid started. This seems to call for some action to clear all areas in the vicinity of aerodromes and I am taking this up.

Edward Hinchley-Cooke, on the basis of a suspect telegram, interrogated a German at the London Hotel and took certain of his correspondence including a letter in code to somebody up north. The code had the appearance of being a perfectly ordinary business one, but the man at the London Hotel was obviously so alarmed that enquiries were made. It now turns out that the individual in the north, Raydt, has confessed that he was a German spy.

The Ministry of Supply has asked that a German at present employed in Wales should be sent urgently to the Royal Ordnance Factory at Irving, Ayrshire to assist in the erection of a machine. He appears to be the only man who knows anything about the job. I said that we would arrange with the local Chief Constable for the man to be sent up under escort, that the Ministry of Supply would have to be responsible for him while he was working in the factory and that the Chief Constable of Ayrshire would look after him at the end of his day's work. The responsibility for any mishap in the factory would have to lie entirely with the Ministry of Supply, and as soon as the man has completed his work for the War Office he would be interned as a technician. It seems amazing that we should be dependent on a German at this moment for the working of our Ordnance Factories.

7 September

A wail has gone up from the acting German Consul in Glasgow who writes to the German Foreign Office from prison: "*Seit Samstag sitze ich hier im Gefängnis von Barlinnie*" ('I have been in Barlinnie prison since Saturday').

Winston Churchill has enquired about a friend of his, Eugene Spier, who has been arrested. I told Edwin Clayton what we knew about him and he seemed satisfied that the man should remain in prison until we had time to investigate his affairs more closely.

8 September

During the night further warning signals by an enemy agent were picked up in the vicinity of RAF Driffield.

The question of domestic servants has once again been raised. Sir Alexander Maxwell is averse to any steps being taken to instruct people in the Services to lay off their alien domestics and he wants them to be dealt with by the tribunals in due course. My feeling is that we should press the three armed services to get rid of enemy alien servants whether employed in or outside barracks, and that any other alien servants should be vetted. At present the army and air force will not allow enemy alien servants in barracks and alien servants only after being vetted. The navy seems to have them everywhere.

It has now been discovered that in the mass of regulations under which we are working it would be extremely difficult to impose the death penalty on a spy, if we happen to catch one. We could only proceed under the Prison Act and the Director of Public Prosecutions thinks that we should meet with a good deal of difficulty in proving our case.

Winston has discovered that Eric Gardiner Camp, who was tried some time ago under the Official Secrets Act for selling plans to the Russians, has got into Napier's works where he has access to extremely confidential work. The management has undertaken to dismiss him.

I have spoken to Monier-Williams about the employment here and the entry of Soviet citizens who are taking delivery of goods from various firms. I told him that we did not like having these people about the works and intended to tighten things up. He quite saw our point but from a strictly departmental view the Board of Trade would deprecate anything which tended to cut down our export trade. He asked that if we intended any drastic action we would let him know beforehand.

We have issued our first warrant on a bank today, in connection with the case of Quen Joyce. We are asking the Westminister Bank to produce the account of Christian Bauer with whom Joyce was in contact. We also intend to serve warrants on the Swiss Banking Corporation and Schroeders in connection with the accounts of various suspect Germans formerly employed at the embassy.

The Home Office is clamouring for information about Spier and we have given our reasons for interning him. These sort of cases of intervention by Cabinet ministers cause a frightful dislocation and a lot of work.

9 September

I have agreed on the procedure with Sir Norman Kendal of Special Branch for sending enemy aliens about the country. In criminal cases the normal procedure is for the chief constable wanting a man to send the necessary escort to fetch him. In the present case, that of Schuftan, a mechanical expert required by Royal Ordnance Factory at Irvine, this procedure does not seem to be necessary. Special Branch will give him a permit to travel and will inform the Chief Constable of Ayrshire that he has been sent off. They will meet him and see that he is placed under the necessary restrictions.

Captain Preston of Anti-Aircraft Command at the War Office reports that various people unidentified in uniform have been asking questions of some of his units. He would like to know what actions his officers should take so he has been told that they should try and satisfy themselves regarding the bona fides of these and, if in doubt, hold them pending enquiries. They should report the whole affair to the security officer at the local command.

We have just heard that we caught a deserter in uniform who has been travelling in a car and changing the index number. It seems probable that he is the man previously reported by Stammers as trying to get information from RAF Observer Corps.

The Home Secretary has now demanded by return the reasons for the internment of Glas. Wickham Steed, Hugh Seton-Watson and the French Ambassador have all weighed in on his behalf. The case appears to be a cast-iron one.

10 September

The question was raised under what powers we could now intern enemy aliens. The answer is that all chief constables have powers under the Royal Prerogative.

Wickham Steed has ask for special privileges to be granted to Holterman, a Social Democrat who has been working in Transport House in efforts to bring about the downfall of the Nazi regime. We took the view that we cannot exempt him at the moment from the normal restrictions imposed on enemy aliens. If we did we should have a flood of applicants from all those who were pleased to call themselves Social Democrats.

Klop has reported that the reason for the German abstention from bombing England or France is that Hitler intends to destroy Poland and then offer to make peace on the grounds that he has taken no offensive action against the allies. Klop also gave us information about an American agent of German origin proceeding to the USA so we have passed this on to Herschel Johnson.

11 September

We have continued enquiries about the interception of telephones and telegrams to Italy. Malcolm Woolcombe has arranged that immediately there is any indication on the telephone of the reporting of troop movements we shall be informed. We then propose to stage a temporary break down of telephonic and telegraphic communication with Rome.

Klop has reported that the South African minister at The Hague is giving out that he has it on the authority of the British government that the *Athenia* was not torpedoed but struck a mine. The Dominions Office is asking for a report from our ambassador, Sir Nevile Bland, about the minister who is Dr Van Broekhuizen. They will then consider whether we should inform de Villers or they should deal with the matter through their High Commissioner.

SNOW, who was arrested under Emergency Regulation 18(b), has been using a wireless set which was given to him by the Germans, under our direction from Wandsworth Prison. He called up three times and received a reply.

We are still getting reports about the man visiting the Observer Corps who travels in a car with a bogus number. The latest information is that he was contacted four times yesterday and said he was an MI5 officer named Bridgeman and on each occasion was released on the assurance of Scotland Yard. This came from Captain Preston in charge of Anti-Aircraft Defence at the War Office I asked him to get chapter and verse if possible. It is difficult to do anything unless we know what chief constable and what officer of Scotland Yard is concerned. I am beginning to believe the whole thing is a myth.

It is difficult to know whether this war is being run by Joe Kennedy, the Home Office or the fighting Services. On 4 September Kennedy was telling Lord Halifax exactly what he thought we ought to do. Great care must be taken by France and ourselves not to set back American opinion by any air action that would enable American opinion to be brought to think that we had been the first to resort to indiscriminate bombardment.

The Home Office is full of appeasement on the home front. The idea is that all aliens in this country, including it seems a large proportion of enemy aliens, should be harnessed into the national effort. For this reason the conditional landing of all aliens is to be cancelled in a week's time. Decisions are taken with regard to control of aliens without any reference to the Security Service, on whom the real responsibility rests. I am going to try and get out some memorandum with a view perhaps to getting the Service departments to weight in and adjust the balance.

I heard yesterday that Rapp, the taxi driver who was down for arrest on account of his association with the German Embassy, drove his own taxi into Brixton Prison with a Special Branch officer inside. The Special Branch man then got out and ordered his arrest.

The Chief Constable of Devon tells us that since the crisis 250 aliens, sixty of whom are enemy aliens, have moved into the Torbay area. He now has a total of some 400 aliens, 120 of who are enemy aliens, and he is getting rather worried about their proximity to the coast. I have suggested to him that he refuse permits and have explained that tribunals are going to deal with enemy aliens. It is also open to him to prevent residence in the vicinity of vulnerable points.

There was a bad mix-up yesterday by the Ministry of Information when they issued some sort of communiqué about the arrival of British troops in France and this was printed by the newspapers. They then sent the police out to confiscate all those which were in print, but finally decided to allow the information to be published. It makes all our efforts to keep watch on leakage of information regarding troop movements through Italian sources rather fruitless.

I saw Herschel Johnson today at his request. He had had a letter from James C. Dunn [*the State Department's political adviser and Assistant Secretary of State*] who was worried because Sir James Paget, the British Passport Control Officer in New York, had established direct contact with the US War Department and the FBI on political and espionage matters. Dunn was anxious that all this information should be bottle-necked through the State Department. I had to give an assurance that we should so inform Paget. Herschel Johnson was careful to explain that this was no personal reflection on Captain Paget and that the State Department was only too anxious to assist us in every possible way. They were worried about the liberal exchange through the police and military owing to the very delicate international situation. I asked Johnson privately what he thought of the leaflet policy. He said "This must be right off the record, but if you want my private opinion I think it is entirely wrong. There is much too much emphasis laid on the note that we are fighting the Nazis. In point of fact we are fighting the Germans and this should be realised."

I saw Commander Rex Howard of SIS. He is anxious to start working on our internees as soon as possible and has appointed Dick Ellis to be in charge of this work. Ellis will have the assistance of Superintendent Jempson of Special Branch and also Thomas Kendrick who is kicking his heels at the Tower of London while waiting for the arrival of German prisoners of war. I suggested we might perhaps pool our resources with SIS in the matter of the interrogation of prisoners, of whom there are over 200. Howard was quite in agreement. I suggested to him that he might perhaps like to interrogate some of the German sailors whom we have already taken off neutral ships.

The Frenchmen, Captains Daru and Beliard, arrived today. The latter is the son of Colonel Beliard who did the same job here in the last war. A schedule has been worked out by which any agent whom the French or ourselves recruits will be inserted in our Black List with instructions that we should be notified immediately of his arrival, but that he is not to be refused leave to land. In this way a man arriving will appear to the port officer as a genuine suspect whom for special reasons we wish to come in and have followed. If a new agent is recruited by Passport Control abroad his particulars will be sent to this country in special cipher by the PCO and we shall then issue similar instructions to ports.

We have had a bad piece of news today. Klop's special source has got into difficulties and wishes to make use of his British passport. No further details at the moment.

Klop's 'special source' was Wolfgang zu Putlitz, formerly the press attaché at the German Embassy in London.

Klop's special source reports of 11 September that the German Foreign Office takes the view that France is not enthusiastic about the war and will welcome any reasonable pretext to conclude peace. Germany intends after the defeat of Poland to start intensive propaganda in France to dissuade the French from fighting for British Imperialism. This will be followed immediately by the putting forward of peace proposals by Mussolini.

Klop's special source considers that our leaflet policy has been a failure. His views are confirmed by a senior representative of the Dutch General Staff, who thinks that the general effect has been unfortunate and the people are contemptuous and irritated by the personal attack on Hitler, whom the Germans regard as the man who holds their fate in his hands which has caused special irritation.

The time has been ill-chosen, the Germans are flushed with success against the Poles and are elated at the inactivity of the British and French. The paper bombardment has been consequently the subject of many derisive jests. It would be better to chuck 15 tons of bombs and then talk.

Other opinions are that the idea is good but that the type of pamphlet is poor. It is suggested that it would be better to say that Danzig, from a German point of view, is not worth a world war, that whatever the outcome Germany at least would be plunged into chaos and Bolshevism, and that if the Germans thought that after a few facile successes against the weakest of their enemies that they only had to make peace proposals for them to be immediately accepted, they were making the mistake of their lives. The Allies could and would prosecute the war to a successful conclusion, namely, the liberation of the German people from a regime which inevitably made Germany world public enemy No. 1.

14 September

Klop's special source and his servant are arriving in this country by aeroplane today, and will be accommodated in a flat in London. We still do not know what has happened.

We are trying to get Dick White's informant to Holland, which may perhaps compensate to some extent for the loss of P.

15 September

The Secretary of State for War, Leslie Hore-Belisha, has been pressing us to take on Pat Hasting in MI5 as a legal advisor. The answer's a lemon.

The Director-General has had a long talk with Sir Claud Schuster who is in charge of setting up the tribunals. Schuster is rather in the dark about the alien situation. He had not realised that about 50,000 were at large and that little was known about their antecedents. He has evidently formed a bad impression of Cooper, from whom he could get no sensible direction. He had not seen our recommendations as to the lines interrogations were to take. The Director-General consulted Schuster about somebody with legal knowledge to represent our point of view in regard to the tribunals. Schuster mentioned his son-in-law Theo Turner who is coming to the office to take up this work. He should be helpful in putting things on better lines.

I heard that Wenninger had left certain property at his apartment in Chelsea. Although I spoke to Sir Thomas Dunlop who said that he was technically inviolable, I asked him to forget the conversation and arrange for John Archer to go down and have a look. There was nothing very exciting there, but certain keys for his safe-deposit were found. Archie Boyle was very keen for Archer to have a look at the safe-deposit. The question is however rather delicate, although I have ascertained that the proprietors are quite sound people and likely to play.

Air Commodore Archie Boyle was Director of Intelligence at the Air Ministry and worked closely with Squadron Leader John Archer, the RAF liaison officer.

Zu Putlitz returned by aeroplane this morning with his servant. He was received by Dick White and is using Dick's brother's flat. Zu Putlitz was convinced that something had gone wrong as he was given a list of agents' names by a member of the Legation Staff, identical with the one that he had given SIS. The curious thing was that one of the names was spelt in the English way. He felt convinced there must be a leakage going on from the PCO's office and it could only be a matter of time before he was discovered and dealt with. The general impression is that the whole situation had rather got on his nerves and that he felt he could not go on. His servant was magnificent and apparently arranged every detail of zu Putlitz's departure. Zu Putlitz had played up 100% until the moment he left the Legation. The Germans at the Hague must now be scratching their head wondering how much has gone west.

The status of Danzigers was discussed without any very conclusive result except that as far as we can ascertain from the Treaties Department of the Foreign Office, they should technically be regarded as aliens and not as enemy aliens. In the middle of the meeting a small boy stuck his head into the room and said "Have you any dirty towels?"

16 September

The Oxford Don, who is a real tiger, brought me a case of a German concerning whom nothing is known but who had annoyed the SCO at Southhampton by wandering about while troops were embarking. The Oxford Don recommended his immediate internment. While cordially agreeing I felt that we were only nibbling at the problem. It seemed highly desirable at this stage that any enemy aliens in the vicinity of ports where troop movements were going on should be interned forthwith. I consulted the Director-General who finally agreed that we should write a letter to Sir Alexander Maxwell at the Home Office. Later, however, he spoke to Maxwell on the telephone. Maxwell has obviously worried at the suggestion as he thought it might be taken as an excuse by certain chief constables to order whole-sale internments throughout the country. He consented however to something of the kind being sent to certain chief constables on the understanding that they would act where they had reasonable grounds for suspecting that an alien was taking an undue interest in service matters. This seems to be the thin end of the wedge and after consultation with Brigadier Allen we decided to drive it well home by drafting a letter for the Home Office to send out to all chief constables and which we hoped would cover them in interning alien enemies who were over-inquisitive regarding any works of importance throughout the country. The Director-General is now try-ing to gild this pill for the Home Office consumption. If it goes through we shall have more or less torpedoed the whole tribunal system.

Norman Kendal spoke to me about the case of Bernard Weiss, the ex-police chief of Berlin who has been interned. We have agreed to release him and have informed the Home Office.

For some reason however Kendal or his deputy Ronald Howe wish to be pre-sent at the interrogation of any enemy aliens sent up from ports to Cannon Row. There does not seem to be any objection from our point of view but it seems to me that they are likely to waste a great deal of their time, and that if one or other of them cannot make himself available the arrangement may be very inconvenient. I am not worrying, because I think by the time Colonel Stephens has interrogated an alien in German (which neither of them understand) for two hours, they will find the proceedings very boring and give up the arrangement.

The Oxford Don has gone off the deep end and has instructed D4 Branch to issue a circular that all Danzigers should be regarded as enemy aliens. This is in direct contradiction to the Foreign Office view. The necessary adjustments are now being made.

17 September

I discussed the question of Russian suspects with particular reference to the Royal Ordnance Factories. There are standing instructions about ROF installations and chief constables have been keeping a special watch over them since the outbreak of war. We have got a list of the more prominent Communists employed at the instal-lations and also a list of the Russians. I have asked B4(b) to get a rough estimate of the total number of Soviet citizens who might have to be interned, and also to let me have a small list of those who are specially suspect.

18 September

John Swift, the Irishman who said he was connected with the underground trade union movement in Germany, returned yesterday. He had in his possession a letter of introduction from the German Bakers Union dated 23 August 1939. As he received his visa from the German Legation in Dublin on 22 August, it would seem that he could not have got it on the strength of this letter. He was also successful in bringing out a number of anti-Nazi leaflets from Germany. He said that he was not searched on account of the letter from the Bakers Union. He refused to give any details as to the people with whom he was connected either here or in Germany. I am inclined to doubt the bona fides of this man and have written again to John Archer.

Special Branch report that the officials controlling the Tottenham Dust Destroyers have received from a Japanese contractor two tons of literature, papers, books, etc which they were asked to burn without making any reference to the police. An official in charge of the Dust Destroyer looked over the literature and refused to burn it. It appears that the Japanese contractor had received the documents from the Japanese Embassy. A recent BJ shows that embassies abroad have been instructed to destroy any papers that they do not feel it essential to keep and to make arrangements for the safety of confidential documents. Samples of the literature are being sent up for our inspection.

An illicit wireless station within ten miles of this office has been picked up. It is in touch with at least five other stations, one of which is in France, and is sending frequent messages by day and night. Our Direction-Finding stations have completely failed to locate it, although signals were very strong. It is believed that the balloon barrage may be having a serious effect on DF work.

Valentine Vivian told me that David Boyle was 'the Mystery Man' who went to Germany just before the outbreak of war and that his purpose was to contact a certain German general whom it was thought might lead a revolt in the German Army.

Valentine Vivian was the head of SIS's Section V, and David Boyle was Personal Assistant to Stewart Menzies, soon to be appointed Chief of SIS.

Wolfgang zu Putlitz and Klop are considering a scheme by which zu Putlitz should come right out in the open and denounce the German regime in the press and on the wireless.

19 September

Lord Hankey has been instructed by the Prime Minister to enquire into the possibility of leakage of information from the UK to Germany and suggest measures to stop it. His first step was to enquire into the methods of wireless interception. This led to a wrangle between the War Office and SIS, and Lord Hankey had not realised that MI5 were not responsible for wireless interception in this country. We have been asked (a) to put up a brief note showing the various methods by which information could reach Germany and any suggestions which we may have to prevent such leakage; (b) a note on Eire in the same sense and (c) a note on any additional powers required to search and arrest. Lord Hankey's interest in these matters prompted by the Prime Minister seems to give us our chance of getting our views represented in the Cabinet and for counteracting home front appeasement and the policy of making this country a place fit for aliens to live in.

The case of leakage of information through John King, one of the cipher clerks in the Foreign Office who was handing it on to the Russians, has developed considerably. Another man is now involved. Arrests have not yet been effected, as the evidence is not complete. They will probably be interrogated under the Official Secrets Act, but it is doubtful whether we shall prosecute.

Our Direction-Finding stations thought they had pinned down the illicit wireless station to the Italian Embassy, but this is by no means certain.

Frequent reports are coming in about German submarine bases on the west coast of Eire. There seems little doubt that something of the kind is going on. We are passing reports on to the Ministry of Defence for their comments. The Naval Intelligence Division is getting rather exasperated and is thinking of putting up a full-dress memo urging that steps with or without the cooperation of Eire should be taken to safeguard the Irish coast. Members of a submarine crew who were captured the other day were in possession of packets of Irish cigarettes.

Commander William Bardwell is very worried about Admiralty petrol storage depots which are being constructed with Irish labour. He wants to have the personnel vetted. I explained that vetting by this department was useless and that Special Branch would probably be unable to cope with the volume and that even if they could the results would be by no means conclusive. It would be perfectly possible for two Irishmen to come over from Eire and do all the necessary damage. At the same time it seemed futile to go on vetting all these people from the Communist or Fascist point of view which we were doing at the rate of some 16,000 a month, while there is no check on the IRA who are by far the most dangerous from a security point of view.

Gravesend telephoned to say that a Dutchman called Grandes had arrived en route for Holland. He was searched and found to be in possession of a number of documents referring to aircraft etc. When questioned he gave the name of [XXXXXXXX] who he said was in the British Secret Service. [XXXXXXXX] who works for the SIS, denied all knowledge. The Security Officer at Gravesend stutters and it subsequently transpired that the name was Brandes.

[XXXXXXX] still denied knowledge but on seeing the papers ascertained that the man was connected with someone else to whom [XXXXXXXX] had given facilities on account of purchases he was making for the Air Ministry.

Poliakov is trying to go to the United States on a lecture tour. He is backed by Lord Tyrrell [a former British Ambassador to Paris] and Frank Ashton-Gwatkin [of the Foreign Office]. The case has been referred to Sir Robert Vansittart with a warning from us.

SNOW has been let out of jail and is proceeding to Holland where he is contacting a German agent. He is to go on using his wireless under our instruction and is sending weather reports which the Germans want.

23 September

Our Direction-Finding stations have definitely pinned down the illicit wireless station to the Polish Embassy. There is no doubt now that previous calculations were thrown out on account of the balloon barrage. There is another illicit wireless station which has been detected somewhere near Winchester.

Zu Putlitz and Klop have worked out a scheme for inducing German airmen to desert. They propose that a message should be broadcast giving details as to a landing ground on some island which can be used by day or night under certain conditions. They think that quite a number of pilots might desert and that in any case the broadcast will have a demoralising effect. In the meantime zu Putlitz has got himself arrested. He went to the Nazi spy film, where he was recognised by a Belgian who was a connection of Sir Robert Vansittart. The Belgian reported him to the police, who took zu Putlitz back to his home. Dick White had to get the party straightened out.

Klop has worked out a useful plan for getting Dick's agent out of The Hague. Her connections are very good and she ought to compensate for the loss of zu Putlitz to a certain degree.

24 September

I discussed with Archie Craig information regarding submarine bases on the west coast of Ireland. The Admiralty is worried about this and is anxious to get up a case to present to the Dominions Office. Their view is that they should be allowed to go inside the three-mile limit in order to control German submarine activities.

Max Knight has put up a note on the British Union of Fascists and the Nordic League. I have asked for some direction as to the policy. The BUF seem to be getting into the War Reserve Police. It seems to me that the time has come to consider whether we go for these organisations as a whole and have them suppressed, or whether we continue to deal with the law-breakers as and when we find them. If we deal with the organisations as a whole we shall have to do it largely on their programme and literature.

25 September

I discussed with Dick White, Francis Aiken-Sneath, Max Knight and Roger Hollis the question of the British Union of Fascists and the Nordic League. My view is that we should take stock of the position and make some definite suggestions for cleaning up these organisations. It is I think worth considering whether in so far as the BUF is concerned the Metropolitan Police Commissioner should not send for Sir Oswald Mosley, confront him with certain evidence from his press and from leaflets and ask him definitely what is the attitude of his organisation in the present crisis. To us it seems that Mosley's future is very much bound up with the success or failure of Hitler, and his purpose would seem to be to impede the prosecution of war. Aiken-Sneath is preparing a note. There seem interesting developments as regards the Nordic League which is evidently trying to penetrate the Peace Pledge Union. This move can only be in the interests of Germany. We hope shortly to have more concrete evidence on this point.

Edward Hinchley-Cooke's pre-war spy Donald Adams has been given seven years' imprisonment.

Donald Adams was a racing journalist implicated in the 1938 mail cover of Mrs Jessie Jordan.

Hordern, the Chief Constable of Lancashire called about the case of Kuchenmeister and left some papers. It seems that people are pressing for Kuchenmeister's return, otherwise the wheels won't go round. I said I did not think we could possibly take the responsibility of having him at large here.

Hordern was most anxious that we should let him have copies of letters that we send to borough chief constables in his area as he has a Special Branch, which he calls his Q Branch, and which deals almost exclusively with matters affecting this department. He was rather upset that he had never been put au fait with the activities of the Auslands Organisation and did not know about the case of Kuchenmeister. I told him that I would see what we could do to put things right.

26 September

A Communist named Goodman who was associated with Claud Cockburn, applied for a permit to go to Paris on behalf of the *Daily Mirror* and *The Week*. His application was backed by Lord Faringdon and others. We turned it down on the grounds that if the French asked us to accept one of their Communists we should have refused him leave to land.

John King, the Foreign Office cipher clerk, has been arrested. He had a safe-deposit for a considerable sum of money in £5 notes. This has been seized and the notes will be traced. Both he and his mistress deny the allegations. They are both under arrest pending enquiries.

27 September

The case of John King is developing in an interesting way. The notes in his safe-deposit have been traced to Henri Pieck, a Dutchman and Soviet agent, and also to the Moscow Narodny Bank. Another man in the code section of the Foreign Office is also involved. His name is Major Grange. He has been suspended pending interrogation. Another individual named Raymond Oakes is being interrogated. It seems doubtful that he is very closely involved.

28 September

Between 7 and 8pm Philip Allen, Secretary to the Home Secretary, rang up about two alleged Dutch inventors, de Voogt and J.R. Carp. Had we any objection to their coming here? It appears that Vice Admiral Tower on the recommendation of an MP called Sir Reginald Clerry (?) had said that he would like to see these people. Tower had made no reference to ourselves or NID. It transpired that Carp has been engaged in some very unsavoury gun-running activities over a period of years. After speaking with the Naval Intelligence Division I was rung up by the First Lord's secretary. I explained to him that Carp was undesirable and that our general experience of these matters was that so-called inventors really try to find out the extent of our progress in any particular line, and that these people might well be acting in German interests, particularly as Carp seemed to be the kind of person who would do anything for money. If, however, the Admiralty was prepared to say that the visits of these people was a matter of national importance we would be prepared to let them come provided that they were given a 48 hour visa and we were told the time and port of arrival.

29 September

C rang up about Dr Yelic, a Croat terrorist who has previously been reported to be in the pay of the Nazis, and is arranging for the assassination of the Prince Regent of Yugoslavia. He is arriving at Gibraltar on an Italian boat on Sunday, travelling under a false name on a Hungarian passport. Can he be turned back? It seems that we have the powers provided the Foreign Office will stand the racket with the Italians and the Hungarians. The matter is under discussion between Foreign Office and DNI.

30 September

I spoke to John Nicholls at the Foreign Office who informed me that it had been decided to bring in the *Conte de Savoia* at Gibraltar on grounds of searching for contraband, and that Dr Yelic would be taken off and interned. It was intended to inform the Italians either at the moment when action was taken or immediately afterwards.

We have obtained a card index of the NSDAP up until 1934. The up-to-date index was probably transferred to the German Embassy but the earlier index was left in cabinets which were sold to a furniture dealer who handed them over to the police. A good many of the people we had not formerly detected have left, there are some 15 or 20 still in this country, whose internment is being ordered.

There has been a flood of applications by firms for the return of Kuchenmeister whom they all say would be of great benefit to our rearmament industry. We are re-stating the case to the Home Office and recommending that if he returns he should be interned forthwith.

I gather that Eugene Spier, Winston's friend, is to remain where he is on account of some last minute evidence supplied by Wickham Steed.

An SIS report on Eire is somewhat alarmist as regards the internal situation. An attempt at revolution by the IRA does not appear to be out of the question.

The Oxford Don is deriving considerable satisfaction at ordering the internment of a complete (enemy alien) company of the White Horse Inn which turned up at one of our ports. He took the view that as they had no means they were better where they were. It now transpires that they were going to give performances at various air force depots. If this is true they are certainly better where they are.

I dined with Gaspa Cassado, the great Spanish cellist, who had just returned from a tour in South Africa and was due to play in Stuttgart on 3 October. He thinks Stuttgart is too near the Siegfried Line and he does not wish to play in Germany as it will spoil his market in the United States.

I October

The *Daily Worker* has made another volte face in its editorial of 30 September. The war is now an imperialist one, and not anti-Fascist. Russia's peace policy must therefore be supported. It would seem to be a case of he who pays the piper calls the tune.

2 October

The Germans issued instructions on 13 September that all Egyptian and Dominion subjects have to report to the police within twenty-four hours. T. A. Robertson tells me that our Direction-Finding organisation is virtually no organisation at all. We require sixty experts at least. At the moment we have 27 amateurs twiddling knobs and hoping they may pick something up. We are asking the Americans whether they can give us any help and if we get a favourable reply Cotton and an expert may go out. In the meantime another station has been located at Belfast. This is interesting as Owens had already told us of the existence of such a station. Owens is sending nightly to Germany both weather reports and reports on military matters carefully concocted. There seems no reason to doubt his loyalty at the moment but he is under close supervision and acting entirely under our orders. When things begin to warm up we hope to do useful work by sending misleading messages.

3 October

We have had a wire saying that Yelic has been taken off at Gibraltar from the *Conte de Savoia*. James Stafford came to see the Director-General today. We talked a good deal about his difficulties on matters affecting permits. He suffers as we do from the lack of direction. It was agreed that if we wanted to turn down a case we should merely refuse on security grounds without giving any further reasons. We should only state our reasons to the responsible minister if the case had to be defended in the House of Commons.

In the meantime, Stafford appears to be taking a certain line of his own. He told us that he had refused a permit to Winston's son who wanted to spend three days of his honeymoon in Paris. The permit was refused owing to insufficient grounds for travel. One imagines there will be a backwash.

Philip Jordan has applied for a permit to go as war correspondent to Paris for the *News Chronicle*. We turned him down for the Ministry of Information and the War Office has for some reason or other assumed that we have refused him a permit. In the meantime the War Minister Leslie Hore-Belisha is fuming and says that in the absence of very special ground the permit must be granted within half an hour. We do not propose to refuse him one as it would obviously be impossible seeing that Jordan is foreign editor. It seems not unlikely however that he will act for Claud Cockburn whose Communist correspondent Goodman was refused a permit the other day.

4 October

The Director-General attended a meeting about the death penalty for spies. The matter appears to have been overlooked in our Defence Regulations. The Director of Public Prosecutions says that procedure by trial for high treason would be far too cumbersome and in a number of cases ineffective. For instance, if a German arrived at one of our ports and was arrested before he had time to do anything, there would be no very good grounds in the absence of special information regarding his mission for preferring a charge of high treason. He could moreover say that he owed no allegiance but to the King and therefore could not commit an act of high treason. It was agreed by all the high legal pundits who discussed this matter that it could not be left to the judge to decide whether a spy should be shot or sent to penal servitude for life. A law should be framed so that if the man was convicted of espionage the judge had no alternative but to sentence him to death on the same lines that he would sentence a murderer. It was of course always open to the King to whittle the sentence down to three weeks if he so desired.

Owens, our double-cross agent, has been contacted by a German, whose identity we are trying to establish.

The two Dutchmen, de Voogt and Carp, are to go back to Holland as soon as we can get them out of the country. They had nothing to say and the Admiralty does not want them. I hope they have learned their lesson.

The American Embassy rang up about a naturalised American citizen of Belgian origin named Henri Kennis who had just left for the USA on the SS *Pennland*. They had been notified by the Belgian police that this man was a notorious bootlegger and counterfeiter who had amassed a large fortune in the States, and now, armed with 600,000 Belgian francs, was proceeding to the United States to organise a petrol supply to German submarines operating in the Atlantic.

Cardiff rang up about Charles Horace Smith, who had left a hotel without paying his bill. His trunks had been opened and had been found to contain a good deal of Nazi literature, addresses etc. We had previous records about this man who had been acting as engineer on one of the Union Castle boats and had drawn attention to his Nazi sympathies. He now seems to be a member of the British Union of

Fascists. He is being charged with obtaining money by false pretences and as soon as he is remanded we shall have a chance of interrogating him.

5 October

Colonel Stephens has been interviewing a number of German journalists who are interned. Some of them are Jews and they all seemed rather distressed at the conditions under which they were living. One complained that he had not changed his socks for three weeks. Stephens replied "Will you kindly sit over there and keep your spats on."

The Ministry for Information published a story today about parcels of butter which had been going from this country to Nazi leaders. This story is absolutely true and had previously been checked up through the Post Office. The sender is one Arthus Hentzen, a Bradford wool exporter of German connections. His solicitor, Mr Early, who is a member of the German Chamber of Commerce, has asked that the article in the paper should be withdrawn by the Ministry and is coming up fife and drum tomorrow morning to see Charles Peake at the Ministry of Information. We have given Peake the background as regards Hentzen and Early.

At the request of the First Lord, Cecil Liddell is going to Brussels to see King Leopold. Winston has a friend, Stein, who professes to have the entrée to the King. I gather Stein has been used for establishing direct contact. Cecil is to take a letter to the King from Admiral Sir Roger Keyes about Stein and to receive the King's answer as to whether Stein is *persona grata*. Winston is looking ahead to the time when the Belgian neutrality may again be violated. He wants to have some plan worked out which would be impossible if any attempt were made to deal with the politicians. The King's influence and control is considerable.

6 October

I discussed the case of Rosinski who was employed by the Military Academy in Berlin until 1936 when he was dismissed owing to his wife being not strictly Aryan. He came to this country and made contact with eminent strategists and was also friendly with Leslie Hore-Belisha. We had always regarded him with suspicion. He was interned at the outbreak of war and subsequently certain specific allegations were satisfactorily explained. We told this to the Home Office who now propose to let him out. I explained to the Director-General that there were two sides to this man's case, firstly the specific allegations and secondly the fact that he was a German and had intimate Reichswehr connections. One aspect of the case had been cleared, but he could not possibly be cleared of the other. He should therefore remain interned. The Director-General put this view to Sir Alexander Maxwell and told him that if the man was liberated it would be entirely on the responsibility of the Secretary of State.

7 October

There are indications that both Harry Pollitt and J.R. Campbell are at loggerheads with the Communist Party on the question of Russian policy. There seems to be a possibility that Pollitt will resign as Secretary-General.

9 October

I discussed with B4(b) the question of the Czech Communist group here. It seems that we might usefully take the opportunity of sending these people to the French. As a group they are apparently anxious to fight the Nazis, although they may engage in subversive activities once they have enlisted. Since however the French have given all Czechs in France the alternative of joining the Legion or an internment camp the probability is that they will know how to deal with them.

The British Mission in Algiers wired us about the activities of one William Mellor concerning whom the French were anxious. He was said to have connections with doubtful aliens in French North Africa. Aiken-Sneath replied that it was unlikely that this man was the well-known Mellor, of the *Daily Herald*, but probably Captain Mellor, a journalist who had had former connections with Morocco and was associated with members of the British Union of Fascists. The reply came back, "The Mellor to whom you refer is a staff officer on this Mission and instituted the enquiry." And then, rather bitterly, "We pointed out the Mellor referred to by the French is Left-Wing not Fascist." We are anxious to reply, "Sorry you've been troubled. Glad to know your present whereabouts which has been duly noted in your dossier."

10 October

We have been asked to receive seventeen Polish cryptographers who are said to be experts in Russian and German ciphers. We have said that we will be guided by the Government Code & Cipher School. I gather however that they do not want all these people and would much prefer to see them in France. Alastair Denniston has already had a talk with them in Warsaw and I believe thought their claims as regards German and Russian ciphers can to some extent be maintained. If this is so they might be very useful.

Everybody is getting worried about Cecil, except me. There had been no news since he left on Thursday except his police pass which has returned from Dover. I expect he had difficulty in getting an appointment with the Distinguished Person.

Cecil Liddell had been sent on a mission to see the King of the Belgians.

Special Material of 5 October indicates that the French are extremely worried about the mysterious Swede who was active during the period immediately prior to the outbreak of war. This man is said to be again on his way to England. There is another individual with whom he is associated who is referred to as "Ballet Russe".

There is some idea that these people are working with the British government on a new appeasement plan.

The 'mysterious Swede' was the tycoon Axel Wenner-Gren, a friend of Herman Goering, then attempting to negotiate peace terms.

11 October

Jack Curry saw Klop last night, who had just returned from Holland. He had a special mission on behalf of the PCO, Major Richard Stephens. Its seems that SIS are in touch with certain disaffected elements in the Reichswehr, who are proposing to organise a coup d'état within the next few days. Their programme is to arrest all the principal leaders of the Party on the grounds that they have sold their country, and laid up large balances for themselves abroad. Hitler is to be the only exception and will be allowed to remain as a puppet head. The army could not attack him on account of their oath of allegiance, but they would see to it that he was rendered entirely innocuous. Two envoys are said to have come to Holland on this mission and were anxious to see a British cabinet minister in order to get some reassurance that if they took over and proposed the restoration of Poland and Czechoslovakia, Germany would be given an honourable settlement. They were told that it was impossible for a British cabinet minister to be involved in a matter of this sort but that if a notice which they had prepared found its way into the *Basler Nachrichten* before Thursday, they could go ahead. The message in the paper is that it is reported that there is a movement by certain elements in the German Army to arrest all Party leaders on the grounds that they have betrayed the State etc.

Klop, in order to get this message through to the *Basler Nachrichten*, approached a contact of his in the Swiss Legation. This was necessary in order to get the use of the press telephone line. The Swiss Legation must have had some idea of what is intended but they put Klop in touch with the representative here of the *Basler Nachrichten*, which is generally speaking anti-Nazi in tone. This representative thought the story was a good one and worth publication, and a message was telephoned through last night. When it appears it will be broadcast two or three times as a news item by the BBC and this is supposed to give the signal for a general revolt. It all sounds rather Phillips Oppenheim but there may perhaps be something in it. In the meantime His Majesty's Government, uninformed, is entirely disconnected with the project.

12 October

Cecil Liddell returned from his journey to Belgium. The King refused to see him, but I gather that he is sending some communication indicating that Stein is *persona grata*. The King's position is a very delicate one, since if either his ministers or the people thought that he had in any way jeopardised the neutrality of Belgium, he might be forced to abdicate. Feeling in Belgium on the maintenance of neutrality appears to be very strong and there will only be a change if some violation takes place by Germany. Stein created a good impression but he is certainly a man of mystery. He evidently has very good connections both in Belgium and Holland.

Cecil saw Winston on his return, who seemed satisfied though somewhat disappointed.

A suggestion has come in through General Fisher from one of his officers that we might scatter dud German banknotes in millions over Germany. It is thought that this would lead to a complete economic dislocation. There may be something in the idea but firstly there is always the chance that the Germans would attempt something similar over here and secondly this practice hardly fits in with the high moral tone of the war! I have sent the suggestion on to Valentine Vivian expressing the view that perhaps when the war has deteriorated through the use of poison gas, bacteria etc a suitable occasion may arise for a venture of this sort.

Klop has returned to Holland. He says that the German diplomatic and journalist staffs are extremely depressed and that Germans generally in Holland are very unpopular. He deplores however the lack of pro-British propaganda. The Germans apparently have an excellent service and see that their papers reach Holland regularly and in large quantities. It is impossible to buy any British paper which is less than three days old.

Eire neutrality is rapidly becoming a farce. A German submarine sailed into Dingle Bay with the crew of a cargo steamer which had been torpedoed, and two British aeroplanes landed in Kilmarnock, but after the necessary repairs had been made were allowed to proceed. A representative of the Civic Guard, who was subsequently questioned, ended with the following remark, "And who in the name of God are we supposed to be neutral against anyway?"

The Marston Press, who print the *Daily Worker*, are also engaged in printing petrol coupons for the Government. The Communists think this is a very good arrangement and are doubtless making the most of it.

13 October

Princess Hohenlohe and her mother have applied for exit permits to proceed to the United States. The ostensible grounds are that her son is seriously ill. Actually she is probably going either to see Hans Wiedemann, Hitler's envoy in San Francisco, whose mistress she has been, or else to consult an American crook lawyer in connection with her case against Lord Rothermere. There is also the possibility that Rothermere may be paying her to leave the country. She had been paid about £5,000 a year by Rothermere to work on appeasement. She is now suing Rothermere for breach of contract and in consequence his solicitors are trying to persuade the Home Office that the Princess is a dangerous Nazi agent and should be deported. Rothermere is considering whether he will now go to the Attorney-General and ask him to give his fiat that the case should be stopped in the national interest. Personally I think that it would be in the national interest that the case should be heard.

A man called Revescz, a Hungarian describing himself as a co-ordinator of information, applied for a permit to leave this country. He was backed by Winston Churchill. In turning up our records we found that the *Deuxième Bureau* regard him as a Nazi agent in the guise of a left-wing refugee. The Director-General told the First Lord who said that he had the utmost confidence in this man who had been his publishing agent for many years and that he was proposing to put him into the Ministry of Information. He thought the *Deuxième Bureau* had libelled him but would like us to make further enquiries. We are doing this, and in the meantime are allowing the man to travel without being searched.

Representations are being made by MPs and others about Ernst Hanfstaengel. Colonel Stephens has interviewed him. Our conclusions are that since he has remained a Nazi Party member and that his son is a member of the Hitler Jugend, and since he has been directly in touch with Hitler regarding his return to Germany right up to the middle of August, he was not a proper person to be at large. He had never published any articles against the Nazi regime in spite of long-drawn-out negotiations and in one instance he had refused to give evidence in a claim against the German government dating back to the last war and had placed all the information at the disposal of the German Under-Secretary for Foreign Office Affairs.

Jane Sissmore has been down to see Percy Glading at Maidstone Prison. "Miss X" had told us some time ago that Glading was very worried because Peters, the Soviet agent, had placed him in charge of certain people who were giving information purely for money and not for Party reasons. Glading did not like these people as he thought they might compromise the whole Party.

When interviewed Glading was rather stuffy at first but gradually, under a good deal of flattery, his own conceit got the better of him. The conversation developed on professional lines and in the end Glading even softened towards "Miss X", when he realised that he had placed her in a very difficult position. His real grievance was against Special Branch in producing the porter at Fawcett Court who swore that Glading had visited Brandes' flat. This he said was a lie. Otherwise he regarded the whole business as a fair cop.

He did not say anything very useful except that as regards the other people who had been working for Peters they were not very far from Whitehall. The inference was that if he knew that, he probably knew a great deal more. Jane is going to visit him again shortly.

Percy Glading had been convicted of espionage in 1938 on the evidence of Olga Gray, an MI5 agent referred to in court only as 'Miss X'.

15 October

The disappearance of Wolfgang zu Putlitz from Holland has caused a good deal of mystery. The Germans are making out that zu Putlitz has gone back to join his regiment at his own request, have asked the Dutch to make enquiries about his disappearance; other rumours about him are that he has gone on a secret mission to the USA and that he has been seen recently at The Hague.

Harry Pollitt seems to have toed the Communist Party line and will not come out in open opposition. Discussion has arisen within the CPGB as to whether the Party should penetrate the army and cause disaffection or whether they should make political capital by objecting to serve.

At 6pm we received a request from MI-l for a note on the Peace Pledge Union. This was required by the Secretary of State for a meeting of the cabinet the following day. I gather that the question of the Peace Pledge Union, the British Union of Fascists, and CPGB had been raised by Winston who was annoyed at seeing Fascist signs written on walls. Our view is that the penetration of the PPU by the Nordic League and the BUF should be exposed through publicity in the press.

A woman has written in from the east coast drawing attention to the large number of kites being flown by children and others. She considers these highly dangerous. I have asked the Director-General whether kites were allowed in the last war.

16 October

Edward Hinchley-Cooke has arrested an Austrian named Kafka who was to be a Nazi spy in the Austrian Legion which is being formed for active service. Kafka is being held temporarily for travelling without the necessary permit from the local chief constable. It seems that he had been attempting to get a list of the legionnaires and he was also found to be in possession of a revolver without a licence.

17 October

Roger Hollis and I saw Frederick Leggett of the Ministry of Labour today. He seems quite satisfied on the whole of the labour situation but is a little afraid of trouble if food prices rise and wages are kept low. Both government and trade union leaders are anxious to avoid an abnormal rise in wages as it will only lead to a great deal of trouble and dislocation after the war when they have to come down. There is therefore a danger of agitation on the lines that the trade union leaders are in league with the government in opposing measures which would be of benefit to the workers. Leggett's policy is as usual to sit heavily on all unofficial strikes and keep all disputes within the unions. At the same time, he is anxious to know of any genuine grievances and to get them removed at the earliest possible moment. Recent troubles have been caused almost entirely by mismanagement of government contract branches who are, he says, without exception the worst employers of labour.

Leggett was interesting about the Prime Minister. He says the trade union leaders do not really trust him. One of them said to him that the other day after an interview at Downing Street, "We left No. 10 at 19 minutes past 12 and we are sure that he told us everything up to that moment, but he did not tell us what he was going to do at 20 to one." Unlike Winston, the Prime Minister seems to talk a language which they do not really understand.

18 October

John King got ten years' imprisonment. The judge told him that he wondered whether he ought to be trying the case at all. In other words whether it was not a matter for a court-martial.

Another illicit wireless station has been discovered and the sender is the messenger of the Civil Lord at the Admiralty. His messages seem to be fairly harmless, but each day he says that he is sending from a different place off the coast. He started on the east coast and came down the Channel and now says he is off the coast of Portugal. This may be a code of some sort reporting on the movement of ships. He is to be raided as soon as he again becomes active.

19 October

I had a long talk with G.P. Slade who is working on questions affecting Eire at the Naval Intelligence Division. I think I succeeded in convincing him that our relations with Colonel Liam Archer of the Ministry of Defence were of a very frank nature and that if any intelligence service were set up in the Eire and happened to go wrong we might lose his assistance, which was of great value to us on getting reports on the activities of Germans in the country. He is going to explain the position to the DNI and suggest that we should in future send reports regarding submarine activities to Colonel Archer and get his reactions. I said that I did not think there was any objection to sending them both through us and through the British High Commissioner, Sir John Maffey. Slade tells me that we are now going to appoint a naval attaché in Dublin.

The Ministry of Information have been ringing up to have our approval to wild stories which the press wish to publish about the Secret Service. The particular paper in question is the *Sunday Graphic*, with Lord Kemsley and House, who both have German connections. The particular article had a good deal about making use of spies when we got them and forcing them to continue their communication with the enemy. If we cut out these particular passages we indicate to the press that they have hit the nail on the head. In a negative way therefore they could quite easily build up a fair picture of our activities. The only course therefore is ban all such articles entirely. This, I gather, is being done.

21 October

A naval attaché disguised as an ex-naval officer is to be attached to Sir John Maffey at the British High Commission in Dublin. It is hoped that he may be able to make some progress on the submarine question.

23 October

On Sunday T.A Robertson raided the illicit wireless at the house of Hammett, the messenger to the Civil Lord of the Admiralty. It was found that the wireless was the property of Hammett's son who had been an enthusiastic amateur for three years. The father denied all knowledge of what his son was doing. Enquiries are proceeding.

Captain Christie and Cornwall-Evans attempted to leave the country today for Switzerland. The latter had in his possession a telegram signed by Sir Robert Vansittart saying "Come at once." As no intimation has been given to the Security Control Officer neither of these people were allowed to proceed and their papers were confiscated.

24 October

The Director-General is staggered by the atmosphere of the Home Office. He says they do not seem to realise that there is a war going on. He arrived there at 9.30 yesterday and was unable to see anybody in authority. He could find nobody for an hour and a half except the charwoman.

As an example of a square peg in a round hole, the Oxford Don recounts that one of his colleagues, an eminent Professor of Medieval History, has been offered the position of Controller of Lard in the Ministry of Food.

Commander Christopher Arnold-Foster of SIS rang up about a somewhat disjointed and cryptic story of an illicit wireless station. I gather that he had intercepted certain messages which indicated that there might be an illicit station on a boat on the Tweed near Melrose. He wanted to know whether we could ascertain whether such a boat was situated there and whether it had a metal bottom. I do not know how we can find this out except by turning the boat upside down, but the Radio Three are working on it.

25 October

Slade of the Admiralty called with Captain Grieg who is to be our naval attaché in Dublin. It has been decided that he is to be officially described as a naval attaché. This, of course, is a confession to Eire in the sense that it recognises her as an independent country. I gave Grieg a brief summary of our relations with Colonel Archer in case he happened to come across him, but said that I thought it would be better he did not refer to our liaison in any conversion with Archer. I recommended to Grieg, although it was actually outside my province, that if it were possible for him to arrive at a point where we could supply Eire with equipment of one kind or another and so place them under obligation to us, we should have much better grounds for interfering in matters affecting German submarine activities on the west coast. I gather that something on these lines is already in contemplation.

25 October

In certain German musical programmes, short sharp sentences are being interpolated which when pieced together form continuous and coherent messages. Evidence tends to show that it is not necessarily the speaker at the broadcast station who is interpolating the remarks, but more probably someone in this country or in France working on the same frequency as the German station. The pause in any programme is used for speaking the message.

26 October

SNOW has returned from Brussels with £470 in notes and a small number of detonators concealed in a piece of wood. He was accompanied by another double-cross whom we put up as a man interested in the Welsh Nationalist movement. SNOW has also had a letter with his salary, which was posted in Bournemouth. He thinks he can establish the identity of the writer. The money is to be banked and SNOW is to receive instructions regarding the appointment of agents.

Dick White has paid a visit to MI7 where he had a talk with Colonel Aylmer Vallance and Major Warburton. MI7 is engaged in trying to establish the movement of public opinion in this country for the information of the General Staff. It also has a close liaison with the department of overseas propaganda, being Sir Campbell Stuart's organisation. Warburton has some scheme for using civilian internees as laboratory material for certain experiments MI7 wish to carry out in order to estimate the effect of their own and Allied departments' propaganda. We explained that these people would not be very suitable material as they have lived here for some time and many of them might very well have the English point of view. We thought that prisoners of war would be much more suitable subjects.

Dick White's informant is doing well in Brussels and looks like being taken on as a member of the local German Legation staff. The latest information is that the Germans have a hundred small submarines based on Heligoland and about twenty large ones based on a secret depot in the Atlantic, locality unknown.

27 October

The SNOW case is looking promising. SNOW and his Welsh friend are to do a course in Germany on intelligence and sabotage. The friend is to start a stamp business, which is of course the old form. It is understood that the Germans are sending messages on the backs of stamps. SNOW brought back with him some instructions on the under side of a postage stamp. These are being brought up by the Post Office. It is believed that they contain information about a man in Liverpool with whom SNOW is to get in touch. In the meantime steps are being taken to look through the mails at Bournemouth and Southampton for envelopes which are similar to the ones addressed to SNOW which contained his pay.

28 October

Brigadier Kevin Martin at MI-1 has suggested that a representative of the *News Chronicle* who thinks he has detected an illicit wireless station, should be shown the apparatus we use and taken round in a van in order to get a cross-bearing. He would then write up the story in the press. The Director-General telephoned Martin to say that we had strong objections to any publicity being given to this matter. It was in our interests that the Germans should regard us as grossly ineffi-cient in these matters, particularly as SNOW is sending them weather reports. If they thought that our organisation was good they might well ask him how it was that he managed to get his messages through.

The French have been talking about running a counter-espionage organisation in Eire. We have sat on this politely but heavily.

29 October

An American Legion is being formed clandestinely in various countries. The organiser in London is Hugh P. Guiller, managing director of the City bank, the Farmers Trust Company. Guiller has made a clean breast of his job to Joe Kennedy who has told him unofficially to get on with it.

31 October

The SNOW party is interesting. The micro-photographs have been brought up and a detailed questionanaire covering an immense variety of subjects has been revealed. SNOW had instructions to get this work done by Eschborn to whom a covering letter had been sent.

At the beginning of the war, as a result of censorship, a telegram was inter-cepted, and Colonel Hinchley-Cooke interviewed a German at a London hotel. He eventually decided to let the man go but made enquiries about the addressee who was Eschborn. The latter was interrogated and virtually confessed to being a German spy. He has since been left at large. SNOW is to go up and see him and will let things develop in the ordinary way. It will be interesting to see what Eschborn's reactions are.

Eschborn, one of three brothers, had been recruited by the Abwehr in 1938 in Cologne under duress. He alone held dual German citizenship and was enrolled by MI5 as DRAGONFLY.

SNOW and his Welsh friend appear to have had an interesting time in Brussels, where they had long discussions with various unidentified Germans. The idea is that they should both be employed on blowing up factories and works of impor-tance in this country, for which ample funds are to be available. There is a suggestion that explosives should be sent by submarine and landed somewhere off the Welsh coast. SNOW was offered £50,000 for anybody who could fly one of our latest aircraft to Germany.

We asked Special Branch to enquire about a man called Stelle who was connected with the Young Communist League They appear to have searched his house on the grounds that he might be a member of the IRA. A complaint has been lodged to the Home Secretary by someone who wishes to know whether the man has been cleared of suspicion. Special Branch have minuted the file saying that they carried out the enquiries at our request. They obviously stretched a point and are saddling us with the baby. We do not however want to let them down as their powers of search under IRA warrant have been very helpful in cases of suspected illicit wireless transmission.

2 November

I saw Brigadier French this morning. He gave me an account of yesterday's meeting. Winston thumped the table. He was anxious that complete censorship should be imposed on Eire and when opposition was raised on the grounds that this might antagonise the Irish government, he said dramatically, "What is that to the sinking of one of our warships?"

3 November

Hugh Fraser, who is an Air Commodore on the Committee of Imperial Defence and a friend of Malcolm Cumming, wished to tell somebody confidentially that he was worried about the security arrangements in the CID. He said there were quantities of copies of Cabinet minutes etc being taken off a roneo machine by girls who were not paid more than fifty shillings a week and that he had grounds for thinking that some time ago a leakage to the press had taken place from the CID. He thought therefore that if we were investigating these other alleged leakages we might do well possibly to put someone into the Cabinet Offices in a suitable position. I mentioned this matter to Jasper Harker for his consideration and told Fraser strictly for his own personal information that we had already been put in touch with Sir Edward Bridges about a possible leakage from the CID. Anything therefore that he could tell us which pointed however indefinitely in any direction would be of value.

I attended a meeting with the Director-General and Jasper Harker in the Secretary of State for War's room. The Secretary of State said that he had been attacked in the Cabinet on the alleged inefficiency of MI5 in not discovering the sources of extensive leakage which was supposed to be going on. The Secretary of State was very anxious to defend MI5 and would like to know what they had to say. The Director-General gave him a copy of the letter that we had had from the BBC indicating that all these rumours about broadcasts from Germany in which the locations of our units etc were disclosed seemed to be without foundation. The BBC have been listening in consistently day and night and had never heard any such broadcasts. They had however received similar rumours which on investigation had proved to be ill-founded. It boiled down to this: that up to the present no one had been able to produce any reasonable qualifications who could say that at such and such a time and on such and such a wavelength he had heard a broadcast disclosing confidential information. The Secretary of State was told that we had an enquiry on foot at the moment regarding a tank unit where the evidence appeared to be slightly more circumstantial but that up to the present the position had not been cleared up. The Secretary of State seemed quite relieved to find that Winston's stories were only a mare's nest. He was not altogether surprised as he said that Winston had told him a few days previously that Randolph and Duncan Sandys had not received a penny of their pay since they joined up. Enquiries showed that they had been paid in full.

6 November

The telephone interceptions to Eire are beginning to come in. So far there have been two instances of fairly obvious IRA activity. They seem to be using aeroplane communication for travel between this country and Eire.

Lady Lees of Dorset has issued a pamphlet on pacifist religious lines which has come to the notice of the *Deuxième Bureau*. They are extremely worried and want if possible to have this literature suppressed at the source. In actual fact the pamphlet is quite mild and cannot possibly be dealt with under existing regulations. We have already condoned far worse things from the PPU and BUF.

7 November

Kuchenmeister has come up again. Various people connected with him in business want him to return in order that he can run our rearmament industry. The whole thing is rather like Alice in Wonderland. The Home Office suggests that he should be allowed to come and take his chances before the tribunal.

The question for decision is whether he is better in Eire where he cannot have direct access to our rearmament industry or in this country under restrictions. I am inclined to say that if the Home Secretary would undertake to place him under close restrictions in spite of any decision of the tribunal, we are prepared to let him come and put his case before the tribunal.

Hugh Stevenson, Anthony Eden's secretary, spoke to me today about his minister's visit to Dulanty. Dulanty is taking up with his government the question of setting up a wireless detecting organisation in Eire but has asked what the approximate cost would be. I told Stevenson that both Secretary of State, the Chief of the Imperial General Staff and Colonel Butler had expressed the view that this equipment should be furnished free of charge. Stevenson thought that the most tactful way of putting it would be to say that we were quite ready to loan them the necessary equipment. Before finally making a decision he would at my suggestion communicate with Colonel Butler at MI8(c).

The Director-General went to see Lord Hankey last night. He told him our difficulties in not having direct access to anyone in the War Cabinet who could exercise the necessary authority in having certain of our recommendations put into force. Hankey thoroughly appreciated our point of view and said that he thought the Minister for Co-ordination of Defence, Lord Chatfield, was really the person who should be responsible. He undertook to sound him out.

SIS had a serious loss in the death of old C last Monday, Admiral Sir Hugh Sinclair.

Today comes the news of another blow. Major Richard Stevens, the PCO at The Hague who has been in touch with certain elements in the Reichswehr, was shot on the Dutch–German frontier last Thursday and his body taken off by the Gestapo. It seems also that Captain Sigismund Best and possibly others were kidnapped. No details are as yet available. The danger is that Stevens generally carried a list of his agents in his vestpocket. Nobody knows at the moment what he had on him. Dick White immediately got into touch with his agent at The Hague, whose identity was known to Stevens and instructed her to make her way to Brussels and return by plane. This she has done, bringing some very interesting information about German intentions in Holland. It seems that the plan was to invade Belgium via the little triangle of Dutch territory by Maastricht. It was thought that this would cause us to violate Belgian neutrality and so give the Germans the excuse to advance on Ostend and Zeebrugge. For some reason or other the plan was called off late on the evening of 10 November, whether permanently or temporarily is not known. The Stevens incident will be a great blow to SIS and also to ourselves, since we lose the services of an extremely valuable agent who had succeeded in getting well in at The Hague.

Major Stevens and Captain Best survived the war in a concentration camp.

SIS has informed us that a German agent who is controlled by one of the double-cross men is due to arrive at Newhaven today. They want him shadowed from the port and kept under observation. It is of the greatest importance that this man should not become aware that he is the subject of observation. As things are at present there is no really satisfactory machinery for carrying out this work. I had a talk with John Adam and Harry Allen and suggested that we should appoint two or three Field Security Police – men in each port for detective work, the idea being that they would go through the B6 school. These people might ultimately form the nucleus of some kind of Port Enquiry Agency. This is very much needed as at the moment we have no real machinery in the provinces. I discussed this also with Harker and pointed out that really our facilities for enquiry at the moment are very little better than they are in peacetime. In some ways they are even worse because we have so many more cases to deal with. We have no thorough means of investigating activities of enemy aliens outside the Metropolitan Police area. In many cases we have to be content with a somewhat colourless report from a chief constable or with postal observation which only involves opening about 10% of the man's letters. At the end of a month's enquiry therefore we are generally very little further forward than we were at the beginning.

14 November

T.A. Robertson has just returned from Belfast. They investigated one rather suspicious case at Portrush, but so far the enquiries are inconclusive. The Belfast detecting station, which is singularly well-placed, has picked up several people believed to be communicating to or from Germany, possibly from this country. Robertson's impression of the local police is somewhat similar to the one I gained more than a year ago. The issue between the Orangemen and the IRA is the thing that really counts and espionage matters are of secondary importance. There is also a certain wildness in the reports which are obtained by Ulster. We hope, through the Command Security Officer who seems intelligent and is well in with the local authorities, to get these matters sifted locally before they are passed on to us.

15 November

Valentine Vivian came over today and told me about Major Richard Stevens. They did not know a great deal as nobody in the original party appears to have survived. A meeting had been arranged at the frontier with certain German staff officers. Stevens, Best and two Dutchmen had been to the frontier by car but nobody had turned up. On the second day they got a message to say that the officers would be there on the following day. When they arrived on the third day they parked the car within forty yards of the frontier. A German car arrived. The officers surrounded Stevens' car and the first man to get out was shot. Then Stevens got out and was also shot. Two men remained in the car, whether the two Dutchmen or Best and one Dutchman, is not known, and the Germans pushed it over the frontier. The Dutch guards and any onlookers were intimidated by the Gestapo and did not dare to intervene. The whole plot was known to the Dutch General Staff and it seems not unlikely that the member of the staff, Colonel Gijsbertius Sas, previously reported on by [deleted] as a German agent, was responsible for giving the show away. Sas, who had been sent to Berlin, was evidently back at the Hague, since a picture appeared of him in consultation with the rest of the staff of *Picture Post* only about ten days ago. The Dutch are terrified and do not wish to make any protest. The French who are also concerned, and have a number of Gestapo in tow, are contemplating some counter-action, which will not perhaps do much good.

Soviet espionage seems to be on the increase. Jane Sissmore has now got a man in the Russian Trade Delegation whom she would like to get at. Unfortunately the premises at 51/53 Hatton Gardens are immune under the latest trade treaty.

We are still looking for a man in the Committee of Imperial Defence who was reported to us by Isaac Don Levine through Walter Krivitsky. We are trying to get Krivitsky himself to come over here if possible and we are also trying to get the man Pieck over from Holland. Both these people should help us clear the matter up.

The spy in the Cabinet Office claimed by Krivitsky was John Cairncross, who was not identified as a Soviet agent until 1951.

It seems that Eire are quite ready to cooperate in the matter of sending wireless experts and that there had been a ready response to Anthony Eden's approach to Dulanty. Two experts have arrived here to undergo a course.

We have stopped two censorship officers from going to Gibraltar. Their names were Harcourt and Chapman. They were friends and one of them is under suspicion on account of a police report, the contents of which are being investigated. We have another very bad case in the censorship.

A woman has written an extremely indiscreet letter to Shishmareff, a suspect American of Russian origin whom we have on check. She told him amongst other things where she was working and that there is a black list and a white list. She thought moreover that Claud Cockburn would be interested to know that he was on the black list. The case is being taken up by the Director of Public Prosecutions.

T.A. Robertson tells me that one of the notes which was paid to SNOW as part of his salary by a woman who posted the letter from Bournemouth and subsequently from Southampton and London, has been traced to Selfridges. Enquiry there showed that she had obtained this note in exchange for treasury notes. An accurate description of the woman has been given. She is evidently in the habit of positing her letters at different places at irregular intervals. A local search of the mails for similar envelopes therefore might not be of much use unless we can find that she makes regular use of one particular locality.

A number of Dutch and Germans have been landed here from the *Simon Bolivar* which was sunk two days ago. As soon as they recover we intend to interrogate the

Germans who were bound for Batavia and may have something to do with German secret service activities there.

Princess Hohenlohe has lost her case against Lord Rothermere and is to be allowed to leave with her mother for the United States. She will have a special exit permit which in the words of the Permit Office "ensures that she and her mother will be put through the canteen."

A long report about her, which is, I believe, for publication in the American magazine *Time*, has been sent to the Home Office by Baron Frankenstein. The report is written by von Hofmanstahl and alleges that Lord Rothermere received very large sums from the Germans in order to carry out his appeasement scheme.

22 November

A statement has been issued by Himmler on the Munich bomb plot that it is attributed to a German subject who was found crossing the German–Swiss frontier. The British secret service is, of course, at the back of it and the Stevens and Best incident has been dragged in. The Germans allege that Major Stevens and Captain Best were attempting to cross the Dutch frontier and were arrested, but state that enquiries are still proceeding as to whether they were on German or Dutch soil. They infer that people in Germany with whom Stevens and Best were in touch they supposed to be disaffected elements, but were in reality agents of the Gestapo. Himmler states however that the Germans had been supplied with a wireless set for communications by the British and had been in touch with the British government ever since.

At about 7 o'clock Percival of MI-1(a) rang up to say that he had a War Cabinet memo on a proposal to set up a secret intelligence organisation in Eire. He had been asked to brief the Secretary of State for the Cabinet meeting tomorrow and wanted a report from us by 8.30am. Percival himself knew nothing about the question and did not know why the memo had been sent to him. I went up to the War Office and found that the memo was based on a report submitted by the Naval Intelligence Division to the First Lord, who had asked for its urgent consideration by his colleagues. I eventually succeeded in getting hold of Stewart Menzies who knew of the existence of the memo but had never been asked to put forward criticisms or been told that the matter was under discussion by the Cabinet. Since he and ourselves were the two people vitally concerned this seemed, to say the least, a little curious. We succeeded in getting out an answer by midnight, which was roughly on the following lines:

The question of reporting on submarine activities and setting up a secret organisation for this purpose might vitally affect the existing relations between MI5 and the Eire Ministry of Defence. It could be done but would take at least two months and a considerably longer period if it were to be really effective. It would moreover necessitate the establishment of secret wireless stations for communicating with the Admiralty. It seemed highly probable that the existence of the organisation would in some way come to the notice of the Eire authorities and that the service they were now rendering to MI5 would cease in consequence. It was therefore recommended that before any drastic step was taken MI5 should get Colonel Liam Archer to come over and discuss with him the possibility of improving the coast watching service.

23 November

I attended a meeting at the Home Office in the afternoon to discuss the question of the export of newspapers and other printed matter and the granting of permits for this purpose. The matter had been brought to a head by the Foreign Office who were disturbed by the fact that the *Daily Worker, Action* and other publications which would entirely misrepresent the situation in this country were being allowed to be exported and read abroad. H.L. Farquhar, who represented the Foreign Office, said he was speaking on behalf of R.A. Butler. He was extremely anxious that something should be done. Walter Monckton was anxious that we should be quite sure that any measures we took were 98% effective, since it was not worth having a political battle on the home front about this question unless we were going to achieve results. He had in mind the possibility of the export of literature of this kind to Eire and its re-export to the continent. Also the possibility of sending individual copies through the mails which might not be detected. Sir Alexander Maxwell disliked the idea of interfering in any way with the existing system and pleaded that by the suppression of minority literature here we weakened the case for which we were fighting, namely, the liberty of minorities aboard. This seems to indicate a complete misconception of the whole position. What we are really fighting for is our own existence and in the second place for the principles for which we stand. Maxwell thought that literature of this kind might have an effect on ignorant native populations, but that it would not have much effect on educated Europeans. This again seems an erroneous theory since only Europeans who have lived here for some considerable time can possibly understand that publications like the *Daily Worker* and *Action* do not really cut much ice. Needless to say no conclusions were reached and a further meeting is to be held.

24 November

I had a long discussion with Stewart Menzies. He tells me that every sort of intrigue is going on by those who want to take over the organisation and that criticisms are being made from every quarter by ignorant people. There is no doubt that SIS is going through a very difficult time owing to the liquidation of Stevens's organisation. General van Orschott of the Dutch General Staff, who was a party to Stevens's activities, has been dismissed and Sir Nevile Bland has been asked by the Dutch government to instruct the Passport Control Office to cease all illegal activities. Similar difficulties are being experienced in Sweden where the government has set up an organisation under one Martin Lundquist to go into the activities of foreign agencies. As Lundquist is thoroughly pro-German and served in the German Army during the last war he is confining himself to enquiries into SIS activities under Passport Control. Menzies says that in a number of cases his agents are being arrested and that it is easier now to operate in Germany than in neutral countries.

25 November

The censorship have picked up a letter addressed to one Moritz Lattmann in Switzerland from someone signing "F.R. Brown" in a foreign handwriting. The decoded message says that the writer has delivered the plans to "our mutual friends" at 13 Kensington Palace Gardens, and that these will be transmitted by bag to Berlin. The letter was posted at Reading. The following action has been taken: All letters to 13 Kensington Palace Gardens from the Reading area are being intercepted. There is a Home Office Warrant on Lattmann and all Swiss mails to Reading. Jane Sissmore has examined the Aliens Register in the Reading district but so far without success. The writer of the letter may well be a British subject of alien origin. A likely firm is Phillips & Powis of Reading who are manufacturing gun-turrets for aircraft.

13 Kensington Palace Gardens was the address of the Soviet embassy.

26 November

The Home Office is still sending us enemy aliens from abroad. They are so-called refugees who succeeded in getting into neutral countries just before the war. We regard these people with the utmost suspicion since SIS have ascertained that the Gestapo are putting a "J" on the passports of agents who they want to get into this country.

28 November

The *Deuxième Bureau* has informed us that the Germans are sending agents over with Hungarian passports.

30 November

Stewart Menzies has been appointed head of SIS but there is no news yet about his second-in-command. A certain amount of pressure is being brought to bear with a view to the appointment of someone from the navy. It is to be hoped that this will not succeed, and that Valentine Vivian will get the post, which in any case is a purely nominal one.

As a compromise between the two leading candidates, Vivian was made Vice Chief of SIS, and Claude Dansey was made Assistant Chief, both of equal rank.

As a result of a conference of B Division sections, Jock Whyte is inclined to think that a woman called Krafft is probably identical with the woman who is paying SNOW. She has drawn £25 on three occasions from her account roughly on the dates on which SNOW was paid. She lives in the Southampton district and she also deals at Selfridges. Two girls at Selfridges have seen her photograph and are inclined to think that she is the woman who changed the treasury notes for a £5 note, but they are not very sure.

1 December

A report has come in from the Security Control Officer at Harwich about Verey lights seen in the vicinity on the dates that the German aeroplanes laid mines in the harbour. The instructions to the anti-aircraft units seemed to have been very remarkable. On the first occasion they had orders that unless the enemy aircraft was acting in a hostile manner they were not to open fire. One begins to wonder whether we are really are at war at all. The local naval authorities were informed of the incident and destroyers were ordered to take a special course on leaving the harbour. HMS *Gypsy* did not apparently follow this course very accurately and was blown up.

3 December

A man called Millbank, a member of the British Union of Fascists, has reported to Special Branch that a Miss Dorie Knowles has asked him to communicate certain information to Germany relating to explosives being manufactured by the firm in which she works. Both the girl and Millbank have been interviewed and we are suggesting to Special Branch that her house should be searched. She is only seventeen, but nonetheless a sophisticated and a confirmed liar. He mother, who is of German origin, is in a mental home.

7 December

The case of Mrs Mathilde Krafft has developed in a very interesting way. An intercepted letter showed that she was going to see W.H. Muller, a somewhat suspect travel and forwarding agents. Richman Stopford got hold of the two girls from Selfridges and identified her on her arrival at the station in London. They picked her up again outside Muller & Co. and are quite convinced that she was the woman who changed the notes into fivers which were subsequently sent to SNOW. After leaving Muller she visited a steamship company apparently with the intention of proceeding to Fiji where it is alleged her husband, who died in 1921, has property. The question as to whether she should or should not have a permit is at present under discussion.

Another interesting fact has come to light. Mrs Krafft has been in communication with Swan & Edgars regarding the despatch of certain articles of clothing to her niece Editha Dargle in Copenhagen. Mrs Krafft was anxious to pack and despatch the goods herself under the export permit granted to Swan & Edgar. The firm replied that they would have to send the goods themselves direct from the shop. The inference is that Mrs Krafft may wish to pack certain messages or correspondence in the clothes. We are trying to get Swan & Edgar to write her a letter saying that they have reconsidered their decision and find that they can acquiesce in her request.

Dick White is sending his informant out with Klop to Belgium. She is to communicate there with the local German authorities and offer her services to the German government as an employee in the Censorship here. If she does not get a satisfactory answer she may proceed to Holland and re-establish her old contacts.

Cooper told me today that the German Jewish Aid Committee and other Refugee Committees are now asking the British government for funds. The matter is being considered by the Chancellor of the Exchequer. I always knew it would come to this.

8 December

SNOW had to go to Antwerp to meet a friend. He is also to be contacted by someone here who will give a password.

I have had long discussions today with Jack Curry and Richman Stopford about office organisation. I have a strong feeling that although we have a few good cases going, we are mainly sifting information which reaches us with the kind assistance of the general public. There is very little attempt to use imagination or make a real drive to collect *agents provocateurs*. We are of course up against many difficulties, not the least of which is trying to follow people in the black-out, but the present means for investigation which are at our disposal seem to be very meagre and when we come to the provinces we are often completely up against it. Stopford is getting out a statement on the SNOW case and its ramifications which are getting steadily wider. When we have got this we may have a better picture and also some new ideas as to how to proceed.

11 December

The Director-General has shown Roger Hollis's notes on Willie Gallacher and Captain Archibald Ramsay to Sir Horace Wilson, who is going to show them to the Prime Minister in connection with the secret session of the House of Commons. These notes emphasise the fact that if anything is said of a really secret nature it is almost a certainty that the information will reach both the Germans and the Russians. Sir Horace Wilson is going to transmit the information to the Prime Minister with a view to his warning his colleagues.

Willie Gallacher, the MP for West Fife, was a CPGB member who reported regularly to the Party's King Street headquarters. Archibald Ramsay was the MP for Peebles who was an ardent supporter of the Nazis, later to be detained.

12 December

The naval attaché in Madrid has telephoned to say that on information received from the Portuguese police, arms are being shipped to Eire. The Naval Intelligence Division is taking the matter up with the Dominions Office.

13 December

[XXXXXXXXX] in the German Legation in Dublin is now sending to the [XXXXXXXXXXXXX] in London torn up pieces of paper which are alleged to come from the German Minister's confidential waste. We have the originals pieced together and they are not uninteresting though somewhat inconclusive. They show connections with the IRA and give details of individuals who are dining and lunching with the Minister. These do not seem useful but we may get something more concrete later.

The Whinfield case is getting really hot. Further examination of banking accounts shows that Mrs Elam passed money to Archie Finlay who passed it to the British Union of Fascists. We have also discovered that Mrs Elam has paid £150 in Bank of England notes into her special account. These notes are said to have some form of cipher on the back. We are getting the original notes and are having them traced. We may in this way ascertain that Mrs Elam's money comes from foreign sources.

A former suffragette who was imprisoned three times, Mrs Norah Elam and her husband Dudley were leading supporters of the BUF. She had been the Parliamentary candidate for Northampton and her flat had been raided by the police in December 1939. She and her husband were interned in August 1940.

19 December

We have taken out a telephone check on David Darrah, of the *Chicago Tribune*, who has been boasting about getting uncensored information out of the country. It may be that he has been using the same methods as the *New York Times*.

Dick White has seen a man called Theo Hesspers who is a friend of Holtermann. Hesspers had an extremely interesting story about the penetration of our organisation in Holland by agents of the Gestapo disguised as representatives of various anti-Nazi political bodies. In particular he mentioned one Morz and a man called Dr Franz Fischer. Both these people had been planted on Major Stevens and Hesspers goes so far as to suggest that Captain Best himself may have been the real nigger in the wood-pile. Best had apparently been in fairly low water and it was noticeable that after he became associated with Fischer that he seemed to be very well in funds.

Before settling in Holland Dr Franz Fischer had been a major coal distributor in Württemberg and a trusted SIS source. He was also a German double agent. The suspicions regarding Captain Best turned out to be unfounded.

Dick White's informant has just returned and SNOW has also arrived back with some very interesting information.

30 December

I had a word with [XXXXXX] about codes. At present nobody seems to be tackling the problem seriously. Colonel J.P.G. Worrledge is by the way of dealing with love codes and today John Maude discovered two ladies in the Censorship who have been given letters in code and told to play with them. They have not got the time nor the knowledge to do so. There is also the question of flower codes. My own feeling is that either GC&CS or ourselves should establish an organisation to deal with the question. It would need somebody at the head of it who has the right kind of mind for the work. [XXXXXX] will take the matter to Valentine Vivian.

31 December

Colonel Stephens is interested in the case of a Mrs Titford. Some time ago a Mr Titford advertised for employment and received a letter from a woman called Margaret Otto who was resident in Czechoslovakia. Correspondence ensued and Titford eventually went over and married the girl in Bratislava. She was very insistent that she should have a British passport of her own and that her name should not be included on his passport. She seemed to have considerable funds at her disposal. She returned with her husband to England and subsequently deserted him. Titford then reported the facts to the police since it seemed that from the girl's side the marriage had been merely one of convenience. One [XXXXX], who has three convictions against him and is working as a police informant, has now stated that he picked up Mrs Titford in Piccadilly and that she took him back to her flat for which she pays £7 a week. [XXXXX] disclosed that he was now employed as a driver by the War Office. Mrs Titford became very interested and asked him to produce his papers which he did. She then suggested that he might like to earn big money and that he could do this if he would come with her to Lausanne to meet her principal. Before he goes he is to meet somebody from the Polish Embassy. Mrs Titford has explained that she has numerous other contacts and that she will require [XXXXX] to act as courier between this country, Basle, Lausanne and Zurich. Mrs Titford has been convicted three times as a prostitute, and has been run by a Jew called Kahn with whom she now seems to have severed relations.

1940

The question of Unity Mitford has been raised. It is reported that she has come out of Germany accompanied by some Hungarian and arrived in Switzerland, that she is in a serious condition and that her mother and sister Barbara have gone over to fetch her.

Lord Redesdale's daughter Unity had shot herself, having fallen in love with Hitler.

I saw Felix Cowgill today and he said that from more recent reports they had had from the Dutch it seemed highly probable that Major Stevens was either shot dead at the frontier or else very seriously wounded.

On the Director-General's instructions I telephoned to Sir Alexander Maxwell about Unity Mitford suggesting that both she and her mother and sister should be thoroughly searched on arrival, the search in the case of Unity only to take place if the medical officer was of opinion that she was in a fit state. Maxwell seemed somewhat reluctant to sanction this at first but finally agreed to the course suggested. I told him that before any action was taken I would let him know what the medical officer's opinion was. After further discussion of this case with SL we came to the conclusion that Unity really ought to be interned under 18(b), and after speaking to the Director-General I arranged to go and see Maxwell between 7 and 8pm tonight.

I told him about the proposal and said that if we had been dealing with Miss Smith or Miss Joyce the probability was that we should not be arguing the case, and that an Order under 18(b) would be made. He was silent at this point but later in the argument said that he doubted whether if the lady had been Miss Smith or Miss Joyce we should take any action. He pleaded that we had done nothing in the case of members of the Anglo-German Fellowship or indeed in that of Carroll of the Link. I said that I did not feel that there was any analogy. Unity Mitford had been in close and intimate contact with the Führer and his supporters for several years and was an ardent and open supporter of the Nazi regime. She had remained behind after the outbreak of war and her action came perilously near to high treason. Her parents had been associated with the Anglo-German Fellowship and other kindred movements and had obviously supported her in her ideas about Hitler. We had no evidence at all in support of the press allegations that she was in a serious state of health and it might well be that she was being brought in on a stretcher in order to avoid publicity and unpleasantness to her family. If I were asked whether I thought the odds were strongly in favour of something being found on her or her parents I should not be prepared to risk my money but in actual fact on the evidence available I had not any right to suppose that she would not be carrying something. In fact in normal circumstances she was just the kind of person who would be crazy enough to do so. Neither was it out of the picture that her mother and sister might aid and abet her. I still thought therefore that she should be served with an Order under 18(b) and that Lady Redesdale and Barbara Mitford should be searched discreetly but thoroughly.

Maxwell was very reluctant to agree to this and thought that we should possibly make ourselves ridiculous, but before I left had agreed to the search of all three and had suggested that possibly an Order under 18(a) might be served on Unity, instructing her to report to report to the police. He tried to see Sir John Anderson, but this was not possible as he had left. He said that he would telephone the Home Secretary's decision to me in the morning.

3 January

Sir Alexander Maxwell rang up today about Unity Mitford and said that the Home Secretary was in entire agreement with his view and had decided that nothing should be done. Nobody was to be searched and no Order was to be served. I reminded Maxwell once more that since Unity was such a public figure there might be considerable criticism if she were left at large. He said that this aspect of the case had been considered. I informed the Assistant Director, D Division of the position and instructions were given to Ferguson to telephone to Sir Arthur Jelf at Folkestone. The Assistant Director D has also informed the Director of Military Intelligence of the Home Secretary's decision in order that he might be aware that the action taken at the ports was not the responsibility of MI5. The Director of Military Intelligence seemed very annoyed and it was gathered that he was proposing to take the matter up with the Foreign Office.

4 January

Unity Mitford has arrived and is reported to have sat up and smiled at the Immigration Officer. There was a good deal of fuss about troops with fixed bayonets who are alleged to have been sent down to deal with the situation. In actual fact there were no troops except the normal guard consisting of about three men. The press are extremely annoyed that they were not allowed on to the quay and there seem to be the makings of a general row about the whole situation as soon as Parliament meets.

<hr>

6 January

The Secretary of State for War, Leslie Hore-Belisha, has gone and many rumours are afloat. It is said that he has got up against the soldiers and committed himself in all sorts of directions to political friends without prior reference to the staff.

I discussed today the Elam case with Francis Aiken-Sneath. We did not find a great deal at the Anti-Vivisection offices outside Scotland Yard indices showing the leaders and deputy leaders throughout the country and British Union of Fascist men employed as taxi drivers. There was also a letter from Sir Oswald Mosley to Mrs Elam more or less giving her a power of attorney in certain matters. There has however been an interesting development in the tracing of the Bank of England notes. Several of them finally reached one Gush, who is Mrs Elam's solicitor. He was interviewed today by Max Knight and John Maude, when he stated that these notes were repayment for a loan by him to Mrs Elam. The latter had asked for the money in order to pay certain debts incurred in Germany. The question of Mrs Elam's internment under 18(b) is under consideration.

We discovered the other day that one Rykens of Unilevers had special facilities from the Foreign Office to travel between this country and Holland. We informed the Foreign Office and asked them the nature of their liaison since Rykens had come to notice in a rather unfavourable light in connection with the Herman Goertz case. Foreign Office has now sent us over their files. They say that Rykens has been a go-between with the Foreign Office and the German Foreign Office since 1938 and that on 19 October 1939 he was asked through a representative of the firm in Holland to go to Berlin to meet Blessing of the Reichsbank who had received the request from Dr Wilhelm Keppler, Under-Secretary of State in the German Foreign Office. No indication was given as to the subject for discussion. Rykens agreed to go but the meeting was postponed and eventually Blessing came to Holland. Blessing said that most people were behind the Führer but that there was a cleavage in the Party. Both the extremists and moderates wanted peace, the former hoping that Hitler could achieve this end by diplomatic means while the latter, who included Hermann Goering, thought that Hitler must go. Peace terms could be discussed on the basis of an independent Poland and Czechoslovakia and the retention of Danzig. It was thought however that arrangements could be made for the Poles to have an outlet to the sea. Rykens told the Foreign Office that one Abs of the Deutsche Bank had been in Holland recently and had said much the same thing except that Poland and Czechoslovakia would have to be demilitarised. Rykens however intimated that rationing in Germany had been tightened up and that the country could continue the war for at least another eighteen months. It was also clear from the files that Rykens himself has apparently been in touch with Admiral Canaris of the German Secret Service. Foreign Office minutes indicated that Sir

Alexander Cadogan thought these overtures were not seriously intended. The Foreign Office seems very skeptical about our doubts concerning Rykens and I think therefore that we ought to give them the full picture of Unilevers as we know it. Personally I feel very doubtful about the whole lot and Rykens in particular.

Rykens had been implicated in an MI5 investigation of Herman Goertz in 1935 in Kent. He was sentenced to four years' imprisonment for breaches of the Official Secrets Act in March 1936, having been convicted of surveying RAF aerodromes in the south of England.

8 January

The Titford case is becoming very interesting. Our informant has been given two photographs of an individual by whom he is to be approached in Bath. He is to obtain from this man the plans which are to be got out of the country. Mrs Titford has given him the sum of £5 and more is to follow. One of the photographs shows the individual in question in civilian attire and the other in German uniform.

A report on Unity Mitford has now been received from the Security Control Officer. Apparently there were no signs of a bullet wound. John Adam takes the view that the Home Secretary has no authority to order that she should not be searched since these powers are vested in the military authorities and not in the Home Office.

10 January

Our informant in the Titford case has extracted from the lady the name of one of her principals. This man is one de Wohl. We have considerable records of him as he is already suspect. The informant has been told to get hold of an officer's uniform which he has done and he is to proceed to Bath tonight. For some reason or other this case seems to hang fire.

We have had some bad news about SNOW. He asked whether the man previously referred to was going to get into contact with him. The reply came that no contact would be established at present. There is a slight impression that the Germans may not be over-confident about SNOW and something may have gone wrong.

Richman Stopford got hold of a letter addressed to Brunck from the Guaranty Trust Company in which it is stated that an account will be opened for $45,000 in New York for Brunck's wife. Our records show that according to Padgham all the payments to Schulzer-Barnett from Admiral Canaris's man in Holland have in the past been made through Brunck. The check on Brunck has produced a letter from Ned Reid who evidently knows Brunck very intimately.

Sir Edward Reid Bt was Guy Liddell's cousin by marriage, a director of Baring's Bank and chairman of the British Banking Committee for German Affairs.

12 January

Matthews' Aliens Branch tells me that before Christmas he was badgered by the Home Office for details about two internees whom Lady Astor desired to spend Christmas with at Cliveden. It seems extraordinary that such a request should be made and even more extraordinary that it should not be met with a curt refusal. It is however symbolic of the present atmosphere.

13 January

A new DMI called Colonel Popovic has been appointed in Yugoslavia. He is said to be more European-minded than the majority of Yugoslav officers. He has told our military attaché that German espionage in Yugoslavia is mainly run by Schiller, the German assistant military attaché who disbursed £1,200 during the month of November. According to Colonel Popovic, the Yugoslavs have arranged matters so that about half the amount paid to German agents during the month is actually received by the Yugoslav DMI who spends it on the veterans of the last Great War unless some of it sticks to his own fingers. He disseminates false information to the German agents through his own people who come back to him and pay him the money they have received. Colonel Popovic says that there are 150 German agents in the country who are left to themselves provided they do not overstep the mark. In the event of a war Colonel Popovic has assured our military attaché that they will immediately be arrested, have their throats cut and be thrown into the old well in the Turkish fortress which lies at the junction of the Save and the Danube. Such are Balkan methods.

14 January

T.A. Robertson has told me of another case of a prostitute, Stella Cleveland, who seems to be intimate with a number of RAF officers. Cases of this sort seem to be on the increase and suggest that as has been previously reported the Germans are getting a lot of information through contacts established with officers. In addition to these two we have the Titford case, if this is in fact a bona fide one. Some doubts have now been cast on [XXXX] whose intercepted telephone conversations are not apparently playing straight.

A German aeroplane came down in Belgium the other day with certain papers found on the pilot indicating projected attack by the Germans on Belgium and Holland. It looks rather as if this may have been part of the scheme for the war of nerves.

17 January

Dick White has been looking into the affairs of the Czech Committee run by Sir Henry Bunbury. It has been somewhat of a shock to Cooper at the Home Office to learn that both Sir Henry's private secretary and his chief assistant, Mrs Ivon Kapp, were Communists. He is quite sure that Sir Henry is unaware of the situation.

---

18 January

Captain Frank Foley, formerly the Passport Control Officer in Berlin, and now the PCO in Oslo, spoke to me today about a very old friend of his, Gustav Schnabel, an Austrian, who is at present working in P.A. Welling & Company, 7 Union Street, EC2. Foley tells me that Schnabel is a really genuine refugee case and when he came to this country he was befriended by Count Mongelas, at present interned. He feels that he would like to write to Mongelas, but has not so far dared to do so in case he might be compromising himself and his family. I told Foley that there would be no objection to his writing and that it would not be in any way counter against him. Foley then asked me whether there would be any possibility for him to travel abroad in connection with his business. I said that this would probably be much more difficult as we had found it necessary to make a rule that enemy aliens should not travel.

There has been a disquieting report from SIS re Eire. A submarine base is said to exist near the mouth of the Doonbeg river in south-west Clare. A submarine comes in three times a week and is camouflaged with a canvas screen. One of the men in charge of the local coast watching station is said to be an IRA deportee. The local Civic Guard appear to be terrorised. It was also alleged that a small tramp steamer was waylaid in Galway Bay by a submarine and made to hand over stores.

Rumours of a secret U-boat refuelling base in the west of Ireland prompted an extensive survey of the coastline, by land and air, but there was none.

Nikolai Aptaker, the Soviet assistant air attaché has asked the firm of Hugh Reece to make him enlargements of photographs of London bridges which appear in an official guide. As no useful purpose would be served in stopping this, we have asked Hugh Reece to let us know of any further developments.

---

19 January

Special Material has now been extended to cover the Papal Nuncio. It seems that he has been visited by the mysterious St. Clair Grondona who has been making the rounds of neutral embassies on what he describes as a semi-diplomatic mission.

There has been a bad slip-up in the SNOW case. Some time ago Jock Whyte wrote to SIS asking them to make some enquiry about Editha Dargle in Copenhagen. The Danish police blundered in and asked her whether she knew a Mrs Krafft, hence a letter from Editha Dargle to Krafft telling her not to correspond in future and a wireless communication to SNOW that his friends are closing down for the time being.

January 22

Stewart Menzies tells me that Halifax has been asked to see Lord Darnley and the Marquis of Tavistock regarding certain peace proposals. I gather that there have been six or seven approaches of this kind. It indicates that the Germans are feeling about but at present their terms are quite impossible. It seems also that these overtures may be a part of what the Germans call *Zermürbungstaktik*, the general purpose of which is to keep this country off the boil. Tavistock is, of course, connected with the British Council for Christian Settlement in Europe which is a mixture of the Link, Nordic League and BUF, and a most mischievous body.

23 January

An article has appeared in the *Daily Telegraph* deprecating the government's policy on failing to intern more enemy aliens. It might almost be written by somebody in this office but, as far as I can make out, it wasn't.

24 January

Dick White's friend is going over to Belgium with Klop. She will be armed with some carefully doctored information.

Applications for exit permits have been received from Claud Cockburn, the Hon. Ivor Montagu and Professor J.B.S. Haldane. We are suggesting that permits to Cockburn and Montagu should be refused, and that as regards Haldane, who apparently only wants to lecture at some university, we should let the Dutch have any information in our possession through SIS.

Cockburn, Montagu and Haldane were all Communist journalists, the latter two later identified as Soviet spies.

25 January

Walter Thomas (the alias adopted by the Soviet defector Walter Krivitsky) has told us the history of the Oldham case. Captain Ernest Oldham was employed as a cipher clerk in the Foreign Office and committed suicide a few years ago. It appears that he approached the Soviet Embassy in Paris who thought he was an *agent provocateur* and turned him down. Later Oldham, who was a heavy drinker and in financial difficulty, went over to Paris and offered actual information regarding ciphers etc. After checking the accuracy of these documents Oldham was taken on and was the fore-runner of John King.

29 January

On 26 January the Socialist Member of Parliament J. Henderson, asked the Home Secretary whether he proposed to put Miss Unity Mitford into a home or hospital under supervision until she was sufficiently recovered in health for detention under the provisions of the Defence of the Realm Act Emergency Regulations 18(b), having regard to her recent hostile associations. Sir John Anderson replied "In the exercise of the powers conferred on me by this regulation to order the detention of persons who have hostile associations it is my duty to consider whether, on the facts of each particular case, detention is necessary in the interests of the Defence of the Realm. It would not be right for me to state in advance whether or not it may become necessary to take any such action in respect to any particular individual."

I saw Ned Reid about Brunck who, according to 'zu Putlitz, has been paying Schultze-Bernet, the head of the German secret service in Holland. Ned said that he had known Brunck since 1926 and was on very intimate terms with him, although he did not have a very good opinion of his bona fides. He first met him when studying banking in Hamburg. After the revolution Brunck formed a company called the Finanz Komptor in Berlin, which Ned found to be a mushroom concern. This puzzled him since it was clear that Brunck was disbursing large sums of money. One day in his cups Brunck disclosed by hints here and there that he was working for the German government and it seemed clear to Ned that he was financing Deutschtum im Ausland in Rumania, Danzig, Schleswig Holstein, etc. His connection with the government was confirmed by a conversation by Ned with the Reichskredit Gesellschaft where a friend of his told him that a mutual acquaintance Brunck had just been calling upon him. A short time before the war Brunck established a firm at the Hague called Hollendische Buitenland and asked Barings to take some shares in the business. The deal was complicated by a suggestion that Barings should be trustees for some unspecified people whose identities Brunck would not disclose. Barings consequently turned down the business. Nevertheless Brunck opened an account for his company with Barings, details of which I have to obtain. It would be extremely amusing if Barings were paying all the German agents in this country.

Sir Edward Reid, Guy Liddell's cousin by marriage, was a director of Barings Bank.

Brunck married a nurse from the London Hospital who looked after him when he was ill. She is of Irish extraction, but more Cockney than anything else. I am proposing to leave her $45,000 account with the Guaranty Trust in New York alone for the moment, until we see what Barings can produce.

30 January

Francis Aiken-Sneath had a meeting with Sir Oswald Mosley on 24 January when he visited the BUF's headquarters to obtain the letter from Claude Duvivier to Alexander Raven Thompson. Aiken-Sneath was accompanied by a Special Branch officer. Mosley himself was standing in front of his desk and did not seem at all surprised at the visit from the police. He adopted at once an attitude of extreme affability and disarming frankness. It seemed clear to Aiken-Sneath that he was anxious to show that the great Führer was as much at his ease with three slow-witted policemen as with kings and presidents. He expended all his charm and explained that he had long been awaiting the opportunity of talking to the authorities. He could not understand why they should pursue a hole and corner method rather than a straight-forward man to man talk which would clear everything up. He had always been expecting the police to tap his telephone and read his letters but apparently they had not done so. He was only too anxious to give any information about BUF finances, which involved an expenditure of about £8,000 a year. This included the cost of maintaining the national headquarters and a small subsidy paid to *Action* which was now fortunately almost self-supporting. As regards the money paid to Mrs Elam he had nothing to be ashamed of and nothing to conceal. There might have been an air raid. His headquarters might have been smashed by a mob and he himself was expecting to be assassinated. He had in fact taken certain precautions. It was necessary therefore to disburse the funds in case anything should happen to headquarters or the leaders. Inspector Bridges then interposed "Well, Sir Oswald, as a matter of fact, we have not come about this money." Sir Oswald did not lose his composure at all. "Ah," he said, "I know, I know. The Elams were friends of young Edward Whinfield, I hear that he has been detained." His face wore for a moment a look of sadness, for the leader is not indifferent to the misfortunes of even the least of his followers. He then went on to say that Whinfield had been one of his parliamentary candidates and that he had disapproved of his gadding about the continent instead of concentrating on his work in England. He would however be very surprised to hear that Whinfield had been working for the Germans. Mrs Whinfield had also behaved indiscreetly and was in fact a very foolish woman. As regards Dr Kruger, Mosley had met him at the Elams. He had met others there, such as Horning and Lord Cottenham. Dr Kruger had written a book about Jews and was an able research worker and not at all the kind of person who would act as an agent. Inspector Bridges again intervened to say that he had in fact come as he wished to see a certain document. Sir Oswald's composure was in no way shaken. "Oh, please, you can see any document you wish," he said. The file was sent for, and in the meantime the leader gave the assembled company a lecture on the foreign policy of the BUF. Not however in the style of his public speeches but as one Englishman to another. He seemed to sense the question which was in the minds of his audience. "I do not want the Germans to win," he said, "I want peace now, before England has been reduced to a dung heap. After the politicians reduce England and the British Empire to a dung heap, they are not going to get me to take over then. I shall retire from political life."

Among other things Mosley said he thought Germany could withstand a blockade for at least seven years, and that there was no possibility of internal upheaval since the Gestapo was the finest secret police the world had ever seen. He did not think Hitler wanted to smash the British Empire. He had had personal contact with him on two occasions and both he and his wife were convinced that Hitler did not want to harm England in any way.

The Duvivier file was then produced and contained the required letter among other correspondence of a harmless nature. It did however contain correspondence which made it clear that certain members of the BUF had an almost unbalanced admiration for everything German. The leader was asked whether he approved of this. He said he quite realised it and it was a great worry to him. In fact he could produce a list of people he had expelled because of their pro-German sentiments. He admitted that an enemy agent would find a pro-Nazi member of the BUF a good cover for his activities. As regards peace movements he said he was willing to support any peace movement led by sincere people whom he could respect. He would have nothing to do with Communists. On the British Council for Christian Settlement in Europe, he said he thought the Marquis of Tavistock was a good fellow but he would have nothing to do with John Beckett who was a crook. He did not think that the latter would work for Germany. Mosley was still in touch with Gordon Canning but did not hear much of him. When the party left the leader's presence they had the impression that he was convinced he had made a profound impression on them. He struck Aiken-Sneath as immensely vain, a bad judge of men and extremely urbane and cunning, and entirely lacking in sincerity. His chief handicap is probably his excessive vanity which must make it difficult for him to take an objective view of any situation. Francis Hawkins is obviously a complete nonentity, very timid and lacking in intelligence, and Raven Thomson, who flitted in for a few moments, looked less stupid but rather dim.

2 February

An elderly statesman with gout,
When asked what the war was about,
In a written reply
Said "My colleagues and I
Are doing our best to find out."

Walter Krivitsky is coming out of his shell and has told us quite a lot. He has as far as possible given us a detailed picture of the 4th Department and the OGPU. He is quite ready to talk about representatives of the OGPU or individuals that he was up against, but he is reluctant to disclose his own 4th Department agents unless we can show him that we already know something about them.

Ivor Montagu has been turned down for an exit permit.

3 February

I have been looking up our file for Engelberg of the German Consulate in New York who was murdered the other day. He was here in 1933 and told us that he used to report on the political reliability of people in the embassy. He then went to Italy and later to Austria where he was doing the same kind of thing. He had very high connections in the Party. I passed this information to the Americans, and have suggested to B2 that they should carry out further investigations into Engelberg's former contacts here.

Walter Krivitsky tells us that some years ago the Jesuits made a very determined effort to penetrate Russia. Krivitsky himself interviewed these people whom he described as extremely tough. Their proposal was that they should be given a free hand to nobble the Orthodox Church and that in exchange they would supply the 4th Department with information about counter-revolutionary activities. They worked for two years and then Stalin kicked them out. I am going to get further details about the matter at my next interview with Krivitsky.

6 February

Ned Reid has sent me a copy of Brunck's account which looks as if it may be of interest. A good many of his transactions have been made with the Reichskredit Gesellschaft, but there are also some payments to private individuals which may be interesting.

Wing-Commander R.G. Bloomfield DSO has written an extremely indiscreet letter to a certain Wallace Groves relating to measures for combating the magnetic mine. The offending passage was in the form of a postscript in Bloomfield's own handwriting. The rest of the letter was typewritten and inoffensive. Bloomfield has been placed under close arrest and Stammers has asked us to make enquiries about Groves, who is in America.

7 February

A secretary of the Chilean Embassy speaking to a friend says, "I like this job. It is quite interesting writing all those letters to the Ministry of Economic Warfare asking them to release cargoes pretending that they are what they are not. It is quite fun. Sometimes they are not what we say they are."

8 February

Klop has just returned from Holland and Belgium. Reports which have reached him from the German Embassy in Brussels indicate that there is now to be a return to *Mein Kampf*. It seems to have been realised that the destruction of the British Empire is an almost impossible task. Generally speaking defeatism is rife amongst the majority of the staff of the embassies at The Hague and Brussels. How far this is a reflection of Germany is doubtful. One informant whom he saw had recently been in the Rhineland where the same sort of atmosphere appears to exist. There is a good deal of grumbling and reference has been made to people being lucky because they are what is known as Left-Bankers i.e. they reside on the left bank of the Rhine which it is anticipated will before very long be French territory. A story was told him about taxis in Cologne. Nobody can get a taxi at the station unless they have luggage. They therefore resort to the practice of going to the station with a large suitcase and coming out again in order to obtain the services of a taxi.

German military information from France and Great Britain is said to be good. The OGPU are working in with the Gestapo and are obtaining a certain amount of information from refugee circles in this country, though not of a very high standard. Information they are getting from other sources is good. The Prime Minister is still thought to have a considerable following in Germany and his presence in the government is believed to have a defeatist propaganda value among a large section of the German people.

Norman Baillie-Stewart's mistress has been discovered here as a Women's Auxiliary Transport driver to the Censorship.

In 1933 Lieutenant Norman Baillie-Stewart of the Seaforth Highlanders had been cashiered and sentenced to five years' imprisonment for attempting to pass information to the Germans. After his release he had gone to live in Berlin.

9 February

Forged dollar and British currency notes are being distributed in the Balkans and Middle East and a gang employed on the same work has been arrested in Canada. This looks like a joint German–Russian plan to discredit British and American currency.

10 February

The Director-General told me today about a case of leakage. Some MP baronet went to France where he saw Prime Minister Paul Reynaud. For no particular reason, Reynaud seems to have disclosed the whole of the Allied plans on the western front. The MP then came back here and started talking.

Lord Killanin also knew Norman Baillie-Stewart, the son-in-law of Mau Gonna Bride. He thinks that Baillie-Stewart who is a very likable person but hotly pro-Nazi might quite easily be acting for the Germans. He did not know that Baillie-Stewart had actually gone to Switzerland quite recently or that he had obtained a visa there for Berlin. He mentioned that Baillie-Stewart was extremely interested in racing. This may be significant as Werner Unland has a contact who follows the same hobby. Information that we had from other sources makes it quite clear that Baillie-Stewart is frequently at the German Legation in Dublin.

12 February

I have passed a report to Herschel Johnson which I received from SIS regarding the leakage of information relating dispatches between Joe Kennedy and President Roosevelt. This appears to come from a reliable source.

13 February

Special Material shows that Sir John Anderson was adamant about the Irish executions and that the Prime Minister, Anthony Eden, and to some extent even Winston, were anxious to find a way out.

I had a talk with Roger Hollis about the Communists in the event of war with Russia. We have a list of contacts in factories and D Division and factory managers are notified about these people. They can therefore be easily laid off in time of emergency if necessary. It would further seem desirable to intern all organisers and members of the CPGB's Executive Committee, but I don't think it would be necessary at any rate in the first instance to make any recommendation that the Party should be declared illegal.

SNOW has returned with £650 in dollars and Bank of England notes. His visit was highly successful and he saw Dr Rantzau and a Mrs Kaller. He was contacted on the way by Samuel Stewart, who sat down beside him in the carriage. They travelled over together and Rantzau told SNOW that he is one of their men. Stewart runs several shipping lines between Belfast, Dublin, this country and Antwerp. He was already suspect and we had intended trying to put somebody in on one of his boats. Rantzau is visiting America shortly and will be returning in April. SNOW brought back with him a letter addressed to one Eugene Hosfall who resides at Feltham. The letter merely states that the writer has forgotten to give Mrs Whinfield's address to Horsfall. Mrs Whinfield is apparently engaged in the purchase of certain books which are to be used for code purposes. This is the same woman whose son was arrested in Switzerland and who is connected with Mrs Elam and the British Union of Fascists.

Mrs Muriel Whinfield, the wife of Colonel H.G. Whinfield, had been the BUF's Parliamentary candidate for Petersfield in December 1936. Her son Peter was detained in January 1940, and she was detained in May 1940. Both were released in August 1942 and emigrated to South Africa after the war.

14 February

Felix Cowgill came to see me today, about a certain Kurt Jahnke, with whom he had been indirectly in touch. At the outbreak of war Jahnke was running an intelligence bureau in conjunction with Admiral Canaris of the Abwehr and situated in close proximity to deputy Führer Rudolf Hess, with direct access to the Führer. Jahnke was a Prussian deputy who seems to have run an amateur intelligence organisation. His whole show was taken over, with himself at the head, by the government just before the outbreak of war. Jahnke had been getting copies of SIS reports and also reports on Imperial policy. He also saw the contents of telegrams or dispatches between Kennedy, the American Ambassador here, and the State Department. His informant here was said to be in the Foreign Office and to be either a clerk or the wife of a clerk. Cowgill was anxious to know whether this Jahnke was identical with a man of the same name who had before Locarno been acting as an agent of the Russian 4th Department.

Kurt Jahnke had been a German saboteur in the United States during the First World War and was suspected of having participated in the Black Tom Island explosion in July 1916. He was known to have been a key intelligence adviser to Rudolf Hess, Reinhard Heydrich and Walter Schellenberg. The source of his information about SIS was never established.

There has been a slight hitch with Walter Krivitsky. We offered him £1,000 and all expenses. Arrangements were made as to how the money was to be paid and Jasper Harker left him apparently in good mood. This morning he asked for a private talk with Alley, and said that he did not wish it to be thought that there was any lack of faith as between himself and the British government or that he had not given us information for other than ideological reasons. On the other hand, he had lost a contract with an American newspaper for $6,500 and his news value was obviously deteriorating with time. He therefore thought that if we were going to give a little nest-egg which would be used by his wife, £5,000 would be a more proper figure. Harker went up to see him and after a great deal of talk and apologies etc the little man threw up his hands and said "All right. Make whatever arrangements you like." The deal was finally settled on £2,000 and all parties seemed satisfied.

The *Deuxième Bureau* have let us down again by passing to their Ministry of Supply information which we gave them about Charles Bedaux. The French Ministry has informed Bedaux that one of his contracts had been held up owing to information submitted by the British government through the French *Deuxième Bureau*, and gave him documents in writing to this effect. Bedaux has now written to Sir Walter Monckton who has passed the correspondence to John Maude. I am taking the matter up with SIS and saying that in future if we cannot get some guarantee as to the handling of our information, it will be very difficult to continue our relations in the spirit of frankness and full co-operation.

Charles Bedaux was a shady French businessman, suspected German agent and friend of the Duke of Windsor.

15 February

Slade of the Naval Intelligence Division tells me that the Admiralty has intercepted wireless communication emanating from some station situated between Dublin and Wicklow. The messages were going between this station and Nauen in Germany. The signals have been taken down and are to be forwarded to us and to GC&CS. Slade was proposing to pass the information to the Dominions Office but I urged him to refrain from doing this as I was not anxious that the Eire authorities should begin searching about for this station until we had seen whether we could do anything with the signals. It might be valuable to us if the station were allowed to continue at any rate for a time.

At John Godfrey's request I saw Lord Rothschild, who is doing sabotage research work for MI(R). He thought that the results of his experiments which were primarily for offensive purposes might also be of use to us in formulating a defensive policy. I told him that broadly speaking we wanted to give an answer to the factory manager who said "You tell me that in the event of trouble sabotage may take place on a wide scale. What do you expect me to do about it?" He saw this point and is going to consult the Joint Intelligence Committee, which is working on the problem. He will also try and keep us posted about bacteriological warfare.

We have had a report today that one Henry Andreae who was anxious to obtain a commission was introduced by a friend of his, T. Usher, to a certain H.I. or I.H. Abelson. He met Abelson at the Charing Cross Hotel and also an individual styling himself Sir Curtis Lampson. He was told that the fee would be £600. When he demurred, he was told that an advance of £300 would probably be sufficient if an undertaking were given that the further sum would be paid as soon as his name appeared in the *London Gazette*. We have put the matter in the hands of Special Branch.

17 February

I spoke to Valentine Vivian regarding an illicit German wireless station in Eire. He says the cipher used is diplomatic and unbreakable, according to GC&CS. There is therefore nothing to be gained by allowing the station to continue. Valentine Vivian thinks we should communicate the facts to Colonel Liam Archer in Dublin.

I spoke to Chief Constable Hordern about the case of Christiansen, manager of a firm which has just got secret contracts worth £187,000. I said I thought the Director-General should lay the facts before the Minister of Supply, Edward Burgin MP, or the Permanent Under-Secretary at the Treasury, Sir Horace Wilson, both from the security angle and on account of the undesirable situation created by Reginald Roberts of the Ministry of Supply being chairman of the company.

Reginald Roberts was chairman of the CO Ericsson Engineering Works Ltd and was also Deputy Director-General of Equipment and Stores at the Ministry of Supply.

18 February

Jock Whyte has brought me the case of Gula Pfeffer. It seems that this woman was at one time in close touch with a certain Fletcher of the Foreign Office whom she, talking to her solicitor, said she had blackmailed. Fletcher in a written statement says that in 1935 he went to Berlin with the knowledge of his department where he met Pfeffer's relations. These include Captain von Pfeffer, whom I believe to be identical with the notorious Captain Pfeffer of the German secret service. It now transpires that Fletcher is employed in the GC&CS. It seems not altogether improbable that he may be the man in the Foreign Office who has been supplying Jahnke with SIS reports and Committee of Imperial Defence policy reports. He might also be the person giving the contents of Ambassador Kennedy's telegrams to President Roosevelt.

19 February

I spoke to Herschel Johnson about the case of Kurt Jahnke and the alleged leakage of Kennedy's dispatches to Roosevelt. He said that the information could only have come from the German Embassy in London or Washington DC and there was no possibility of leakage in the ciphers since all their telegrams were by special cable route and not by wireless. I told him that Sir Alexander Cadogan was aware of the facts and he expressed his intention of speaking about the matter on the occasion of his next visit to the Foreign Office.

21 February

Lord Tavistock left Stranraer for Northern Ireland yesterday morning. According to our informant it was his intention to get into touch with the German Legation in Dublin regarding certain peace proposals which he is going to put forward in the name of the British Council for Christian Settlement in Europe. If these proposals are not considered he proposes to start a campaign.

I decided after consultation with C, Stewart Menzies, and Slade, that the Eire government should be officially informed through the British High Commissioner Sir John Maffey about the illicit wireless station near Dublin and that we should simultaneously inform Colonel Liam Archer, asking him to let us have full details in due course.

22 February

I discussed the case of Fletcher with Felix Cowgill of SIS's Section V. His enquiries made it even more probable that Fletcher is at least the Foreign Office contact who was in touch with Kurt Jahnke. If this is so he has played his cards fairly well by reporting certain facts to his superiors as and when they happen. There seems little doubt that he has known von Pfeffer since 1935. His SIS file indicates that he has made two attempts to obtain the release of Gula Pfeffer, one by representing that she is harmless and the other by suggesting that she might be a useful double-cross agent.

23 February

I attended a meeting at SIS in order to discuss the case of Fletcher of the GC&CS. The SIS Chief, Valentine Vivian, Felix Cowgill, Alastair Denniston, Richman Stopford and myself were present. From Denniston's description of Fletcher it is obvious that he has a kind of secret service kink. He has never been very content with his ordinary cipher work and has always been trying to get into something more exciting. He likes to imagine himself as a kind of cloak and dagger man, and is given to relating hair-raising stories about himself which have absolutely no foundation in fact. There was a curious incident at the outbreak of war. Colonel Vivian received a letter in a foreign hand-writing from a woman. She stated that Mr Fletcher had told her at the time of the 1938 crisis that his life would be in great danger and that if she wanted to know about him she should communicate with Colonel Vivian at Room 46, Foreign Office. On this occasion Fletcher was sent for, confronted with the letter, whereupon he became as white as a sheet and almost hysterical. He wanted to know whether he was going to be sacked. He was told that he had behaved in an extremely indiscreet way by giving Colonel Vivian the kind of publicity which he did not in the least desire and if he did anything like that again his services would probably be dispensed with. The letter was then torn up and the incident closed. My impression of Fletcher from what was said is that he is the kind of fellow who must be in the limelight at all costs, and that if he is the source of the leakage this is more likely to be his motive than money. It was generally agreed that the odds were about 60–40 against him and that very careful enquiries should be made about his habits and associations before any action was taken. There is really nothing to interrogate him on since he has very carefully covered himself in his association both with Gula Pfeffer and with Captain von Pfeffer. It seems also from an earlier report that he met Jahnke on at least one occasion. We are going to try and get a look at his banking account though I doubt whether this will disclose anything much.

26 February

According to a report that I have had from Ned Reid, the son of the Dominican Minister in London has been selling Dominican passports at £100 a time to German Jewish refugees. His father has discovered what is going on and has kicked him out.

29 February

Axel Wenner-Gren, a wealthy Swede with an estate at Nassau and the largest yacht in the world, has confided in the Governor of the Bahamas that he carried out delicate negotiations between the Prime Minister and Hermann Goering at the outbreak of war. He is now reported to be in Europe and it is said that he is associated with the American government in peace efforts. He is said to be in Rome and to be going to Berlin. He is particularly concerned with saving Finland and in this sense may be playing the German game.

The Czechs have given us a magnum opus on the German intelligence organisation and counter-espionage organisation. Jopson is translating it.

N.B. Jopson was a linguist from GC&CS.

2 March

There has been a letter from Lord Hankey stating that he has looked into the affairs of SIS and that he has now been ordered by the Prime Minister to investigate the activities of MI5. He would like in the first instance to have a rough chart covering our various duties and, having studied this, he would like to discuss the department in all its aspects with the officers concerned.

Lord Hankey, Minister without Portfolio in Chamberlain's Cabinet, subsequently submitted a report of MI5, SIS and GC&CS. As his private secretary was John Cairncross, the Kremlin received a copy too.

Nabil continues to act as an intermediary between the Gulbenkians. It seem that both father and son had committed acts which, had they become known, might have involved them in serious consequence. In time of war these acts would have amounted to high treason. Probably the reference is to supplies of oil to the Germans, since I know through David Williams, who is employed by the Anglo-Iranian Oil Company, that large sales to Germany were going on immediately prior to the outbreak of war.

The immensely rich oil tycoon Calouste Gulbenkian and his son Nubar fell out and were never reconciled. Both men had a close relationship with SIS but were suspected of having traded with the Nazis.

Madame Maisky, using the alias Mrs Buck, has ordered from the Co-op shop a sixteen ounce tin of Flit. She was anxious to know whether it killed fleas.

SIS material from Italy indicates that the policy against the Jews has been relaxed. It was originally enforced in order to curry favour with the Moslems. Italy is still divided on the German question. Mussolini, Parranici and General Achille Starace are still inclined to stick to the Axis but with reservations. Those in favour of a break are Ciano, Grandi, Balbo and the King.

I dined with John Maude and Victor Rothschild last night. We had a long discussion about sabotage. He is quite ruthless where Germans are concerned, and would exterminate them by any and every means. He outlined our problem as he saw it. He thought we should first try and classify our vulnerable points and factories in this country and place them in groups. We should then get the opinions of some of the managers to how it would be possible to put the works out of action or damage the products without undue risk of detection. The methods would have to be fairly simple ones which would be carried out by any of the employees. We should then go to the chemical experts and find out what they could do by subtler methods. Having established these facts we should suggest counter-measures and also lay down certain guiding lines for diagnosis when trouble occurred. Rothschild thought that to put such an organisation on a proper footing it would be necessary to have the services of someone with a fairly complete knowledge of the scientific world. Scientists were generally specialists in a rather narrow field and to obtain the proper advice it was necessary to know exactly where to go. He would also advise the employment of an engineer. Re the remainder of the staff one would have to see how things developed. In addition to chemical sabotage we discussed bacteriological warfare. He said that Professor William Topley, who is an expert in these matters, had been rather disappointed by the lack of enthusiasm expressed by MI5 in the early stages of the war and that there was in fact a feeling in the newly constituted Committee of Imperial Defence (CID) that MI5 were neglecting their duty by not tackling the problem. He was very anxious that I should see Group Captain William Elliott of the CID and discuss the matter. Lord Rothschild mentioned the existence of a rocket bomb known as 'the UP bomb'. I gather that this is a somewhat epoch-making invention but whether it has reached the production stage or not is not clear. It is the first that I have heard of it but it may of course be known to the D branches. It is obviously desirable that every possible step should be taken to prevent a leakage about this information to the Germans. We shall probably find that it is being made in a small tin shack in a corner of a field and that anybody can get inside with the aid of a tin opener.

This was a reference to the possibility of an atomic weapon, word of which had reached Lord Rothschild, MI5's adviser on sabotage and scientific issues.

Dick White is doing well with his Czech liaison. He has already unearthed three Gestapo agents and three Communists who have joined the forces.

Gladwyn Jebb rang me up last night to say that the Americans had heard that Sumner Welles' apartment at Claridge's had been fixed up with microphones. Could anything be done to verify this?

Sumner Welles was the American Under-Secretary of State, visiting London.

8 March

I saw Herschel Johnson about Claridge's. He had obtained his information from an ex-American diplomat formerly employed at Berne named Einstein who had married a member of the Ralli family and settled down in this country. Occasionally he spent a holiday in Italy, where he met Count Carlo Sforza, the former Italian foreign minister, who had told him that some time ago the Italians had fitted Claridge's up with microphones. I subsequently arranged with Henry Maine for the inspection of the suite by a Post Office expert. This was done through a friend of Maine's named Miles Thornewill, who is a director of the Savoy, which also controls Claridge's, the Berkeley, and the Meurice in Paris. In his capacity as a director Thornewill asked for the master key and took the expert in. So far as could be ascertained there was no microphone installation, but it might well have been built in and plastered over in such a manner as to make it undetectable unless the walls were pulled to pieces. I explained the situation to Herschel Johnson who has spoken to the ambassador. The latter thought that no chances should be taken and therefore decided to reserve rooms at the Dorchester. In the meantime Thornewill is anxious to get rid of the manager at Claridge's, a member of the Fascists. He is, in fact, prepared to sack the whole staff rather than lose American custom. Herschel Johnson bears no malice against Claridge's and in fact does all of his entertaining there but he told me that on at least one occasion when Norman Davies had stayed there he was quite convinced that his papers had been gone through.

9 March

The telephone check on Rickatson-Hatt, editor-in-chief of Reuters, shows that he is hard up, has many woman friends, and that he talks indiscreetly on the telephone.

Nothing has been disclosed so far as to his sources of information except that he evidently did have a talk with Noel Mason-Macfarlane, who was not impressed by him and said so to the DMI.

After he left Reuters, Bernard Rickatson-Hatt was appointed an adviser to Montagu Norman, the Governor of the Bank of England, and before his death in 1967 was a pioneer of commercial television with Associated-Rediffusion.

11 March

The British Union of Fascists has a secret military organisation known as the Fellowship of the Services run by one F.G. Geary. The organisation was anti-Communist in 1936, is now anti-Jewish and closely allied with the BUF. It is also pro-Nazi and each member is armed.

I lunched with Miles Thornewill today and discussed the case at Claridge's. He is very anxious to get rid of the manager and to satisfy the Americans in any way he possibly can. I said I thought it would be best if he refrained from taking any action against the manager until Sumner Welles had left Europe. In the meantime I promised to have a talk with the Americans and ascertain their reactions.

12 March

Harold Gibson of SIS says that Czech claims to have arrested 15,000 German spies in a year are not exaggerated. Their intelligence service costs a large sum and was regarded as first call on the Government.

FRANK, Max Knight's informant, has gone to meet Barlen in Holland. Barlen had communicated with Heath who is interned and should have been prosecuted for espionage. FRANK will pose as coming from Heath.

14 March

Major E.W. Gill of MI8 has produced the deciphers of some interesting messages emanating from the Frankfurt area, which it would appear are destined for German agents in France or Luxembourg. It seems highly desirable that there should be collaboration with the French both in the deciphering of these messages and also in subsequent investigations. One of the messages indicates the Germans are taking an active interest in the movements of one Sebillon, who is obviously working in the French Legation in Luxembourg.

15 March

SIS is rather worried about a payment which has been made to Frank Foley by a man called Zellner. Personally I do not think there is anything in it. Foley who was a friend of the family in Berlin, and was the PCO there, probably lent the money on account of exchange difficulties.

SIS's concerns were probably prompted by the knowledge that before the war some PCO had been implicated in the illicit sale to desperate Jews of entry visas to Palestine. Just such a scandal in September 1936 had led to the suicide of the PCO in the Hague, Major Hugh Dalton.

16 March

Dingli is apparently off to Italy again on some hush-hush mission for Downing Street. We started to interrogate him on his business at the War Office but got a warning from Stewart Menzies that we had better not probe too deeply. It seems entirely wrong that this kind of thing should be going on without our knowledge.

18 March

Klop has been seeing Hammer, the German economic expert at Berne, who is generally pessimistic about Ribbentrop's policy *vis-à-vis* Russia. He thinks Hitler is still looking east but that he will try and break our resistance through extensive air attacks on our ports, including London. He does not believe in an invasion of Holland, or Belgium, but thinks that had we intervened in Finland, Germany would have gone into Scandinavia.

Klop was struck by the contrast between the German and British Legations at Berne. At the German he found feverish activity, piles of leaflets and propaganda of one kind or another. At the British, he found the military attaché, Brigadier Wyndham Torr, sitting well down in his chair, his head back and his fingertips together in clerical fashion. When Klop expressed a wish to see the ambassador, for quarter of an hour Torr had tried to dissuade him. Eventually, pointing to the ceiling, he said "The ambassador is up there. Perhaps you will excuse me from taking you up but my left leg has gone to sleep." A messenger was sent for and Klop was shown into the august presence.

19 March

An order was recently issued by the Field Security Police in France that copies of the *Daily Worker* should be confiscated if found. A copy of this order was sent to Maurice Fyrth here by his brother, who seems to have passed it on to Ronald Kidd and also to D.N. Pritt MP, who is going to make use of the information. The question of a prosecution is being considered, but in any case the officer will be dealt with.

Denis Pritt QC, the Labour Member of Parliament for North Hammersmith from 1935 to 1950, was also a Soviet agent.

20 March

The French have discovered a complete set of blueprints of the Renault works at the Russian Trade Delegation so they have instituted a close watch on the Soviet Embassy. When Suritz complained, he was told that this was as nothing compared with the watch kept on the French and other embassies in Moscow.

27 March

The Drogheda IRA radio station has been active again, at 1600 hours on 24 March. We have told Colonel Liam Archer in Dublin.

29 March

A Maltese named Dalmanin has offered us the text of the Brenner Treaty between Mussolini and Hitler for the small sum of 5m lira! He said that he had made the acquaintance of Edda Ciano and that she would be prepared to obtain this document for the above consideration, which was to be paid partly in jewelry and partly in Swiss francs. Jack Curry interviewed Dalmanin at the War Office. He seemed to be a rather simple-minded sort of fellow, and when asked how he could expect us to part with such a large sum of money to someone we knew nothing about, he had no real answer so he has gone away to think again.

I lunched today with Miles Thornewill. He has evidently made up his mind to get rid of the Italian manager of Claridge's and he wants to know if we know anything against one van Thuyne, a Belgian, whom he proposes to put in. I promised to let him know unofficially.

Miles Thornewill remained with the Savoy Group until his death in 1974. The Italian general manager, F.H. Cochis was dismissed and interned, and was replaced by H.A. Van Thuyne who worked at the hotel until April 1968.

31 March

Mrs Gertrude Plugge, wife of the Member of Parliament, is going rather far with the Egyptian Ambassador. He is now trying to use her in order to get information about her husband's activities.

Captain Leonard Plugge was the Conservative MP for Chatham until 1945.

1 April

Fletcher of the GC&CS is going to France for eleven days on a bicycling tour. We discussed the possibility of sending over two girls with him on the boat, but the plan fell through as it was found he had already left.

Harold Flecher was a Cambridge mathematician.

Derek Sinclair is running three double-cross agents at the moment. Dawkes's inter-mediary Henri is now *brûlé* but Kutzner, writing from Rome, has made another approach. A new contact is one Bernie Kiener known as RAINBOW. This man was a friend of a certain Schutz who confided in Kiener before leaving this country that he had had a special mission here for the Reichswehr. Schutz has now written to Kiener who went over to Holland or Belgium where contact was made with a man from Hamburg. The third of the double-cross people is an Irishman named Clarke who is in touch with the Dutchman called Simon. There is some doubt about Clarke's bona fides.

RAINBOW was a piano player in a dance band working in Weston-Super-Mare.

---

2 April

A German agent named Durrent gave himself up in Egypt some time ago and is being run by Raymund Maunsell of the Middle East Intelligence Centre. He men-tioned that one of his contacts was a certain Fursen of Aabenraa, in Denmark, and an early file on the SNOW case mentions Fursen. The place in Denmark where he resides is the same one from which Andresen communicates with Werner Unland. This is interesting and it may be that Fursen and Andresen are one and the same person.

---

5 April

On the introduction of Wood, I saw General van Oorschott, the Dutch Director of Military Intelligence. I discussed with him the possibility of his giving us his assis-tance in the event of an influx of Dutch refugees. He thinks that in such an eventuality we should ask for him and one of his assistants, and he believes that such a project would be favourably received. He could also arrange for records.

Early in November Colonel Sas, the military attaché in Berlin came hot-foot with a story that he had been approached by a German officer who had been his intimate friend for many years. This officer had told him in strict confidence that Holland would be invaded in the early hours of 12 November. Colonel Sas was very excited and said he wished to see the Queen of the Netherlands. Van Oorschott regarded this as merely a move by the Germans in the Nervenkrieg since he had had similar reports from his frontier police who had been in touch with the Germans. An old general was called in to give an independent opinion and he said that if a German officer gave away important information, it could be taken as a certainty that he was acting under instruction. Van Oorschott said that the reports about the purchase of Belgian uniforms by German agents was also part of the general bluff. It was ridiculous to suppose that these uniforms could not equally well have been purchased or made in Germany. Van Oorschott did not dis-close in any way that he suspected the bona fides of Sas who of course was reported to us by [XXXX] before the war as a German agent who was in constant touch with the German Legation at the Hague.

Sas's informant was probably Colonel Hans Oster, of the Abwehr, who was later to be arrested and executed by the Gestapo for complicity in a plot to assassinate Hitler.

7 April

SNOW has reported, on his return from Antwerp, that the *City of Sydney*, now en route for Mauritius, has two bombs on board which were placed there at Amsterdam. We have ascertained that the ship never touched at Amsterdam, and that she has been out thirty-three days. This may quite well be a plant and I am advising that we take no action. The Director-General and Jasper Harker agree.

SNOW has been given over £1,000 in notes and is to be visited shortly by an Indian, maybe Sethia?

SNOW was asked by his Antwerp contact to find out where the *City of Sydney* was and to wireless her course. He is to send a message to say that the steamship company refused to give the information and to ask whether he can enlist the co-operation of Stewart. This may produce some useful reactions.

SNOW has picked up a crook called CELERY. T.A. Robertson has a long statement from CELERYwho is wanted by the police. SNOW has told him among a heap of other things that he is the key man in the British and German secret service so T.A. Robertson has called him severely to order.

CELERY *was Walter Dicketts, a former World War I air intelligence officer cashiered for dishonesty.*

The Germans want SNOW to recruit another agent who is to go over to Germany and do a course of sabotage. They have also spoken of a form of micro-photography which enables a whole message to be put into the size of a pin's head. This information fits in with something that Derek Sinclair has heard recently.

8 April

I have heard from the Foreign Office that the alleged assassination plot is directed against the King of England.

17 April

There was a meeting of the Bacteriological Committee in the afternoon which was attended by Jasper Harker. Lord Hankey was in the chair and about thirty other people were present. Lord Hankey evidently seemed to think that MI5 ought to be doing something more than they were, but no issue was raised as regards our responsibilities and no decision of any consequence seems to have been reached.

19 April

A War Office document marked Most Secret about the disposition of our forces in certain eventualities in Turkey and Thrace has been discovered in a dustbin in Whitehall Court. It was given to the police by a patriotic dustman.

A man called Thomas [XXXXXX] who had been working in SIS has been interned under Emergency Regulation 18(b) for gross indiscretions when in a state of intoxication. He is a member of Laurence Grand's party and was telling everybody exactly what he was going to do.

20 April

Richman Stopford has interviewed Carlin on the Fletcher case. Carlin seems to know more than he is prepared to say. He intimated that he distrusted Fletcher since the latter had heard of Pfeffer's arrest and had talked for an hour on the telephone in a room by himself, and then went out and bought several bottles of Chartreuse which he proceeded to consume to excess. He was obviously very agitated. We are going to compare the statements of Carlin, Fletcher and Pfeffer and then draw up a questionnaire for interviewing Fletcher.

The French illicit wireless section has intercepted one of SNOW's messages. We are telling them to lay off.

21 April

Richman Stopford tells me that the Indian who was to visit SNOW has not turned up. SNOW has informed his principals and has been told that owing to unforeseen difficulties this man's visit has been delayed.

I spoke to the Director-General about Victor Rothschild. He has agreed to take him on as a part time member of the staff. This also apparently has Lord Hankey's approval.

22 April

The Lascar who is being awaited by SNOW has turned up, bringing with him the two wireless valves. Rolph, who received the valves, succeeded in tracking the Lascar back to the *City of Simla* which had just done a trip from Southend to Antwerp and back.

A former World War I MI5 officer, William Rolph acted as SNOW's sub-agent, but in May 1940 was found to have been selling him genuine information. He gassed himself at his flat in Dover Street while MI5 considered what action to take against him.

24 April

Frank Foley, the PCO in Oslo, seems to have done extremely well. He was the only British officer to join up with the Norwegian forces in the early stages of the campaign. He destroyed all his documents and one of his wireless sets. He took the other with him and joined the Norwegian headquarters when C opened communication with this country. Our military attaché who has since turned up reports that had it not been for Foley it is quite likely that the Norwegians would have given in. Foley was able to encourage them by promises of support from this country. Another wireless set has since been flown out to Foley, and three others are operating with the various British contingents. These have all been supplied by SIS since other apparatus of the kind seems singularly out of date. The sets, I gather, are designed by [XXXXXXXXXXXX] and SIS have them operating from German territory and from all over the continent. Stewart Menzies believes that they are extremely difficult to pick up and doubts very much whether any monitoring system however widespread will be effective against them. If SNOW's set is a sample of the best the Germans can do, it would seem that we are fairly well ahead in this matter. It would not however be safe to assume this, particularly in view of a statement by two German prisoners of war which was overheard at Cockfosters to the effect that they got very useful information from Scapa Flow about the movements of ships.

26 April

Valentine Vivian in his Irish reports mentions a man called Rickett who is the intermediary between the IRA and Germany. This man has been attending secret IRA meetings and seems to be in communication with German submarines off the west coast of Eire.

27 April

It has been established that the individual who sent the Lascar with the two valves for SNOW is almost certainly Obed Hussein, a disaffected Indian, who has been residing in Antwerp for some time and is well known to Indian Political Intelligence.

7 May

Two Goanese have turned up at SNOW's office. They want to know whether the valves have been received. Efforts are being made to identify them with a view to having them followed whenever they arrive here.

An underground account of the CPGB has been discovered at the National Provincial Bank. It is the executory account of one Stalker of the International Brigade who was killed in Spain. The account is manipulated by Miss Howard who lives with Bill Rust. She has paid fairly large sums to Eva Reckett, Shand and others. The account seems to be fed by Miss Howard. Further enquiries are being made.

Ken Stalker, fighting with the British battalion of the International Brigade, was killed on the Jarama front in February 1937. Bill Rust had been secretary of the Young Communist League and became a leading member of the CPGB.

9 May

According to the press and SIS the Dutch have arrested a number of important German agents. These include de Rantzow and a commander, probably the two individuals who have been in direct contact with SNOW. Arrangements have been made with the Dutch by which we shall see any papers obtained. It will be interesting to see what arrangements are now made for communicating with SNOW.

11 May

An Austrian, Ruben Glucksmann, is to be interned and Kate Rank, his British secretary of Polish origin, is to go in under 18(b). Both these people are connected with the Eastern Trading Company, which was formerly run by Ehrenlieb, the Russian 4th Department agent.

14 May

Hermann Goering's nephew van Rosen, a Swede, has arrived here. He was apparently in Germany two days before the invasion of Holland. He was a KLM pilot and had fought against the Russians in Finland and on his return from there he had seen Goering who was interested in his technical experiences.

15 May

I arrived at Droitwich about five o'clock and found Colonel Liam Archer at his clinic. We told him that although it was our original intention to discuss particular cases, recent events in Holland had very much brought home to us the dangers of something similar happening in Eire. There was this probability which had a certain amount of supporting evidence. Archer said that as far as he could see there was nothing to prevent the Germans landing in Eire and he did not see how any resistance could be maintained for more than a week.

Archer seemed to think that if the Germans landed in Eire there would be general resentment and a certain amount of resistance but he thought there might be quite a number of people who would say "Oh, well, they are here in force, we can't do anything about it" and be prepared just to accept the situation. He was quite emphatic that Eire would be thinking about her independence and that many people would not mind Great Britain getting a licking. On the other hand somebody who had expressed this view to him concluded by saying: "But what would happen to us if they did?"

Archer was quite interesting about the Communists. He said that they were getting $150 a month from Earl Browder of the CPUSA. It was evidently a new development that this subsidy should come from the United States. Some members of the Party were associated with the IRA. Our whole interview was most friendly and cordial, and before parting we promised to find out what negotiations had been going on between the government of Eire and the British government and to advise him accordingly as to whether he should return to Dublin at the earliest opportunity.

16 May

SNOW has received a message to say that Dr Rantzau will meet him somewhere in the North Sea on 22 May. SNOW is to go out in his trawler if he considers it safe, otherwise he will let the captain deliver the message. The crew are not to be informed and the trawler is not to carry arms.

18 May

Stewart told me an amusing story which came up on Special Material. The Americans ordered 25 camp beds from Harrods, but as these were described as cots in America, 25 baby cots arrived at the embassy. An irate official told Harrods that he was talking from an embassy and not from a crèche.

Glucksmann, the Soviet 4th Department agent, has been arrested and his office has been searched. He has a large amount of interesting correspondence and seems to have a large number of bearer cheques for large amounts. He has been questioned but appears to have been mostly in tears and frequently asked for water. Edward Hinchley-Cooke is carrying out the interrogation as the man is an Austrian and there is no doubt that he is an important Soviet agent. All his answers to questions are completely unconvincing.

19 May

Max Knight has seen Herschel Johnson about Tyler Kent, the employee of the American Embassy who is associated with Anna Wolkoff and has evidently been getting secret documents out of the embassy. It seems likely that these documents may have leaked to the Germans. Johnson was very perturbed since Tyler Kent has access to the embassy ciphers and has previously been reported as being somewhat pro-Nazi and associating with a woman of similar views. It has been decided to raid Tyler Kent and Anna Wolkoff tomorrow.

BISCUIT, who was put in on SNOW in such a way as to preclude the possibility of SNOW realising that he was an agent of ours, has now made it clear that SNOW is double-crossing us. He has indeed said as much to BISCUIT. Personally I think SNOW just regards the whole business as a money-making concern and gives a little to both sides. Probably neither side really trusts him. He has not been in a position to give the Germans very much from this country, except information which we have planted on him. In view of this development it has been decided to let the North Sea meeting take place. SNOW and BISCUIT are to go out on the trawler and hang about the fishing ground until dusk. Instead of then going to the rendezvous the captain will sail to some other point and bring the boat home. This will keep SNOW out of harm's way and ensure that he does not get wind of any impending action. Meanwhile a submarine will play about in the vicinity of the rendezvous and if another submarine turns up it will be torpedoed, if a trawler, it will be captured and we hope with Rantzau on board.

BISCUIT was a petty criminal, Sam McCarthy, who concluded that SNOW suspected he was also a double agent loyal to MI5. Fortunately their boat failed to keep the rendezvous with a U-boat in the North Sea and returned to Grimsby unscathed after it had been circled by a Luftwaffe aircraft.

20 May

Special Material: The Latvian Minister has proposed to the Afghan Minister that they should go fishing. The Afghan Minister has invited the Chinese Ambassador to join them. The latter has accepted with pleasure, remarking that there is nothing like fishing for the deep contemplation and discussion of grave issues and events.

Stewart Menzies told me what I believe is an authentic story in connection with Winston's recent visit to the French. He found them in a terrible state about the possibilities of tanks arriving in Paris. Winston said "That's all right, they will have to get out to relieve themselves and then you can shoot them."

21 May

At 7pm today I attended a meeting at the Home Office which lasted until 8.45. The Home Secretary Sir John Anderson, the Director-General, Sir Alexander Maxwell, Charles Peake, Sir Alan Brooke, myself and Max Knight were present. Anderson had our original memo which was turned down about ten days ago and wanted to have detailed information in support of the various statements made. Max was extremely good and made all his points very quietly and forcibly. I did not interfere at all except on one or two occasions. Anderson began by saying that he found it difficult to believe that members of the British Union of Fascists would assist the enemy. He had been studying the recent number of *Action* where Mosley appealed to the patriotism of its members. Max explained that this was merely an example of how insincere Sir Oswald Mosley really was and how many of his supporters simply regarded utterances of that kind as a figure of speech. He then went on to describe something of the underground activities of the BUF and also of the recent case against Tyler Kent involving Captain Archibald Ramsay. Anderson agreed that the case against Ramsay was rather serious but he did not seem to think that it involved the BUF. Max explained to him that Ramsay and Mosley were in constant touch with one another and that many members of the Right Club were also members of the BUF. Other subjects dealt with were the somewhat sinister

activities of John Beckett and other members of the BUF who appear to be collecting arms.

Sir John Anderson said that he needed to be reasonably convinced that the BUF
might assist the enemy and that unless he could get such evidence he thought it
would be a mistake to imprison Mosley and his supporters, who would be
extremely bitter after the war when democracy would be going through its sever-
est trials. I longed to say that if somebody did not get a move on there would be no
democracy, no England and no Empire, and that this was almost a matter of days. I
did strongly stress the urgency of the matter and said that surely, rather than argue
the fine points of these various cases, wasn't it possible to make up our minds
whether the BUF was assisting the enemy and if we came to the conclusion that it
was, wasn't it possible to find some means of dealing with it as an organisation.
Anderson rather skated over this but he seemed to have a great aversion to locking
up a British subject unless he had a very cast-iron case against him. He was, however, I think considerably shaken by the end of the meeting and he asked us for
further evidence on certain points which he required for the cabinet meeting
which was to take place tomorrow evening. Either he is an extremely calm and
cool-headed person or he has not the least idea of the present situation. The possibility of a serious invasion of this country would seem to be no more than a vague
suggestion.

22 May

A representative of the BBC came here this morning to say that in his opinion the
New British Broadcasting station which is of course a German one, was putting
over information in code. He had made a careful study of broadcasting methods
when the Germans took Poland and also when they took Holland. They had
destroyed the Polish broadcasting stations and had taken their wavelengths. In the
case of Holland they had left the stations standing and had taken them over. There
were strong indications that in the event of an attack on this country the New
British Broadcasting station would try and monopolise the air and issue instructions and misleading information to the public.

The last three days have been the worst I ever spent for some considerable time.
The news has been so bad that it made me feel physically sick. I am much heart-
ened today by the re-taking of Arras and the reported flank attack by the British
Expeditionary Force. There was a rumour that Marshal Gamelin has shot himself.
The trouble on the Meuse was apparently due to the fact that the troops were
mostly French colonials who ran.

25 May

The Director-General told me this morning that he had had an interview with
Neville Chamberlain who had questioned him on Fifth Columnists here. The
Director-General told him that he was worried about Czechs and also about

other aliens. He then went on to see the Prime Minister. The latter was not available owing to a meeting, but Desmond Morton was there. It seems that the Prime Minister takes a strong view about the internment of all Fifth Columnists at this moment and that he has left the Home Secretary in no doubt about his views. What seems to have moved him more than anything was the Tyler Kent case.

At about 6 o'clock Stephens had a telephone message asking that he and I should go up to the Privy Council to see Clement Attlee and Arthur Greenwood [*the deputy leader of the Labour Party*]. I could not understand how they had got hold of my name. Before going I rang up the Director-General to ask his permission. I told him that I proposed, if I were questioned about internment, to tell them exactly what I thought, and he agreed. Attlee and Greenwood gave me the impression that they thought there was some political intrigue or graft in the Home Office which was holding things up. I told them quite frankly that I did not think this was the case. I went over the whole ground, explained how enemy aliens had been let into this country freely for a period of five years, how the War Book contained directions for their probable internment in categories immediately after the outbreak of war and how Sir Samuel Hoare had reversed this policy early in September and substituted the tribunal system. This has meant that the organisation of MI5 had been swamped and for the last six months had been engaged on work of relatively small importance which had largely been abortive. I said that in my view the reluctance of the Home Office to act came from an old-fashioned liberalism which seemed to prevail in all sections. The liberty of the subject, freedom of speech etc were all very well in peace-time but were no use in fighting the Nazis. There seemed to be a complete failure to realise the power of the totalitarian state and the energy with which the Germans were fighting a total war. Both Greenwood and Attlee were in agreement with our views. They said that they had been charged by the Prime Minister to enquire into this matter.

31 May

The Anna Wolkoff–Archibald Ramsay case is going to be interesting. Anna Wolkoff has come perilously near to high treason. She has obtained information of vital importance to this country from the American Embassy through Tyler Kent. She has had documents photographed by a man called Smirnov, and there is some evidence to show that she has passed this information to the Duca del Monte in the Italian Embassy. She has moreover endeavoured to plant agents both in the censorship and MI5. There is little doubt that Captain Ramsay has been cognisant of her activities.

Wolkoff was sentenced to ten years' imprisonment. Kent received seven, and was deported to the United States at the end of the war. Archibald Maule Ramsay, the Member of Parliament for Peebles since 1931, was detained under Emergency Regulation 18(b).

4 June

The general opinion now appears to be that SNOW is once more on the straight and narrow path. Personally I doubt it, although he has given us certain information which has proved to be reliable. We have just heard that two bombs were found in the *City of Sydney* at Mauritius.

7 June

Downing Street is worried about some land which is in the property of a Dutchman in the vicinity of Chequers. It is said that he has ploughed up his fields all round Chequers and that the deposit thrown up is mainly chalk. Enquiries have been made and it has been found that the Dutchman was naturalised some time ago on the recommendation of Neville Chamberlain and Mr Cleverley, Sir Horace Wilson's son-in-law.

9 June

We have now arrested one William Gaskell Downing, an AID inspector and his German mistress Lucy Sara Strauss. When Downing's room was searched eight Winchester repeater rifles were found, with telescopic sites and 2,000 rounds of ammunition. No adequate explanation was forthcoming as to why he was in possession of them. He also had photographic representations of an AID pass and an Air Ministry pass that were found. He said he had done this in order to keep them as souvenirs. The possibility of his prosecution under section 1 of the Treachery Act 1940 is being considered.

11 June

The blow has fallen, and the Director-General and the Deputy D-G are leaving us. Harker is to take over with Charles Butler as his Deputy and myself as Director, B Division. I am terribly sorry for the Director-General and his Deputy. It must be a frightful blow to them as being the two pioneers of the whole show.

As the new Prime Minister, Churchill ordered Sir Horace Wilson to dismiss Sir Vernon Kell and his deputy Sir Eric Holt-Wilson. Lady Kell, working as a volunteer at the canteen in Wormwood Scrubs, announced to the assembled staff, "Your precious Winston has sacked the General."

24 June

We have formed a new section under Dick Brooman-White to deal with the Celtic movements. The Germans had obviously done a good deal of work in the Breton Movement and it may be that to some degree they have done the same here.

John Maude has discovered that the military, particularly 55th Division in the eastern counties, have badgered the local police into giving them a list of people with whose bona-fides they are not altogether satisfied. If and when the balloon goes up the military intend to take the law into their own hands and arrest these people. We have got hold of these lists which do not seem to have much in the way of common-sense basis. One man's only crime appears to be that he is a dentist. Another is a member of the Peace Pledge Union. The Prime Minister had apparently heard of these lists and was wondering why the people had not been arrested already.

26 June

This office is being absolutely inundated with ridiculous enquiries from every possible quarter and the worst come from the highest circles. We have asked the Director-General to try and get some broadcast urging the public to report more accurately and to take steps to verify their facts as far as possible before. I have also suggested that something should be done to ensure that stories are fully sifted here before being passed round to the Prime Minister, Cabinet ministers and other officials. We are now harassed by a number of amateur detectives in high places. The bow and arrow story is still going on and we have had to answer a five-page letter from Antony Bevir, the Prime Minister's secretary, who is still unconvinced. I really think it must be accepted that we probably have more experience of mare's nests than anybody else. I have asked the Director-General to take the matter up with Lord Swinton.

3 July

Cecil Liddell heard this afternoon that the French fleet was being sunk in the Mediterranean. News was also received about the *Arandora Star*, which went down with so-called Category 'A' German and Italians on board.

3,528 Nazi internees were drowned in the Atlantic on 2 July when the U-47 torpedoed the Arandora Star *which was carrying them to internment camps in Canada.*

13 July

I have just heard about an officer who has leaked about an Admiralty plan known as SACKBUT and ACCORDIAN. A medical officer had blown into Cable & Wireless and asked about hospital accommodation in the Azores. It looks as if we had some scheme either for operations in North Africa or in Portugal.

SNOW has been in communication with the other side. They first of all wanted him to give them the name and address of a suitable individual in the north of England or Scotland who would be prepared to receive explosives. They subsequently cancelled this and asked him to find out whether his friend in the Welsh

Nationalist Movement would be prepared to act in this capacity. This may possibly indicate a change of plan. Some time ago we heard that the points for invasion were Anglesey, Scotland and the south-east and east coasts. The latest message to SNOW may mean that the Germans will go for Ireland first and subsequently for Wales. On the other hand it seems to be an indication that an attack here is not likely to be impending. In fact the indication from SIS sources are confirmation of this view. Nothing is expected for about ten days at least, and some think that Spain and Portugal are the first objectives, with Gibraltar as the final object of attack.

The whole German machine seems to have concentrated on defeating us through propaganda. As regards espionage the Germans were in a position to have everything they wanted for the asking. Our rearmament industry was penetrated and under our system of government there was nothing to prevent the Germans from getting almost any information they required. As regards sabotage, it would obviously be wrong to take a complacent view. It may be that the Germans are holding their hands until the day of invasion, when we may see things going up, either through the agency of the IRA or possibly certain elements of the British Union of Fascists. Up to the present however practically nothing has happened in the way of sabotage, and we know that the Germans are making approaches to SNOW to obtain the necessary contacts. We also have the incident of the two Afrikaaners, so-called, and the Indian Obed arriving in the south of Ireland with two suitcases full of bombs. Neither incident suggests anything very thorough in the way of organisation. Just at the moment the main line seems to be broadcasts by the New British Broadcasting Station and other stations. While I feel it likely that there are a few German agents here, possibly transmitting by wireless, I do not envisage anything in the nature of large bodies of individuals going out to stab us in the back as soon as the Germans invade this country.

16 July

At Herschel Johnson's request I lunched today with Harvey Klemmer of the American Embassy who has been instructed by Joe Kennedy to produce a report on the Fifth Column. I gave him as general a picture as I could on the situation here. I had the impression that he or the ambassador was apprehensive about the desire of this country to see things through. He wanted to know whether I thought there was any danger of this country packing up if we were bombed incessantly for two to three months. I said that on the contrary, the more we were bombed the more we would dig in our toes. I asked him for his own views. He seemed to have gained a rather superficial impression that we had not really got our heart in this war and that there was a possibility of the country thinking it was better to come to terms. I could have given him some arguments in support of his theory, but I did not think it would be good for him, as they might well have presented a false picture. In fact I did my best to get him to believe that there would be no compromise here of any sort or kind. In the meantime I heard that one Edgar Mowrer, a representative of Frank Knox of the Ministry for War or Marine in the United States, had instructions to get similar information for his chief. Lord Swinton had instructed Brigadier Holt-Wilson to get in touch with him and find out what he wanted. He is to be given information purely on the organisation and legal side. I am a little frightened about this arrangement which may become a fifth wheel on the coach.

18 July

SNOW has had an interesting message. It is proposed to drop somebody in Ireland or this country. Information is requested as to documents and formalities required for getting to this country from Ireland. I am suggesting that a man should be dropped in Ireland and should be given instructions as to how to obtain a visa from Passport Control. These instructions should be of a kind which will make his identity apparent. We can then pick him up when he lands. It is very important that he should not fall into the hands of the military or the parashots either here or in Ireland until we have got his whole story and instructions.

Gooch has returned from Liverpool. He has arranged with the Liverpool police for a close watch to be kept on Beppu, who is expected back from Ireland in the course of the next few days. Gooch managed to get into the consul's office and to make arrangements for finding out the combination of the safe. As soon as this has been done, Gooch will go up and have a look at the contents.

20 July

Cecil Liddell has got an interesting link-up on Werner Unland. A firm here called Raw Furs, which is reported to have IRA connections, is associated with another firm called Thora in America with German connections. Thora in turn is run by a firm Grondhal of Stockholm, who paid money to Unland.

The Eire authorities appear to be arresting a certain number of Germans.

A suspected German spy, Werner Unland had left England shortly before the outbreak of war and his mail in Dublin had been intercepted by G-2. Unland had corresponded with addresses in Hungary, Spain and Belgium, and was eventually arrested in May 1941 and sentenced to five years' imprisonment.

27 July

A Group 1 message has been intercepted between Ireland and Germany and refers to a man called Donahue, presumably a German agent, who is coming over here in the course of the next few days. A new branch has been formed in the office called the O Branch, which is to deal with organisation. I should have a lot to do.

Group 1 was the Radio Security Service designation for suspected Abwehr wireless traffic intercepted on monitored frequencies.

31 July

Anna Wolkoff and Tyler Kent are coming up for trial. It has, however, been decided not to prosecute Captain Ramsay, at any rate for the present. Originally a conspiracy charge had been contemplated.

2 August

The Irish have now given us a fairly full report about Henry Obed and his two Afrikaaner friends, but there is still much detail that we should like to know. They have brightly told us that no useful purpose would be served by our sending an officer over to interrogate these people. Obed had in his possession a letter addressed to one S.B. Kahn, an Indian in Liverpool. This man was arrested by the Liverpool police and is being sent down to the interrogation centre. We hope to have some other Indians to keep him company.

Henry Obed was arrested by the Garda with two South African students, Herbert Tributh and Dieter Gaertner, having landed in Baltimore Bay from a yacht, the Soizic, *which had sailed from Brest. All three were sentenced to seven years' imprisonment at Mountjoy.*

9 August

I lunched with Somerset Maugham, who is writing four articles for the American press, one of them on the Fifth Column. The Director of Military Intelligence had asked me to go and see him. He said his task was rather a difficult one because although he wanted to arouse Americans to send a sense of danger with which they were faced, he did not wish them to get the impression that this country regarded the position as hopeless and was not worth supporting. I gave him an outline of the foreign organisations of the Nazi Party, explaining that I thought that as far as this country was concerned, and in fact America and many other countries, it was the basis of the Fifth Column activity. I then went on to give him an estimate of what I thought was the position at the moment. I said in fact that I didn't anticipate anything very frightful in the way of Fifth Column activity. He said that what I had told him was most interesting but actually very helpful in so far as his report was concerned. He had apparently just written one article for some American periodical on the French collapse. He said that when something so complete and unexpected happened one had to go back to fundamentals. He thought that the root cause was that the French had grown to attach more importance to money than to more spiritual things.

10 August

John Dickson Carr has done a very good report on the funds of the British Union of Fascists which have been invested in a number of trust companies. A great deal of trouble had been taken by the party to cover up the origin as far as possible. So far investigations disclose that there is a balance of some £11,637.

13 August

An interesting case has come to light. We have records dating back some years showing that one Stanislas Seymoniczky, who has used a variety of other aliases, was either a member of the OGPU or the 4th Department. This man succeeded in getting over here with a number of refugees at the time of the French debacle and he was accompanied by a woman called Alta Lecoutre. We now find that they are ensconsed in the offices of General de Gaulle, the woman being secretary to André Labarthe, who is supposed to be in charge of technical equipment. Labarthe has a very sticky record as one of the people who were deeply involved in the Spanish arms racket on behalf of Moscow. This looks like developing into an interesting case. We have sent a wire to Walter Krivitsky in Canada as he is almost certain to know these people.

Seymoniczyk's wife, Alta Lecoutre, was Labarthe's secretary, and had been the mistress of Pierre Cot, the former French Minister of Air. All three were Soviet agents.

19 August

I attended Bow Street Magistrates Court where I gave evidence in the Wolkoff–Tyler Kent case. I merely had to state that two of the letters found in the possession of Tyler Kent addressed to the American Embassy were written by myself. One referred to the Brandeis case and the other to certain secret wireless operations. I said that both these letters would be useful to the enemy. McLure was prosecuting and I was cross-examined.

20 August

BISCUIT has returned from Lisbon with an up-to-date wireless set in a suitcase and £950. He met Dr Rantzau in Lisbon and his whole visit seems to have been a thorough success. He gleaned a certain amount of information regarding local German activities particularly those of Dobler, who is the head German agent there.

21 August

A German named H.K. Bruin who came over here in the guise of a refugee from Belgium and Holland, is a self-confessed German agent. He had been in possession of a wireless set with which he had been communicating weather reports and other information to the Germans. He had also been instructed to give them early intimation of the advance of British troops into Belgium. This I gather he had done. He was working for Dr Rantzau. The question now arises whether this is a shooting case. There is no doubt whatever that Bruin was a German agent and very little doubt that he was operating against us and he was certainly operating against our allies.

Seymoniczyk has been followed and had a meeting at the Serpentine Lido with a man who was subsequently identified as Nolte, a Dutchman. Nolte has considerable intelligence background. He is said to have been working for the French and has quite recently offered his services to us. In the meantime things are obviously leaking through General de Gaulle's office. Very secret operations in contemplation involving the landing of de Gaulle's forces at Dakar were only supposed to be known to de Gaulle and his chief of staff. Now they seem to be known to almost everybody on the French mission including André Labarthe. We shall have to tell the DMI that until the organisation is cleaned up they should not be given any confidential information at all.

Lord Rothschild had an amusing interview with the Beaver on the subject of Loewy. He described the general scene when he arrived. There were about a dozen people in Beaverbrook's room all talking in groups. Beaverbrook went out for about an hour and left them all sitting there. When he came back he was called upon to go to Downing Street. Rothschild went with him and started his business in the car on the way. He waited 1½ hours outside 10 Downing Street in the car, and had a further talk with Beaverbrook on his return. After this he got ten minutes of private conversation. The dialogue went something like this:

Beaverbrook: Well, Rothschild, you have come to see me about the Loewy people, about those eight people. I am surprised that somebody with your name, your liberal views, your position and reputation, should go in for this witch-hunting. Those poor Jews have been hunted out of Germany, and now when they come here they are hunted back into concentration camps. You should not be involved in this persecution and you should not be in MI5 witch-hunting. You should be leading your people out of the concentration camps.

Rothschild: The members of the Loewy firm that I came to see you about are not Jews. They are what is known as Aryan.

Beaverbrook: They are Jews.

Rothschild: They are not.

Beaverbrook: They are Jews.

Rothschild They are not.

Beaverbrook: I am not going to start an argument. Now are you anything to do with that man Captain or Group Captain Archer?

Rothschild: He is a colleague of mine.

Beaverbrook: You know I fired him. I fired him because he said a terrible thing to me, something that would do this country a great deal of harm with its traditions of harbouring political refugees. He said that if those poor Jews were left out that the public would hang them on every lamp post. Anybody who says that to me gets fired at once. You ought not to be associated with those witch-hunters.

Rothschild: Do you think then that MI5's investigations into Nazi agents in industry are of no value?

Beaverbrook: No value at all. Even if these Loewy people are agents, they can do no harm.

Rothschild: Couldn't they sabotage plants?

Beaverbrook: No. I watch them very carefully.

Rothschild: Couldn't they convey information to the enemy about the geographical position of your extrusion presses, and about the Ministry of Aircraft Production's aircraft capacity and production?

Beaverbrook: I don't care if they do know where the presses are. It is not easy to bomb a press even if your so-called agents were signalling to them. As regards our capacity, I hope the Germans do know. I said what it was on the transatlantic telephone at 9 o'clock this evening.

Rothschild: So really you are quite happy about having these people about. You remember what happened in France and Holland.

Beaverbrook: I was in France at the very last moment before the government fell, and I can tell you it was nothing to do with so-called Fifth Column activities. The French were a decadent and beaten race. That poor Jew Mandel was the only one who had any spirit in him. I watched him trying to carry the whole country. You know I have not always been pro-Semitic, but when a people get persecuted I go on to their side. I am the only liberal member of the Cabinet, and I am sticking up for them everywhere. You ought to stick up for them too, instead of persecuting them. It is disgraceful.

Rothschild: Well, if you are quite happy about having dangerous people in your employ, I will say nothing more about it.

Beaverbrook: (a little apprehensively), Well, what is your case against them? I must have logic and I must have my presses. If you take men away I can't have my presses.

Rothschild: Your own industrial adviser Sir Charles Craven says it will make no difference if these people are taken away.

Beaverbrook: How the bloody hell does he know? What is your case against them?

Rothschild: In two cases we consider that the people are German agents, or at any rate strong Nazi sympathisers, and our source of information has been some Czech intelligence officers who have known these people for a considerable time. It is no good your saying that Loewy has confidence in them. Loewy is quite unreliable. He told me that Eugene Hilt, an Englishman who had been in his employ for some time, was perfectly reliable, when the witch-hunters knew perfectly well that he was actively conspiring with the German embassy and the German Chamber of Commerce to break Loewy. The thing I have against the others is that they were members of the German Labour Front.

Beaverbrook: The German Labour Front is a trade union.

Rothschild: It isn't. It is an espionage organisation.

Beaverbrook: Everybody in German after 1934 had to belong to the German trade union. Therefore it means nothing.

Rothschild: But these people became members of the German Labour Front not in Germany in order to work, but in a free country.

Beaverbrook: That poor Jew Loewy wants to go to Canada now. He comes and begs me every day to let him take all his people over there.

Rothschild: Well, I take it you are not going to agree to having these people removed.

Beaverbrook: You produce your case. You have not produced anything yet. Then I will consider it. I do not want Nazi agents in the Ministry of Aircraft Production.

Rothschild: Thank you very much for letting me come and see you.

Beaverbrook: Good-night. You should not be in that organisation with witch-hunters. It ought to be abolished. I do not think there is any danger from Nazi spies in this country. I do not think it matters if they are at large.

25 August

According to a code message the Germans are very anxious to find out the strength of our forces in Northern Ireland.

26 August

Roger Hollis has been all through the documents of the Executive Committee of the CPGB which were in Eric Godfrey's possession, and made a comparison between Moscow's short thesis on the war situation and utterances made by Moscow as related by Jay Lovestone to the Dies Committee in Washington DC. Moscow's instructions are that the imperialist war must be gradually converted into civil war, that no steps should be taken to oppose a German landing in this country since a short period under a Nazi regime would be the quickest way of bringing about a Communist revolution. Jay Lovestone said that Moscow was working on similar lines in the past in Germany since they held the view that it was much easier to bring about a revolution after a Fascist regime than after a Social-Democratic one.

27 August

SNOW is in daily communication with the Germans, and arrangements are being made to land an agent by parachute. A suitable spot is being found, the location of which will be communicated to the Germans. The great difficulty is to get the man down alive and to prevent the Local Defence Volunteers from getting at him. The German proposal is that a house should be taken in an out of the way spot where this man and other agents could be accommodated.

6 September

I returned at mid-day to find that in my absence four Dutchmen had landed in a boat at Dungeness on 3 September. Their names were van den Kieboom, Meier, Pons and Waldberg. They had been instructed to report on British defensive measures on the coast near Dungeness and on army reserve formations in depth from Dungeness to Ashford and thence to London. They said that there was a concentration of mounted troops equipped with mules at Le Touquet. This information was confirmed to some extent by SIS sources and they had been told that an invasion would take place before the middle of September. In the meantime they were to report anything they could with the small transmitting sets in their possession. They were to work in pairs. Each pair had £60 in English money and food for seven days. They were given no contacts in this country and in fact they were singularly badly directed and to anybody with any knowledge of conditions in this country should have been apparent that none of these could hope to succeed. All of them had been misled about conditions in this country, probably as an inducement to them to come over.

I found on my return that William Charles Crocker had resigned. I gather that he was not prepared to accept the position which we had to find for him but that he had had a row with Lord Swinton as the result of which he had retired not only from this office but from the Centre as well. Personally I am very sorry in a great many ways that this has happened, as I am sure that he could have done very useful work here. The real mistake is that he was pitch-forked into this office on half-baked information of the situation. For this I am afraid he was to some extent to blame.

7 September

A parachutist descended during the night from a height of 15,000 feet. He had been stunned by his wireless set and was found lying in a ditch at Denton, Northamptonshire at 1730 hours yesterday. He was dressed as a civilian and was in possession of a German automatic and a wireless set which could transmit and receive. It was of similar pattern to that now in possession of SNOW. The man's name is SUMMER. He is a Swede of German origin. He had been dropped by a Heinkel plane and had embarked at Brussels. He had intended to land at Birmingham and thought that on landing he was somewhere near Stratford-on-Avon. It transpired that he had been in England as late as December 1939 when he had stayed with friends at Boughton. He was in possession of his National Registration Certificate. He had been trained at Hamburg. Colonel Hinchley-Cooke took down a statement from him at Cannon Row police station and he was then sent on to Latchmere House.

Quite a number of reports have been coming in from SIS regarding the imminence of invasion. SIS is in touch with two people in Portugal who have been approached by the Germans and it has been suggested that they should be allowed to come here and that we should test them out.

8 September

Carrigan has been on a very secret visit to Eamon de Valera. He was asked to find out what de Valera's terms would be for the abandonment of his neutrality. I gather that de Valera is quite intrigued and is thinking things over. The move is inspired from the highest quarter here.

According to Group 1 intercepts the Germans are worried about the four men in a boat [*landed at Dungeness*] and also SUMMER and his friend TATE, whose identity has not been disclosed, on condition that TATE's life will be spared if and when he arrives in this country. This is interesting confirmation that these six spies, who have been thrown into this country in the most inefficient manner, are apparently part of a serious German organisation. SUMMER is not apparently interested in his own life but merely that of his friend. He himself is quite prepared to be shot as a spy and is apparently a student of philosophy. Owing to his German parentage and his admiration of the German regime he joined the German army but was, however, reluctant to become a spy, so having taken the job was prepared to see it through and determined not to give away his friends. Malcolm Frost and Max Knight seem to have succeeded in persuading him that the Germans had given him a very raw deal and had sent him over here ill-equipped and under somewhat false pretences. He came round eventually to this view and agreed to work his wireless set, which he had up to then refused to do.

I saw Kenneth Strong from military intelligence this evening. He had just had an interview with the prisoners. What puzzled him was that the Germans should have given their agents details of their plan of attack. The details they had given more or less agreed with what we had received from other sources and from aerial reconnaissance etc of the dispositions of enemy forces. This made it difficult to believe that the spies had been sent over here to mislead us. Strong has a great regard for German efficiency and cannot bring himself to believe that they could have been so stupid, as to send these men over here without having schooled them properly and worked out plans by which they could be really effective.

9 September

We had a heavy raid last night and a raid at Northolt today. We are sending SUMMER down to Buckinghamshire where he is going to get into communication with the other side.

We are getting CHARLIE fixed up in Manchester where he is to be ready to receive another agent with a wireless set. We have also got a place waiting in Wales for three more agents who are due to arrive.

10 September

A meeting has been held with military intelligence to discuss policy in regard to communications sent to the enemy though our various agents. Are we to encourage them to invade or are we to try and stall proceedings? The DMI was rather in favour of encouraging them to come over but on referring the matter to the Chiefs of Staff it was decided to let them have the truth about the strength of our defences. The question of getting the necessary information to transmit was also discussed. This was to be done through MI9 except in the case of the Air Ministry where Archie Boyle will continue to let us have information for SNOW. Felix Cowgill is not very satisfied with the plan to obtain information through MI9. His whole experience is that we ought to go very high. The heads of the intelligence are too important to give us the chicken-feed and important enough to give us the really vital stuff. Whenever you ask something of the kind you are always told to refer the matter to someone else, when the result is generally unsatisfactory and the delay considerable. Personally I think Cowgill is quite right but I am afraid we are committed to the MI9 scheme until it breaks down, which it undoubtedly will.

Lord Rothschild has recovered his Home Farm at Tring, which he gives to the office for the use of those who want a night's sleep. This is getting more and more necessary.

11 September

Colonel Liam Archer has written to say that he has unearthed the wireless set we told him about. Some time ago he had been interested in a German named Preetz who had left the country. Preetz had subsequently returned under the name of Mutcheell and was associating with a man called Donoghue. This is the Donoghue who we were looking for as the result of an intercepted Group 1 message. Both Preetz and Donoghue have now been arrested and a wireless set has been found in their possession. We have asked for the fullest possible details.

Cecil Liddell has put forward a scheme by which an Irish mission should be attached to our forces if we are called in to assist the Eire government in the event of an invasion. He feels that it is extremely important that the military should not attempt to deal with any Fifth Columnists in Eire except through the Eire mission. If it is necessary to arrest anybody he should immediately be handed over to the mission for necessary action. This is I think an extremely important and urgent matter. A memo has been prepared for DMI on the subject. There is also a suggestion that suitable liaison officers with the British forces should be appointed for the purpose of maintaining contact with the Eire missions.

12 September

SUMMER has succeeded in getting through to the Germans and has received a reply. He explains that he had been experiencing considerable difficulties.

13 September

I have asked Valentine Vivian to arrange that we should receive in future copies of Group 10 messages which come from the United States. These are very important if we are to have a complete picture of the Rantzau organisation. The Poles, Czechs and Hungarians all appear to be transmitting by wireless without any supervision. I am not so worried about the Czechs but I think the Poles should certainly be supervised. I have asked the Radio Security Service to take down the Hungarian messages and if they cannot be deciphered I propose to ask for the removal of the military attaché, who is transmitting the special cipher unknown to his minister. He is, moreover. notoriously pro-German.

14 September

A warning has been sent to all chief constables about Kuhirt and Peter Schoder who may have landed here. We are still on the lookout for SUMMER's friend, TATE, alias Leonhard. We know his wavelength, which has not come up and there is also a rendezvous between him and SUMMER on 20 September.

15 September

Last night SUMMER sent a message telling his employers that he was in the vicinity of Oxford but had met with considerable difficulties. This morning SNOW received a request from the other side to go to the assistance of a Swedish friend who was in the fields near Oxford. He has agreed to do this and has suggested High Wycombe railway station as the rendezvous.

The Director of Naval Intelligence, Admiral John Godfrey, rang up in the evening as he was worried about these wireless messages which he did not understand. He told me they referred to a meeting which was to take place at 11 o'clock on Monday. I showed him that the meeting would be covered and he seemed satisfied. In actual fact we are sending down B6 (a) to see that SUMMER does not escape and (b) to ascertain whether the Germans send anybody to observe what takes place.

16 September

I have arranged that we shall in future form a small committee to deal with SNOW and double-cross agents. It will consist of Malcolm Frost, Dick White, Jack Curry, T.A. Robertson, Felix Cowgill and myself. [XXXXXX] of SIS has put in an excellent report of his examination of the prisoners. He seems to have come to precisely the same conclusions as Dick but he adds a certain amount on the lay-out of the wireless stations etc. It has been decided to amalgamate the two projects.

There is yet another strange incident, when Klop called on Gregor Harlip at an unexpected hour and a mysterious stranger came in, much to the embarrassment of Harlip and his wife. Klop had a very definite impression that this man was a German agent.

The meeting between BISCUIT and SUMMER took place. There was no-one else there. The Germans have expressed their warm thanks to SNOW for his services.

I hear that there is considerable confusion in the Irish Home Guard due to the fact that the orders are given in Gaelic. As nobody understands the language, they never know whether they are being told to pile arms or open fire.

Cecil Liddell has got a reply from Colonel Liam Archer about Willi Preetz. We have got a description of his wireless set, and photograph and further details are to follow.

André Maurois' wife, writing from New York to a Miss Varley of Ross-on-Wye, talks of her husband's book and his story about Paul Reynaud which is apparently authentic. Helen de Portes, Reynaud's mistress, was his undoing. She destroyed his sense of duty. His so-called accident was perhaps a double suicide. It occurred shortly after a discovery in Spain of suitcases filled with 50m francs, which had been carried across the border by two minor *attachés de cabinet* of Reynaud. Arrested, the two men declared that the money belongs to Reynaud and mostly to Madame de Portes, who was killed in the accident. To William Bullett, the American Ambassador, who visisted Reynaud in Montpelier Hosptial, Reynaud said: "I have lost my country, my honour and my lover."

SUMMER's friend TATE has been captured near Cambridge. He had a Danish passport and answers to the description we have. He said that he was a refugee and that he had landed some time ago. He first said he came on a yacht with brown sails and then on a ship propelled by motor. A gypsy has told the police that he had a friend with him at 8 o'clock yesterday evening. Every effort is being made to trace this individual and also a wireless set if one exists.

Wulf Schmidt, alias Harry Williamson and codenamed TATE, was arrested in the Cambridgeshire village of Willlingham on the morning of his arrival.

Dick White and Malcolm Frost have been interrogating SUMMER all day but without result. He sticks rigidly to his story although it has many discrepancies.

Colonel Stephens rang me up late in the evening to say that TATE, the new arrival, had broken down and was prepared to go out and assist in the discovery of his wireless set.

TATE's wireless set, which was a two-way one, and also his code, parachute etc, were found. He explained that he had been dropped from a height of 3,500 feet, had been caught up in some telgraph wires and for a brief moment was in a searchlight beam. He eventually succeeded in extricating himself from the telegraph wires but damaged his foot on landing. He could not add a great deal to what SUMMER has already told us, but what he has to say is interesting confirmation. I discussed with Frost the question of running TATE. We came to the conclusion that it was essential that he should try and establish connection, since if the Germans thought he had been caught SUMMER and SNOW might be compromised. TATE had an address on him of Lopez in Lisbon and we are considering writing to say that the set had been damaged. It was recollected, however, that the Lopez address had been to some extent compromised by the capture of the other prisoners, so we dropped this idea.

I have just been told that the officer from MI9 who was present at the interrogation of TATE yesterday took it upon himself to manhandle the prisoner without saying anything to Colonel Stephens, Dick White, or Malcolm Frost. The interrogation broke off at lunchtime, when Colonel Alexander Scotland left the room. Frost, wondering where he was, followed him and eventually discovered him in the prisoner's cell. He was hitting TATE in the jaw and I think got one back for himself. Frost stopped this incident without making a scene, and later told me what had happened. It was quite clear to me that we cannot have this sort of thing going on in our establishment. Apart from the moral aspect of the whole thing, I am quite convinced that these Gestapo methods do not pay in the long run. We are taking the matter up with DMI and propose to say that we do not intend to have that particular military intelligence officer on the premises any more. I am told that Scotland turned up this morning with a syringe containing some drug or other, which it was thought would induce the prisoner to speak. Stephens told Scotland that he could not see TATE, who was not in a fit state to be interrogated. Actually there was nothing seriously wrong with TATE.

After the war Colonel Scotland published The London Cage, *an account of his experiences as an interrogator questioning prisoners of war in Kensington Palace Gardens.*

Colonel Stephens has given an amusing account of Osbert Peake's visit to Latchmere House where he saw two German spies. The conversation with Charles van dem Kieboom was pleasant and ended on the note that he (Peake) hoped that Kieboom "would not be here long". Conversation with Carl Meier was perhaps equally unfortunate in that he asked this spy, who had been pitched on to these shores by the German secret service, whether he had arranged with his relations to send him clean laundry each week. Peake was closeted with Dr Harold Dearden for some time and told him that he intended to rely on him as a private source of information.

Osbert Peake MP was the Parliamentary Under-Secretary of State at the Home Office from 1919 to 1944. His daughter was one of C's secretaries.

24 September

I dined with Anthony Blunt and Guy Burgess at the Reform Club. Just as I was going away at about 11.30pm a Molotov breadbasket descended. Three incendiary bombs fell just inside Pall Mall and all sorts of people were rushing about in dressing gowns with bags of sand. When I got into the Mall the whole of St James's Park was lit up as if by Roman candles. I saw at least a dozen there and several in the Mall itself.

3 October

We had another long discussion about the three people who arrived in Scotland. Vera is beginning to break. She has mentioned the Duchesse de Chateau Thierry as a person with whom she was to establish contact. Our files about the Duchesse are interesting. They show that she was introduced to My Erikson, a highly suspicious woman who had been employed here as a domestic servant, by Rantzau, with the suggestion that she was hard up and might be approached. The correspondence in our files shows that the Duchesse's daughter was in touch with a Dr Henry (also known as Dr Heinrich), with whom she was negotiating on behalf of her mother. Her mother was to provide introductions for Dr Henry's friends to ambassadors. Vera now confirms that the Duchesse was employed by Rantzau to set up a salon in this country. She had been paid quite a lot of money but had not produced any very astonishing results. Vera knows Dr Henry as a person who frequented the Duchesse's salon. It is interesting to note that about this time attempts were being made to set up a similar salon in Washington. This all came out in *Confessions of a Nazi Spy*. We are having very close observation both on the Duchesse and on Henry. She was a Dutch Jewess who was subsequently divorced and she then married Chateau Thierry, who is living apart from her now.

Vera Erikson had been delivered by a Luftwaffe flying-boat to Scotland on 30 September with two companions, François de Deeker and Werner Walti, and all three had been arrested the same day. The men were later hanged, but Vera was never prosecuted. They had been recruited in Hamburg by the mysterious Abwehr spymaster Dr Rantzau, later identified as Nikolaus Ritter.

4 October

Interrogations are still going on and De Deeker and Walti absolutely refuse to say anything except that they cannot understand German. Vera has told us that De Deeker is an extremely important man who could easily be exchanged for some prominent British subject. She is evidently very much in love with him, and refuses to disclose his true identity. We are inclined to think he may be Werner Ulm who is mentioned by all the other prisoners as the one who did a great deal of instruction work at the spy school at Hamburg. It is said that he had already been to England and had been picked up by a German plane in Norfolk, obviously an untrue story.

5 October

Another parachutist has arrived. His name is Karl Grosse, and he has a British pass-port in the name of Alfred Phillips which it is suspected he obtained in Luxembourg. He is a German who returned to Germany from America via Japan after the outbreak of war. He has a one-way set and maps of the Liverpool area. His instructions were to hike about and report on morale (or as he put it morals), road-blocks, weather conditions, etc. We had already heard about him from TATE. He is going to work his set and we propose to run it as a very obvious double-cross in order to enhance the value of SUMMER and company. Grosse is a poor fish who never wanted to be a spy. He joined his regiment and when a sergeant asked who spoke English he rather foolishly put up his hand. Before he knew where he was he was an indifferent spy dropped down from the air into Northampton.

SUMMER was a well-established Swedish double agent, Goesta Caroli, who had parachuted into England in September 1940. Karl Grosse, a soldier in the elite Brandenburg Lehr Regiment was enrolled as GOOSE.

I saw the Vice Chief of the Imperial General Staff with Roger Hollis. He wanted to know about Communism. He was worried about the morale of the troops dur-ing the winter and the possibility of their being affected by agitation. On the whole his views seemed very sound and sensible. We reassured him but I pointed out that in our view two things were necessary, first that the Government should anticipate events rather more intelligently i.e. it should not allow the Communist Party of Great Britain to get the credit for putting people into the underground or in large shelters in the East End which had formerly been locked up at night; secondly, that if the regulations were contravened strong action should be taken and the reason explained to the public. The CPGB had been allowed to make a lot of capital out of the case of Mason who would quite openly preach mutiny. If the facts had been given to the workers it is doubtful whether Mason would have got any sympathy. It is very necessary to explain that membership of the CPGB has a very strong sig-nificance when acts of this kind are committed. The tendency of the Home Office is always to avoid the issue of CPGB membership.

Vera Erikson shows signs of going on hunger strike. She has been removed to Holloway Prison.

7 October

Two French officers and a Czech arrived yesterday. The Czech has confessed to being a German and there are grounds for thinking he is a spy.

Lord Swinton came down today and cross-examined us about the spy cases. The Prime Minister had evidently been asking why we had not shot some of them. I told Swinton that we understood that we had been given a more or less free hand to promise a man his life if we thought we were going to get information and that information was really by far the most important matter to be considered. He said that we had no authority to grant a man his life and quoted some minute of the Centre. On looking this up we found this to be quite irrelevant. It merely referred to the Director of Public Prosecution's attitude in these cases, which was that if we wished to prosecute we should not offer a man any inducement to talk. Swinton said that in future nobody was to be offered his life without his authority. I am still in ignorance of what Swinton's position is. I have seen no charter, and all we know is that he appears to think that he is head of MI5 and to some extent even of SIS.

Communication with Blenheim Palace is frightful. At the moment there are only two lines and one of them is not working. Whenever you ring up you are told that your name will be put on the waiting list. We have been promised five lines but quite clearly we need twenty. What seems to have been overlooked is that everybody down at Blenheim has to keep in touch with his outside contacts, and that if connection is not made those in the country will become completely isolated.

MI5 had moved half of its departments from its cramped prewar offices in Horseferry Road to Wormwood Scrubs Prison, known as The Centre, and sent the other half to Blenheim Palace in Oxfordshire.

8 October

Group messages show that the Germans are making use of wrecks for the installation of wireless sets. It is presumed that they establish themselves in the funnel. The Admiralty are taking stock of the position of these wrecks and it is intended to intercept one of the most promising. If anything is found there will be a reasonable excuse for looking at the remainder. There is no doubt that some of them are extremely well-placed for the purpose of giving information about our shipping, and also for directing an invading party.

Cockfosters reports indicate that the Germans do not like our wire rockets. These rockets fire a coil of wire into the air which is held up by parachute.

Trent Park, at Cockfosters, was the Air Intelligence interrogation centre where downed enemy pilots were accommodated, and their private conversations recorded.

G.J.M. Libot, a Belgian, H.L.L. Jonasson, a Swede, and one de Lille, also a Belgian, arrived at Plymouth in a cutter called *La Parte Bien*. They had been recruited in Antwerp for espionage work and were to sail ships between French ports, the UK and Ireland. They had been recruited by Otto Voigt, who is known to be working for the German secret service. They were it is believed destined for Le Touquet but preferred to land here.

All three were imprisoned at Camp 020 until the end of the war as it turned out that they had landed accidentally in England, having got drunk en route from Brest to Le Touquet, where they had intended to collect more agents.

Developments in connection with the big case are as follows: Ronnie Reed was instructed to try again to establish contact with the TATE transmitter and if successful to send a message in the form already agreed. He was also instructed to send a message on the GANDER transmitter purporting to operate from somewhere near Northampton. The message was to consist of weather reports, a report as to roadblocks, and the general morale of the public. Reed and GANDER will compose the message and have it approved by T.A. Robertson or Colonel Stephens. The former at a meeting yesterday with the Director of Military Intelligence Home Forces obtained approval to any message which stated that the road blocks were strong and that morale was good.

TATE and GANDER were both Nazi spies who had been 'turned' into double agents in captivity at Camp 020, MI5 interrogation centre at Ham Common, commanded by Colonel R.W.G. 'Tin-Eye' Stephens. Ronnie Reed was a skilled amateur wireless operator who remained in MI5 after the war.

T.A. Robertson and John Marriott interrogated Vera Erikson at Aylesbury Prison, and in their view she had no connection with espionage and her introduction of the Duchesse to Rantzau had an entirely innocent explanation.

Major Tommy Robertson was head of MI5's B1(a) section dealing with double agents, and his subordinate John Marriott, formerly a solicitor, became Secretary of the XX Committee.

Arrangements are being made to take over the Old Parsonage at Hinxton as the Home for Incurables.

The Old Parsonage was to be used as an isolated safe-house in Cambridgeshire to accommodate trusted double agents, among them SUMMER who was to attack his guard and escape.

9 October

There have been developments in South Wales. G.W. has received a letter from Miguel Piernavirja.

G.W. was a retired Welsh police inspector, Gwylym Williams, who worked as a double agent, ostensibly having been recruited by SNOW.

Walti appears to be beginning to break under interrogation. He now admits to having arrived by seaplane and states that it is true that he had come to London to hand over his wireless set at a rendezvous at Victoria Station. The B6 Watchers and Special Branch were instructed to cover the meeting.

Albert de Jaeger (codenamed HATCHET) is now at Latchmere House and Jiri Graf has been moved to the Alban Court Hotel, Harrington Gardens.

De Jaeger and Graf had been interrogated at Camp 020 before being enrolled as double agents HATCHET and GIRAFFE.

At our meeting today it was decided to rope in the Duchesse, her daughter and Mr and Mrs Henry on Saturday.

G.W. has received a letter from a man on the paper of the Tuscan Hotel. The writer says that he met a friend of a friend of Mr Kettering in Madrid and would very much like to see G.W. at the earliest possible moment. "KETTERING" was a pre-arranged password between SNOW and Rantzau and company. It was changed about two to three weeks ago to "KETROCH". G.W. will see the writer but not before we have checked up on his bona fides. The interrogation of Vera indicates that she was formerly a 4th Department agent working under Serge Ignatieff, whose mistress she was.

Vera Erikson admitted under interrogation that before the war she had worked as a spy in Paris for the Soviet military intelligence service, the GRU.

10 October

We had a conference about the German agents who formerly frequented the salon of the Duchesse. It was decided we should act on Monday.

I had a long talk with Albert Canning and explained to him the general lay-out. I also had a talk with Malcolm Frost and Major E.W. Gill. Canning was quite outspoken about William Charles Crocker and the employment of Leonard Burt, etc. He said that there were many people coming up in the Branch who could not get out of their heads that at the conclusion of the war, when he (Canning) and others of high rank retired, Burt and his minions would be put in to take their places. Canning said that he had done his best to dispel this idea but without success. He also said that there was a general feeling in the Branch that we had not been satisfied with the work his officers had been doing and therefore wished to set up our own detective force. I told him exactly how the whole thing had happened and that we were in no sense responsible. I also made it quite clear that we were thoroughly satisfied with the work Special Branch was doing.

The head of the Special Branch since 1936, Albert Canning had opposed the transfer of five of his detectives, led by Leonard Burt, to MI5. Malcolm Frost had been seconded to MI5 from the BBC where he had been an expert on wireless.

We had rather hoped that we had discovered the identity of François de Deeker. SIS had papers about H.L. Abbas who seemed to have been closely associated with Rantzau and whose description seemed to fit. Abbas has an uncle in London called Hector Abbas and we have decided to have him interviewed.

G.W. has met his Spaniard. He was given £3,500 in a tin of talcum powder. He is to report on factories in the west of England and on the Welsh Nationalist Movement and is also to work up something in the sabotage line. In the meantime he has been asked to obtain an intermediary between himself and the Spaniard whose name is Del Pozo, henceforth known as POGO. G.W. is very incensed at having the money taken away from him and threatens to resign. Marriott managed to calm him down. He is a rather unpleasant type who is obviously on the make. Enquiry about POGO shows that he came here under the auspices of the British Council and on the recommendation of Sir Sam Hoare. The British Council are trying to arrange for him to visit the forces and show him as much as possible. They seem to think this is a good plan, as the Falange, to which POGO quite openly belongs, gets all its news from Germany. On arrival here POGO told the Immigration Officer that he did not want Spain to enter the war and hoped that Germany would win. It seems a curious thing that our authorities should not be really wise to the fact that any member of the Falange, which is in fact a Spanish Nazi Party, must be right in the German camp. The Air Ministry has been somewhat cautious and had arranged a tour of certain aerodromes in the north of Scotland. The Army, on the other hand, without reference to us, arranged for POGO to visit 7th Corps HQ and other units. The Navy I think turned him down. A number of names and addresses were found on POGO when he came in, one of these being a Spaniard, Escobar. He is a member of a Falange and of the Spanish Club. His address has also appeared in the papers of Enrique Buena, a Spaniard who had been arrested by the police for taking particulars of air raid damage. The police, thinking he was a nitwit, had released him. An interesting point about POGO is that he has expressed a keen desire to the British Council to be allowed to take part in an air raid on Berlin. This opens up all sorts of possibilities. My suggestion is that when we have got as much out of him through G.W. as possible we should accede to his request. POGO bomber would however return to some home for incurables where he would be kept for the remainder of the war. A notice would appear in the papers to the effect that three of our bombers did not return. In this way we should avoid any complications with the Spanish Embassy and we should not endanger the position of SNOW or G.W.

SNOW was another valuable Welsh double agent, Arthur Owens, who had been in radio contact with the enemy since September 1939. Del Pozo's sponsorship by the British Ambassador in Madrid, Sir Sam Hoare, was a major embarrassment to Hoare.

Hector Abbas, interviewed by Special Branch, denied that the photograph of de Deeker was that of his nephew L.H. Abbas.

A photograph of a Robert William Wilkinson, engineer, has been obtained, which corresponds reasonably with Vera's description, but this man does not appear to be identical with the Lincolnshire Fascist of the same name.

A message has been sent to the other side enquiring as to the bona fides of the Spaniard who had written to G.W. and the following reply was received "Man with password Kettering is OK. Is man of Captain for propaganda and sabotage."

As a result of G.W.'s meeting with POGO and the latter's statement that he was visiting Glasgow, the local police were asked to try and pick him up if at any time they were certain that he did not know he was being followed. Dick Brooman-White later telephoned to say that a man answering to POGO description but wearing glasses had been followed to an address in Glasgow. A Home Office mail and telephone intercept warrant is to be put on to the address. Doust was consulted as to the possibilities of installing microphones in POGO's flat and in the meantime a Home Office telephone intercept warrant has been imposed.

SNOW is reported to be feeling his oats again after a long period of quiescence. He must be watched very carefully, and the question of putting a microphone into his new house is being considered.

SUMMER attempted to commit suicide after interrogation.

SUMMER was interviewed at Latchmere House today. After the interview Colonel Stephens was left with the opinion that he has not double-crossed us while working for us.

SUMMER survived the war and subsequently returned to his native Sweden.

I met Lord Swinton today and explained the POGO story to him, in which he seemed very interested. At the conclusion I said that it was necessary that not one word of it should go any further at this stage. He entirely agreed. I then asked him exactly what he wanted us to report to him in future, as I had rather got the impression from our previous interview that he had no confidence either in myself or in Dick White in so far as the handling of this case was concerned. He seemed slightly embarrassed but protested that he had every confidence in the way we were running the case but not in our desire to keep him informed. I said that we had no wish to withhold information from him provided it went no further.

I went on to the see the Director of Military Intelligence in order to get his cooperation. I told him the story. He asked that we should get in touch with Colonel Eric Mockler-Ferryman, BGSI Home Forces. If he agreed to an innocuous tour he should communicate with the DMI who would put the thing through to the public relations department in a perfectly normal way. I went on to see Archie Boyle who was thrilled with the story and pleased to find that he sounded a note of caution. He is out to play 100%. POGO is to visit Leuchars and some other aerodrome. The question of a visit to Mildenhall will be considered later.

Macolm Frost is arranging to give POGO a lunch at the BBC, which is more or less common form for people sponsored by the British Council. [*3 lines deleted*]

We are also taking steps to tap his telephone and keep him under close observation. I thought of trying to put in an Irish agent as the intermediary between G.W. and POGO. This might give us a new line.

The watch on POGO will be begun by B6 tomorrow at Atheneum Court.

The Director of Military Intelligence Home Forces was told the true story of POGO. He seemed quite willing to play, but was a little worried owing to the fact that POGO had been given permission by the War Office to visit the 7th Corps HQ on 16 October. The DMI feels that he is not in a position to be responsible for allowing this visit to take place owing to the fresh information. We are going to get in touch with the DMI War Office.

Later the DMI War Office was contacted and said that he would get in touch with Home Forces and cancel POGO 's visit to 7th Corps HQ.

We have arranged with Miss Franks that a Spanish-speaking gentleman will take up residence in POGO 's block of flats as of tomorrow.

14 October

The lunch party at the BBC arranged for today has been cancelled as POGO has been mislaid. It has not therefore been possible to complete the arrangements for the installation of the microphone in his flat.

Dick Brooman-White reported that he had found a contact who might be able to produce a suitable go-between for G.W.

Later a Tory MP, Dick Brooman-White headed MI5's Spanish section.

15 October

The Huggins' were bombed out of their flat last night without casualty to themselves although five people were seriously injured.

Margo Huggins was Guy Liddell's secretary.

Incidentally, while he was up, John Mariott produced one of his clerihews on the subject of myself:

> They can't diddle
> Guy Liddell.
> He's sufficiently deep
> To look asleep.

I saw Sir Alexander Maxwell in the afternoon and gave him our 18(b) orders for the Duchesse, her daughter and the two Henrys. He began by studying each case individually and expressed the view that they seemed rather thin.

16 October

De Jaeger told us an interesting story of his work for the German secret service in Lisbon and has expressed his willingness to work for us there. Unfortunately as he has been away for some time it may not be possible to work him back.

Arrangements have been made through Commandant Howard to sign on GIRAFFE and SPANIEL with General de Gaulle. Nothing has come up on the telephone check of Oulpe. We are trying to find out his telephone number and will put on a check.

A Polish recruit recently arrived from Lisbon has reported to the Polish Deputy Director of Military Intelligence here that he was approached in Lisbon to work for the Germans. John Bingham is going to interview him after consultation with Felix Cowgill.

John Bingham (later Lord Clanmorris) was a skilled MI5 case officer. Major Cowgill headed SIS's counter-intelligence branch, Section V.

Vera does not identify the photograph of the Lincolnshire Fascist R.W. Wilkinson as Rantzau's London agent.

Walti and De Deeker are still holding out on us. It appears likely that the latter is aware that he is being listened to.

All the cells at Camp 020 were wired for sound so conversations among the prisoners could be recorded.

SNOW arrived back in London this afternoon but is not to transmit till tomorrow, when he will make apologies for the delay and explain that travelling is now very difficult.

It has been decided that TATE is to pose to the other side as Harry Williamson, a British subject educated in Denmark. As a result of failing to establish contact he had almost given up hope and had decided to resign himself to living here for the rest of the war and had accordingly not gone to the trouble of obtaining information for which he had been sent over. Now he has established contact, he will set out his job and is awaiting instructions.

TATE was of Danish origin, but he retained his false identity as Harry Williamson for the rest of his life, living in Luton.

17 October

A telephone check on POGO is now working. [*1 line deleted*] Captain Russi, who is going to do the listening, was shown round today and arrangements have been made for him to stay on the premises.

Arrests and interrogations of the Chateau-Thierry group were carried out today. From this it would appear that Mackenzie corroborates in general Vera's story. She was certainly his mistress. According to him Vera was wounded in the chest while she was in London and he understood that it had been done by a hired assassin of her husband, Serge Ignatieff. Philip de Froberville turns out to be a Squadron-Leader. Action against him has been suspended pending a report on the case.

SIS are continuing enquiries into the new arrivals by the *La Part Bien*. It is now almost certain that the Belgian, Libot, is a German agent.

18 October

Another canoe has been discovered in the Hythe reaches bearing the name *Claudinette*. Our Regional Security Liaison Officer in Kent has been asked to organise a thorough search and to consult the military as to whether it would be possible for someone to land at the point where the canoe was found without disturbing the land-mine mechanisms. The Admiralty is being furnished with details of the two canoes for their views.

20 October

B24 has got an interesting case about a registry office girl being run by a Mrs Newitt. She is of German origin and was formerly placing servants under the direction of the German Embassy.

23 October

I was summoned to the Old Bailey to give evidence in the Wolkoff trial but owing to a legal argument as to whether the court was competent to try Tyler Kent, I was not called. Kent's counsel took the line that as the offence had been committed when Kent was a diplomat he was privileged.

24 October

FRANK, in an excess of zeal and imagining he was making a contact with a German agent aroused the suspicions of the Grantham police. Ronnie Haylor smoothed out the situation and FRANK is coming back to report.

I attended at the Old Bailey again. I merely had to testify that I had written certain letters to the American Embassy which might be useful to the enemy. I was asked by Kent's counsel whether I thought these letters would be useful to some political party in the United States which was interested in showing up a connection between the British and American services. I said that the documents could be used for this purpose by unscrupulous persons. I was then asked whether these two documents were isolated instances or whether the correspondence was a considerable one. I said that it was considerable.

25 October

FRANK told his story to John Marriott this morning. It appears that he was picked up by a man calling himself Frank Cullen, who made all the overtures. Cullen was in fact Inspector Curry who, in accordance with the usual custom in Grantham, had been notified by the management of the hotel of the arrival of a stranger who merited observation. FRANK'S telephone call to T.A.Robertson on the previous Wednesday had been tapped and had been regarded as suspicious by the police, who were led by it to think that both FRANK and Robertson were undesirable characters. Ronnie Haylor cleared up the position and FRANK left Grantham with a promise of every assistance from the local police.

28 October

The telephone check on Mrs Harris, POGO's girlfriend, has produced one curious feature – it is remarkable how many different accents and methods of speaking are adopted by this woman. According to the person to whom she is speaking she employs at various times a marked foreign accent, a slightly American accent, a Cockney accent, and a comparatively educated and fluent English accent. When speaking to POGO she appears to be a rather elderly woman with a poor command of the language, just as on other occasions she speaks fluently, quickly and with practically no accent at all.

27 October

We have established contact with [XXXXXXXXXXX] of the Rumanian Legation. He is prepared to give us all the information we want, and should I think be able to help us with the Rumanian cipher.

31 October

I had a conference today with Archdale and Gilbert Lennox about the possibility of a general comb-out of General de Gaulle's entourage. The difficulty is to get a comprehensive list, since Meffre's position is rather difficult. He is evidently unpopular and there is some suggestion of sending him to Africa. Archdale, who incidently is Tom Archdale, whom I have known for years, says that there are some very good people in the de Gaulle entourage, that the older men who are at the top are extremely reliable but are surrounded by dubious Left politicians such as André Labarthe.

Mademoiselle Baudelot has arrived with a number of letters sewn in her skirt. These letters were from John Freeman of Madrid and Lisbon, and were addressed to Rickett, Dame Rachel Thornhill, Loewy, and certain banks. The Duke of Westminister and Rickett immediately weighed in when they heard that Baudelot was held. It seems that she is the Duke's mistress and that since Rickett is also involved there must be some oil in the picture somewhere. Freeman seems to be connected with a man called de Lazovert, a Russian residing in Madrid. There are two plans, one to create a revolution in Morocco and the other to place agents in France.

2 November

We have broken Jorgen Borresen, a Dane, who had been to Greenland from Oslo on the SS *Furenak*. Ostensibly he was on a trapping expedition but in actual fact it is believed he was concerned with setting up another meteorological station. He was captured by the Fijof Nansen, taken to Iceland, sent on to Southampton and arrived there on 18 September. He gave us important information regarding the Arctic stations.

4 November

The following interesting fact has emerged in connection with TATE's transmitter. Before he was provided with the one he is at present using he was given one which was a much larger instrument, which he said was used by parachutists in Holland and Belgium. They told him that he would be given a special combination in order to open the back of the transmitter to put it into operation, and that if this combination was not used (that is to say, if it was opened by someone unaware of the combination), the instrument would be blown up by a small bomb which was to be placed inside.

5 November

The possibility is being discussed of SNOW demanding a meeting with the other side and Northern Ireland is suggested as a suitable venue. It is agreed that SNOW should take the line that he was dissatisfied with the evidence of German incompetence and inefficiency and that, unless his complaints could be cleared up satisfactorily at an interview, he was contemplating throwing in his hand altogether.

7 November

POGO has badly blotted his copy-book by getting tight and giving an indiscreet interview to the *Daily Express*. He told the *Express* that he hoped Germany would win. We have sent over a violent protest to the other side who have replied apologetically. It seems that POGO has been superimposed on their system by some outside body, probably the Propaganda Ministry.

10 November

The SIS agent in touch with POGO is of the opinion that the latter is changing his views and becoming more Anglophile on account of his treatment here. POGO is rather upset by the Ministry of Information broadcast to Italy which attributed to him the view that although the Italian Air Force may be good, the Italian infantry is hopeless. POGO realises that he did in fact say this but only when he was slightly drunk. So far as can be ascertained he proposes to stay here for another four or five months.

11 November

Victor Rothschild and I saw Rickett at the [XXXXXXXXXXXXXX]. We had the room miked [XXXXXXXXXX]. Rickett was exactly what I expected. Although I think he was lightly nervous at first, he very soon got into his stride and waving his cigar in the air subjected us to a perfect tornado of bluff. He tried to make out that Betty Baudelot had nothing to do with the project at all and was a brainless female (in his own words "her brains were in her bottom"). Rickett's own interest soon became clear. He wanted to have a monopoly for the supply of oil to the sheiks in Morocco. This would act as an inducement to them to revolt. They would also be given other commodities such as tea, tobacco etc. Rickett, Freeman and de Lazovert were to arrange this if they could get the necessary backing. Baudelot had evidently been used to get Rickett and company in touch with the Prime Minister's entourage through the Duke of Westminster. Westminster's sole interest seems to be the woman. Rickett told us a lot about himself and his many financial deals. He said that he had had a lot of experience in dealing with orientals and that he always worked through women. He said that he always put on a good show for them over here and that they appreciated getting it for nothing whereas in Paris they had to pay through the nose. It was in this way that he got them to make concessions. One point of specific interest emerged about Miss Reid. Rickett said that he had planted her in the Iraq Legation. We are investigating the case of Miss Reid because she went to some obscure mission to Italy for the Iraq Legation in the early days of the war.

12 November

We have been trying to get Betty Baudelot down to London for an interview. Westminster has sent a note and a medical certificate to say that she is ill and unable to travel. This is obviously a put-up job.

I have suggested to Valentine Vivian that we ought to try and get at Admiral Canaris. If we could stage an interview somewhere in Portugal we might make use of the information about him which we got from Walter Krivitsky. There is no doubt that he was in Russian pay.

13 November

I saw Walter Monckton on the subject of General F.C.J. Fuller. Everybody is getting worried about Fuller's articles in the *Sunday Pictorial* and particularly those which he prepared for the American press and which had to be carefully censored. Monckton told me he had had three-quarters of an hour's talk with Fuller, whom he regarded as rather deep and sinister. It was suggested to Fuller that possibly certain passages in his articles might be harmful to this country and cause alarm and despondency abroad. Fuller asked what the offending passages were and when these were shown to him he said that he could see no harm in them. He refused point-blank to alter any of his articles. Monckton has seen the American press who agreed to pay for Fuller's articles but not publish them. Monckton agreed that it would be unwise to touch Fuller at this moment although he thought that he should be carefully watched. This we are doing by every possible means.

14 November

The other side has asked SNOW if he could obtain a visa to Canada via Lisbon in order to meet Dr Rantzau. SNOW has made it clear to the other side that there is a long waiting list for Lisbon. He had suggested Eire, but Rantzau is apparently not prepared to go there. BISCUIT has been ordered to lie low, and this message was sent to the other side. They replied asking where Lielow is.

18 November

We had a meeting of the Wireless Committee to discuss the possibility of putting some constructive proposals about making use of our double-cross system. There are three main objectives (1) to keep our agents sufficiently well fed with accurate information so as not to lose the confidence of the enemy (2) to control as many of the enemy's agents in this country as we can in order to make them feel that the ground is covered and that they need not send any more of whose arrival we might not be aware and (3) by careful manoeuvring of these agents and a careful study of the questionnaires, to mislead the enemy on a big scale at the appropriate moment. I heard today that Jane Sissmore had been sacked for insubordination. This is a very serious blow to us all. There is no doubt that she was completely on the wrong leg but somehow I feel that the incident should not have happened. I am trying to think whether there is anything to be done.

20 November

I went down to Blenheim Palace and saw Jane Sissmore at the Bear Inn in Woodstock. She seemed to be quite normal and in a fighting mood. She was determined to put forward her views in high quarters. I asked her to do nothing for the moment in case it were possible to smooth out the difficulties. I felt that if Sir David Petrie was coming over to look into our affairs she might perhaps be given a chance of talking to him.

21 November

The SIS agent reports that POGO has recently written to his chief in Spain stating that his stay in this country has convinced him that Great Britain is invincible.

I had a long discussion with the Director-General and Charles Butler. I told the Director-General that I thought that Jane Sissmore had no technical right of appeal but that in view of her long and devoted service she certainly had a moral right. Both he and Charles took the view that she had no right at all, and that if the Director-General's authority was questioned in this matter he had no alternative but to resign. They neither of them thought that there was any possibility of her returning to this office even though she tendered an apology.

25 November

I had to go down to Blenheim Palace in order to explain to the Regional Security Liaison Officers that Jane was no longer in charge, and had in fact left the office. I said that nobody regretted this more than I did but I had done everything possible to smooth things over, but that an impasse had been reached. I was sorry that I could not say any more except that I hoped everybody would continue working as before. I had a long discussion with Jack Curry about the whole business and also with Colonel Alan MacIver who is carrying on for the present. I also had a talk with Charles Butler. He is very depressed and does not feel that he can stick it much longer.

26 November

Gilbert Lennox rang me up in a great state of mind. He wanted to see me some time before 5pm as he had received instructions to go to Downing Street at 5 o'clock. I rather wondered whether he was going to be asked to take over the office. I thought it best to get this clear and told him that in my view neither he nor I were suitable, and if anybody was to come in Valentine Vivian was far the best choice. He entirely agreed with me. When he got to Downing Street he found that Lord Croft, presumably on the advice of the DMI, had written to the Prime Minister saying that all was not well with MI5 and he had better have a talk with Lennox. Lennox told the Prime Minister what he thought about this office and also about the Centre. The Prime Minister then replied that he did not know why Lennox had come, to which the answer was "Because you sent for me". The Prime Minister said that he always left these matters in the hands of Major Morton and he would be glad if Lennox would have a talk with him at once. The Prime Minister seemed worried about the Bob Boothby case, which he thought had been badly represented by MI5 and he took the opportunity to make a long political speech while walking round the Cabinet room. Lennox went straight on to Desmond Morton who was more understanding. He told Lennox that Sir David Petrie was on his way here to enquire into the whole organisation.

Bob Boothby MP had been obliged to resign over allegations that he had exploited Czech war bonds, using inside information.

27 November

Charles Butler saw Lord Swinton and gave him his views about the office. He suggested that Swinton should have a talk with me, but this did not go very well. He said "You see, Guy thinks I'm a bloody shit." Charles protested vehemently but without making much headway. He mentioned Malcolm Frost and told Swinton that he thought him a snake in the grass, neither loyal to MI5 nor to Swinton himself. Swinton seemed worried about this.

30 November

Ham Common was bombed last night in one of the worst night raids we have had in London. There was a direct hit on the main building, and three casualties, among the guard. Bruhns, one of the internees, had a serious skull injury and is not expected to live.

There have been three interesting developments today. Firstly, Group 2 has been broken. These messages are between the principal stations in western Europe and

Berlin and should give us a great deal of valuable information. Secondly, GIRAFFE, our Czech agent, has received a draft from the Swiss Banking Corporation for £50. It comes from the Banco Santo Spirito e Commerciale in Lisbon. What seems to have happened is that the White Russian director Ulpe of the London Merchants Bank where GIRAFFE was originally told to apply has tipped off the Swiss Banking Corporation. The payment is from the account of Pallhares. Thirdly, there is the discovery of a South African who has been in hospital for seventeen weeks and says he is suffering from loss of memory after a motor-accident. We think that this man is probably a German agent, a South African, who we were expecting and that he probably damaged himself slightly when coming down. His loss of memory is merely a cover and he is making extremely intelligent use of it. He tells all sorts of stories and if they do not check up he throws the blame on his memory.

2 December

The case of POGO is getting rather difficult. The Ministry of Information has told him that he is no good and he had better go home and meanwhile the Spanish Embassy seem to have come to the same conclusion. We cannot stop him without endangering the position of our agent and without causing an incident with the Spanish government which the Foreign Office is very anxious to avoid. We are going to try and get the British Council to smooth things over and then place POGO in the hands of Bill Cavendish-Bentinck of the JIC in order that he can be fed with interesting Foreign Office news. Cavendish-Bentinck will take the lines that a great mistake has been made and that he has been deputed to put it right.

3 December

I saw Henry Hopkinson today and asked him to slow up the departure of POGO. He said he was doing everything he possibly could to smooth down the embassy. There was no immediate prospect of POGO going because he could not get a seat on the plane.

6 December

I saw Lord Swinton today. I said that first of all I should like to try and put something right. I had been told that he thought I was moved by certain personal feelings against him and I was in consequence obstructive. I wished to say that this was entirely untrue. I was only interested in doing my work as efficiently as possible and that I was very grateful to him for all he had done to put over my point of view with other departments. He seemed to accept this. I then went on to speak about Malcolm Frost. I said that I did not see how there could be any peace in his office while he remained. He was obviously an intriguer first and foremost and was so regarded by everyone here. This was no isolated incident. T.A. Robertson had told me months ago and I had pressed him to remain where he was. What I felt was that this was for the general interest. I now felt that this could not continue and that Robertson and the double-cross business must come back where they belonged. Swinton did not demur but he was anxious that Frost, for whose ability he evidently had certain regard, should not be isolated on account of what had happened. He thought that after his talk with him the latter would not misbehave himself again. We then discussed the reorganisation. He was full of Horrocks' achievements as a re-organiser of the Treasury etc. I told him that while I had the very best personal relations with Horrocks, I sometimes wondered whether he fully understood what he was trying to reorganise in our office. I had already spoken about the registry and the impossibility of getting anything looked up either now or in the near future, and I had also studied the reorganisation plan. Swinton pulled out a copy of this, which I was under the impression that he had not yet seen, as it was still the subject of discussion amongst ourselves. I pointed out that the main purpose of it was to create an active espionage section to which all cases of any importance should be thrown up. I did not think that this was a practical arrangement, and I gave the example of a case of Russian espionage. I explained that various forms of information would be coming in and that reference would be made to people and incidents which would only be known to someone who was making a close study of the Communist movement in this country and abroad. It was therefore imperative that any such case should be run by the Communist section and not by the active espionage section. Swinton seemed to see the force of this argument. Lastly, I spoke to him about Jane Sissmore. Swinton told me that he did not think that it was perhaps proper for him to discuss the matter. She had submitted a memorandum with a request that she should be given an interview. He had consulted with the Lord President who thought that she had no technical right, but had a moral right. Swinton was proposing to see her in front of Harker and Butler. I said that if he thought it improper that I should speak, I would say no more. He thought a little and then asked me for my views, which I gave him, though I said they would only be of a general kind. I said that she had always been in a rather privileged position as a court jester, but that on this occasion she had undoubtedly overstepped the mark and committed an act of gross insubordination. She was therefore completely on the wrong leg. Secondly, and on this point I spoke with some feeling, the office had lost the services of an extremely valuable officer. She had served for twenty-four years and I regarded her as far more efficient than most of the men. It was therefore little short of a disaster that her services could no longer be utilised. Thirdly, I wanted to say that discipline within the branch had become a very difficult matter owing to lack of confidence in the management and a feeling of frustration caused by the various difficulties which for one reason or another were preventing officers from carrying out their duties in a manner satisfactory for themselves. There was no inducement for anybody to stay here unless they felt that they were doing a job of work for the country. It was therefore essential that when orders were issued affecting their work they should be consulted and their views considered. There was at the moment very little machinery for such consultation and differences had arisen in consequence. I thought these could easily be smoothed out if appropriate action were taken.

8 December

Dick White has just produced another *magnum opus* based on the intercepted Group messages and what we have learned from the captured agents. We are now beginning to get quite a good picture of the German espionage organisation.

10 December

I met two Americans at Waterloo station today. They are Hugh Clegg and Clarence Hince, previously reported as Florence Hince. We had all expected to see a glamour platinum blonde and were much disappointed. We told him so and he seemed to think it was a good joke.

Clegg and Hince had been sent to London by the FBI Director, J. Edgar Hoover, to study British intelligence organisations and procedures.

11 December

I lunched with Hugh Clegg and Clarence Hince of the FBI and had a long talk with Clegg. They have an enormous programme which covers studying everything from SIS to the fire brigade. They were desperately anxious to wipe out the impression left by the Leon Turrou incident. Clegg told me that he now covers the whole of the western hemisphere both for espionage and counter-espionage. He looks as tough as a gangster but is, I think, a very good fellow.

Former Special Agent Leon Turrou had written a book about the arrest of Gunther Rumrich in 1938, claiming all the credit for the FBI, whereas the original information had been supplied by MI5 and delivered to Washington DC personally by Liddell.

17 December

Mrs O'Grady has been sentenced to death. Personally I doubt whether she is guilty of anything more than collecting information. She probably pictured herself as a master spy, and cannot bring herself to say that there was really nothing behind it all.

Mrs Pamela O'Grady, an Isle of Wight landlady, had volunteered a false confession to espionage after she had been spotted acting suspiciously near Sandown. Her sentence was reduced to fourteen years' imprisonment on appeal.

19 December

I lunched today with Sir Nevile Bland. He wanted to know whether we had anything about a man called G.R. Strauss who writes in the *New Statesman* and *Nation*.

He made some very insulting remarks about Bland's broadcast on Fifth Column activities in Holland, and I gather that libel proceedings are contemplated.

A prosecution is being staged against Mrs Nicholson. She is the wife of Admiral Wilmot Nicholson. They are both mixed up in the Right Club and were connected with Anna Wolkoff and Tyler Kent. The Admiral is rather a passive member and strongly anti-semitic and with a bee in his bonnet on the subject of corruption in high government circles. Mrs Nicholson on the other hand is a much more active member of the Right Club and has a strong pro-German background. In May 1940 we heard that she and her husband claimed to have obtained from Anna Wolkoff the full story of our Norwegian Expeditionary Force. Later in May we were told that Mrs Nicholson had made a copy of some document which Anna Wolkoff had obtained from Tyler Kent. Almost simultaneously we heard that a servant employed by the Nicholsons was handed a sealed envelope by Mrs Nicholson with instructions that she was to take it home and hide it and that if she was questioned she was to say that it was Admiral Nicholson's will. The servant handed the envelope to the police who found that it contained two sheets of notepapers with pencilled writing very much abbreviated. It was clearly a copy of one of the US embassy telegrams. The handwriting appeared identical with that of a Right Club card found in Captain Ramsay's property, and when compared was nearly the writing of Mrs Nicholson. She was arrested on 26 May and admitted that the document was hers, that she knew Anna Wolkoff and had met Tyler Kent. She refused at first to say who had given her the document of which she had made a copy, but later admitted that it was Anna. She was detained and subsequently interned under Emergency Regulation 18(b). The contents of the telegram dealt among other matters with the now famous American destroyer deal. At that time the matter was considered so secret that the prosecution of Mrs Nicholson was out of the question. Now the law officers of the Crown consider that she should be dealt with under the Official Secrets Act and Defence Regulations.

27 December

I went on to Tring where we spent a cheerful evening. Dick White is very interested in a Mrs Marston who has come over from Lisbon where she had been seen in company with an agent of Wimmer & Company. Wimmer has a strong German background. Mrs Marston is staying at Oatlands Parks, it is alleged, with a Portuguese.

Dick also told me about the case of Admiral Emile Muselier. A letter had been produced by Commandant Howard, alleged to have been written by General Rozoy of the Vichy Consulate, to the Second Secretary of the Brazilian Embassy, a man named Frederico de Chermont Lisboa, and carried by Mademoiselle d'Anjou, his mistress. The letter disclosed that Muselier had warned Vichy about the Dakar project.

Admiral Muselier was Charles de Gaulle's deputy, and the allegation that he had betrayed the Dakar expedition to the Vichy forces was a grave one.

I went to see Desmond Morton today about the Admiral Muselier case, showed him the letter, and explained to him very carefully that while we had verified the text as far as possible, also the paper, the signature and the stamp, there were two weak links in the chain between the source and ourselves, namely the Adjutant Collin, who had not got a very good reputation, and a mythical man called Gomez who was supposed to be an attaché at the Brazilian Embassy. Morton got very excited about the letter, which he said he thought had all the appearance of being genuine and said that he would like to show it to the Prime Minister at once. I made it quite clear to him that we should not have brought it to his notice at all if we had not heard through a junior member of Howard's office that the contents of the letter had already been communicated verbally to Colonel Angenot, de Gaulle's Chief of Staff. It followed therefore that it would be all over de Gaulle's headquarters within the next twenty-four hours. I said that if he was going to show it to the Prime Minister, I hoped he would make it absolutely clear that we could give no guarantee whatever about the source of the information. Otherwise I foresaw that it might recoil on our heads if MI5 were too inclined to hold the thing up pending verification, and that we had done absolutely right in bringing it to his notice immediately. He thought that the Foreign Office should be informed immediately. Kenneth Younger and I then went round to see Henry Hopkinson and told him the same story.

1941

We have now obtained three more letters from Commandant Collin who says that he has obtained them from the same source. They deal with a variety of matters and all incriminate Admiral Muselier. His Chief of Staff, Lieutenant Villers also seems to be involved. We can find nothing wrong with the text of the documents so Kenneth Younger is giving them to Desmond Morton under the same safeguards.

At about 10 pm I was rung up at Tring by Jasper Harker. He said that the Prime Minister had given orders for the arrest of Muselier, Villers and Mademoiselle D'Anjou. I offered to come up but he said he did not think this was necessary. He and Kenneth Younger went to see Desmond Morton, when Kenneth once more emphasised our doubts about the source of the information. Morton said that the Prime Minister had given his order and there was nothing to be done but to carry it out. Colonel Angenot was fetched and attempts were made to get hold of General de Gaulle. He was away on leave and it was found impossible to get into touch with him. Angenot rather regretfully agreed to the action suggested. Although he thought the documents bore the stamp of genuineness he would have liked General de Gaulle to have seen them before the arrests were made.

The Home Secretary was visited by Jasper Harker and Desmond Morton and gave the necessary orders to the police. Luckily we had already warned Albert Canning during the afternoon that some action might be taken. In deference to Angenot's wishes no action was taken against Moret, Admiral Muselier's Chief of Staff, but at his request Mademoiselle Herincx was put on the list as it was thought that if there was any conspiracy by Muselier she would be the most likely person to have documents. The police took action during the course of the night. Mademoiselle D'Anjou was found in bed with Frederico Lisboa and Mademoiselle Herincx with a Dr de Kerguelen. This is the first occasion on which they had slept together and it was his birthday. The police saw fit to bring in the doctor on the grounds of his association with Mademoiselle Herincx. Lisboa, hearing the police entering Mademoiselle d'Anjou's flat, thought that they had some complaint about the blackout and hid in the lavatory. He eventually emerged and claimed diplomatic privileges. While he could not object to the flat being searched he refused to allow the police to touch any of his own clothes.

Lieutenant Villers could not be arrested till 8am as he was on night duty at the Free French headquarters, and it was found that the Admiral was down at Windsor spending the night with a lady friend. He eventually rolled up at about 9am. By way of precaution the police pulled in his valet and chauffeur. The Admiral protested mildly and said he hoped the matter would soon be cleared up as it would create a very bad impression in the Free French Navy.

2 January

I interrogated Mademoiselle d'Anjou, but could get no change. She protested that she had never carried any letter from anybody connected with the Vichy Consulate or Free French Forces to Lisboa. When I showed her the letter in which her name was mentioned she seemed genuinely unable to interpret it.

3 January

I went down to Praewood this morning to discuss with Valentine Vivian what we should say to Hugh Clegg and Hince about the intercepted Group messages. It was agreed that we should try and find out how much they knew before disclosing our hand. We had common ground to begin on since they already had information about Group 10.

I saw General de Gaulle at the Foreign Office at 4pm and he seemed very sore about the arrest of the Admiral. He began by saying that in his opinion the documents had been forged either by the British Intelligence, by his own Security Bureau or by the Vichy Consultate. He then put forward a number of points, none of which either Sir Alexander Cadogan or I thought were in any way conclusive. They were in fact all very weak points. He eyed me with the gravest suspicion and at one moment hinted that the documents might have been forged by Kenneth Younger, who was the only person who had seen the originals. I assured him that this was not so, and that he could rule the possibility out of his mind. I countered his points to some extent but owing to the obviously very tense situation I thought it was better not to criticise his judgment too strongly. He gave me the impression of being a very conceited man. At the conclusion of the meeting he asked what we were going to do. I said that we proposed to continue the enquiry. He said what was the use of continuing the enquiry if the documents were forgeries. We said that we thought it desirable that the case should be cleared up to the satisfaction of all concerned. He said that he proposed to see the First Sea Lord, Sir Dudley Pound, tell him that he had interviewed Commandant Collin, and that he was satisfied that the documents were forgeries, and ask for the Admiral's immediate relase. Cadogan said he had a perfect right to do this if he wished.

In the evening I went through the Muselier papers at Scotland Yard. There was nothing in them of any real consequence. Among his property was an opium smoking outfit.

4 January

I saw Commandant Collin and his friend Stieglhember at Adjutant Howard's flat. They had again to give an account of their doings the night before, when it was alleged that they had both been to the Brazilian Embassy and seen Gomez, whom they now stated to be Barboza, one of the attachés. Stieglhember told me that he had waited on the ground floor while Collin had gone into Barboza's room. I asked him to give a description of Barboza which seemed to embarrass him rather. I then tackled Collin and he said that while Stieglhember had remained on the ground floor he had gone up to the fourth floor where he had seen Barboza. I then had Stieglhember and Collin in together. I said that one or other of them was obviously lying, and I wanted to know the truth. Stieglhember then confessed that in actual fact he had remained outside the embassy and that he had lied to me because he had lied to Howard the night before and had to be consistent. He had lied to Howard because he wanted to support his friend Collin in a story which he believed to be true.

This all seemed very unsatisfactory, and I went away with serious misgivings about the whole business. Admiral Sir Gerald Dickens of the Spears mission visited Muselier on Friday and thought the prison conditions at Pentonville were very severe. It was therefore arranged that the Admiral should be removed to Brixton. He was visited there today by General de Gaulle's ADC Commander Collet, and Kenneth Younger. The ADC told the Admiral that all would be well as the General was quite convinced that his arrest was due to "*un coup monte par les gens de Vichy à Londres*". The Admiral seemed in fairly good spirits.

5 January

Kenneth Younger and I spent a long time getting out a report on the Admiral Muselier case up to date. The conclusions were that no evidence had been discovered among the papers of those arrested in support of the documents, that nothing had been discovered which would seriously challenge the text of the document but that their origin was still in doubt.

7 January

George has returned from Lisbon with £800, a high-class transmitting set concealed in a gramophone and secret ink in a specially made cigarette holder. He had a long story.

George was the MI5 double agent codenamed DRAGONFLY.

8 January

Commandant Collin was pulled in last night and has confessed that he forged the documents in the Muselier case. He says that he was inspired by Adjutant Howard, with an idea of re-instating himself and giving the French Security Service a boost.

He told us that when the first document was produced, dated 5 September, Howard had looked at it and then told him that it was no good as the things recorded did not fit in with the date. A few hours later he returned with an identical document dated 5 August. On this we decided to pull in Howard, who confessed that the two documents had been presented to him and that he had accepted the second one as being genuine and completely forgotten to inform us of the facts. I find it rather difficult to believe either Collin or Howard. Howard would have sufficient background to forge the text of the documents, and it is still possible that somebody else may be behind Collin. I find it difficult to believe that Howard is really a bad man. He had been reporting about Admiral Muselier and his entourage for some time and the whole business has become rather an obsession with him. I am inclined to think that when he saw the document, even though the date had been changed, he just could not or would not believe that it was not genuine.

Kenneth Younger had a curious scene with Inspector Cain of Special Branch who certainly behaves in a very odd way. He suddenly gets wild theories about a case, but in the end seems to get at the facts with fair efficiency. He got it into his head that Kenneth was withholding some important information. In fact at one moment he thought Kenneth might have forged the documents. He started grilling him as if he were a pickpocket. Kenneth got rather annoyed about this and went for him. He then sent the two sergeants out of the room and asked him why he had got sore. Kenneth said that he was not accustomed to being talked to in that sort of way and thought it was time Cain got a slap in the eye. After this Cain very much changed his tune and smoothed it all over by taking Kenneth to dinner at the canteen. He then discovered that Kenneth had been in the office since 1936 and had also been in control of a region since the beginning of the war. This was evidently rather a shock to him. Kenneth's youthful appearance had evidently misled Cain who thought he was a young pup just down from the university who knew nothing about anything.

Incidentally, an amusing incident occurred at the outset of the case, when Inspector Cain first interviewed Frederico Lisboa. The latter was very worried at the accusations, and hinted to Cain that as he was the official at the embassy in charge of the issuing of decorations and orders, if Cain would lay off him he would see what he could do for him!

It emerged during Kenneth's conversation with Inspector Cain that the appointment of the CID men to our office had caused deep resentment among the officers of Special Branch who felt that they had lost promotion in consequence. They thought that if we had wanted police assistance it should have been drawn from Special Branch and not CID. Personally I think they are quite right. In fact it is exactly what we told Lord Swinton and William Charles Crocker would happen. It will obviously take a very long time before this sore is healed.

The question of the suppression of the Communist Party is under active discussion. Frederick Leggett [*of the Ministry of Labour*] thinks that both the *Daily Worker* and the Party should be dealt with and is supported in this by Ernest Bevin. Herbert Morrison thinks that only the *Daily Worker* should be suppressed. I gather that he and Bevin do not get on. Leggett feels that the trade unions are losing their grip and that it is time something was done by the government which will give them the support they need. Possibly he is right, but at the moment there is no serious dislocation due to Communist activity.

9 January

I spent the day between Scotland Yard and the Foreign Office on the Muselier case. I first saw Anthony Eden and told him more or less what the position was. He wanted me to put up a note in conjunction with William Strang, and Malkin the legal adviser, which he would show to the Prime Minister at 4 o'clock. He did not seem to be very concerned about it all, as the baby was obviously with the Prime Minister who would have to eat humble pie to General de Gaulle.

I went back to Scotland Yard where I had a long interview with Commandant Collin and also with Howard. Collin confessed to me the whole story. He did not implicate Howard beyond saying that he had on one occasion remarked that the only kind of information that was any good was a document. It was this that had given Collin his cue. He would not say that Howard had asked him to forge the documents. Howard tells the same story but did not give a convincing explanation as to why he had not reported the alternative date on the first document. He insisted that he had had a complete lapse of memory. William Strang and I and Malkin composed the document for the Prime Minister and Eden returned shortly after 4pm, saying that the Prime Minister had ordered the immediate release of all those arrested. I then went to see Herbert Morrison and explained the position to him. He said he would issue the necessary orders. He was slightly critical of our action, but understood the position when explained that the documents had been put forward with the greatest reserve.

10 January

Desmond Morton tells me that the Prime Minister has given an order that the Attorney-General is to enquire into the whole circumstances of the Muselier case and to consider a prosecution.

11 January

A German named Karl Haushoffer, in whom Jack Curry was interested several years ago on account of his work on geopolitik, has written to the Duke of Hamilton whom he knew personally some years ago. His letter dealt with family matters and concluded by saying how much he would like to see Hamilton if ever an opportunity arose. He said he could meet him anywhere on the continent. Hamilton is now a squadron-leader in the air force. We have approached Archie Boyle who is prepared to send Hamilton on some mission to Lisbon. The whole case looks rather like a peace offer of some sort.

13 January

I saw the Attorney-General today on the subject of the Admiral Muselier case. He was very pleasant about it all. I explained to him exactly how the case had arisen, that the action taken had not been on our advice. We had in fact only presented the documents because there was no alternative and had emphasised the fact that the source was not verified. He went through General de Gaulle's points with me, and agreed that there was very little in them one way or another.

An unpleasant incident occurred this afternoon. SUMMER, one of the parachutists, knocked down his keeper, then tried to throttle him, and finally tied him up. He got hold of a motorcycle and canoe from a neighbouring barn and set forth in the direction of Newmarket. Here he fell off his bicycle, and handed himself over to the police.

Clearly SUMMER can never be allowed to use his wireless transmitter again and he will have to remain under lock and key.

14 January

Gilbert Lennox told me about the arrangement for the departure of Lord Halifax. Elaborate precautions have been taken by Inter-Services Security Board. Bogus luggage had been sent down to Liverpool which was to be placed on board the Port Jackson and SNOW was asked to put over a message indicating that Lord Halifax would be on this boat. When they got to Liverpool they found that the ship was not going to America at all, and the bogus luggage was thereupon transferred to the Warwick Castle with the necessary publicity. In actual fact, Halifax is leaving on a cruiser from Scapa Flow and Winston, accompanied by a pack of journalists and half Wardour Street, are going up to watch the incident and have it filmed. This is all by way of a publicity stunt for America. After all this was well under way Gilbert Lennox was told that he was only one of seven people who knew about it all. He suggested that as Winston and the cameramen were all going on a special train, the Railway Executive, not to speak of the porters, must know all about it, apart from other publicity in Fleet Street. This seemed to come as rather a surprise. It will be little short of a miracle if we don't lose the Port Jackson, the Warwick Castle, the cruiser and Halifax.

16 January

We had a long discussion this morning about SUMMER and that of the other people with whom he has been associated. We have all come to the conclusion that somehow or other SUMMER must be eliminated. This not however an easy matter. In the eyes of the Germans he is known to BISCUIT and he has also been in touch with TATE. Through BISCUIT he is known to SNOW. If therefore we report that he has been captured the Germans may think that the whole organisation has been compromised. Various ingenious suggestions have been made. The best I think is that Biscuit should report that Summer is on the run, that he has put his wireless into the cloakroom at Cambridge station, and sent the key to Biscuit. Later we could say that he has been picked up by the police for failing to register and later still Snow can put forward another candidate who will use his set.

Max Knight has got a curious case involving the purchase of a large amount of dollars by a man called Conyngham at prices ranging from 4/10 to 7/-. Conyngham was introduced to one of Max's agents by Lonsdale, the ex-Mayfair boy. He has already passed $65 to Conyngham at the price of 4/10. I have asked Leonard Burt to find out whether there is an ordinary criminal motive for transactions of this kind.

Lonsdale was a member of the gang led by the Marquis of Bristol that robbed and beat a London jeweller.

17 January

I attended the lunch at Claridges given by Herschel Johnson for Hugh Clegg and Clarence Hince. I had a talk with Herschel afterwards about Axel Wenner-Gren. He said that if I would give him a note he would send it over to Washington DC by bag and made the suggestion that somebody should say something privately to the Duke of Windsor. He quite saw the point that a warning from that quarter might be more profitable than one from here.

The Swedish tycoon Axel Wenner-Gren had taken up residence in the Bahamas and had begun cultivating the Governor, the Duke of Windsor.

The dollars case is developing. There is to be a meeting on Sunday morning at which it is suggested that two notes of $1,000 each should be passed. The whole set-up is on Edgar Wallace lines. We are consulting the Criminal Investigation Department and shall probably pull in the lot.

Hugh Clegg has come clean about the Group 10 messages. He tells us that he has some thirty double-cross agents placed in various factories and that he is feeding the Germans with misleading information. Contact between these thirty agents and the Germans is maintained by one courier who apparently brings the funds.

The FBI had been developing its own double agent system, based on William Sebold, but the Radio Security Service had been intercepting their wireless traffic from New York. Evidently the FBI initially had been reluctant to share this information with MI5. The entire spy-ring, led by Frederick Duquesne, was rounded up in June 1941.

20 January

T.A. Robertson and Felix Cowgill had a meeting with Rainbow today, which appears to be satisfactory. Rainbow's principal, Schutz, has been in Barcelona. This confirms what we thought some time ago.

23 January

I attended a meeting of the Twenty Committee today when various schemes were discussed. We are to go ahead with Plan I, which is a scheme for getting the Germans to bomb a wood on the assumption that it is full of ammunition. We also discussed Stringer's plan for telling the Germans that all our troops are going to have some special identification mark in the event of invasion. The idea is that the Germans should use this identification made and that we should not. The suggestion is being made to Home Forces who have I gather already given a good deal of consideration to the problem. This is known as the BLUE BOOT PLAN as Stringer's suggestion by way of illustrating his meaning had been to tell the Germans that all our troops would have their right boot painted blue and that our troops should be issued with tins of blue paint to add conviction to the story.

The Twenty Committee met, for the first of 226 weekly meetings, for the first time on 2 January 1941. Accordingly, this was the third meeting, and Plan I, to use TATE *to persuade the enemy to bomb a non-existent ammunition dump, failed.*

24 January

SNOW has had a message asking him to bring over to Lisbon certain secret information which another German informant has obtained in this country, on the subject of infra-red. The other side want to know how their informant can get the information to SNOW without the latter having to disclose his identity. SNOW has also been told that he can give SUMMER's wireless set to Sam Stewart "who is believed to be all right".

25 January

I spent between three to four hours during the afternoon discussing with Dick White, T.A. Robertson and Felix Cowgill the answer which should be given to the SNOW message about infra-red. SNOW was rather inclined to put the thing on a high plane and meet the man himself. This had obvious disadvantage since if we wanted to arrest the individual concerned it would be difficult to do so without compromising SNOW. J.C. Masterman was rather in favour of cracking down as he felt that if the information was really vital and could not go SNOW was likely to be compromised anyhow. Eventually we decided to draw the other side on the question of whether their informant had a wireless set, and to suggest that within the next twenty-four hours at a given time the unknown informant should drop his information through a letterbox. If a message came back to the effect that the meeting could not take place we should at least have ascertained whether the informant has a wireless set.

I had about two hours benevolent cross-examination by the Attorney-General today on the Admiral Muselier case. Generally speaking, he seemed to think that our letter in which we said that we were "fairly reasonably certain about the authenticity of the documents" did not perhaps sufficiently show the red light, even though we had stated that the man Gomez had not been identified and that Commandant Collin was not an entirely satisfactory person. He thought it was a pity that we had put in the word "entirely". He then asked why we had not pursued more active enquiries after the first document had been obtained. I pointed out to him that we had proceeded in the normal manner to try and find out what Collin's contacts were and who was behind him. This could only be done by observation of one kind or another and under present conditions of the black-out was bound to take a considerable time. Had we adopted the course that we were eventually forced to adopt, namely to tell Collin that we had no confidence in him and that we wished Jannings to accompany him on his visit to the Brazilian embassy, it would have been impossible for us, as in fact it was now, to find out who if anybody had been at the back of Collin. It was therefore only when we came to the conclusion that it was imperative to clear the matter up immediately that we did get hold of Collin, tell him that we did not believe his story, and insisted on his being accompanied by Jannings. He seemed to think that this was a reasonable explanation. I have the general impression that he is going to place a small amount of responsibility on us for what ultimately happened. I gave him a very clear picture of my first verbal interview with Desmond Morton, of which he made a careful note. The information was evidently new to him.

I had a long talk with Inspector Cain of Special Branch about the Admiral Muselier case. I had seen Gilbert Lennox previously and he had been asked to go round and talk to Cain on certain aspects of the case. Cain's manner to Lennox had caused considerable annoyance. I don't think he means anything very much but he is undoubtedly somewhat of a megalomaniac. He has an unfortunate and somewhat offensive manner. This is now the experience of three of our officers, Kenneth Younger, Derek Tangye and Lennox. He generally starts by being very melodramatic and putting forward some rather fantastic theory but eventually he seems to settle down to the point. I told him that he ought not get the idea that we have got anything to hide or have had any part in aiding or abetting Commandant Howard. I explained to him exactly what our relations with Howard had been and exactly how the case had started. I emphasised that from the very start we had put forward the information with the greatest reserve and that while we could not see any flagrant discrepancies in the text, we had never been satisfied about the source. Action however had been ordered without any further reference to this department. Cain had previously made some rather wild statements to Lennox, one of them being to the effect that Norman Kendal was gunning for me.

I February

I saw a representative of the Ministry of Economic Warfare today, who wanted to talk to me about the case of Sofino. The firm's headquarters were formerly in Brussels but by a ruling of the board they were transferred to wherever the seat of the Belgian government might be. This was thought desirable as if they were operating from enemy territory their profits would obviously be liable to be taken over by the Enemy Trading Department. It seems that the MEW have definite evidence that Sofino and/or its subsidiaries have been trading with the enemy and further that they have transferred a large portion of their assets into dollar securities in order to avoid confiscation and taxation. Negotiations are going on for a settlement and very large sums indeed are involved. They run into millions. The representatives of Sofino here are a firm called Runaples, on the board of which are Lord Swinton, the former Home Secretary Reginald McKenna MP and the King's former private secretary, Lord Wigram. The legal representatives are man called Diplock and a Jew of Russian origin, Idelson. Through these negotiations, which were initiated at Swinton's request, the firm made it quite clear that they accepted the position of being domiciled here in view of the presence in this country of the Belgian government. A telegram has now been intercepted showing that they are trying to get the board to rescind their resolution but the company being domiciled with the Belgian government had to change the domicile to New York. The reasons are obvious. Diplock now wants to go to Lisbon in order to discuss matters with Richard, formerly head of the Belgian office of Sofino and an extremely tricky customer. The MEW does not want him to go until they have got some agreement out of Sofino about their assets in America. Equally they do not wish the company to know that they are trying to obstruct Diplock's journey as it might make them less reasonable about the assets in the United States which we can only get hold of by bringing pressure on the score of enemy trading. I said that I did not see how we could obstruct Diplock's journey, which was really a matter for the MEW. I do not however think that he is likely to get a passage either by boat or plane for some considerable time. Walter Simon of the MEW said that as long as he did not get there during the next two weeks he thought it would be all right.

2 February

The parachutist is at Brixton hospital and he says his name is Josef Jakobs and that he was in a concentration camp at Oranienburg. This may be true but it is a story that we have heard before. He had with him £500 and this is more than any of the other agents have brought. He had one address on him, that of Mrs Lily Knips, 9 Compayne Gardens, NW 7, reputedly a Jewess with whom Jakobs intended to communicate. Jakobs said that it was eventually his intention to go to America where he had an aunt.

It is difficult not to be skeptical about these people. Firstly it seems almost incredible that if Jakobs' story is true the Germans could imagine that he was going to be of any real value to them. Secondly, why did they give him a registration card with no letter prefix? Incidentally it was one of those about which SNOW sent numbers. If they had wished to alter the letters or the numbers, that would have been different, but to rule out the prefix and put in numbers instead would seem to be rather more than a clerical error. Did they intend that Jakobs would be captured, on the assumption that they know that these XX agents send weather reports and other information which though limited is at least accurate? If he had a number and name submitted by SNOW and SNOW was not trusted, they might have sent him over to test SNOW in some way although it is difficult to see exactly how, since SNOW could perfectly well say that he had been captured owing to the blunder about his registration card. A better test would seem to have been to try and place him in direct touch with SNOW. Another point which occurs to me is that the Germans must now be wise to the game of collaring an agent and forcing him to use his wireless set in our interests. There is in fact evidence that they are doing it themselves. Surely therefore they would have some arrangement, for example the dropping of the first letter of the prefix by which an agent could indicate that he was not acting under compulsion. We know that in some ways the Germans are extremely crude and sketchy in their methods and this may of course be the explanation but I find it difficult to believe. Jakobs has already agreed to assist us to make use of his wireless set.

4 February

In the morning we had a meeting with Jack Curry and others concerned in the Gregor Harlip case. It was agreed that we should take action on Thursday and that Hubrich, Ruth Glover, Lengyel and Heintz should be arrested. Max Knight is making all the necessary arrangements with the police. The case looks promising and there is no doubt that the ramifications are fairly extensive. Harlip is to be left untouched for the moment but we are taking steps to gauge his reactions when he learns of Lengyel's arrest.

5 February

We had a Director's meeting this morning at which a few minor matters were discussed. I lunched with Thornewill who told me about the incident at the Savoy Hotel when there was a Communist demonstration. He was anxious to have some cut and dried arrangement with the police, since the Workers Challenge broadcasting station is urging the Communists to send up a bunch of toughs to turn the Savoy upside down. The complaint of the Communists is that the rich eat omelettes at the Savoy while the poor can only buy one egg a fortnight if they can afford it. For this reason they think that the Minister of Food, Lord Woolton, should go. What is interesting is that the incident took place on 29 January and that the broadcast had been made at 8pm on 31 January. The broadcast showed that the account given must have been from somebody who was actually present. There was a certain amount said in the papers on 30 January but not I think anything on the lines of the Workers Challenge broadcast. The probability is that the information went to the *Daily Worker* who handed it to the Soviet Embassy who in turn passed it out by diplomatic cipher.

SKOOT has returned with a long and interesting questionnaire. He is to go to Paris in about a month's time, in order to undergo a course before being sent to America. What is interesting is that he has been told to get his secret ink from GIRAFFE. Once more we come back to the family.

SKOOT was the SIS codename for Dusan Popov, a Yugoslav lawyer and playboy. Later he was to be adopted by MI5 as TRICYCLE.

7 February

The Radio Security Service has picked up a message (on 2 February) showing that a parachutist has landed on 31 January and intends to communicate again on Sunday. He has given us his prefix so we may be able to pick him up. T.A. Robertson's idea is that we should give him a bit of a run in order that we may find out exactly how much these people can ascertain if they are left to themselves.

The Harlip case seems to be developing in rather an interesting way. We are holding Lengyel and Hubrich and the reactions of Harlip and his wife when they heard that Langyel had been arrested were said to be highly significant. I have no details at present.

8 February

We have had a reaction about infra-red. The documents will not be ready until the day before SNOW leaves. It has therefore been suggested that SNOW should look at them and try to memorise the most important points. He should then put them away in a safe place until his return when they should be micro-photographed, and sent over by some other channel. We are now faced with the problem of dealing with the individual who comes to the rendezvous. My inclination is to bump him off, but there are many difficulties.

10 February

The alleged parachutist's transmitter from this country was heard again on Sunday but turned out to be a communication between Paris and Cracow. This is reassuring.

We have just heard that one of our AID inspectors in America has written to the German consul in Boston offering his services. The Americans are going to deport him with his letter and we shall deal with him when he arrives.

I attended a meeting at Kinnaird House with Lord Swinton in the chair. Representatives of the Home Office and General Spears mission were present, to discuss ways and means of dealing with Frenchmen who arrive in this country. It was agreed that we would supply the Spears mission with the names of all Frenchmen passing through the Patriotic Schools. This would enable them to meet any queries put to them by General de Gaulle. We said that it was essential that we should not be forced to give reasons if people were being detained. This is especially important as sometimes we get SIS agents who have come through by saying that they are coming to join de Gaulle's forces. There are also cases of Frenchmen whose qualifications are such that they may be of use to us or to SIS. We do not therefore want their names bandied round the Free French Forces.

I went on from this meeting to the Director of Naval Intelligence's room where the Wireless Committee was assembled. Sir Findlater Stewart said that he would, if the Committee agreed, approach Sir John Anderson and ask him to take the responsibility for matters affecting the civilian population.

We then discussed the question of passing the information obtained from questionnaires to FOES. FOES is an inter-service organisation which puts itself in the position of the enemy intelligence service, and tries to work out what the enemy is likely to do. It is therefore important for them to have as much information as possible known to be in the possession of the enemy. It was decided that the three Service representatives on the committee should make a paraphrased version of both our questionnaires and SIS questionnaires and that this should be given in strict confidence to FOES.

The Japanese assistant military attaché A. Nakamo, is obviously doing intelligence work. Special Material shows that he is trying to get information about the movements of our ships to the China Seas and that for this purpose he has been in touch with some European. We are having him kept under close observation and also putting Lord Sempill under observation. The Japanese are very difficult to watch as to a European they all look alike and there is the additional difficulty of the blackout and four exits from the military attaché's office.

Lord Sempill had long been a Japanese sympathiser and had been warned that his association with the embassy could endanger him.

Lady Howard, alias Manci Gertler, was interned the other day. Personally I always thought the case was very thin and it never amounted to more than that she had a very large number of acquaintances from whom she might have been able to extract valuable information.

The Hungarian-born wife of the 6ᵗʰ Earl of Effingham was a member of the BUF and was detained for five months. She was released from Holloway Prison in July 1941, and her marriage was dissolved in 1946.

13 February

Brigadier Leonard Hawes came to see me as he has instructions to form a Jewish Division but was worried about the Revisionists. He was in close touch with Chaim Weitzman who thought that the Jewish Agency should be entirely responsible for vetting those who joined the Division. This is to be composed of Jews from all over the world. Weitzman is also arranging for skilled Jewish technicians to come here from America. I told Hawes that I thought that he would be well advised to leave the vetting in the hands of Weitzman who was obviously interested in seeing that the division was a really good one. If the Revisionists were in any way responsible, undesirable people would creep in and the division would be used as a sort of political debating ground. I gather all of the various departments of state are now concerned with the issues of some statement about the project. It will need very delicate wording if it is not going to give offence to the Arabs. Although there may be considerable advantages in the scheme both from the point of finance in America and technical skill, I cannot help feeling it is a blunder, since the whole project will be used as propaganda against us both by the Arabs and by the enemy. It will, moreover, pin us down to granting concessions to the Jews in Palestine after the war. It is one of those things which are done in times of crisis and which are bitterly regretted afterwards.

14 February

The whole of the Rumanian Legation has refused to return to their country. The Foreign Office has insisted that six of them shall go otherwise Sir Reginald Hoare and our Legation party will not be allowed to leave Rumania. Radu Florescu is amongst those who refused to go. Attempts are being made to persuade him to leave on the understanding that he can come back.

15 February

One of Lord Beaverbrook's Allied technicians, whose entry is being facilitated, has arrived from Lisbon. His name is Kovalsky and his nationality is Belgian. [XXXXXXXX] was found in his wife's possession and GIRAFFE's address in his. The arrival of somebody from Lisbon had previously been signalled in an ISOS message.

Andrew Rothstein is anxious to know where the War Office print their documents. He also wants to publish in some paper or other a statement to the effect that a professor who is being used as a Russian expert in the Ministry of Economic Warfare is rabidly anti-Soviet. The suggestion is that this is a cover for the professor who may in reality be a Soviet agent. As regards the War Office printers, Roger Hollis is going to consult Alf Wall of the Printers Union with a view to finding a suitable plant for Rothstein.

Andrew Rothstein was one of the founders of the CPGB. Alf Wall was a trade union leader and a member of the Security Executive.

17 February

We had a discussion about STORK, who has refused to go into his house at Hendon as his wife is going to have a baby. This is unfortunate as we have had the place carefully miked. We could not tell him about the locality before as he would have been on the premises, which for obvious reasons would have been undesirable. The house will however be very useful for other purposes. We are telling STORK that he has got to go and do his transmission from some specific place. We hope to get a line on premises from one of the Post Office people in Dollis Hill.

MI5 established a safe-house in Crespigny Road, Hendon, next to the home of Edward Pouton of the Radio Security Service, and wired all the rooms for sound so they could accommodate double agents.

3 March

There has been some news about SNOW from Lisbon. He and CELERY are by way of returning. The indications are that their visit has not been altogether a success although SNOW tells us that he has an important contract.

7 March

Sir David Petrie has been officially appointed Director-General and is to come in on Monday.

8 March

SIS is in a great state about the publication of a book called *The Diary of a Staff Officer,* which in addition to criticising the French and British commands in rather an outspoken manner makes reference to work affecting the GC&CS. I have communicated first with Mr Ray of Methuens, the publishers, and then with Dick White's brother who is a partner in the firm. 1,900 copies have already been issued and since further demands are being made by the booksellers, most of them must be in the hands of private individuals. Meanwhile another 7,000 copies are in preparation and are to go out on Tuesday next. Dick's brother tells me that the book was submitted and passed by all three service representatives before Christmas and it was then published serially in the United States. It is possible however that the offending passages may have been omitted. A few copies have gone to Canada and the book has been extensively reviewed here in the press. I am suggesting that the 7,000 copies should not be circulated and that the Censorship and D4 should be warned against letting any of them out of the country. I feel that if we do more than this we shall only be drawing attention to what we are anxious to conceal. We shall be in a better position to decide on Monday.

The anonymous author, Colonel Gribble, had served as an Air Intelligence liaison officer on the staff of Air Marshal Sir Arthur Barratt, the Commander-in-Chief of the British Air Forces in France.

Stewart Menzies, Gilbert Lennox and I saw Gribble at the War Office. He admitted that he knew the messages came from a very secret source but he thought that he was amply covered by having submitted his diary for censorship. He admitted however that he had shown the document previously to his agent in order to see whether its contents were likely to interest the public if they were published in book form. It was explained to him that certain passages constituted a grave indiscretion and that it was in the public interest that he should co-operate with us in doing anything possible to pick up the pieces. We eventually agreed that even though the offending passages had appeared in the *Saturday Evening Post* it would be better to issue the new edition in amended form. Gribble was to tell his agent that he wished to make certain amendments in the text and therefore that he would like the return of the proof copy from America before any further action is taken. As regards the *Manchester Evening News* who were asking permission to publish the book in serial form, it was decided to see first whether they were proposing by their own selection to exclude the offending passages. If not, we should have to say that the book could not be published serially until certain amendments had been made which the author considered desirable in the light of subsequent information received.

SO2 have been giving a great deal of trouble. They act in a very slipshod and indiscreet manner. The result is that all their people get rounded up and some of Stewart's as well. This I gather is what has been happening in the Balkans. In the afternoon Dick White's brother came down and we discussed details about Gribble's book. It was apparent that if the offending page was taken out it would be quite clear that a new one had been gummed in. We therefore decided to buy up the whole of the second edition which was already bound and have arranged that the offending page in the other two editions should be removed altogether, with those which were joined to it. These would be collected before the new amended pages were delivered to the printer.

The Nora Briscoe case is developing. Max Knight is introducing a German agent and there is to be a meeting when he will get the documents. This case was first brought to my notice on Saturday. One of Max's agents was asked to tea with Molly Hiscox, where he met Nora Briscoe, who is the wife or mistress of Jock Houston, the interned member of the British Union of Fascists. Briscoe said that she was working in quite an important section of the Ministry of Supply and that she had been copying all documents which she thought would be of interest. She is of German origin and has a son who is being brought up in Germany. She is now looking for some means of getting the documents through to the Germans.

Molly Hiscox was convicted in March 1941 of unauthorised possession of official documents supplied by Mrs Briscoe, and was sentenced to five years' imprisonment. In 1944 she was engaged to Jock Houston.

SNOW 's wife has received a telegram from him saying that he is very ill and asking that she and the baby should go out to nurse him. Even if this were possible we should certainly not agree to it.

CELERY has also cabled that he expects to be home in about three weeks' time, from which it appears he is making his own arrangements. In the meantime SIS has been asked to arrange for SNOW 's return here as soon as possible.

Richman Stopford arrived in England for a few days and confirmed the report that CELERY's connection with us is fairly generally known in Lisbon.

SKOOT left for Lisbon this morning taking with him notes on his questionnaire and notes about the Ministry of Supply circulator for which he was asked and certain particulars of mine fields put forward by the Naval Intelligence Division. All these notes were written in secret ink on innocuous correspondence from Friedle Gaertner (his girlfriend), BALLOON and his business cover. After immense difficulties he obtained the diplomatic visa for Portugal and arrangements have been made for him to obtain an American visa from Portugal and an Egyptian visa from New York. He can get into touch with us in Lisbon and will be contacted both by us and by the FBI in America. In America he will stay at the Waldorf Astoria.

BALLOON was a former army officer, Dickie Metcalfe. He and Popov's Austrian girlfriend, Friedle Gaertner, were recruited as double agents.

POGO has approached our embassy in Madrid offering to disclose the names of German agents working in England in return for a British passport. His reason for this course is his theory that he is being hunted by the Spanish secret police, but we have decided that this may be an attempt, either to embroil our ambassador or to penetrate our service and that therefore no agreement should be entered into until POGO gives us a good deal more information.

Nora Briscoe has been pulled in with all the documents. The meeting room was miked and Max Knight and Special Branch were in the adjacent room listening in. It was clear that important documents were being discussed and Max came to the conclusion that action should be taken immediately.

17 March

I lunched with Max Knight and he told me all about the Briscoe case and showed me the documents which are voluminous and cover a wide field. If the information had leaked it would certainly be a very serious matter. They relate to the location of factories, shortage of materials, establishment of submarine bases in Northern Ireland, etc.

18 March

After lunch I discussed with Valentine Vivian and Felix Cowgill the question of Jack Hooper, who is working with Commandant François van t'Sant, the head of the Dutch Combined Intelligence Bureau. It seems that there has been some inter-office intrigue with Claude Dansey employing an agent to watch him. He is apparently associating with Mrs Tregenna who is of foreign extraction. I do not think there is anything in it except sex but we are going to make further enquiries.

Jack Hooper was a former employee of the Passport Control Office in The Hague, an SIS station known to have been thoroughly penetrated by the enemy.

20 March

Enquiry shows that in the Briscoe case we were consulted by the Ministry of Supply about this woman's employment on 31 January 1941 but that they had already taken her on on 20 January 1941. We replied that she had German and Fascist associations and we did not think her appointment was desirable. This case should be a lesson to other departments.

A shorthand typist at the Ministry of Supply, Mrs Briscoe was a widow who had been a member of the Link. When arrested in March 1941 she had been found in unauthorised pos-session of official documents, and had been sentenced to five years' imprisonment.

21 March

We have just captured Otto Kretschmer, the German ace submarine commander. A member of his crew says that the other submarine ace Gunther Prien is some eight weeks overdue and it is thought that his submarine has been sunk.

Otto Kretschmer, captain of the U-99, sank his last ship, the Swedish freighter Korshamn, *on 17 March. He and all but three of his crew were captured by HMS* Walker, *and the news was announced to the House of Commons by Winston Churchill. Gunter Prien's U-49 had penetrated Scapa Flow in October 1939 and sunk HMS Royal Oak. Later he also torpe-doed the SS* Arandora Star, *but was sunk by HMS* Wolverine *on 7 March.*

22 March

There has been some rather disquieting news about SNOW. It seems that the Germans were not satisfied with his traffic and went for him. He evidently felt him-self cornered and admitted that he had been operating under duress. In spite of this he alleges that he been given a sum of £10,000 and a new contract. This seems very curious but there is no chance of getting at the facts until he returns and we are expecting him back next week. In the meantime CELERY is apparently making his own way back by sea. SNOW has suggested that he aroused suspicion through obtaining a passage so easily on the aeroplane. I am disinclined to believe this as he had very good commercial reasons for travelling. There is also the rather curious fact that at one moment he wanted his wife and child to join him in Lisbon. It may be that he has lost his nerve. The whole thing is rather unfortunate but it was bound to come to an end sooner or later. We shall have to get other strings to our bow.

There is rather reassuring news about TRICYCLE, formerly SKOOT. He is to come here on a special mission instead of going to America. It is possible that he is required here in order that he can take SNOW's place and that this is why a change has been made.

Intercepted Group messages have indicated that a woman named the Countess de Jonghe, *née* Savitsch, was possibly a German agent. The German secret service was in touch with her and interested in getting hold of her passport. She subsequently applied for a visa in Lisbon and although the application showed that she had received a Spanish transit visa at the request of the German authorities her application was granted. Her husband, the Vicomte de Jonghe, a Belgian subject, is at present employed by SO2 and has apparently been communicating with his wife in Lisbon through the Belgian bag. The Vicomte is considered to be all right although he has some curious connections. He joined the Belgian Army on 10 May and somehow managed to get over here. He has had a very adventurous career according to his own account. He married the Comtesse de Jonghe by proxy after living with her for four years. Fortunately Tommy Harris knows de Jonghe fairly intimately and may be able to get some line on the wife. In the meantime we have issued instructions that if she arrives she is to be brought to Nightingale Road where she will be examined on the strength of her Spanish transit visa. It is just possible that she has played up to the Germans in order to get an exit visa to visit her husband but on the whole this does not seem very likely. It is difficult to make any decision about the handling of her case until she actually arrives. We shall be in a better position to make up our minds when we have searched her baggage and heard what she has to say for herself. Her husband is extremely talkative person and will undoubtedly tell his wife everything that he is doing. There will then be the danger of the information going through the Belgian bag.

Max Knight and Tony Gillson came to see me about Heron, who has produced some interesting information about Alexis Hochberg, the younger brother of Prince Henry of Pless, now interned. For some reason the German government wishes Hochberg to sell his property rights in Poland to his brother for the sum of $5m. The exact purpose is not clear but it may be that the Germans wish to give some air of regularity to the proceedings in order not to offend local public opinion. The transaction has been carried out through a bank in Switzerland and the deal was to be concluded in Lisbon. Heron is obviously anxious that the transaction will go through as he will get a large rake-off. He wants our assistance in facilitating the exit here of Mrs de Havilland who will have a power of attorney to complete the deal in Lisbon. This is obviously going to be the kind of basis on which we shall be expected to work with Heron. In actual fact Heron in this case is telling us nothing that we did not know before. Herbert Hart, who has been doing the case of Prince Henry of Pless, has the full facts. Heron has produced another story about Cunninghame who was arrested on our information a short time ago for a confidence trick. His *métier* was to steal suitcases. He had disclosed to the police that he had found in a suitcase a document, the property of W.J. Hooper. This document was relating to Soviet espionage. When questioned by Max, Cunninghame said that he had taken no copy of the document. Heron, who has been asked to act for him in his appeal, now says that he did take a copy. Max wants to know if in the event of this copy being handed over, Cunninghame will get a remission of sentence. I have said that the first thing is for us to see the document. In actual fact I do not see how this disclosure will benefit Cunninghame in any way. The incident does show however that Heron is able to get useful information, although there is obviously going to be a *quid pro quo* in each case. What I think he really wants to do is to legalise some of his more dubious dealings with the underworld.

---

28 March

Joseph Laureyssen, the Belgian seaman who sent a letter in secret ink to Lisbon, is now beginning to talk. He appears to have got his orders from some Dutchman in the Port of London so further enquiries are being made.

There have also been developments in the George Armstrong case. He is the AID inspector who communicated with the German consul in Boston. He appears to have told a fellow prisoner who was being released that he could arrange for the necessary travel documents to the United States through a certain "Queenie" who had a café in Bute Street, Cardiff.

George Armstrong was arrested in the United States and returned to Cardiff to face trial in London. He was convicted under the Treachery Act and executed.

SNOW and CELERY arrived back yesterday by air, with £10,000 and explosives concealed in soap, and an electric torch in a fountain pen and pencil. Their stories will need a lot of sifting.

SNOW and CELERY had been to Lisbon to see their Abwehr controllers, but unexpectedly CELERY had been taken to Hamburg where he had survived three weeks of interrogation.

---

29 March

I saw the Director of Naval Intelligence in regard to a BJ which denoted leakage of information to the Japanese by some contact on the subject of the *Asaka Maru*. The Japanese have turned this ship into a naval warship in order that it could go through the Contraband Control. Negotiations have been going on and some contact of the Japanese Embassy who is also in touch with somebody in the Admiralty had given away information about our intentions. I suggested Lord Sempill was a possible, and said that the case should be fairly clear if the

Admiralty made enquiries within their office. The DNI took this opportunity to discuss the question of Sempill and he is evidently rather worried and wants if possible to get the matter finally cleared up.

We have just heard that a Dutchman called Jan Willem Ter Braak has been found dead in a shelter at Cambridge. He had evidently shot himself and had been dead for some thirty-six hours. His Dutch papers were out of order and did not show any authority to land. He had lived in Cambridge for about four months. He had arrived about 4 November with a small suitcase and a parcel, and he had a brand new registration card. On form, I should say he was undoubtedly a parachutist, and probably one whom we expected at about that time.

We have now got some definite information about Ter Braak. There is no doubt that he was the parachutist who was reported to have come down near Bletchley. We have obtained his wireless set which was in the cloakroom of Cambridge railway station. The joke of it is that in spite of our instructions to the police Ter Braak has been living within fifty yards of our RSLO in Cambridge. It seems that his landlady did report his presence to the local police who merely said that they expected he would register before long. The man had been trying to get a ration book having run out of food and money, and he presumably decided to shoot himself. The question of tightening up regulations will have to be gone into very seriously, although I think in this case the police were almost entirely to blame.

Ter Braak seems to have shot himself in desperation, although his true identity was never ascertained.

I attended a meeting of the Wireless Committee in the morning and T.A. Robertson and J.C. Masterman were present. The principle subject of discussion was the case of SNOW and CELERY. Masterman gave a masterly exposition of the case. He put forward the various hypotheses: (1) that SNOW had not given away the whole show to the Germans as he alleged he had, that he had intended this story to enable him to go into retirement with a foot in both camps; (2) that his story was quite true, that Dr Rantzau still thought that he had his uses and could in any case be employed as a paymaster and that eventually his place could be taken by CELERY; (3) that SNOW was a rogue and had been from the start. In this case he would merely have been telling them what they knew already, namely that he was in touch with the British Intelligence but really working for the Germans. Masterman pointed out that the story of CELERY was still obscure. It was not clear whether he had actually gone into Germany or not or whether he was working for us or wholeheartedly for the Germans. A good deal more sifting would have to be done before the position is cleared up.

7 April

A report came in during the night to say that two enemy agents had been arrested somewhere between Banff and Aberdeen. It transpired subsequently that their names were Erick Gustavssen Glad and Helge John Neal Moe, two Norwegians who had been landed by a seaplane and come ashore in a rubber boat. They had a two-way wireless set, a bicycle each, formulae for explosives and other sabotage material, two cameras (one cine and one contact), revolvers and £100 each plus some dollars. They also had alternative suits and nail clippers believed to be for cutting wires. If they conclude their messages with the name "Henri" the Germans are to assume that their traffic is controlled. They are being brought down to London.

8 April

SO2 have asked whether we can supply them with Princess Hohenloe's letters for publication in America. They apparently want to help one of their contacts there. I have said that I think it is extremely undesirable since Hohenloe might well retaliate by the publication of Lord Rothermere's letters which he wrote to Hitler, and also Hitler's replies.

SO2 was the Foreign Office's clandestine sabotage and subversion department, later to become Special Operations Executive. Lord Rothermere was the proprietor of the Daily Mail.

9 April

Colonel Stephens reports that the two Norwegians, Glad and Moe, are genuinely anxious to assist this country. He recommends that they should be removed from Camp 020 and taken out to dinner. I have arranged with Leonard Burt to have two men on guard outside John Bingham's flat where they will be staying.

10 April

Last night's party with the Norwegians has raised doubts in the minds of those present. Certainly a number of difficulties have to be got over. Tor Glad appears to have joined the Germans at a very early stage after the invasion of Norway. He was for a time employed in their censorship but maintains that he helped a lot of his countrymen to join up with the Norwegian forces. John Moe seems to be rather under the thumb of Glad.

Dick, T. A. Robertson, J. C. Masterman, John Marriott and myself had a long discussion about SNOW and CELERY. It was agreed that the only safe course was to assume that Dr Rantzau knew about our controlled agents and that he probably knew as much about it as SNOW or CELERY. On this assumption SNOW can be of little if any further use to us but the fact that the Doctor has given him £10,000 and the explosives shows that he wishes himself to keep the party alive. The reasons for this may be a wish to maintain his own prestige, a wish to use SNOW as paymaster or for contacts in the event of invasion and the belief that he can learn a great deal by studying information which we allow to go over, because it will tell him what we regard as unimportant and what we regard as important. The fact that he wishes to keep the party alive is a strong argument for closing down on it and it is also desirable that we should put the onus of ending it upon him. SNOW will therefore be informed tomorrow that we propose to send a message on Saturday to the effect that his health and nerves have collapsed and that he must throw in his hand. He will also ask what he is to do with his transmitters and his explosives. The advantages gained from this course will be (1) we shall be able to observe SNOW 's reactions which may help us to decide how far he has involved himself on the other side and (2) we shall be able to watch the Doctor's reactions since he must either himself break up the party by refusing to answer or send some sort of reply and instructions to SNOW. If SNOW accepts the decision without comment or a suggested alternative we shall then tell him that we believe CELERY's story that SNOW never warned him, which we regard as a foolish and treacherous act on SNOW 's part. It is possible that this statement may elicit from SNOW further accusations and possible information about CELERY.

TATE in the meantime will go over with renewed and urgent requests for money. He will explain that he cannot send any valuable information because his money is running so short, that he dare not spend it on travelling about to procure information. If he is not helped at once he must throw up the sponge. Here again we shall be able to decide according to the Doctor's reply what is to be done with TATE and the Doctor will have the responsibility of breaking up the party with consequent loss of prestige to himself. If SNOW really did tell the Doctor that his traffic was controlled the Doctor must know that TATE is also controlled.

We shall hold CELERY in play until we have more information through SNOW and TATE. CELERY will write a letter which will be sent to Lisbon as though it had been carried over by a ship's steward or seaman in which he will say that he is trying hard to go over to Lisbon again according to his instructions but that it is becoming more and more difficult to obtain a seat in the plane and he cannot be sure when he will be able to obtain one. In the meantime he would welcome further instructions if they can be conveyed to him.

This meeting was held after Dick White had examined both SNOW and CELERY and then confronted them with each other in order that they could argue out the discrepancies in their statements. Dick felt confident that Dr Rantzau knew that SNOW and CELERY were under the control of the British Intelligence Service but that he had decided to use both of them as agents against this country. Rantzau probably saw a certain advantage in the situation as SNOW and CELERY might in these circumstance be able to get through port controls carrying with them large sums of money and equipment for sabotage. The Doctor may have accepted SNOW's word that his agents in Wales were not compromised and could therefore be used for sabotage purposes. It seems fairly clear that CELERY did not know the party was blown before he went into Germany. SNOW may have been prevented from telling him by the Doctor who was anxious to test CELERY independently or he may have been activated by motives of personal spite and jealousy against CELERY. It was curiously noticeable that in spite of the unpleasant things that SNOW and CELERY had said about each other they did not embark on any serious recrimination, and in the end seemed quite ready to go on working together.

11 April

The investigation into the case of Jan Willem Ter Braak, the Dutch parachutist found dead in a shelter at Cambridge, is beginning to reveal a good many holes in the net. It seems that there is some system by which these people can obtain temporary ration cards. Herbert Hart is going into the matter in great detail.

I had a conference with Dick White and B2(a) about the Norwegians as we are not yet satisfied as to their bona fides and there are still a number of enquiries to be made. We do not intend to put them on the air for the moment. It is proposed that we shall eventually put over the story that they have given themselves up to the authorities and handed over their sabotage equipment, having posed as bona fides refugees who joined the German secret service in order that they might escape to this country. They hid their wireless set and have now got taken on, one in the British Army and one in the Norwegian Army, or possibly in some other form of employment. I have suggested to Valentine Vivian that he should communicate with William Stephenson with a view to getting the FBI to vet a dozen or so of the technicians who are coming to this country and introduce them to his German friends as possible agents for the German service. In this way we could build up quite a nice little show, which will set Dr Rantzau's mind at rest.

Jack Curry, Roger Hollis and I had a conference today with Valentine Vivian and David Footman about building up some organisation to deal with contemporary social movements. Our objective is to collect authenticated inside information on important politico-social movements in all European countries and Great Britain and the United States on their aims, leading personalities, and practical chances of putting their ideas into effect. It is suggested that Roger Fulford and possibly Guy Burgess will undertake this work in close co-operation with Footman.

12 April

Dick White has had an interesting conference with all those concerned in the Laureyssens case. It seems fairly clear that Laureyssens had a number of visiting cards of a lady in Lisbon and he also had a good many copies of her photograph. Moreover he had been seen associating with other seamen at a café in Erith. Most of the people who had seen him thought that he was a dull-witted Flemish peasant.

It seems more likely that he is quite an intelligent German agent and that his protestations about not being able to read or write in spite of the fact that he carried on him a very good pen and pencil are quite valueless. What he is clearly doing is to give the visiting card and a copy of the girl's photograph to any seamen who might make a good German agent. They are told to call on her when next in Lisbon if they want to have a good time. She is, of course, merely a German recruiting agent. It is significant that the address on the visiting card was different to the address for the same girl that Laureyssens had in his notebook.

A merchant seaman, Laureyssens failed to confess under interrogation at Camp 020 and because the original evidence against him, a letter written in secret ink to a cover-address in Lisbon, had been destroyed in the laboratory accidentally, he was never prosecuted but detained until the end of the war and then deported to Belgium.

16 April

The Germans have been informed that SNOW is seriously ill. They have replied that they hope he will soon be better, that he must make his own arrangements about his wireless set, and that if he can resume his former activities later on so much the better. They will continue to listen for him at the appointed times.

SNOW was detained at Dartmoor Prison until the end of the war, when he emigrated to Canada.

17 April

TATE had been pressing the Germans to let him have some money. They have suggested dropping some by aeroplane and sending a larger amount later c/o the Post Office at Watford.

I saw Air Commodore Charles Medhurst of Air Intelligence and he promised to make the necessary arrangements, to see that the aeroplane was not attacked in the particular area where it is proposed to drop the money.

21 April

MUTT and JEFF are now established in the villa at Hendon, where they have succeeded in establishing contact. Generally speaking, we are more satisfied about their bona fides but personally I feel that JEFF has rather too much German background to enable us ever to regard him as reliable.

MUTT was John Moe, and JEFF was Tor Glad, the two Norwegians who were accommodated at Crespigny Road, Hendon. Moe proved highly reliable whereas the volatile Glad later had to be interned.

26 April

MUTT and JEFF are going on the air on Monday with their full story. They are going to say that they have, after considerable adventures, given themselves up as refugees and succeeded in getting through the various examinations to which they have been subjected, and that they await the decision of the authorities as to how they are to be employed. Ultimately we hope to work them into the position of examiners to the existing immigration authorities. This may give us considerable help in sorting out bodies of refugees who arrive in the future.

The Germans are arranging for someone to come over and give TATE his money. This man is described as "the man from the Phoenix in Hamburg". We intend to arrest both him and TATE. Elaborate precautions to effect the arrest are being planned.

27 April

It is reported that Marschner, the German parachutist who came down in Eire, was intending to visit Werner Unland.

Under interrogation by the Irish G-2, 'Hans Marschner' turned out to be Sergeant Gunther Scheutz, a 29-year-old German.

2 May

I lunched with Herschel Johnson and warned him that Grotwohl was getting information from the US Attorney-General Francis Biddle. I also told him about Scanlon's association with Artaza, the Spanish Consul in Newcastle. As regards the latter I said we were particularly anxious that no sort of indication should be given to Artaza that we regarded him with suspicion. Lastly I told him that one of Averell Harriman's commission, I think a Colonel Green, was shortly to receive a visit from General F.C.J. Fuller and I thought it advisable that Green should know about Fuller, although the purpose of the meeting was probably only to get Fuller's view about tanks and mechanised warfare.

An expert on mechanised military tactics, General Fuller had been very sympathetic to the German cause before the outbreak of war.

6 May

David Lloyd George has changed his views again. Several months ago he was all in favour of a negotiated peace. He still feels that we cannot win the war and that the most we can hope for is a stalemate and in view of our recent reverses he no longer thinks that the moment is opportune for peace negotiations. He thinks therefore that we should speed up our war effort to the maximum and that having achieved a few successes we should then come to terms with the Germans. He is surrounded by a group who to some extent hold the same views as himself. The principal people are James Horrabin [*of the* News Chronicle], Leslie Hore-Belisha and Sir James Wardlaw-Milne [*the Unionist Member of Parliament for Kidderminster*]. The whole group consists of about ten people and they are leading the attack on the government in the House of Commons today. No personal attack on Winston is contemplated and Lloyd George's ultimate object is to get into the Cabinet on his own terms. An offer was made to him some time ago but he would not go in as he felt that his hands would be tied. He would only join the government if he is to be the big noise on policy.

Arthur Donaldson, the dissident Scottish Nationalist, has been arrested and two others called Hope Campbell and Haig. Campbell was a deserter evading conscription. Haig, who is associated with McGibbon, was found to be in possession of firearms, two or three rifles, a few revolvers and some ammunition. The prosecution was undertaken on the instigation of the Lord Advocate.

Arthur Donaldson later became Chairman of the Scottish Nationalist Party.

7 May

SNOW remains interned and so far has not asked to see anyone. There is a proposal to send CELERY to Lisbon to see if he can induce a German agent called Sessler to sell out. RAINBOW is angling for a full-time job but so far the Germans have not bitten. He has received no pay since January. TRICYCLE arrived back at the end of last month and continues to give the same very favourable impression. The Germans have swallowed his deputy BALLOON and also GELATINE, with whom we hope to open up new lines. TRICYCLE is going on to America and brought some money for GIRAFFE but gathered that the information of the latter was not regarded very highly. TATE has been awarded the Iron Cross first and second class. DRAGONFLY is still somewhat suspect. We have put over a story about the German Consul in Madrid which ought to cause a good deal of confusion in the minds of the Germans.

MUTT and JEFF have been asked to say what questions were put to them during their interrogation. This presents a useful opportunity. We are going to frame the questions in such a way as to assist us in sorting out so-called refugees when they arrive here. We shall try to base them on the documents being carried by MUTT and JEFF and show that they cannot easily get away with excuses for not having their papers in order. This we hope will lead to further laxity on the part of the Germans. New arrivals will be questioned and if they give the answers that we gave the Germans we shall know where we are.

Mrs Nicholson has been acquitted in spite of the fact that she admitted that she had made notes from cipher telegrams which she had received from Anna Wolkoff. Her husband went into the box and admitted that he had also taken notes. Their excuse was that they thought the Prime Minister was conducting some intrigue with President Roosevelt and that the matter might be of importance from the national point of view. The former Attorney-General, Sir Patrick Hastings KC, made a clever move in putting the husband into the box and bamboozled the jury into thinking that a British admiral could not possibly commit an act of treachery and that therefore his wife must be innocent. The Solicitor-General regards the case as one of the worst miscarriages of justice that he has known since he was at the bar. The question now arises as to whether Mrs Nicholson should remain interned under 18(b). The probability is that she will be brought before the Advisory Committee.

A qualified physician, Mrs Christobel Nicholson was a member of The Right Club and was detained under 18(b) immediately after her acquittal. She was not released until September 1943, whereas her husband was never arrested.

8 May

One of Max Knight's people came to see me today about the case of one John Manifold, a lieutenant who has succeeded in getting in to MI8. He is a Communist and intimately connected with the headquarters of the Communist Party. Gilbert Lennox is making enquiries about him, but I gather the War Office is anxious to get him transferred elsewhere as soon as possible. I have passed the case to F Division to deal with although as far as I can see most of the work will have to be done by me. This is rather a typical example of how the lines cross. I have to protect B5(b)'s agents and deal with the War Office because this can be done more conveniently from here than from the country.

10 May

We have bought two bloodhounds and their keeper. They will be available to all regions for tracking down parachutists.

12 May

Ned Reid has unearthed several interesting accounts in the course of his banking enquiries. It is found that one Yusuf Kemal is at present in Hungary and has paid out notes which have passed through the hands of one Lessing who is doing counter-espionage work for the Germans at Ankara, Pugh, a German suspect, POGO, and SNOW. He has also found four cases of payments to Communists being made in Lisbon.

Lieutenant Manifold was hit by a bomb on Saturday night and is temporarily laid out. This disposes of our difficulties at the moment.

13 May

Today's sensational news is the arrival of the deputy Führer Rudolf Hess in a Messerschmitt-110. He apparently landed near Glasgow on the night of 10 May.

Ivone Kirkpatrick of the Foreign Office has definitely identified him. He has a broken ankle and is in hospital in Glasgow in charge of the military. He seems to have been carrying some sort of message to the Duke of Hamilton from Professor Karl Haushofer. We knew about Haushofer before the war. His great subject is geopolitik. He had written to the Duke immediately after the outbreak of war and had sent him another letter last September saying that if there was ever a chance of seeing the Duke he could come to Lisbon. This letter was sent to a cover address and enquiries were started on the assumption that the Duke's bona fides might be in question. As these led to nothing it was suggested to the Air Ministry that they should get him up and suggest that possibly he might go to Lisbon in some official capacity. There was a good deal of delay and eventually the Air Ministry produced his brother. After further delay they got hold of the Duke himself. He explained that he had known Haushofer for some time and expressed his willingness to go to Lisbon if suitable cover could be found. The Air Ministry eventually decided that it would probably be better not to send him at the present moment. It is difficult to say what Hess's motive is in coming here. He has probably fallen out with the party on what he regards as a fundamental issue. He may resent the approach to Russia as he was violently anti-Communist and become embroiled in some kind of intrigue. Possibly his life was in danger and he decided to escape. Alternatively he may have come over with some kind of peace offer. The Germans may have thought they could only convince us of their sincerity by sending a man of high standing.

The statement in the press about Hess being mad would merely have been put over to cover up the fact that the Germans are putting out peace-feelers. Personally I doubt this hypothesis very much. It seems to me too far fetched.

Liddell's account of the Duke of Hamilton's correspondence with Professor Haushofer tends to scotch the theory that there had been an elaborate British plot to lure Hess to England.

14 May

I saw Lord Swinton yesterday. He told me that Hess's story was that he was still an admirer of the Führer but that he was appalled by the slaughter and destruction and wanted to see if there was not some way of stopping it.

I saw Walter Monckton and explained to him our point of view about Hess. I thought that it was highly necessary that we should be kept informed of what he was saying and that there should some record of the conversations of the people who visited him and their impression. I realised that the whole business was on a very high plane. At the same time we had a very definite interest, since Hess was nominally in control of the secret service organisation known as the *Innere Dienst*. An occasion might arise when the conversation could be led onto this ground. Monckton said that he quite understood our point of view and that they would make arrangements for me to see Ivone Kirkpatrick as soon as he returned. I also discussed with Monckton and Charles Radclyffe certain indiscretions by the press which had come to light. Air raid damage was being telephoned all over the country and in particular from Belfast where references have been made to movements of ships. Radclyffe said he would see the editor of the *Daily Express* and get him to instruct his reports not to send in information which they knew could not possibly be published.

15 May

The 'man from the Phoenix' who was to bring TATE his money has been picked up by a War Reserve policeman at Colney. He was asking his way to the nearest hospital. The policeman suspected him and on finding his papers were not in order took him to the nearest police station. Here he was searched and a sum of £500 and $1,400 dollars was found on him. The police superintendent, having had his instructions from our RSLO about suspicious persons carrying large sums of money, immediately came to the conclusion that the man was a spy. On being questioned he said that his name was Karel Richter, that he had landed in a boat ten miles west of Cromer on the previous night and was making his way to the Regent Palace Hotel where he had a rendezvous with an unknown person outside the barber's shop. He was to hand over to this person the sum of £450. He had undertaken this work as he was formerly in a concentration camp and saw a chance of getting away to America. It was for this reason that he had the American dollars.

16 May

I attended a meeting of the Wireless Board, which had been called at my request. At a previous meeting the Board had requested that CELERY should not be sent abroad again without their approval. Personally I feel that in this matter the Board are rather exceeding their functions, but as we want their help and co-operation it is probably better to comply with their wishes. I explained that CELERY's idea was to proceed to Lisbon where he would try and make contact again with Georg Sessler who had travelled with him to Berlin and Hamburg on his previous visit. It will be remembered that Sessler appeared to be strongly anti-Nazi and quite ready to sell out and go to America if a suitable opportunity could be found. It may have been that Sessler was merely posing as an anti-Nazi in order to draw CELERY out and discover his true colours but it seemed to us that there was at least a chance of winning over Sessler since he was an admirer of Hess and the occasion seemed somewhat opportune. I pointed out however that we were running a certain risk if we still proceeded on hypothesis 1, namely that SNOW had never divulged to Dr Rantzau that his traffic had been controlled. If he had not done so this would account for the continued confidence of the Germans in TATE, which fact had been confirmed by the arrival yesterday of Richter. I explained that J.C. Masterman and T.A. Robertson were seeing SNOW today at his request but that if he did not make some sensational disclosure to the effect that he had never given the traffic away I thought that we might profit by allowing CELERY to go to Lisbon. The board agreed to this course of action.

I saw Henry Hopkinson and explained our point of view about Hess. He said that the matter was still on a very high plane and that Hess was not in the mood to discuss matters on our level. He told me that so far only the Duke of Hamilton and Ivone Kirkpatrick had seen him. I asked him about the microphones as I thought that a record of his conversations might be interesting, particularly if some of the appeasers were allowed to go in and see him. He told me that this matter was in charge of C and that all arrangements had been made. Hopkinson promised to keep our point of view in mind and I told him about the Gula Pfeffer letter and the importance of the *Innere Dienst*. I thought that Pfeffer's letter might possibly give us the opening we wanted.

Karel Richter has broken over the weekend. It now appears that he was dropped by parachute near Hatfield. He was taken to the spot and produced his parachute, wireless set and crystals and valves which he was bringing for TATE. It seems fairly clear that he is not the Richter who was commonly known as Clark Gable. Richter had been working for a Dr Schiltz. In the meantime we have been on the air and complained that the money had never arrived.

Cecil Liddell has discovered that Marschner is identical with Gunter Schutz. There seemed a reasonable possibility and the matter was confirmed by RAINBOW without the slightest hesitation.

Cecil Liddell and I flew from Manchester to Dublin to see Colonel Liam Archer of G-2. The flight which took 1½ hours was in a blacked out aeroplane and uneventful. We landed at Colinstown and I imagine must have passed straight over Lambay. Archer met us at the aerodrome and we went to his house to discuss. He was highly interested at the identification of Marschner with Gunter Schutz. I gave him a general picture of our work here and he seemed to have reached the same conclusions as ourselves about the German intelligence service. His experience so far of all the agents who landed in Eire, is that their plans were singularly ill-conceived and badly carried out. Marschner had been spotted wandering about by some woman who kept a hostel for the local police. He had asked his way and she became suspicious about him. The police were informed and he was easily rounded up. He had in his possession a wireless set, £1,000 in British notes and American dollars, a small microscope, a photograph of Werner Unland and a piece of paper identical with the paper on which Unland had written a number of his letters. This paper had brown streaks on it and a white border. He said that he was going to make contact with Unland and that the wireless set was to be fetched by some German agent who would come over from England. Archer does not believe this story so Unland has been arrested and was extremely evasive when questioned. He is admitting nothing unless the documentary evidence pins him down. Archer is firmly of the opinion that Marschner was intending to operate his wireless set in conjunction with Unland. Marschner's passport is a South African one but it was quite clear from an examination of it that the photograph had been changed and that the signature slip underneath it had been signed after it had been stuck on to the passport and covered by the embossed stamp.

Marschner had a story of a meeting with a British agent but Archer does not believe this. He thinks the story is put out in order to make the Eire authorities think that Schutz was not operating against them but against this country.

---

23 May

On my return to London I found that there had been a lot of excitement about the Hess-Haushofer case. Lord Swinton had written a rather offensive letter to the Director-General complaining that it was an outrage that he should not have been informed about this matter last November when the original letter was received. He argued that as the case was one of high political importance it should have been brought to his notice immediately. Everybody who was concerned in this case has been asked to give an account of himself. I have expressed the view that though the case was interesting one there was no particular point to it until we had found out what Haushofer's intentions were. There had been a certain delay in the Air Ministry getting hold of the Duke of Hamilton after we had satisfied ourselves that he was not intriguing behind the back of the government but had we known that he had had a previous letter from Haushofer in July 1939, which he had shown to the Prime Minister, we might have taken a different view and approached him direct at the outset. This was one of the disadvantages of Downing Street intelligence. As things had worked out it seemed a very good thing that Hamilton had not made contact with Haushofer. Had he done so, Hess would probably never have come here, since Haushhofer would have realised that any attempt to discuss peace terms would be quite useless.

The Germans have suggested a new plan for getting money to TATE. He is to take a bus No. 16 at 4 o'clock on a certain date from Victoria bus station. There will be on board a Japanese. TATE and the Japanese would get off at the first stop and get into the next 16 bus. The Japanese would carry *The Times* and a book in his left hand. TATE would get alongside him and ask him whether there is any news in the paper. The Japanese will then hand him the paper which will contain the money.

A message came though from SIS to say that a woman with good legs, not a Portuguese, was arriving on the plane from Lisbon. She was a German agent and had her instructions written into the margin of $50 notes. Some difficulty was experienced at the port as three ladies arriving on the plane appeared to qualify.

The most suspect was a Mrs Taylor who said she was the secretary of Pitt-Rivers but nothing could be found on her of an incriminating nature and therefore she had to be released but she is the subject of further investigation.

Mrs Taylor had been the BUF's Womens District Organiser for Sheffield before the war. An enthusiastic Nazi, Captain George Pitt-Rivers had taught in Germany and was detained under 18(b) between 1940 and 1942.

25 May

We had a further discussion about the Japanese party when it was decided not to follow. A watch is to be kept on likely people at their homes and at Berkeley Court and the embassy. The Special Branch officers who will be on the bus would proceed to Berkeley Court and the embassy as soon as the Japanese gets off and B6 will be on observation both before and after 4pm. An attempt will be made to get a photograph.

27 May

A message came through for TATE last night. The Japanese party is to be repeated on 29 and 31 May. On the night of 27/28 May four birch tree branches, each a metre long and with money in the thick end, are to be dropped near Luton. Two 200-pound bombs will be dropped in the direction of Charlton and the birch sticks will fall on the continuation of this line at a distance of roughly one to two kilometres from the second bomb crater. The Germans say that the failure of the Japanese meeting was due to delay in transmission which had to go by a roundabout route.

29 May

TRICYCLE is to go to America as an import and export merchant, as he cannot get the backing of his own Yugoslav Legation to proceed as a representative of the Ministry of Information. He has, nevertheless, got a letter from Walter Monckton which should be of assistance to him.

I have just heard that the Japanese party has been successful. We got £200 in brand new English notes in series. We took a photograph of the Japanese and he was subsequently trailed by two Special Branch women to the Japanese Embassy. There was some anxiety at one moment as things did not go according to plan. TATE and the Japanese, instead of getting off at the first halt, got off when the policeman held up the bus at a crossroads. They were therefore unable to take the next bus and four went by before they could get on board. This was rather disconcerting to the Special Branch men who were waiting for them further up the road. Fortunately Special Branch had arranged for a champion cyclist to follow up the bus. He saw what happened and went on ahead and warned all concerned.

The Japanese was identified as one of the assistant naval attachés, Lieutenant-Commander Minitory Yosii.

30 May

A Major Carter, who looks after the papers of the Chief of Staffs Committee in the War Cabinet, has leaked to a solicitor friend about the evacuation of Crete. He said that this policy had been decided on and gave details of the numbers to be evacuated each night. The solicitor revealed the whole thing to his fellow fire-watchers, one of whom happened to be a secretary employed at the Admiralty.

31 May

I spoke to the Director-General about Del Campo. He was reluctant at first to agree to the plan by which the bogus Del Campo would plant himself on Artaza. He has now agreed to let this go forward. I am very glad as Dick Brooman-White and Tommy Harris had taken a great deal of trouble.

Major Carter has been arrested and is to be tried by court-martial. Edward Hinchley-Cooke tells me that he is a very decent fellow. He had risen from the ranks and has many years service.

4 June

I arranged with Valentine Vivian about Semmerlbauer and Maas who are to be got down from Knapdale. Rudolf Hess is going to see somebody of consequence and wants a Nazi to be present as a witness.

5 June

Captain Savage of Special Operations Executive called today about one Arthur G. Sant, who had put forward a proposition for dropping unbreakable gramophone discs with appropriate speeches by parachute in German occupied territory. Sant was getting difficult and threatening to call in assistance of Members of Parliament. It was agreed that we would have Sant up to Room 055 and hint to him that if he did not behave himself there was such a thing as the Defence of the Realm Act.

6 June

ISOS traffic shows that CELERY is being treated with some skepticism. Georg Sessler is going to meet him and Dr Rantzau is returning from Cyrenaica.

We again discussed the case of Sam Stewart. It was decided that J.C. Masterman and I should interrogate him. I would cover the early party and Masterman would deal with SNOW's information. T.A. Robertson and Victor Rothschild would simultaneously interrogate Caldwell, and Baxter would deal with Davies.

Certain members of the Polish forces in Scotland have been plotting to kidnap and murder Rudolf Hess. It is difficult to say how far the matter has gone but it is of course the kind of thing they might attempt to do. We are taking steps to get hold of either the commanding officer or the officers themselves and explain to them what serious harm they might do both to their own cause and to the Allied cause if they attempt to do anything of the kind. This quite apart from what might happen to themselves. I think the Poles imagine that Hess may be making peace overtures and that this will be listened to by the British government. Nothing, of course, could be further from the truth.

It was evidently a great shock to Samuel Stewart to find himself under arrest. I went over all the early ground, where he found no difficulty in crossing most of the fences. The only really interesting point was brought out with reference to his association with an apparently quite harmless German named Pohl. This man was a refugee and had left for Haiti. He assured us that he had not had communication with this man whatever after he left this country. He then went on to explain how, in his position as the shipping agent, he would of course have facilities for passing letters out of the country. J.C. Masterman then took up the interrogation on the subject of his journey to Antwerp and subsequent relations with SNOW. Stewart's memory has been very good up to this point, but he soon became hesitant and evasive. He admitted that he recognised the photograph of SNOW and recalled having travelled with him on aircraft to Antwerp in February 1940. He said that he had met him on the aerodrome. In fact, he met him on Victoria Station and travelled with him to Folkestone. He said that he had lunched with him at Antwerp and had seen him there on one other occasion. He had never seen him in this country nor had he kept up the acquaintanceship. Masterman had read him out the gist of some telephone conversations with SNOW and asked him whether these were consistent with his statement that he had entirely dropped the acquaintanceship. He was obviously rather confused and when asked whether he had seen SNOW on any other occasion made a further denial. He was then told that we had positive evidence that the German secret service had confidence in him and it was suggested to him that he should consider very carefully what people he had seen at Antwerp and Hamburg and how this confidence in the minds of the Germans could have been built up. It was on this note that we left him.

Sam Stewart has applied to see his solicitor and the Home Office is reluctant to refuse this request. This means that his solicitor could warn everybody concerned in the case to keep their mouths shut, and will seriously impede our investigations. I went to see Sir Alexander Maxwell who was reluctant to give a definite refusal. He thought it would be best if the prison governor should tell Stewart that he should write to his solicitor. The letter would then be submitted for censorship and would probably not reach the solicitor until Monday. This would give us the necessary time to complete our enquiries. This is a typical illustration of how difficult it is to carry out investigations properly in a democracy which is fighting a totalitarian enemy.

I saw Valentine Vivian today and Richard Gambier-Parry was also present. I told him that in our meeting of the Radio Security Service committee we had discussed very carefully the importance of building up our staffs concerned in the production of ISOS. It seemed that Gambier-Parry was also going to intercept an increasing volume of material and it was therefore necessary for all those concerned in its production to increase their staffs. I thought also that it might be necessary to get higher authority to say that our requirements were to be met without the usual obstructions. The material was pure gold and everything should be done to develop it 100%. At present we only took 20% and even then we have difficulty in producing it.

CELERY has returned with an interesting report about Georg Sessler who returned to his project of selling out on the Germans provided he could get a free passage to America. He has further succeeded in confirming to himself that CELERY is working for us and this may have been his sole object. There is, however, a 30% chance that he is quite genuine in his desire to get away. He has told CELERY that he will be back on about 29 June and will apply to the barman at the Concha Bar in Lisbon for a note giving him instructions how to meet CELERY or his nominee. At this meeting the plan for Sessler's escape to England will be laid down. Dick White was very keen to go over to Lisbon himself to arrange this and to have a look at the SIS organisation on the spot. Personally this I think would be entirely wrong. It is obviously desirable that we should send somebody however, otherwise the job will not be carried through to our satisfaction.

Georg Sessler never defected and ended up living in Aix-en-Provence.

Dick White and I dined with Klop Ustinov. He gave us a rather sorry picture of his difficulties in Lisbon. He refused to work any longer under his section leader in SIS. One gathered that another job is to be found for him. He told us that quite adequate machinery existed in Lisbon for carrying out our enquiries and that he could only assume that the delays were due to a shortage of staff at head office and perhaps to some degree at Lisbon.

A Spanish captain called Martin Ocrana has turned up with high-grade secret ink disguised as VD medicine. When he was examined it was found that he had never had VD.

We have decided to send Cyril Mills to Lisbon to make the necessary contact, as it would obviously be impossible for CELERY to get another visa.

I saw Samuel Stewart at Brixton Prison and I went over the previous ground very carefully with him. He had recalled quite a number of things and I impressed upon him how important it was from his point of view to provide us with some explanation of his build-up with the German secret service. He gave me certain particulars, but nothing which could really explain matters.

RAINBOW has been further questioned. He admitted that he had been out taking photographs with Schutz and had seen him using a micro-camera. When asked why he had not told us this before, he said that he had spoken to Derek Sinclair about eighteen months ago.

The illicit wireless has now been found to be in the possession of the Poles, who were trying to communicate with one of their agents in Warsaw. They should of course have informed either ourselves or SIS what they were doing. It was only when the head of their service was pressed that he made enquiries and found that one of his subordinates had been operating for the last six days. While a good deal of time has been wasted it is at least satisfactory to think that the Radio Security Service has located the station.

Dick White and J.C. Masterman saw SNOW yesterday and went over the whole ground of his relations with Sam Stewart. His story was fairly consistent and in some respects amplified the information he had previously given. Personally, I think Stewart has got a lot to explain. The general impression is that he did wet his feet some time ago, although he can never have become very deeply implicated. Probably the Germans had a talent-spotter on him and came to the conclusion, owing to various small services he had rendered them, that he was the kind of person who could be easily approached. Things may not have gone further than this, but the general indications are that some kind of service was rendered at one time or another.

19 June

We had a Radio Security Service meeting. It was decided that the question of the circulation of Hugh Trevor Roper's analysis of ISOS should be discussed privately between him, Felix Cowgill, Dick White and myself. Dick and I feel that there is value in the work that he is doing. Cowgill's point is that he only wants the material to circulate if it is properly blanketed. Trevor Roper has a scholarly approach to the whole question and perhaps a better understanding of the system than anybody else. He is, however, somewhat of an intellectual snob. It was decided that if there was disagreement on the RSS Committee, Ted Maltby and I should take the matter to the Director-General and C, and if it further became necessary, to Lord Swinton as the final arbitrator.

22 June

I had a meeting at Bletchley Park at 11.30 which lasted till 4pm, with Richard Gambier-Parry, Ted Maltby, Felix Cowgill, Valentine Vivian and Alastair Denniston. We discussed the requirements that would have to be met in connection with ISOS and get a concrete programme. Gambier-Parry said that he expected a 65% increase. He hopes to have thirty double-channel Y stations making a total of 120 sets in the first year and he will add another 60 in the second year. At present the Radio Security Service is only listening to what is Group material. They are doing no research work and no policing of service traffic, neither are they taking any Italian secret service material, which might well be interesting. Further they are doing no figure cipher work. If RSS is successful in breaking Enigma another 65% of material will be added to the existing flow.

23 June

I saw Stewart Menzies about Section V. He had obtained the necessary sanction from Sir Alexander Cadogan and very much welcomes the assistance we are to give in personnel. He said that the Finns had for some time been decoding the Russian ciphers and passing the information to the Germans. I gather that we also have had the benefit of this service. We have now been obliged to inform the Russians of the position.

25 June

I had another discussion with the Director-General and Max Knight about the Manifold case. I pointed clearly that our objective should be the safeguarding of ISOS rather than the possibility of obtaining information which might incriminate Manifold. I thought that if Manifold were interrogated and denied any close connection with the Communist Party he would be bound to associate his removal to other spheres with any feelings that he might have about his political views. This might possibly lead to difficulties. On the other hand if he gave a free confession, the army might wish to kick him out. We should not have sufficient information to intern him under Emergency Regulation 18(b). He would be disgruntled and we could not prevent him from passing information which he might have obtained in MI8 to his Communist friends, if he has not already done so. I thought that if he could be transferred in a military intelligence capacity to some remote island this would probably be the best solution. I learned that the Director-General later decided he should not be interrogated.

26 June

The Director-General has looked into our domestic agency project and it has his full approval. We are going ahead and I understand that several quite useful applications have already come in. The question of having some relations with the Russian intelligence service has arisen. I feel that they should know a great deal about German espionage activities against this country. The approach is rather a delicate matter and we are proposing to open the ball with the Czechs.

27 June

Tin-Eye Stephens has had a row with Harold Dearden and it all arose from a rather trivial incident. Dr Dearden, as might be expected, went to William Charles Crocker and has written a rather carefully worded solicitor's letter. It was suggested that Tin-Eye should send an acknowledgement and suggest that Dearden should take a few days leave but I said I thought this might perhaps be unwise. It would probably be better to acknowledge the letter and say quite simply that as Tin-Eye was not in a position to accept Dearden's resignation he had forwarded the papers to the Director-General. I have sent the papers down to the D-G who is in the country and suggested that he should see Dearden personally and then decide whether the incident can be smoothed over, whether he should accept Dearden's resignation or whether he should conduct some enquiry into the incident and the relations between Stephens and his officers. I thought that an enquiry of the kind indicated would probably strengthen our hands when questions arose at a later date.

A man is expected from the other side in the course of the next two to three weeks and he will be bringing money for DRAGONFLY. Arrangements have been made for him to deliver this money at a special address where he will hand it over to the woman in charge.

28 June

There is a curious association between Almassy, the brother of the Count Almassy who has been working for the Germans in Egypt, Lisboa, of the Brazilian Embassy and Matsumoto of the Japanese Embassy who is known to engage in espionage. We are rather well-placed in this matter and hope to get useful information.

2 July

The Director-General has seen Dr Harold Dearden and Tin-Eye Stephens, and neither of them appears to desire to continue under existing conditions. The D–G has ordered Toby Pilcher to hold an enquiry before he decides whether to accept Dr Dearden's resignation.

Horsfall-Ertz has admitted before the Advisory Committee that he knew Mrs Mathilde Krafft and Kruger. He said that he had formerly denied this as he was threatened with the Treachery Act. We have decided to interrogate him further as soon as we have got hold of Mrs Krafft.

Commander Neville of the Naval Intelligence Division has brought over what would appear to be an interesting espionage case. The German standing orders taken from a captured submarine disclose that they have accurate information about our minefields and it is alleged in one instance about a projected minefield. The Admiralty does not think therefore that the leakage could have been through our ciphers being compromised, but I have detailed Herbert Hart to carry out the investigations, and have said to Neville that he must be given free access to all relevant documents.

3 July

I sent the full report about the Polish plot case to the Director-General today suggesting that he might wish to show it to Lord Swinton. It has disclosed that some seventeen Polish officers and possibly two British subjects had worked out a scheme to assassinate Rudolf Hess but it seemed that as the plot was due to take place on 19 May the project might well have been abandoned. Stephen Alley says that the Poles are always formulating plots and schemes, most of which never materialise, but that you can never be quite certain that they will not go off the deep end without much warning. The Poles seem to think that Hess may have come here to offer peace negotiations and that the British government may succumb to the idea of leaving the Poles in the hands of Germany.

The Director-General was very annoyed that this matter had not been previously brought to his notice. He felt that if anything should happen his position and that of the whole office would have been quite untenable. He had no fault to find with the way in which the enquiry had been conducted. I said that I quite agreed that I should have informed him but that I had no intention of deliberately withholding the information. The fact was that my day was so full that if I could not get into him at a given moment it was sometimes difficult to recollect what I had told him and what I had not.

4 July

I had lunch with Laporte, who is now Chef de Cabinet to Admiral Muselier. He gave me a long account of himself, how he had left *Le Matin*, gone to the Agence Fournier, and on the outbreak of war had been sent to this country as assistant air attaché. When the collapse came his chief returned to France but he asked Archie Boyle that he himself might be interned. This was done and when he emerged he was posted to Muselier's staff. We discussed the Muselier case at great length and I think I convinced him of all the various difficulties which we had encountered. I explained to him how the whole thing had happened and how I hoped for once and for all the suggestion had been dispelled from the minds of the French that we were in any way trying to pry into their private affairs. We had helped to set up Howard's Bureau merely because we wanted some representative French body with whom to deal on security matters. We were interested in French security matters only in so far as they affected the security of this country and we felt that the closest cooperation is necessary. We had a great deal of machinery at our disposal and we could undoubtedly render a great deal of assistance to the French. Laporte was very friendly and I think he will be a useful ally. I am going to introduce him to Kenneth Younger when I come back from the regions. In the meantime he gave me the name of a woman called Jeannette Hart who, he said, was pursuing the cipher officer.

CELERY has got an offer to go to Brazil or to work for SO2 in France. I am going to try and get Section V to use him in Brazil.

Mrs Mathilde Krafft has been arrested.

5 July

I saw General Sir Alan Hunter and Colonel James Coats about the Polish plot. Hunter knew Alfgar Hesketh-Pritchard who was one of the Englishmen thought to be concerned, and seems to be of an SO2 type. He attached himself to the Guards at the beginning of the war and was rather a nuisance. He was a very good shot and interested in sniping. General Hunter suggested that as Hesketh-Pritchard had been at RAF Ringway parachute training centre with de Rema we might interrogate him about the whole affair. He could be very useful to the plotters since he would have access to the Guards' mess at Pirbright and might find out quite lot about Rudolf Hess. We also considered the question of putting checks on the Poles in Scotland and London. Edward Hinchley-Cooke is to go down to Camp Z on Monday with Coats in order to acquaint the commandant with the position and study the general layout.

Alfgar Hesketh-Pritchard was to be killed on a mission in Yugoslavia for SOE in 1944.

I saw Peter Loxley at the Foreign Office and told him about the case of Comtesse de Jonghe who has now arrived here carrying a Belgian bag which seems to have been opened. It was decided that we should draw the attention of somebody at the Belgian Embassy to this fact when returning the bag.

I also saw Stewart Menzies and explained the position to him and he agreed to this procedure. He told me that Hess had attempted to commit suicide by throwing himself over the banisters but had only succeeded in breaking his leg. His mental state is said to be improving and he may possibly broadcast, at some future date. He is not so suspicious about his food being poisoned as he was.

Madame de Jonghe has been interrogated and seems to have given a fairly good account of herself. We have tried twice to return the bag to the Belgian Embassy but on each occasion have not succeeded in finding a responsible official who could take it over.

Anthony Blunt rang up to say that the Spanish Consul-General was going out on Tuesday. We decided that if his bag was not properly sealed by the Foreign Office that we should send him back or take it over and return it ourselves.

I saw de Rema about the Polish plot to murder Rudolf Hess. De Rema made a very good impression and he has obviously handled the whole business with great ability and discretion. He thought that it would be wise for him to go up to Scotland on some pretext in order to find out whether there were any developments there. He could sound out Colonel Sosabowski and also visit Fort William, where the Poles had a special training school. I suggested to him that it might be a good plan if some minister of standing, preferably the Prime Minister if he could spare the time, could visit Polish units and explain to them our aims and objects in the present struggle and the meaning of certain political events which took place in this country. They would not then be worrying their heads about irresponsible statements made by politicians in the House of Commons and elsewhere. I thought too that something in the nature of entertainment would also be a good thing, and suggested films with Polish captions. De Rema was enthusiastic about both ideas and pressed me again and again to get something done on the lines suggested and said the great thing was to keep the minds of the Poles occupied during their leisure hours. They were intensely patriotic and desperately keen to be in the fight but there were times that they felt very much at a loose end. It was during these moments that they were likely to be scheming and hatching plots. I mentioned this matter to the Director-General and he is having it taken up by Lord Swinton. De Rema told me that they were having a certain amount of trouble with the older men who felt that it was a point of honour for them to join the parachute troops. The result of this had been rather serious. The jump apparently affected their hearts, they became unconscious and then injured themselves when landing.

The Director-General and I saw the Lord President, Neville Chamberlain, and Lord Swinton about the Polish plot. The Lord President seemed satisfied with the action taken and agreed with us that it was essential that de Rema's position should in no way be compromised. He thought however that Alfgar Hesketh-Pritchard might be interviewed since this could be done without raising difficulties for de Rema. He thought that we ought to endeavour to reach a position where we could disclose the whole matter to the Polish authorities without jeopardising de Rema's position, as he felt that if any incident occurred the results would be disastrous whether it was successful or not.

12 July

Gehrdt van Wijk, who arrived here from Spain a short time ago, has now confessed that he was sent here by the Germans. He originally had a business in Spain but on mobilisation he joined his regiment in Holland. After the defeat of the Dutch forces he applied to go back to Spain and was approached there by a German agent called Pablo and suggestions were made to him that he should work for Germany. He was reminded that his wife and family were still in Holland. He was first sent on some financial mission to Holland but was not able to bring the negotiations to a successful conclusion. Finally, it was suggested to him that he should go to England and after considerable difficulties he managed to get away from Lisbon. He had been instructed in the use of secret ink.

13 July

There was a discussion last week by the Security Executive on the CPGB and enlistment in the army. The general opinion seemed to be that Communistically-inclined workmen might be less harmful in the army than the factory, but the whole question is to be referred back to the army. The general, most important, point as to whether Communists enlisted in the army should be eligible for officer rank, does not seem to have been raised.

15 July

I lunched at the Savoy with William Charles Crocker and he seemed in very good mood. Before lunch we had a cocktail with Newnham, the ex-editor of *Truth*, Gordon-Lennox, Michael Arlen and Commander Grenfell, who had just written a book on sea power. Gordon-Lennox remembered having met me at the house of Brocas Burrows and having talked with me about Russia. He wanted to get hold of me for some time. I told him he could ring Room 055. I am not very anxious to meet him, as I do not altogether trust him.

16 July

The Twenty Committee has got a plan known as MIDAS. The idea is to get the Germans to send over a large sum of money which will be held here by some selected individual who will make the necessary payments to agents in the United Kingdom. TRICYCLE has succeeded in getting the Germans to bite but they propose to send over their own representative who will effect the disbursements. He will get the money from our agent who will be reimbursed by the opening of a credit which TRICYCLE will take with him to America.

The office of the Japanese naval attaché has, with characteristic impertinence, asked some electrical institute here to give them full details about the grid system. The writer of the letter is Willis, who has been known to us for some time.

We do not think Willis engages in espionage but he knows which side his bread is buttered.

DRAGONFLY has had quite a success in putting over a story about a possible invasion of Norway. ISOS material discloses that his report is confirmed from other sources.

17 July

MUTT and JEFF 's plan for assisting the immigration authorities in the examination of Norwegian arrivals seems to be developing satisfactorily.

The Spanish press attaché, Alcazar de Velasco has returned owing to the spineless attitude of the Foreign Office. Lord Swinton and the Lord President have expressed the view that he should not come, but just before we had been notified of this fact, not directly but through Valentine Vivian, we had given the Foreign Office what we felt was an overwhelming case for declaring Velasco *persona non grata*. The day before the man arrived they sent us over their files which concluded with a minute in the following terms: It seems that Velasco is likely to be with us again before long. The only action taken had been an attempt to enlist the support of Alba and his Counsellor, Villaverde, who was to try and persuade Alcazar not to come, but if he failed it was felt that nothing could be done without running the risk of reprisals. Swinton was extremely annoyed that the case had not been reinforced by his view and that of the Lord President and doled out a raspberry to me in front of the Director-General. On examining the minutes of our file I found that the Director-General had approved our action. He readily recognised the position and very generously took the file over to Swinton and told him that the fault was partly his, for not writing to him instead of Valentine Vivian and partly the Director-General's, for not weighing in and making use of the ministerial backing at an earlier stage. It is very refreshing to have a chief who is ready to stand up for his officer and the department.

22 July

Findlater Stewart is worried about TATE's reply to a request for information about Coventry. He thinks that if TATE is allowed to report everything that he has seen, Coventry will inevitably be bombed. He has accordingly amended the message which now gives the impression that a great deal of dispersal has taken place. He wishes to raise the whole question of policy with the Wireless Board.

Herbert Hart who is continuing his enquiry into the leakage of information about our minefields, has now discovered that there is another document which shows quite clearly that at least four of the minefields were disclosed to the enemy through charts taken from the sunken submarine *Shark*. This document proves Hart's previous conclusions that the information contained in the original German document was probably obtained from operational charts, taken from sunken warships. If we had had the second document before, we might have been saved a good deal of time and trouble.

23 July

There has been a bad case of leakage regarding a special convoy which is proceeding direct to Malta. The result has been that one destroyer has been sunk, a cruiser torpedoed and one of the supply ships torpedoed. The cruiser has got back to Gibraltar and the rest of the convoy, including the damaged supply ship, is going on. It is clear from an Italian intercept that the approach of this convoy was known about on 16 July. Enquiry shows that the security arrangements for the assembly of the goods and the convoy were absolutely lamentable. Packing cases arrived labelled 'Malta NAAFI', telegraphed in an obvious code about the arrival of stores and the Crown Agents notified at least a hundred firms about goods required for Malta. There were, moreover, a number of ships in port while the loading was going on and a good many of them left for Eire and other destinations before the convoy.

24 July

BALLOON has got a cheque for £350 from Lisbon.

I saw Sir Alexander Maxwell about Joseph Lenihan and he agreed to his being detained at Camp 020 and suggested that pending the clearing up of his case he should be detained under the Arrival From Enemy Territory Act.

25 July

We had a conference about Joseph Lenihan and we came to the conclusion that the only use we could make of him would be by impersonation. Lenihan was dropped in the Curragh with instructions to send weather reports to Sligo, and to proceed to England in order to obtain information about air raid damage. He had given himself up in Northern Ireland because he had a criminal record in the south. He is wanted for unlawful assembly, presumably in connection with an IRA meeting, and has also done time for fraud. The Irish have already discovered his parachute, and his set, which has not so far been taken, is left at a house on the Eire side of the border.

The Group traffic shows that three Norwegians who arrived here a short time ago, are in fact German agents. The principal is a man called Ingard Nilsen and another is named George Lunde. The ship in which they arrived is the *Hernie*. One of them is now on a coastal vessel, another at a London hotel, and Nilsen has been sent to join the Norwegian force. We are taking steps to pull them in. The Norwegians, when questioned, said they had never been very satisfied about them.

26 July

A man, Karl Streser, has been discovered in Dorset in battledress and he states that he's a German and that he came here with a Hitler Jugend party in 1937. It has been discovered that he is a deserter.

Roger Moore of the Royal Ulster Constabulary has come to an agreement with his contact in the Garda Siochana by which we are to be lent Lenhan's wireless set for eight days. We are to lend the auxiliary one-way set to the Eire government for a similar period. Before the agreement was signed the matter was referred to Eamon de Valera.

We have scored a great success with Alcazar de Velasco. He has handed £50 to G.W. in the presence of Luis Calvo. This money was a repayment for a sum borrowed by del Pozo. Alcazar has promised to obtain another £500. I hope the Foreign Office will now be convinced that we were right in saying that Velasco was a German agent and should be declared *persona non grata*. The trouble is that we are not able to get rid of him owing to the delicate source of our information. We may, however, succeed in working him to our advantage.

Our agent has discovered that Lisboa has a report on our aircraft. Matsumoto, with whom she is also acquainted, has under the influence of drink, disclosed that the Japanese contemplate an attack on the Dutch East Indies.

THE SNARK, also known as KISSMEQUICK, has arrived with the meagre sum of £10.

27 July

I spoke to Bill Stephenson about the case of Max Jordan of NBC and he said he would look into the whole matter on his return. There had been so much wire-pulling that it was almost impossible to know where we stood.

28 July

I saw Bill Stephenson again and he told me about certain technical apparatus which the Americans were using. They have a very good camera which can be easily concealed in a wireless set. There is no click, it merely makes the ordinary wireless noises. The Americans also use a special device for tapping in to telephones. This can be clamped on an outside wall and is apparently very effective.

29 July

We had a Radio Security Service meeting at which ISOSOCLES was discussed. This is the Vichy–Berlin Group traffic which we do not normally receive. There have been at least three cases where we have not been informed about matters which have a definite counter-espionage interest. The meeting felt that they could not properly assess priorities unless they were in possession of all intercepted material. I was asked to take this matter up with Valentine Vivian or C.

We had another meeting about Joseph Lenihan and decided that we should abandon the idea of using his set. We propose to send a message in secret ink indicating that he has managed to get over here and has established contact with an IRA friend in Liverpool and will ask for instructions. We shall have to keep him permanently at Camp 020 but we may be able to work him through a cut-out.

I learned that during my absence there had been a certain amount of trouble with MUTT and JEFF. JEFF and his keeper had apparently got rather tight in Aberdeen and had ended by getting themselves arrested. The chief constable was extremely annoyed because he had not been informed about their presence in the area. He was also deeply shocked that MI5 should conduct their affairs in such a manner. Unfortunately we cannot explain to him the full facts and the difficulties in running the double-cross business. JEFF was apparently asking very indiscreet questions in pubs and taking down the answers in his notebook. This very naturally aroused the suspicions of the publican who informed the police.

There has been a great anxiety over Plan MIDAS. TRICYCLE made a number of mistakes and began by sending his telegram from Eric Sand instead of Eric Glass. This led to endless complications but the situation cleared up when we found that instead of somebody from their side arriving to collect the money, TATE received instructions to do the job. It then became clear that what we thought to be an independent plan by the Germans to build up TATE and make him a centre for running agents was in the minds of the Germans, Plan MIDAS. The two plans were married and all is now well. TATE is in the position of paymaster and we should before long have £20,000 to our credit in New York.

Two Frenchmen, called Poullain and Gonhouilou have arrived at the Royal Victoria Patriotic School with a curious story. They are both journalists of some standing, and one of them was formerly editor of *La Petite Gironde*. They say that on the excuse of going to Morocco to buy up a number of French papers they succeeded in getting an exit visa. They had previously had conversations with highly placed individuals at Vichy including General Hunziger whom they regard as being anti-Nazi. In Morocco they got in touch with a member of the French air force called Giradot who had some plot to overthrow Vichy elements in Morocco and take command. The success of such a venture seemed somewhat problematical at the moment since the navy was anti-British, the air force ready to take orders from its high command and the army doubtful. It has been suggested that Poullain should intimate to Giradot after the French broadcast on 5 August whether he was to start to a revolt or whether he was to try and come over here to join General de Gaulle. As this was a matter of high policy we felt it difficult to release these two Frenchmen until we had some idea of the view taken in high quarters here. Being a bank holiday, nearly all those concerned were away. We succeeded in getting in touch with the Director of Military Intelligence who agreed that we could not hold these men any longer without causing a good deal of trouble particularly since one of them was a personal friend of Admiral Muselier. The DMI did not think that a putsch in Morocco was desirable at the moment and undertook to get in touch with Desmond Morton. In the meantime they are being seen by Willoughby of the Spears Mission and will be fixed up at the Cumberland Hotel for the night.

6 August

RAINBOW has received a letter in Portuguese. One of the full-stops on examination has been found to contain a message of a hundred words. RAINBOW had been warned that he might expect some communication in this form. The process is micro-photography.

SNOW's son has made a suggestion that he should go to occupied France and make contact with a number of our agents. He intimated that he had some sort of contact with the Germans which would make him acceptable if he went to Lisbon. After an hour and a half's interrogation by T.A. Robertson and J.C. Masterman he confessed that he had before the war supplied information about the aerodrome at Biggin Hill to his father's postbox address in Hamburg. We have now to decide whether he would be locked up. He is a frightful little worm.

There is a story going about Fleet Street that the Prime Minister has gone to meet President Roosevelt, who is on a cruise in his yacht *Potomac*. The story is said to have reached this country via the Trans-Ocean German News Service in Lisbon. The story of the meeting happens to be true. It is not surprising that it has been leaked, because Brendon Bracken has been hinting to the press that they will have a grand story before long. They certainly will have a grand story if the Prime Minister and the President go to the bottom of the Atlantic.

Special Material shows that Grotwohl has passed the story on to someone in the Greek Legation and that John Dulanty is talking about it to Joe Walsh. The whole matter seems to have been handled extremely badly. The whole press knows about it here and doubtless the story is raging across America like an advertisement for a new toothpaste.

A German by birth, Professor Grotwohl was naturalised in 1869 and from 1903 to 1912 he worked as Professor of French at the Universities of Bristol and Dublin. He also worked for the Daily Telegraph *and was on the payroll of the Greek, Rumanian and Saudi Arabian Embassies. He was later connected with the Poles and with the Turkish and Argentine Embassies, and acted as an unpaid secretary for Selwyn Lloyd MP at the Foreign Office. He had been close to Dr Siebert, doyen of the Nazi press corps in London, and passed information to the Japanese Embassy.*

14 August

I lunched with Valentine Vivian and the Director-General when we discussed the question of BJs. I tried to press home my point that if we were to make a proper study of developments here it was essential for us to have as much information, both positive and negative, as we could obtain. BJs were especially valuable since it was in communications of this sort that they expressed their innermost thoughts.

Valentine Vivian was rather inclined to take the view we should limit our requirements. I said that it was for this reason that I had suggested that Anthony Blunt should
do down periodically to GC&CS and make notes. This would save everyone a great
deal of trouble and avoid filing a large amount of this material in our office.

After the meeting I had a long talk with Felix about the difference between our
two departments. A good deal of suspicion had arisen in his mind on account of a
number of minor and rather trivial incidents which he had pieced together. What
he had really liked doing more than anything else was running special agents. It had
been a great wrench for him to hand over TRICYCLE and the situation had been
aggravated because he thought that T.A. Robertson's people did not trust him to
do his work and felt that they had to give him minute instructions about what
TRICYCLE had to do abroad. He felt that he was becoming merely a postbox. I tried
to explain to him that there was a certain feeling here that he was reluctant to give
us information about what was happening abroad, and that this was vital to our
work here. I did not think there could be any dividing line between us. We ought
to have a free run of his files and he ought to have a free run at ours, since our
interests were identical. At the moment I felt there was a hiatus and that for that
reason the information in our two departments was not being properly collated. I
think the meeting did a great deal to clear the air, at any rate I hope so. I drew his
attention to the vital mass of information which I thought wrongly had been often
referred to as being of purely local significance. We wanted details of cafes, rendezvous, enemy and neutral organisations abroad, otherwise we had nothing to pit
against the stories of arrivals from abroad at the RVPS. It was essential that this
information should be carefully carded and readily available.

15 August

Josef Jacobs was shot this morning after trial by court-martial. Edward Hinchley-
Cooke saw him a few hours before and was very impressed by his pluck and calm
bearing.

A cousin of Toby Pilcher's, who is commanding a battalion of the Guard at
Windsor is under arrest for communicating information obtained from an intelligence summary to Kenneth de Courcy.

25 August

I learned on my return that Campkin, whom we had recently sent to Section V, had
committed suicide but there is no reason to think that he had any sinister motive.
He apparently suffered from some nervous disease for which he had been receiving
treatment. He may have taken an overdose of the drug which was given to him and
under its influence placed his head in a gas oven. All his papers have been examined
without result.

Helmik Wallem, one of three Norwegians who arrived on the *Hernie,* has broken after interrogation at Camp 020. He admits that he is a German agent; that he

was sent over here in order that the British might employ him as a double-cross and send him back to Norway where he would have operated a wireless set under control. He says that his colleagues Nilsen and Lunde are not involved.

Plan MIDAS does not appear to be working quite as we arranged. The traffic indicates that the money is to be used for building up an organisation under TATE rather than for payment of other agents already established. This is deduced from the fact that DRAGONFLY used to receive his money from other sources. TRICYCLE has arrived safely and our £20,000 has been safely banked in New York.

26 August

We had an RSS meeting at which the question of Hugh Trevor Roper's notes and their circulation were discussed. Those notes are excellent value in explaining the significance of ISOS material. For some reason or other Felix Cowgill does not wish them circulated to the recipients of ISOS. Ewen Montagu is pressing for them and Oliver Strachey of GC&CS wants them too.

27 August

I spoke to the Director-General today about the RVPS and said that we were very anxious to put Jim Hale in as our intelligence representative. He took exception to this on account of Hale being a lawyer. He said that lawyers were all right when they had briefs but that policemen were better at attracting information from people about whom nothing was known. I said I did not think his argument applied in Hale's case since he had considerable experience in this office and had done a lot of useful interrogation work. It was obviously no good pursuing the matter at that stage.

SNOW's son has been interned under Emergency Regulation 18(b).

28 August

There has been an interesting development in the *Hernie* case. Helmik Wallem, George Lunde and Ingard Nilsen arrived on 8 August. On 11 August there was a statement in the Norwegian broadcast about Quislings in the Brandt Club which I imagine is a club in Oslo. ISOS mentioned on the same date that the safe arrival of the Norwegians travelling on the *Hernie* had been signalled through the Norwegian broadcast. Nilsen stated that he heard a Norwegian broadcast on 11 August with the statement about the Brandt Club and that this was the signal for the party's safe arrival. We wondered how the message had reached the Norwegian authorities. There is a good deal to be cleared up here. There is a suggestion that the information may have been passed to the Norwegian government by Bjorkelund, the Norwegian Consul in Lerwick. One Oxenwald is concerned with the Norwegian broadcasts at the BBC and it transpires that his wife is actually the owner of the *Hernie*.

Martin Forrest came to see me. He is very anxious that RSLOs should be given instruction in *agent provocateur* work. There is I think a good deal in his suggestion. While we are probably doing as much as we can about long-term espionage and about new arrivals I feel sure that there remains quite a lot to be done in the Fifth Column field. I am sure that there are a number of people who would be prepared to assist the enemy in time of invasion. For the moment they are dormant and only by provocation will they be induced to show their hand. I am arranging for a meeting at which specific cases shall be discussed in considerable detail by the officers who have been handling them. I am also suggesting that RSLOs should bring any suitable cases for general discussion and advice.

MUTT has been asked whether a German agent would be likely to get in here in the guise of a deserter, and what his fate would be likely to be. We have replied that the English are so gullible that provided he had a good story he might quite easily get away with it. We thought however that it would be preferable that he should be an Austrian or Sudeten German.

Arrangements are being made for Kuznetzoff to be seen by some member of the Soviet Embassy. In the meantime he has been writing his early history which is quite interesting. He has done quite a lot of espionage work for the Soviet Government.

There has been a little trouble with Joseph Lenihan who was being held under the Arrival from Enemy Territory Act. We had to get an 18(b) order but we refrained from serving it as we did not wish to upset Lenihan before he had been seen by Moore of the Royal Ulster Constabulary. Moore still thinks that Lenihan made some contact in Southern Ireland before crossing the border. There is a gap of three days between the expiry of the Arrival from Enemy Territory and the serving of the 18(b) orders. This has been made clear to the Home Office and I do not anticipate that we shall have any trouble.

The DMI does not want CELERY to go to Brazil. T.A. Robertson and I went to see him and persuaded him of the desirability of this move. He agreed that CELERY should go provided we could obtain the sanction of the other members of the Board. Personally, I think the DMI is rather going outside the province and had he refused to let CELERY go I should have raised the matter with the Director-General. The question of sending agents abroad must be a matter for SIS and ourselves. It would be an impossible situation if we had to consult the Directors of Intelligence every time we wanted to send a man out of the country.

2 September

I attended a meeting at the Foreign Office with C and Sir Alexander Cadogan, to decide about the suggested exchange of Gerlach and others for a number of our diplomats and consular officers. I had previously drawn C's attention to the fact that Gerlach was a secret service man and should therefore be exchanged on a secret service basis. He made this point very clear to Cadogan and said that had he been acquainted of what was going on at an earlier date he would have suggested Richard Stevens as an exchange for Gerlach. Cadogan was afraid that if such a suggestion were now introduced it would wreck the negotiations which had been going on for months. He accepted the principle however put forward by C. I mentioned Baron Oyenhausen as another man who should bargained for on a secret service basis. He is not included in the present party and his status will be borne in mind in any future negotiations. It seems that the Prime Minister had put in a last-minute suggestion that we should bargain with the Germans captured in Iran instead of with Gerlach and company, but the Foreign Office turned this down, on account of the negotiations being so far advanced. Cadogan thought that if we could effect one exchange confidence would be established and other exchanges would be possible.

3 September

G.W. has received £160 through Luis Calvo from Angel Alcazar de Velasco. This is merely in payment for a bogus document showing divisional signs. Alcazar is apparently extremely pleased with his purchase. He will doubtless sell the pup to the Germans at considerably larger sums and in due course be reprimanded for making such a fool of himself. We now have a fairly clear case for having him declared *persona non grata*.

4 September

A Belgian seaman named Alphons Timmerman has been arrested and has confessed to being a spy. He had with him all the requisites including secret ink.

5 September

There has been an interesting ISOS case. It became apparent that three Norwegians, Sverre, Stefansen and Elverstadt, were preparing for some expedition. The message said Iraq but it was difficult to see why three Norwegians should be going to that country. Hugh Trevor Roper discovered that the 'Q' was probably a misprint for 'X' and that the 'R' was probably a misprint for a 'D'. This left IDA in inverted commas since X is used for this purpose. IDA is the speller in German Morse code for I. This leaves I in inverted commas and from the context it seemed likely to be Iceland. A telegram to Iceland has produced a reply that a boat called the *Hornfjell* recently arrived with eight crew and passengers, three of them being

Saetrang, Stefansen, and Elverstad so they are all being sent over here for examination. This case is a clear indication of Trevor Roper's value.

General de Gaulle seems to have thoroughly blotted his copybook, in Africa, Egypt and Syria. He has been talking a lot against the British and saying that he would like to place his movement under the American flag. The Prime Minister is extremely annoyed and has given orders that no department is to have any relations with him for the time being. As this order has never reached us we are in the ironical position of being his only friends.

General de Gaulle has apparently become very swollen-headed while Admiral Muselier, on the other hand, has made a declaration of loyalty to the Prime Minister. There is some anxiety lest de Gaulle should attempt to leave the country and we have been asked to do what we can. Our task is not an easy one since in the classic phrase "it is important that his suspicions should not be aroused in any way".

I had a talk with William Malkin about Alcazar de Velasco. I told him that we had caught him out but that we did not wish to make use of this information. Alcazar had talked a great deal in an anti-British and pro-Nazi way during his stay in this country and I hoped that the Foreign Office could make use of this information in telling the Spanish authorities both here and in Madrid that he could no longer be regarded as *persona grata*. An alternative suggestion, that a question should be asked about him in the House of Commons, was not favourably received. I said that our object would be achieved if we could let it be widely known in Falange circles that people of the type of Alcazar could not come here and act in the way he had with impunity. If this were not done we might expect to see more of his kind. Makins said that if I would let him have a note he would take the matter up.

I had a conference with Dick White, T.A. Roberston and Grogan about inks. Tests are going on twice a week on different days of the week but so far, nothing has been discovered.

It was decided:

1. to continue the major test on Lisbon mails for another two weeks and then to try all major towns in Spain and Portugal where it is known that cover addresses exist.
2. that Dick White would consider, after consultation with Major Cowgill, the circulation of a list of cover addresses obtained from secret sources to Censorship at Bermuda, since a recent case has shown that at least one of these addresses is common to both agents in this country and in America.
3. that copies of all information about the dates of each major test be sent direct by Mr Grogan to SIS. SO2 have said that they are not affected, although exactly why I cannot understand.

4. that Major Robertson would consult with Major Cowgill about having certain of his letters submitted to the major test, since it would obviously be suspicious if all the letters from his agents bore no trace of a test. Grogan pointed out that we should not get an exaggerated view about this because even though a bi-weekly test was going on it would never be possible to say that a letter on a certain date should have been tested. Much would depend on the office of origin of the letter. If it came from Scotland there might be anything up to a forty-eight hour internal delay.

5. that Major Robertson would consider the advisability of putting through an [XXXXXXXXXXXXXXXXX] letter on a day that a major test was being made.

6. that Major Robertson would make enquiries about BASKET's ink and other inks being used by the Germans in order to see whether they can be successfully brought up and expunged.

Further enquiries have been made about the Norwegian broadcast in the *Hernie* case and as far as we can see at the moment, the broadcast was an extraordinary coincidence. Before the departure of the *Hernie* the question of Quislings in the Brandt Club at Bergen had been a matter of general talk and speculation in Norway. As a matter of hot news certain data on this subject had been transmitted from Stockholm via the Norwegian legation through the Norwegian section of the BBC here. By coincidence, those travelling by the *Hernie* had chosen a reference to the Quislings in the Brandt Club as their code message signifying their arrival in this country.

It is now established that Oxenwald's wife did not own the *Hernie* but one of the other boats that had been suggested for the expedition. There is still a certain amount of doubt about Olssen, the Norwegian vice-consul at Lerwick, who is to be questioned. It is clear that in future we shall have to arrange that Norwegians at Lerwick are sent straight down to the Royal Victoria Patriotic School without making contact with either the consul or the vice-consul. The present arrangement, by which the Norwegian authorities and local representatives of SO2 make contact in the first instance, will have to cease.

10 September

The Royal Ulster Constabulary has received a request through their contact in the Garda Siochana for information about Dr Hermann Goertz, the German spy who got five years' imprisonment here sometime before the war. He served about three and a half years and was released before the war. It would be interesting know how the Eire authorities have got hold of his name.

In the meantime he reconstructed the document and also gave us certain coded messages with the *en clair* underneath. These should prove valuable to GC&CS. I think we are well out of a difficult situation.

I attended a meeting of the Wireless Board to discuss the vetting of wireless traffic and secret ink communications, in answer to questionnaires put to TRICYCLE. It was decided that this should be done by the local Joint Intelligence Committee in

Washington DC. I put forward a paper about sabotage which had been prepared by B1(a). We wanted to get it accepted in principle that in order to build up MUTT and JEFF we should be allowed to blow things up. We thought there was an advantage to be gained from getting some sort of control over enemy sabotage activities in this country. If we could satisfy them that they had an organisation for the purpose they would be less likely to attempt anything of the kind through other channels. It was thought on the whole that we should use service, rather than civilian, establishments for the purpose since the inevitable activities of the press, police, etc could be more easily controlled. We have, in fact, been asked to blow up food dumps and we shall have to think out ways and means for inducing the enemy to concentrate more on bomb stores or the like.

11 September

Nakimura has applied to go to Stratford and thence to Leamington Spa. Desmond Orr thinks that he will almost certainly lose his way and go on to Coventry and the Director of Military Intelligence is anxious that we should have him followed and, if possible, catch him out. This all seems to me to be rather a waste of time as it would be much simpler if there was a general ruling that attachés could not go to any places of military, naval or air importance and that if they applied to go elsewhere they should be confined to a radius of five miles. I have arranged with Scotland Yard to have Nakimura followed.

12 September

Desmond Orr is in a fever about the Japanese. It seems that Anthony Blunt has made careful arrangements about Nakimura and was going to have him watched at his hotel at Leamington Spa so he therefore called off the police observation by Scotland Yard. Orr says that this has let him down in the eyes of the War Office and everybody else. I told him that it was entirely my fault for thinking that I was dealing with the case *de novo*. Had Anthony been here, I should of course have asked him to make the arrangements and he would then have told me that this had already been done. Orr seemed to think that he ought to have been kept informed of every move in the game. He did know in fact that certain arrangements were being made by the Deputy DMI who approached Orr with the suggestion about Scotland Yard. Carlisle, of MI(L) was au fait but evidently did not tell the Deputy DMI.

There has been an interesting sabotage case. It was noticed that a curious white powder was coming out of a large tin of eggs which had been imported to this country from Shanghai on the *Tacoma Star*. On further examination it was found that the case was packed with magnesium and contained a clock bomb of a type which has been definitely identified as German. A large number of the tins had already been taken away and placed in cold storage, and the labour involved in digging them out would be so colossal that a chance will have to be taken. The indications are that the tin was not tampered with *en route* and that it was probably filled by the packing firm. Enquiry in Shanghai shows that the firm is Henningsen & Company and that the head of the packing department is a White Russian named J.M. Kopelman.

13 September

The Twenty Committee has started a new idea which is be known as Plan TRELLIS. A bank representative here with a German background goes to Lisbon and says that he has been sent there by the British to act as a double-cross. He declares that he is thoroughly pro-German and suggests he should be taken on in his present role as a German agent. They will know that anything he sends from this country will be under control. He will, however, have the opportunity of sending them other information and will of course be able to visit them from time to time. He suggests further that they will be able to learn something from our misleading traffic. He will ask for a wireless set.

15 September

It has been arranged that TATE shall be caught in the general round-up of those who have not registered, but that his excuses shall be accepted by the authorities here. This will result in his having to do certain work which will restrict his movements and make it easier for us to decline to give certain information. RAINBOW has received an [XXXXXXXXXXXXXXXX] concealed inside the packing of a tin of coffee. The ink was on a small piece of cotton-wool which has to be dipped in water. The whole package came through Customs and Censorship without the slightest difficulty.

Guy Burgess came to see me about Peter Hutton of the News Department of the Foreign Office who had disclosed to our Swiss contact information obtained from telegrams between Stalin and the Prime Minister. Hutton had done this in an off-the-record talk and was nervous lest his Swiss friend might have passed the information further, since enquiries were being made as to how Freddie Kuh had become so well informed on the subject of these telegrams. The fact is that all these people in the News Department have their pet journalists and that there is rivalry among all members of the department in being sought after by the most prominent journalists. The journalists, of course, like to go to the people who will tell them most and the result may well be deplorable. The difficulty in this case is that if Hutton is made a scapegoat our very important relations with our Swiss contact may be jeopardised. I think we shall have to tell William Codrington and suggest to him that this incident should be used more as an occasion to tighten things up generally in the News Depertment than to take drastic action against one individual.

Guy Burgess had recruited the Swiss press attaché, Eric Kessler, as a source codenamed
ORANGE.

I have just seen the papers of the Reverend George Henry Dymock, who is a rector, aged 62, and has been more or less associated with Fascist activities since 1935. The police at Bristol have been making enquiries about him but could get no further. They asked for our assistance and M/Y was sent down. She provoked the old man by suggesting that they should compile a seditious pamphlet and circulate it secretly. She also hinted that in time of invasion there might be a possibility of cutting up telephone wires and blowing up bridges. She got quite a strong reaction and in the course of conversation with Dymock and Drewer, who is now interned under Emergency Regulation 18(b), it emerged that Dymock had a number of Fascist uniforms concealed on church property so the police decided to search. The uniforms were discovered and the Regional Commissioner made an order for internment and submitted it for confirmation to the Home Office. M/Y had arranged a special code and pseudonym for corresponding with Dymock before his arrest. He got frightened when she sent him a telegram and gave a copy of it to the police saying that he knew nothing about its contents or the sender. In the meantime, he telephoned to M/Y instructing her not to come near him. The Home Office eventually decided to reduce the 18(b) order to a Restriction Order under 18(a), prohibiting Dymock from moving outside his parish without reporting to the police. They also reported him to the bishop for a raspberry. In minuting the Home Office file on this case Arthur Hutchinson and Frank Newsam both took exception to the *agent provocateur* methods of MI5, and Hutchinson went so far as to say that the Secretary of State would strongly disapprove of the use of agents in this way. I put up a strong minute to Director-General saying that if these methods cannot be employed to investigate the Fifth Column field we cannot be responsible for its investigation at all. Quite clearly, the ordinary methods will lead us nowhere, and it is clearly part of our duty to find out exactly where doubtful elements would stand in time of invasion. This can only be achieved by provocation. My own view is that action under the Defence of the Realm Act should, generally speaking, be taken now only if it can be based on evidence other than the spoken word or action which can be directly attributed to provocation. Otherwise, the suspect should be placed on the invasion list. I do not think however that any exception can be justifiably be taken to the methods employed in obtaining the information. In the case of Dymock, the evidence about the uniform – although obtained as a result of provocation – related facts which had taken place long before the agent ever met Dymock. Toby Pilcher has some doubts about the lengths to which provocation should go and he thought that there was a limit. I agree, but I do not think it was reached in the Dymock case. Theo Turner feels that as neither the Secretary of State nor Sir Alexander Maxwell have commented on Hutchinson or Newsam's observations, we should let sleeping dogs lie, otherwise we may get our wings clipped. If, on the other hand, we are attacked we have a good case. I think there may be something in this argument, but it will be for the Director-General to decide.

16 September

The Prime Minister wants a report on Japanese contacts in this country. I have asked Anthony Blunt to compile this and to send it to Peter Loxley who will collate it with other information from the Foreign Office.

I spent the night with Charles Butler, and discussed with him to a fairly late hour my various difficulties. We became rather heated about Jack Curry. Charles, I think, has never quite forgiven him for his support for the malcontent at Buckingham Palace. I said that I thought Curry had been placed in an almost impossible position. I think that in the end Charles saw my point, and is going to say a word to the Director-General about Curry's possible transfer to B Division.

Jack Curry had supported Edward VIII and thereby made himself unpopular during the Abdication crisis.

17 September

Colonel Stephens rang me up early this morning to say that Saetrang, one of the Norwegians who arrived on the *Hornfjell*, had committed suicide, by hanging himself from a water pipe with his scarf. He had stripped himself to the waist and gagged himself by stuffing a handkerchief down his throat. He had only been interrogated for three minutes on his arrival on the previous day. He had been told that he had information which connected him with the German secret service and that he had better consider the advisability of making a written statement. He had been seen by the guard at 4am and must have committed suicide sometime between four and six o'clock.

On arrival at the office I got hold of Edward Hinchley-Cooke and Edward Cussen in order that we could make arrangements for a coroner's inquest with the least possible publicity. They have made arrangements to do this effectively, through a tame coroner in the north of London.

19 September

Director-General has agreed to a £500 guarantee to CELERY's employer on whose behalf he is going to Rio de Janeiro.

Scrongheim, of the *Hornfjell*, has amongst his kit a bottle of medicine which he says is for VD. He is not at present suffering from any such disease but we are taking a test to see whether he ever had suffered from such a complaint. The medicine can also be used as a very high-grade secret ink and has been used by the Germans on a previous occasion. Scrongheim was a close friend of Saetrang.

I lunched with Valentine Vivian and we had a long talk about America. I said that I doubted whether Bill Stephenson was equipped to deal with our particular enquiries. There had been no action so far on my letter of April last, that technicians should be recruited for double-cross work, and the Joe Kennedy case revelations in the American press were extremely damaging to our work. We had never received any details about the case and we had never been told of the proposed action. Surely if the relations with the FBI were so good this could have been done? Vivian agreed that the present situation left much to be desired, although he thought from reports he had seen that Stephenson was sufficiently equipped to deal with these matters.

It now transpires that the interest of the Eire authorities in Dr Goertz arose from the arrest of certain members of the IRA, but we hope to hear more next week when the Garda Siochana will be paying a visit to the Royal Ulster Constabulary. At T.A. Robertson's suggestion a comparison has been made between the handwritings of Goertz and that on the document known as Plan KATHLEEN which was found at the house of Stephen Carroll Held about a year ago. There is no doubt that the two are identical. We may therefore infer that the parachutist who had left his parachute and wireless equipment plus a considerable sum in dollars at Held's house was probably Dr Goertz.

Plan KATHLEEN was a German scheme to drop paratroops near Davis Head and Lisburn, and isolate British troops garrisoned in Belfast from the rest of Ireland.

The Germans have under sentence of death one Oloff de Wet, a South African. He is charged with espionage or conspiring against the state. They are suggesting that he should be exchanged for someone under sentence of death here and have asked for the names of any suitable candidates. As de Wet has not been employed by any known organisation in this country or in South Africa this may be a ruse to get us to disclose what agents we are holding in captivity. We could, of course, give them Karel Richter, or Finkelstein of the Jan Mayen expedition.

21 September

There is an interesting prisoner of war report. A wireless operator from the crew of the U-570, which was captured off Iceland, has said that from the beginning of the war until the middle of October he was in a Norwegian ship owned by a German company and was sending reports by wireless about English shipping movements. There were three people on board, including an officer. The ship was about 3,000 tons and generally sailed under the Norwegian flag. Last September the prisoner of war was on a fishing smack somewhere in the vicinity of Calais setting up communication with wireless units. It seems probable that he was on the ship which we picked up in the early stages of the war in communication with Hamburg. The code was similar to that used by SNOW, and it was the interception of these messages that really led to the development of the Group traffic.

The U-570 had surrendered to a Hudson of Coastal Command after being depth-charged. Only four of the young, sea-sick crew had any combat experience and they were pleased to be captured by a Royal Navy trawler. U-570 was later put into service as HMS Graph and her commander, Kapitän Hans Rahmlow, survived the war as a PoW at Bowmanville Camp, Ontario. Three of his subordinates were court-martialled by fellow Kriegsmarine prisoners at Grizedale Hall. Two were acquitted of cowardice but Leutnant Bernard Berndt was convicted.

177

He later escaped on a mission to sabotage the U-boat in Barrow-in-Furness, but was shot dead by a Home Guard.

23 September

In the afternoon we had a Radio Security Service meeting. The importance of developing the South American traffic was stressed since it seemed fairly clear that both the Germans and Japanese were collaborating in building up an intelligence service in South America which was to work in with the north and which might to an increasing degree operate against ourselves. There was already evidence that agents were being sent to West Africa and South America. I mentioned the prisoner of war report about the man from the U–570 who had in the early days of the war been employed on a 3,000 ton Norwegian ship in Scandinavian waters for the purpose of reporting on British shipping by wireless. Hugh Trevor Roper is going to frame a questionnaire for this man, and Ted Maltby will make the necessary arrangements with Thomas Kendrick. Herbert Hart mentioned that according to ISOS a German agent was travelling between Vigo and Eire. It seemed likely that the ship on which he was working was the *City of Antwerp*. I think this is one of Samuel Stewart's boats.

Lord Swinton came at 6pm to discuss the Prime Minister's anxieties about various British subjects who were making contact with the Japanese so we went over the whole ground with him. He will reply to the Prime Minister, who had become very excited about the whole matter on account of a BJ, that for certain reasons Grotwohl should be left at large, that Lord Sempill should, in accordance with our advice given years ago, be removed from the Admiralty, that Edwards was openly receiving £4,500 a year from the Japanese, and it was believed was of certain value to the Foreign Office, that Swinton would speak to McGrath, that George Sale knew very little but was inclined to put business before the country, and that Piggott was a pathological Japophile, but honest.

Commander McGrath, a director of Cannon Boveri, was a near neighbour of the former Japanese Ambassador in Bucharest. George Sale was a director of Sale Tilney, an export–import firm doing business with Japan. Until 1930 General F.S.G. Piggott had been military attaché in Tokyo.

24 September

Victor Rothschild is anxious to send someone to Gibraltar to go into the case of José Munoz, a Spaniard who has given us specimens of German sabotage material and is by way of acting for a German organisation in Madrid. We are a little inclined to think that Colonel H.G. 'Tito' Medlam, the DSO Gibraltar, is having his leg pulled. Most of the material that he has got seems to be rather out of date but it may be that Munoz is trying work himself in as a double-cross.

I went on to see the Assistant Director of Naval Intelligence about the case of Strachan of the HMAS *Bulolo*. It had been noticed when this boat was refitting in Baltimore in August last that Strachan had visited Joe Kennedy at a place called Pocono Pines. The local consul had commented on this, and when asked what he was doing there Strachan said that he had got particulars of the place from some travel agency and had gone there on holiday. Strachan, who is secretary to the captain, is apparently unpopular in the wardroom. I visited the chartroom and found that the *Bulolo* is now at Simonstown and that she had been escorting convoys between there and Freetown. It seemed now that she might be destined for South American waters but in any case there was no prospect of her coming here. It was decided that after getting certain further details from SIS, a signal should be sent to the captain instructing him to interrogate Strachan.

Mrs Gladstone came to see me about the agency and I asked her about Acworth and Van der Willik. She said that the conclusion that she, Dickson and Shepherd had come to was that Van der Willik was a good man and very loyal to Acworth who he thought had been wrongfully dismissed. They thought that Acworth was keen and hardworking but rather simple. Without guidance they thought he might get into difficulties. Acworth, who I had seen on the previous day, was very worried about the agency. While he accepted his position he thought we should be losing a good man in Van der Willik. He was himself very keen to stay on and run the agency with Van der Willik as he felt it was the only decent job that he had been able to do since the beginning of the war. Acworth had also seen Theo Turner, who had formed a good impression of him. Both Acworth and Van der Willik have got the secrecy bug developed to the nth degree. Acworth evidently thinks that only about three people should know anything about their work. I asked him how the office was going to make use of his organisation if it did not know of its existence. He did not seem to have any real answer to this question, and from what I saw of it I very much doubt whether he will ever submit to any close control. I do not think he would mind working under Theo, but it seems rather a bad organisation to have two agencies working apart from each other. I am proposing to have a conference about the whole matter as soon as Dick White returns.

Mrs Gladstone's employment agency specialised in placing domestic staff in embassies in London, and was controlled by the Security Service as a very useful source of information.

T.A. Robertson and J.C. Masterman are a little worried by the lack of questions from the other side regarding a possible invasion. This might be due to three things: the Germans may be fully informed that we do not contemplate invasion; they may wish that for the time being their agents here should not be inquisitive and so run the risk of being detected. This would imply that they wished to keep them in position until such time as they themselves contemplate invasion of this country. The only other supposition is that they do not trust their agents in this country.

Herbert Hart has produced an ISOS message today showing that SO2's people in Norway are in considerable trouble and the Germans seem to have successfully planted an agent on them. I do not know how they are going to get out of their difficulty but I sincerely hope that they will be prevented from issuing a warning to some agent who may in fact be under German control. This, however, is a matter for SIS.

27 September

Felix Cowgill rang me up to say that Vieja, concerning whom José Munoz had had a conversation with Tito Medlam, was almost certain to be our old friend del Pozo, whose name was Pierna Vieja. He certainly fits the description and this makes it fairly clear that Munoz is really a German agent, as in fact we thought from the beginning. The question now arises as to whether we should attempt to get hold of both José Munoz and del Pozo and bring them over to this country. This needs a great deal of careful thought. If they are to come we shall certainly have to get the Foreign Office into line, otherwise they will succumb to representations by the Spanish government. There is another awkward feature, namely del Pozo's relations with G.W.

29 September

I had lunch with Derek Tangye, who told me that he was communicating political information to Lord Swinton which had little or no importance from an office point of view. Swinton did not ask him any direct questions about the work of the office but often gave him rather obvious openings. He took the line that everything was going smoothly. I explained to Tangye that a good deal of ill-feeling had been caused between ourselves and Section V through people telling Swinton of our difficulties. I thought that these difficulties should be settled on our own level, and that only if we reached an impasse should we ask Swinton to arbitrate.

Anthony Blunt has been going into the Turkish mission and ISOS shows quite clearly that the Germans have planted somebody on them. We have got the services of the British officer in charge of the mission and he seems intelligent and is going to keep his eyes open. We are also taking other precautions.

Colonel Dudley Clarke, who is the link between GOC Egypt and Raymund Maunsell, came to see Gilbert Lennox, who brought him down to me. He has many double-cross schemes and controls both rumours and purveying false information through Maunsell's channels. Evidently his operations have been very successful. His rumours go through Istanbul and Lisbon. I said that if we had a really good liaison and knew more about his schemes we could probably give him considerable help but the main difficulty is communication. We decided that it would be necessary to have some sort of code within a cipher in order to ensure secrecy. Two of his schemes seem to have been particularly successful. The Italians were allowed to believe that an attack on British Somaliland was imminent. The purpose of this was to keep their reserves out of Abyssinia and in the end the Italians seem to have become so positive that an attack was impending that they withdrew all their forces from British Somaliland, almost without firing a shot. Another plan was devised to make the enemy think that we had very large reserves in Cyprus whereas we had hardly any troops at all. The scheme was worked out on a big scale and in considerable detail, even down to officers being made colonels and generals and dummy tank battalions being moved. What really stands out in contrast to our operations here is that the GOC makes his plans and asks the local Twenty Committee to support them, whereas here we reach a point where we have to put forward two alternative policies which go no further than the Directors of Intelligence. In other words, in Egypt the GOC makes the running, whereas in this country it is left to us. Admittedly the conditions are somewhat different but it rather bears out what we told the Directors of Intelligence at the beginning, namely that they had a machine but they do not make proper use of it.

30 September

We have had a message from SIS to say that our old friend Frederick Rutland is arriving at Foynes, en route for England. It is said that he has been asked to leave the United States in order to avoid an awkward prosecution. We may have some difficulty in going to the Americans about this case since some years ago SIS put in an agent on him and when we were anxious to tell the Americans about Rutland they prevented us in case their agent should be compromised. On present information it is not possible to say whether the awkwardness is due to a belief by the Americans that we have been running Rutland, or to a fear that American negotiations with Japan will be embarrassed. We propose to give Rutland a normal search and then keep him under observation for a fortnight pending some further information from SIS.

I had a discussion with J.C. Masterman and T.A. Robertson about POGO. It was decided that both José Munoz and POGO should be encouraged to go to Gibraltar and that as much of their story should be extracted from them as possible. We feel that we cannot very well bring POGO over here and intern him without seriously jeopardising the position of G.W. We shall probably therefore send him back to Spain after we have heard his story. The question of Munoz will be for further consideration.

3 October

I had another talk with Gilbert Lennox, Dudley Clarke and T.A. Robertson. Since Raymund Maunsell cannot pay us a visit we are going to fix up an arrangement with Dudley Clarke, by which we shall be informed of all his counter-plans and receive instructions from him as to exactly what he wants us to do. I emphasised that it was very important that we should have as full knowledge as possible of the measures he himself was taking. I also told him that without running serious risks we could not embark upon a policy of downright lying. We could, however, put forward tentative half-truths.

Plan STENCH is in operation. Porton Down is being asked to make a special gas mask which will contain certain ingredients which will puzzle the German scientists. They will think that because we are introducing these ingredients we have some very special gas about which they do not know. The mask will also have earpieces in order to give the impression that we have some new gas which affects the ears. There have already been rumours about such a gas. It has not yet been decided how this gas mask is to reach the Germans. DRAGONFLY has received £1,000, ostensibly in payment for the right to sell his cosmetics in certain countries.

We had a Radio Security Service meeting. We are now intercepting 216 stations and there has been a steady rise in the decoded traffic.

I discussed with J.C. Masterman and Christopher Harmer the MUTT sabotage scheme. A site has been discovered on a food dump and the proposal is that nobody should be warned. Normally there are two firewatchers on duty. Personally, I feel somewhat apprehensive about the whole scheme and I have suggested that, as a preliminary, Harmer should carry out an examination of the site both in the daylight and at night, since I think we must be satisfied that nobody would really be wandering about. Even then there would be likely to be a risk that one of the two firewatchers might take it into his head to stroll round the buildings. There is also the possibility that the machine might not go off. This would necessitate everybody being warned and the site being roped off until some expert could dismantle the machine. Publicity would be bound to result. Lastly, there is the question of getting some suitable notification in the press. How exactly is this to be done and what will be the result? Will a horde of press representatives arrive on the site and make enquiries? All these matters will have to be carefully explored. I think the principle is right that we should if possible satisfy the enemy that something is being done. Similar measures were taken in the last war with success.

Kathleen Harriman of the International News Service, the daughter of Averell Harriman of the American mission, is acting as a representative of the Hearst press and sending her stuff out through the bag. I have suggested that we should ascertain from press circles that she is a representative of the Hearst press and that we should establish through Censorship that she sends no telegrams or letters to her paper. We can then suggest to the American Embassy that they might look into the question.

A man called Johnson, using the name Robert Adair, has deserted from his ship and has been arrested by the police. He has confessed that he was sent here by some Hearst paper on the instigation of Senator Gerald Nye, the isolationist. He has to collect as much data as he can about the state of our armaments etc for publication in the isolationist press.

Lord Swinton rang up to say that he had learned from Edwin Herbert that the Americans have known about the microdot for some considerable time. Herbert had given Swinton to understand that this information had been sent over by Bill Stephenson but had never reached us. I said that I could not believe this was possible. We had known that Stephenson was inclined to say that he had sent material and when we made enquiries found that he had not. It was, however, quite clear that the FBI were being extremely cagey about the information they obtained. They should have kept us informed about their big spy case, and should certainly have consulted us before taking action. I rang up Valentine Vivian and told him what Swinton had said. He thought that there might quite well be a misunderstanding between the discovery of the microdot and the discovery of microphotography. We have all known about microphotography for some considerable time but the first we heard of the microdot was from RAINBOW.

On looking through BALLOON 's traffic, I found that he had reported on an ammunition dump situated on Lord Swinton's estate. This had apparently escaped notice both by the Air Ministry and the Home Defence Security Executive. BALLOON was communicating in secret ink but had not sent the letter off. The necessary amendments have been made.

12 October

There appears to have been some mistake about Frederick Rutland wearing a uniform. The watchers evidently mistook somebody else for him. Rutland has been to a friend in the Air Ministry and also to somebody in the Ministry of Aircraft Production and has offered to act as a double-cross agent against the Japanese. So far he does not appear to have made any contact with Japanese here. It seems unlikely that he will, but I should like to be quite sure on this point before making a direct approach to Rutland. In the meantime I am proposing to find out if possible something more from SIS in America. John Maude appears to have had some hand in Rutland's departure from America. Apart from this, and the very meagre press survey already received, we are largely in the dark. I should like to ask the Americans for further particulars, but before doing so I want to be sure that their agent, who several years ago was in touch with Rutland, will not be compromised.

17 October

Cecil Liddell has returned from his visit to Northern Ireland. Sir Charles Wickham had written a very stuffy letter about our refusing to let him pass on certain information relating to Dr Hermann Goertz and the fact that he was the writer of Plan KATHLEEN to his contact in the Garda Siochana. Sir Charles Wickham had evidently misunderstood the whole position. He does not realise that Liam Archer and Dan Bryan have always been at great pains to conceal [XXXXXXXXXXXXXX] that they obtain any information for us, and that our position is therefore an extremely delicate one. The fact is that Northern Ireland is so concerned about the IRA and obtaining information from the South that they are not inclined to give much consideration to other matters.

ISOS discloses that the Germans have two agents in our embassy in Ankara and that they have had access to our diplomatic bag.

One of the spies was the Ambassador's Albanian valet, Elyesa Bazna, and the other was his chauffeur.

Colonel Tito Medlam, our officer at Gibraltar, called to discuss the case of José Munoz and POGO. From what he said, I am not so inclined to think that Munoz is double-crossing us as I was before. Munoz has now given information about a plot to blow up two ammunition ships in the harbour. These ships lie within 150 yards of the Spanish port. Munoz, whose real name is Dominguez, is to go out with a party and lay a mine on which the ships will drift with the changing tide. We shall know more about Dominguez if this operation really takes place.

José Munoz was arrested in June 1943, following an explosion at the fuel depot on Coaling Island, Gibraltar. He later pleaded guilty to charges under the Treason Act and was executed in January 1944.

21 October

I discussed the José Munoz case and we decided that we should allow the present arrangement to take its course, and that if it petered out we should try and give Munoz some direction with a view to his committing some further act of sabotage which would be under our control. We thought that in such an eventuality it would be worthwhile sending an officer to Gibraltar in order to make personal contact with Munoz and absorb a certain amount of local colour. While we had formerly been skeptical about Munoz's bona fides we now thought that there was a reasonable chance that he might be genuinely working for us.

We lunched afterwards with Tito Medlam and put our suggestions to him. He agreed but said that if we were sending anyone to Gibraltar it was essential that he should speak fluent Spanish. The only people we could send would be either Dick Brooman-White or Tommy Harris. Brooman-White would, I think, be preferable as he has more experience.

I saw Max Knight and asked him whether he would like to have Egerton-Johnson, whose contacts I thought might be very valuable to his organisation, and he seemed pleased at the idea. He is also anxious to get hold of Duncan, and had a conversation about him with Theo Turner. He thinks he may make something of Duncan, as he regards him as a willing learner. I asked Max about Harald Kurtz. He told me that the latter had written to Sir Alexander Maxwell, which ought to forestall any approaches to the Home Secretary by Oswald Hickson. Kurtz had been lured into making a rather foolish statement to Hickson about Ben Greene. Ben's brother Edward had got into touch with Kurtz and had got him to deny a certain allegation alleged to have been made against Ben Greene; and his brother Edward then manoeuvred Kurtz into Hickson's office with a view to his making a statement on this subject. Hickson asked Kurtz whether he was a government agent. Kurtz replied "No". Hickson then asked him a number of questions connected with the evidence that Kurtz had given before the Advisory Committee, and involved Kurtz in a denial of all the statements he had given in evidence. These denials followed naturally on his statement to the effect that he was not a government agent. The whole matter was obviously a trick by Hickson, aided and abetted by Edward Greene. I suggested to Max that it might be a wise move to ensure that no Parliamentary Question was put down on the Order Paper about Kurtz since once this was done an answer would have to be given, and Kurtz's name would have been exposed. We subsequently arranged this with Abbott in the House of Commons Table Office.

I saw Paddy Beaumont-Nesbitt for a few minutes as he is on his way to the Middle East, Singapore, and Washington DC. I arranged for him to attend a meeting of the Twenty Committee in order that they could put him thoroughly in the picture with regard to feeding information to TRICYCLE. The Twenty Committee have raised the question of communication with the Middle East on plans to mislead the enemy. Arrangements have been fixed up with Dudley Clarke, but the latter has now got himself into difficulties in Spain. He has been imprisoned by the Spanish authorities, presumably on his way to Switzerland. I am afraid that after his stay in Lisbon as a bogus journalist he has got rather over-confident about his powers as a secret service agent. It would be much better if these people confined themselves to their proper job.

25 October

Donald Fish came in to tell me that Dan Corrigan had started a new racket, posing as being able to get people out of occupied territory. He has got hold of a wealthy Czech from whom he required a sum of £1,200 to carry out the preliminary negotiations with the parties concerned. If he is successful he wants a further sum. The Czech does not mind what he pays as long as he can get his relatives over to this country. I have suggested that he should deposit a credit in a bank which would be payable on production of goods. The Criminal Investigation Division is going to try this on and see what happens.

I had a talk with Acworth about his agency. He is so bitten with the bug of secrecy and to some extent with the sense of his own importance that I am rather apprehensive about getting him into line. I told him that while I fully realised that either his departure, or that of van der Willik, would for a time seriously dislocate the machine, I did not regard either of them as indispensable. I have told him to put forward a memo on the agency for discussion.

The Director of Naval Intelligence is being very troublesome about Frederick Rutland. Having pinned his faith on him and found that he had made a mistake, he is now trying to say that we have made a bungle of the case.

I had a talk with Machell about *Inside Information* and some form of censorship has been suggested. I have asked Machell to analyse the information in the column over a period in order to establish which of them are true and which are not. If the majority of the information is false or more or less a matter of public knowledge it will not be of much use to the enemy and therefore not worth censoring. Censorship might in fact enhance its importance in the eyes of the Germans if by any chance they were in touch with any employee of the *Daily Sketch*. It would follow that if a particular item was censored that it was probably true. The same arguments apply if it were thought possible or desirable to use *Inside Information* indirectly as a means of misleading the enemy.

Stewart Menzies spoke to me about the Pyrene Company, with which I believe W.B. Phillips was at one time connected. It was always thought that Phillips' news service acted in some way as a cover for a mild form of American espionage organisation in this country. Fellner, an American who is representing Bill Donovan over here, let slip that he was visiting one Christie at the Pyrene Company. Stewart thinks it might be worth while looking into this matter. A further point of interest in this connection is that while coming out of Claridge's with a representative of SIS, Fellner met Sir William Wiseman who rolled up in a large limousine. Wiseman, who was formerly an SIS representative in the United States during the last war and subsequently associated with Phillips, gave Fellner some form of recognition. Fellner seems to be in charge of a section of Donovan's co-ordination department which receives information from the FBI, the immigration authorities, the Treasury and the three services. They have more or less taken over the functions of the Dies Committee and are beavering into the origin and activities of all societies which may be engaged in un-American activities. Fellner, who was formerly an American consul in this country, is quite pleasant but gives the impression of being a little bit shifty. We had heard about him through our agent who is in touch with Luis Calvo, the Spanish agent who is working under Alcazar de Velasco. It seems that Calvo and Fellner both have the same mistress in the person of a Russian girl called Natasha Anton. Fellner has evidently told Natasha that he is a great spy-catcher. She, knowing that he is a man who always blows his own trumpet, does not believe him. Perhaps this is just as well.

There have been a very large number of arrests of members of the IRA in Ireland. This is probably due to the previous arrests of Stephen Hayes, and Sean McCaughey.

Stephen Hayes, the IRA's Chief of Staff since April 1939, was sentenced to five years' imprisonment and gave evidence against McCaughey, who was sentenced to death and then reprieved. He died on hunger strike in Portlaoise Prison five years later.

3 November

I went over to see Valentine Vivian and found him with Dick Ellis who had just flown over from New York at 26,000 feet in an atmosphere of sixty degrees below zero. He had eaten a large meal and drunk half a bottle of brandy before starting since he could not get any food on account of having to wear an oxygen mask the whole way. The journey took eight and a half hours, starting from some desolate spot in Newfoundland.

Ellis said that Bill Stephenson was very het up about the criticims that he had received over the Joe Kennedy case. Ellis thinks that what is really wanted is somebody who had more knowledge of what we are doing over here. He feels that our side of the work has to a considerable extent been neglected, owing to the enormous amount that is being done on security co-ordination lines. He says that Ronald Sinclair has been doing very good work and cannot understand why we have not heard more about it. To give him his due Sinclair did write to me suggesting closer co-operation on our lines. The only result was that Stephenson and Section V took violent exception to what he said and insisted on having the letter withdrawn. Ellis was all in favour of my going out with Felix Cowgill.

I had a word with Stewart Menzies, who told me that active enquiries were going on at the embassy in Ankara since it had been discovered that a blueprint of one of our guns was missing from the military attaché's office. We knew this in fact from ISOS, but it was only after telegrams had been sent out from the War Office suggesting that something was wrong that the facts became clear. There is obviously somebody purloining documents in the embassy. The bag to which the Germans had access, according to ISOS, was one brought from Cairo to Ankara by our assistant air attaché. In addition to a certain amount of information about C's activities in Istanbul, it contained re-cyphering tables. Had the military attaché reported about his blueprint it would have been known that probably these tables were compromised at a much earlier date. Luckily they have not yet been put into operation and the necessary action has been taken.

The leak was eventually traced to the Ambassador's valet, Elyesa Bazna, an Albanian, code-named CICERO by the Sicherheitsdienst, who routinely copied the contents of Sir Hughe Knatchbull-Hugessen's safe.

Stewart also talked to me about Leonard Plugge MP, who has been talking in a very defeatist manner to the Pasha. Anthony Eden has got very excited about this and wishes to know what is being done. Stewart has calmed him down. In point of fact, there is very little that can be done unless the government is prepared to put Captain Plugge inside, which he rightly deserves. He doesn't care a damn about this country and is merely concerned with filling his pockets.

4 November

Lord Swinton rang me up about a company known as WAF. The principals in this firm are a man called Bergl and another called Warschauer, both Germans and at one time members of the German intelligence service. Warschauer is interned for good and proper reasons. It had been proposed to place a rather confidential wireless contract with this firm. The chairman is Sir Herbert Williams MP, who is also chairman of a select committee for investigating expenditure by contracts departments. We advised against the employment of WAF and it had been decided to give the contract to the British Acoustic Company. They could, if they so desired, call in a representative of WAF for technical advice. They would in any case have made the recording set as WAF are merely a skeleton without a factory. This action had apparently caused a certain amount of trouble politically, and we were asked whether the position would in any way be changed if certain members of WAF were got rid of. Swinton wanted me to see Burton of the Ministry of Supply.

SIS has information that the Eire government has discovered codes and ciphers, and a wireless set at Brittas Bay.

I had a long talk with T.A. Robertson and Dick Brooman-White about the Luis Calvo case. Brooman-White is very anxious to arrest Calvo and possibly a number of other Spaniards who have been working here for some time. T.A. Robertson's contention is that if Calvo is arrested there will be a serious reaction on G.W., and that in view of the slightly dicky position at the moment of the B1(a) organisation it would be undesirable to throw a spanner into the works.

6 November

Craufurd and I saw Burton of the Ministry of Supply about WAF. Major-General Theobald Butler was also present. I think we persuaded Burton that WAF was of no consequence whatever as a company, that its directors were undesirable, its chairman was trying to grind his own axe, and its financer Svarvasy was a shady alien financier with a bad reputation in the City. Burton, who seemed to accept our view, said that he thought the present arrangement should stand and that the WAF should not be given the contract.

Valentine Vivian attended the Twenty Committee in the absence of Felix Cowgill who has been showing Lord Swinton round Section V, and there was one rather controversial issue. G.W. might possibly be compromised if Luis Calvo were arrested. Ewen Montagu took the view that the Director of Naval Intelligence would be extremely annoyed if he was not previously consulted. The view taken was that as Calvo and G.W. had been used as a mean of transmitting false information to the enemy, the services were naturally concerned if the enemy was now to discover the truth. Vivian took a very useful hand in the argument. He thought that the services had a case for requesting consultation, but that their point of view might be carried too far. In putting information through these channels they had to realise that they took a certain risk since any agent was liable to be compromised at any moment through no fault of his or anybody else's. They could not, therefore, claim priority rights over the handling of an agent merely because he had been used as a channel for transmitting their information. On the other hand, the Security Service and SIS should do everything in their power to meet the wishes of the services.

Lord Swinton came over to discuss the case of Karel Richter. He read my minute in which I had pointed out more on the undesirability of the present procedure. I had suggested that in future the matter should be dealt with by a statement in the House of Commons to the effect that it was not the intention of the government to publish details regarding the apprehension and execution of spies, and that the House should not assume that because no details were published spies were not being caught and executed. This would leave our hands free. Swinton said that he would have to consider this matter rather carefully. As regards the particular case of Richter he thought that it would be unwise to press for a reprieve since the information would undoubtedly leak out with results which would be detrimental to B1(a)'s organisation. There were two alternatives, either to proceed as usual, or to suppress the notice of the execution and make a special appeal to the editors. My fear was that the bare mention of Richter's name in the press might cause the Germans to make a thorough enquiry into our traffic, and possibly with disastrous results, since Richter was linked with TATE, and TATE with TRICYCLE and RAINBOW, and TRICYCLE with BALLOON and GELATINE. There was, in addition, the legal difficulty since Richter had made an appeal in which he stated that he knew that TATE was under government control. Edward Hinchley-Cooke has got Richter to withdraw this statement, which is in no way relevant to the normal legal appeal. He had told him that he can put this in with his appeal to the Home Secretary if his appeal fails. T.A. Robertson and I had a consultation about the case afterwards and decided that it was best to let it take its normal course.

DRAGONFLY has received a message instructing him to write a letter to FATHER, which was to be signed in the name of a Belgian who has passed through the Royal Victoria Patriotic School and been absorbed into the Belgian army. The letter asks for a meeting but it is not clear, however, whether the Belgian or DRAGONFLY is to meet FATHER. This is probably a reply to FATHER's urgent request that somebody should establish contact with him. The matter is interesting as an indication that if the Germans wish to conduct urgent business they have to do it through one of the family.

9 November

Plan GUY FAWKES went off at 4am this morning. The bombs were successfully placed but while the superintendent was keeping watch a War Reserve policeman appeared on a bicycle. He saw Christopher Harmer waiting in the car and asked him what he was doing. Harmer said he was waiting for somebody. The constable then became inquisitive and Harmer was obliged to refer him to the superintendent. The constable was threatened with every possible penalty if he said anything about what he had seen. Unfortunately, however, he was not told to leave the site. As soon as the fire started he raised the alarm and one bomb was extinguished before it had really exploded. A portion of it, and also of the suitcase, have been discovered and enquiries are being made. The two night-watchmen were obviously fast asleep. One of them said that he could not imagine how the fire could have started since he had visited the site only ten minutes previously. In actual fact he had never moved from his hut. Press and Censorship have been asked to issue the necessary D-Notice.

10 November

I discussed with the Director-General the cases of Frederick Rutland and Gerald Hamilton, and it was decided that a letter should be written to Rutland saying that in all the circumstances we had no use for his services. It was felt that no useful purpose would be served by interning him as he would in all probability be released. If, however, war breaks out between this country and Japan, the matter could be reconsidered on the grounds that he was of hostile association. Rutland has been thoroughly scared and I do not think he is likely to do anything. The Director-General has decided to write to Sir Alexander Maxwell about the case of Hamilton expressing his disapproval of the findings of the Advisory Committee.

Dan Bryan turned up today. He has given us some interesting details about Dr Herman Goertz. It appears that hue and cry after Goertz has nothing to do with the cases of Stephen Hayes and Sean McCaughey, the two members of the IRA recently arrested. Bryan says that the police got on to some woman called Helena Malone and that through her they were led to a Mrs McCaughey who had a boarding house at Dunlaoghaire where Goertz has apparently been a lodger for some months. Goertz had been brought to this boarding house by some people called Farrell. Just before the house was raided Goertz seems to have escaped to the Farrells' house and then got away to some bungalow at Brittas Bay. The people with whom he was staying had a rubber boat which had been bought in Dublin. There would seem, therefore, to be some possibility that Goertz has been picked up either by a ship plying between Eire and the Iberian peninsula or by seaplane. Bryan says, however, that as far as the Eire authorities know, there has been no seaplane in the vicinity of Brittas Bay, neither have there been any submarines in the Irish Channel. It is possible that Goertz may have boarded some vessel making for Lisbon but this could have only been done by means of a prearranged plan. The hunt for Goertz is still going on. While at Dunlaoghaire Goertz had an HMV radio receiving set and this was one of two purchased by a man named Redmond in Dublin. Goertz took the set with him and it is possible therefore that it may have been converted into a transmitter. It is not quite clear to me how the Germans knew of the existence of Goertz, but I dare say we shall find this out in due course.

Victor Rothschild has seen Ernest Wood of SOE in connection with Plan GUY FAWKES. Inspector Greeno of CID has discovered a part of the bomb. The CID made enquiries some time ago at the request of SO2 about the loss of a similar part and therefore recognised it. Wood appears to have fenced quite well and suggested to Greeno that he should consult Victor.

11 November

We have an extremely interesting case which centres round Stella Lonsdale, the wife of John Lonsdale, the 'Mayfair Boy'. Stella, who was in France, appears to have been caught by the Germans. She was at liberty for some time but was eventually arrested when in possession of a diagram showing the location of a petrol dump. According to her own account it had been her intention to pass this information on to the British through the American consul at Nantes. She was imprisoned and threatened with the death penalty, but according to her account she was reprieved owing to the intervention of one René whose identity she refused to disclose. René she says is working for the British although in the employ of the Abwehr Stelle at Angers. The head of the German organisation at Anger was Meissner who subsequently went to Paris. René had sent Stella into French unoccupied territory, and she had apparently become acquainted with certain facts relating to the British Secret Service activities in France. She knew the history of a man called Gaessler who had in fact been sent over to France with a transmitter. Stella said that he had offered his services to the Germans but had eventually been imprisoned. She gave a number of other details which according to SIS are substantially correct. It will I think be necessary for us to obtain the fullest possible facts from SIS before we shall be able to establish how far Stella can be regarded as genuine. On present form we are inclined to the view that René, if he exists at all, has been running Stella and that he is in fact a German agent. His technique, in posing as one who is pro-British, would be quite sound. He might expect that Stella would work more rapidly for him and would communicate more facts to him about the British organisation than she would otherwise do. It is quite possible of course that Stella's story has been entirely invented and that she is in fact collaborating with René, and there are many points in her story which struck us as extremely weak. On the other hand, her information about SIS agents is substantially true, though most if not all of it was known to SIS already. Stella herself wants to go back to France where she says she has contact with the *Deuxième Bureau*. We propose to discuss this proposition with her solely in the hope that she will in this manner ultimately disclose her hand.

At the Director-General's meeting today Toby Pilcher raised the case of Oswald Hickson and Ben Greene. Hickson is to give evidence before the Advisory

Committee and also Max Knight's agent. Hickson wants a transcript of the notes and Maxwell agreed to his having these. We feel that this may create an awkward precedent and that the official notes of the Advisory Committee should not be allowed to pass into the hands of a private individual. This seemed to us to be particularly important in the light of the coming debate on Emergency Regulation 18(b). The Director-General asked Toby to consult Sir Alexander Maxwell.

T.A. Robertson has seen the Commissioner of Police about Plan GUY FAWKES. The Commissioner knows that the CID are working on the case but he has not told Sir Norman Kendal about the plan.

I forgot to mention that Dudley Clarke was released three weeks ago. The circumstances of his release were to say the least of it peculiar. At the time he was dressed as a woman complete with brassière etc. Why he wore this disguise nobody quite knows. He seems, however, to have played his cards fairly well, since his speedy release can only be explained by the Germans having intervened on his behalf. It will be remembered that he made contact with a man he believed to be a German agent in Lisbon. This man was in Spain at the time and believing Dudley Clarke to be an important agent who was ready to assist the Germans, intervened with the Spanish police. Dudley Clarke is now on his way home. Nobody can understand why it was necessary for him to go to Spain. Before he is allowed to go back to the Middle East he will have to give a satisfactory account of himself. It may be that he is just the type who imagines himself as the super secret service agent.

14 November

The Stella Lonsdale case has been handed over to T.A. Robertson who is rather keen to use her as a double-cross but before doing so wishes to know much more about her character. It is also essential that we should have the fullest possible particulars from SIS.

I had a long talk with [XXXXX] at the Travellers' Club and he told me all about the Frederick Rutland case. It seems that his organisation sent several telegrams and letters from New York and found it extremely difficult to get any answer. The full facts of the case were known to them four or five weeks before Rutland left the United States. He could not understand why the first intimation to us was the projected arrival within forty-eight hours of Rutland's arrival at Foynes. It seems that Rutland was definitely implicated in the case of the Japanese language officer at Los Angeles who was arrested some months ago. Rutland, realising the delicacy of his position, had offered his services to the American authorities, saying that he had extremely good commercial connections with the Japanese and that he would be very pleased to work them. His suggestion was turned down and he next appeared in Washington DC where he visited our air attaché, du Boulay. John Maude got hold of him and thought it would be a grand idea to use him as a double-cross. John never consulted anybody and it was only by accident that [XXXXXXXXXX] heard about the case. Knowing Rutland's record he warned John to lay off. Rutland, in the meantime, had gone back to Los

Angeles. Finally, Percy Foxworth of the FBI told [XXXXXX] that the Americans proposed to arrest Rutland. They did not, however, wish to have the scandal of bringing to trial an ex-member of the British air force. They thought therefore it would be better if we made arrangements to send Rutland back to England forthwith. He was summoned to Washington DC, where John Maude suggested to him that it would be a good thing if he went back to England to discuss his project. Rutland seems to have jumped at this. Several days after Rutland had arrived here Bill Stephenson got a telegram from SIS asking who he was and all about him. As he had already sent three telegrams and one if not two reports he rather wondered what was going on. The Americans have evidently been watching Rutland for several years. They always wondered why we had never put our cards on the table. They thought perhaps that he was one of our agents and they had been waiting for us to tell them. I anticipated some sort of situation like this arising when some years ago I suggested that we should give full details of Rutland's case to the Americans. The objection at the time was that Rutland was tied up with an SIS agent and it was thought that there might be awkward disclosures if the Americans started to make enquiries. The services of the agent were eventually dispensed with more or less at our request. C agreed with us that any form of espionage in the United States was a mistake and likely to jeopardise good relations. There was nothing that this agent was finding out that could not be found out by asking.

15 November

T.A. Robertson and I had lunch with [XXXXXX]. He told Robertson quite a lot about TRICYCLE. TRICYCLE had now made contact with the enemy. He was rather resentful at first about his treatment but he now seems to have hit it off with the FBI and also with the SIS representative. He has been given introductions which have given him the build up he requires. He was very anxious to know about the fate of BALLOON and GELATINE since if anything had happened to them he thought his position might not be very secure. These are the kind of matters on which Section V evidently do not consider it necessary to keep us informed.

17 November

A suggestion has been made that we should employ Joseph Lenihan as an agent on a boat between this country and South America. I have looked through his file. I do not believe his story about his escape from the Channel Islands. I think he was anxious to get away and conceived the idea of offering his services to the Germans partly as a means to this end and partly in a spirit of adventure. If we are going to make any use of him it seems to me that we shall have to wipe out his past completely and give him a fresh identity. He could give away a certain amount of information about Camp 020, etc but it would be difficult for him to talk to the Germans without disclosing his identity, but if he did he would have to explain how he came into the hands of the British authorities.

I had lunch with Roger Fulford, and he is rather concerned about the Duke of Bedford. There is a movement to have him arrested because it is thought that his propaganda will do a lot of harm in the United States. Fulford I think rather wisely considers that his arrest would do more harm than good since it would give the Duke an enhanced importance. At the moment it is like a voice crying in the wilderness. Lord Swinton's view and I understand Herbert Morrison's is that if the Duke is not dealt with there will be a cry of one for the rich and another for the poor.

18 November

We had a Directors' meeting and I raised the question of Irma Stapleton. From the transcript notes taken by mike of her last interview with John Bingham posing as a representative of the German secret service there seemed no doubt that she was prepared to go to any lengths and that she could quite easily bring out a whole shell from the factory where she works. She has swallowed our bait hook, line and sinker. If we went on with the case there seemed little doubt that we could get her seven years' at the Old Bailey. We were to some extent forced to adopt these methods because if we interned people under 18(b) because we felt they were a potential danger they were almost invariably released. I rather wondered how far it would be worth the expense and trouble of trying to get a woman of this type sentenced to seven years, particularly since the case could not be held in an open court. The Director-General said he would give this matter his consideration.

We had the famous meeting with SIS: Stewart Menzies, Valentine Vivian, Jasper Harker, Dick White and myself, with the Director-General in the chair. The Director-General made a few introductory remarks and the rest of the meeting, which lasted one and three-quarter hours, was taken up with a discussion between Vivian, Dick and myself. The D-G asked me for my views and I tabled them in the form of a short memo which was read by all present. I said briefly that it was the responsibility of the Security Service to combat the activities of the German intelligence service wherever it was directed against this country or the British possessions, including Egypt and Palestine. It was for this purpose that it was essential that we should make a comprehensive study of the form, workings and agents of the German intelligence service. The collection of such information from foreign territory was the responsibility of SIS and from British territory including Egypt and Palestine of ourselves. In each of these territories the Services must of necessity overlap. I felt that in the best of worlds we should both be houses in the same office but that since for a variety of reasons this had not been considered possible, we had to strive for the next best thing, namely complete and frank interchange of information on all questions affecting the German intelligence service. I did not think it would be sufficient to confine this to anything in the nature of an exchange of periodical memoranda. We could only do it by the closest collaboration even on matters of detail. I had never wished to suggest that everything that SIS obtained should be thrown to us to digest and assimilate. We had always regarded it as their function to pass on in a palatable form information after it had been co-related with any other facts already in their possession but we did feel that as the executive responsibility was in our hands we should receive all relevant material in order that our picture might be as complete as possible. Vivian did not dissent from these views in general but said that he did not quite see how to define the limits of our interests. He thought that if we had everything relating to the German intelligence service from all parts of the world we should be duplicating the functions of SIS. I said that I did not see that this was necessary. We had never had any difficulty about it in the past when he himself had been in control of Section V and that provided Felix Cowgill would allow his subordinates to collaborate in a perfectly free and friendly manner I did not see why there should be any difficulty. Vivian then passed on to our standards of secrecy. Felix was apparently horrified because so many people knew about ISOS. Dick replied that at least fifty people knew about it in Section V and I asked how many people knew about it on the G side. Stewart said only four or five. I found this difficult to believe. I should be surprised if it were not known to a great many more on the G side. I then asked why it should be considered that our officers were in any way less reliable than those employed in SIS. There did not seem to be any answer to this question. Vivian then questioned the carding of ISOS. We said that we had to card it because we were working on it every single day, that we carded it in a limited way, i.e. we covered those areas to which we attached the most importance. Vivian suggested that this was duplication of the work being done by Section V. I said that if he carried his argument to its logical conclusion there would be no point in our having ISOS at all. Vivian then produced the Frederick Rutland case which, he said, had come as a great shock to Felix. A comparative table had been prepared showing the information given to the Director of Naval Intelligence by SIS and by ourselves. Felix held that the Rutland case had nothing to do with the DNI and that therefore information should be refused to him. We had on the contrary sent him a very full statement of the case including references to certain information obtained from BJs. I said that while I quite agreed that the DNI was interfering in a matter which was not his concern, I could see no harm in the action we had taken since the BJs were already in the DNI's possession and the remainder of the information was old and was in fact made use of by us in breaking Rutland down. We had lost nothing in the process since the letters which were shown to him were dated 1935, and the methods for intercepting correspondence were known to all. We had to work with the DNI and if by peaceful means we could satisfy him that he had made a fool of himself we were quite prepared to do so. I then referred to another aspect of the Rutland case, namely that although the full facts of this case had been known in America for five weeks we were only given forty-eight hours' notice of his arrival at Foynes, and heard nothing of any consequence until [XXXXXXX] arrival. This was just the kind of thing we wanted to have the full facts about. Before the meeting broke up I referred to the Stella Lonsdale case. It was essential that in a case of this sort we should be given the fullest possible information. It was only by the most detailed collaboration that we could really get at the facts. Stewart said he would be only too pleased to let us have any information about this case that we required. The D-G took a strong view about Felix, and he thought that he ought to be sent away for a long period. He had grossly overworked himself and had in consequence taken up a very narrow bigoted attitude. I think all present agreed that the real difficulty was Felix's personality.

20 November

Irma Stapleton was arrested last night. She had brought an empty shell out of the factory, and a note in her own handwriting giving the position of Wade's garages. She also gave John Bingham full production figures for Wade's garage. Her reaction was immediately to denounce Bingham as a Gestapo agent who she was intending to hand over to the police at the earliest opportunity. She insisted on making a statement which is said to be a tissue of lies. Bingham was arrested at the same time and carried away struggling and handcuffed. This morning she was remanded at Bow Street for fourteen days.

The Director-General asked me to come down and see William Dwight Whitney, who is Bill Donovan's representative over here and will have a small staff working under him. He is to have an office somewhere in Bush House which will be for press and propaganda. This will act as a cover. His main purpose is to collect as much vital information as he can which has any bearing on the part being played by the United States and the possibility of her entering the war. This information will go direct to Bill Donovan in special cipher for the President. Lastly, he is to try and lay the foundations of some organisation for penetrating the continent both on SIS and SOE lines. It seems to me that this is going to complicate life considerably for SIS. It is bad enough having an English SOE but if there is to be an American one as well I fear there may be a major disaster.

23 November

On the evening of her arrest Mrs Irma Stapleton produced a 22-mm Oerlikon shell, unloaded but apparently passed by inspectors, a two-pound anti-aircraft shell igniter and a 22mm shell base plug. She also gave in her own handwriting the address of the Royal Ordnance Factory at Stone, in Staffordshire and the production figures of Wade's Chain Garages which are stated to be accurate, as well as the addresses of the other units of Wade's factory organisation. The Naval Intelligence Division says that the production figures are confidential although they do not regard the shell as such. Mrs Stapleton is provisionally charged under Defence of the Realm Emergency Regulation 2(a), in that she obtained certain articles of ammunition and information concerning the same and endeavoured to dispose of them to the enemy.

25 November

David Boyle came to see me about George Knupfer who is associated with a young White Russian organisation known as Mladoross. Knupfer is bringing an action against the *Daily Express* who said that his organisation was working for the Nazis. Brendan Bracken MP wants to support the *Daily Express* if they are on a good wicket, and has asked C for his assistance. C has told him that he thinks Mladoross is suspect and Bracken now wants to place the *Daily Express* solicitors in touch with MI5.

---

26 November

As I rather anticipated, a Parliamentary Question has been put down on the Order Paper about Harald Kurtz. It is to the effect that since the information he gave to the Advisory Committee in the case of Ben Greene has been admitted by the Chairman to be false, will the Secretary of State say what action he proposes to take. As far as we know the Chairman expressed no such view, and we strongly object to Kurtz's name being placed on the Order Paper. Toby Pilcher is going to see Sir Alexander Maxwell and say that if the Question has to be allowed Kurtz's name should be omitted. He should merely be referred to as "the material witness". The Director-General considers that this incident amply justifies his contention that informants and agents should on no account be forced to appear before the committee.

---

28 November

Craufurd came to see me about Denys Boyd-Carpenter, who had informed us that he was receiving correspondence from a German officer named Karl Bruckner, who was employed on intelligence matters in France. These letters were said to reach Boyd-Carpenter via Spain. Boyd-Carpenter had said that he last met Bruckner in France in 1937 but we were inclined to disbelieve this since his passport which was dated 1934 must have expired in 1934 and had not been renewed. Craufurd went to see him with an 80a order and asked him to produce the letter. He found Boyd-Carpenter in bed and with a certain amount of difficulty got from him a letter authorising Craufurd to obtain the correspondence from Bruckner from Vernon Bartlett to whom it had been sent. Our files showed that Vernon Bartlett had been interested and that Isobel Cripps, Stafford Cripps' wife, had also had copies which she had sent to some high-up in a hush-hush department. We have now had a letter from Boyd-Carpenter's solicitors apropos of Craufurd's visit. The solicitors explained that their client periodically went into a trance, when interesting facts were revealed to him. He attached great importance to the information he received but knowing that the authorities would not be likely to pay any attention to psychic transmission he had felt bound to invent the story about receiving the information by correspondence from enemy occupied territory. The solicitors had realised that their client had committed a breach of the regulations and hoped that we would take a lenient view of his conduct. We have now got to concern ourselves with finding out what circulation has been given to Boyd-Carpenter's letters and to warning those concerned that they are wasting their time.

I had a talk today with Alex Kellar about George Knupfer and the Young Russian organisation known as Mladoross. There do not appear to be any grounds of a substantial kind for saying that this organisation is pro-Nazi. In fact most of our evidence is in the contrary sense. I saw David Boyle later and gave him the facts. He is going to draft a letter for C's signature to Brendon Bracken telling him that the *Daily Express* seem to be on rather a bad wicket.

SO2 has got a couple of tame Russians who are to be dropped in Germany. I presume this means that they are collaborating with the 4th Department. I am going to try and find out since there may possibly be an opening for obtaining Russian information about German intelligence organisation.

2 December

The Director-General saw myself and Victor Rothschild about the Dorothy case. He has made up his mind that there is nothing to be gained by allowing the wireless set to go in in the biscuit tin, since Walter Wegener was already interned. I tried to explain that the project had a definite intelligence value. If Walter started to transmit we hoped to learn firstly whether there was any subversive organisation among the internees in the Isle of Man and secondly whether Wegener would communicate to the Germans that certain of his former collaborators in Siemens Schuckerts were now at large and could be made use of. The Director-General felt that if Wegener used the set he would ultimately have to be arrested and that our connivance in the whole matter would then come out. I do not think that this is necessary. We should be able to arrange matters so that no difficulties of this kind arise. As things stand at present Toby Pilcher is to express his opinion on the merits of Wegener's case from the point of view of his continued internment, since unless his more recent intentions are made clear to the Advisory Committee they will probably recommend his release.

3 December

MUTT and JEFF have at last re-established contact. Satisfaction was expressed about Plan GUY FAWKES, but subsequent requests for money have met with no response. It is still difficult to assess the exact position of MUTT and JEFF in the eyes of the enemy. The whole case is being reviewed.

4 December

I had a talk with the Director-General about the Dorothy case and explained to him what the advantages were from the intelligence point of view. Firstly we hoped to find out something about a possible organisation among the internment camps in the Isle of Man and secondly we thought that Wegener might indicate what representatives of Siemens Schuckert were still in internment and could be relied upon from the German point of view. He has now agreed to let the scheme go forward.

Dr Goertz's arrest has now been confirmed and has been published in the Irish press. So far we have no details.

5 December

I went with Edward Cussen to the Ministry of Economic Warfare this afternoon where we saw Farrer and Vickers. The Assistant Director of Naval Intelligence joined us there. He stated his case to Vickers and it was finally decided that Cussen should interrogate all those at MEW concerned with the leakage. From what Vickers said I do not think we should have much of a case against Postan although he has clearly talked very indiscreetly. His excuse will be that the loss of the *Barham* had a very important bearing on work that he was doing and that the Admiralty representative had mentioned the matter to him in this connection.

There has been an interesting development in the Stella Lonsdale case. She has sent a wire to a man called Boulanger in Marseilles who she previously told us was her lover and had no connection with intelligence work. She asks of Boulanger whether he has given news of Solange to Rene. Stella has already told us that she had false papers in the name of Solange. Lonsdale's sister who is a great friend of Stella's has been spending the nights with her at the flat. The mike revealed that Stella was nervous about her conversation being overheard. It looks more and more as if she were a German agent. She is undoubtedly a clever woman. She was shown a photograph of von Einem and almost too hurriedly handed it back saying that she had never seen him before.

7 December

I went over with Edward Cussen to see Commander Neville. We showed him the statements which Cussen had taken from those in the Ministry of Economic Warfare who were connected with the leakage of information regarding the sinking of one of HM ships. I told Neville that in Cussen's view the case would not look well in court if a charge was brought under Defence of the Realm Act 3. There was however ample evidence for disciplinary action. Neville said that he thought we should complete the enquiry by interrogating Wilson but unfortunately Wilson was having a day off.

8 December

Dick White told me about the case of Ingwald Johanson who came over as captain of a boat some time ago and took back with him to Norway three SIS agents who were handed over to the Gestapo. Johanson's wife is now residing somewhere in Scotland. Steps are being taken to see whether she is using a transmitter. Johanson brought with him a man called Sollum who came under suspicion some time ago and is now undergoing imprisonment for some infringement of the Aliens Order. Sollum has been employed as an agent by Nagel of the Norwegian *Deuxième Bureau*.

We have decided to intern Frederick Rutland under Emergency Regulation 18(b) since he is now of hostile associations. Further the Americans are asking whether he has been interned. If we leave him at large they will certainly think that he was acting as one of our agents while in America.

11 December

I returned at midday. While I was away Special Material indicated that an Englishman had correspondence which was of a compromising nature and had to be destroyed. He was in conversation with Nakimura. It was felt that the Englishman could only be Lord Sempill and his apartment and office were subsequently raided. Only a few Air Ministry and Admiralty reports of no particularly interest were recovered. He has, of course, committed a technical breach of the regulations but we are fairly confident that he had not retained the documents for any ulterior purpose. There was a scare later in that the ambassador's house in Grosvenor Square contained a transmitter. Post Office wireless vans were quite confident. It transpired eventually that the transmissions were from a house occupied by the Poles in an adjoining street. The Foreign Office was quite prepared to let us go in if we found anything to search all the other embassy premises. They were fortified in this idea by the news that our chancery in Tokyo had been searched for wireless equipment. The Foreign Office is now considering whether we should in any case search all Japanese embassy premises, on grounds of reciprocity.

12 December

Colonel Dudley Clarke was shipped some little time ago from Gibraltar to England, but was torpedoed, returned to Gibraltar, and finally sent to the Middle East for disciplinary action. There are some interesting photographs of him in female attire which have been obtained from the Spanish police.

13 December

We had a discussion about the case of Lord Sempill when it was decided that Colonel Hinchley-Cooke, Edward Cussen and Inspector Grant of Special Branch should summon Lord Sempill to Scotland Yard and question him about the telephone conversations. Colonel Trevor Wilson of SIS had been seen and emphatically expressed the view that the speaker was Lord Sempill. He discounted the suggestion that it might have been Edwards on the grounds that he knew Edwards' voice quite well.

15 December

I lunched with Hugh Trevor Roper, who is very worried by the capabilities of Kenneth Maidment in connection with the pioneering work which it has been decided to do in Canada on Japanese ISOS. He thinks that the only really suitable man is E.W. Gill who did all the pioneering work on the German ISOS. Trevor Roper thinks that the matter ought to be brought to the notice of Lord Swinton. There are obvious difficulties here as we should be interfering in a technical matter of which we have no real knowledge. I am fairly confident that Trevor Roper is correct in his view. We shall have to see what we can do.

Sir Francis Lindley has been seen in connection with the Lord Sempill case. He states that at the time of the first telephone conversation Sempill was in fact attending a meeting of the Japan Society, that he did not leave the room and that afterwards he accompanied Sir Francis for a period of about twenty minutes. This statement in fact corresponds with the report of the watchers who give quite an accurate description of Sir Francis. It looks therefore as if the first and second conversations were not related. The second one in which some uneducated Englishman speaking to Nakimimura delivers a message on behalf of "Bill S" is still unexplained. Personally, I think it undoubtedly refers to Sempill who has denied that he has communicated either directly or indirectly with any member of the Japanese embassy since the outbreak of war. The message delivered to Kamimura was to the effect that Bill S had been going through a difficult time but that everything was being taken care of. Nakimimura was to remember that Bill S had not communicated with him since the outgreak of war. The implication was that in fact he had so communicated.

16 December

John Senter came to see me about the case of Frederick Strauss, a so-called railway expert in SOE. They had at last decided to get rid of him, having discovered that he was an accomplished liar and a pilferer of the petty cash. Characteristically, we have been asked to look after him.

17 December

The Deputy Director-General held a meeting on the subject of Lord Sempill where all aspects of the case were discussed with all concerned. It was agreed that in the light of the evidence available it was almost impossible for Sempill to have been a party to the first telephone conversation. There were three witnesses and the watchers to corroborate the fact that he could not have had access to the telephone at the material time. On the other hand it seemed at least probable that Edwards might have been the man who rang the embassy. It will be remembered that Colonel Trevor Wilson had discredited Edwards on the grounds that he knew his vice. We were able to say however from our records that on two or three occasions we had established that Edwards was the speaker when Colonel Wilson's department had been unable to identify him. We also had a report from our informant in the embassy that it was Edwards not Sempill who had been responsible for a conversation about the retention of the services of Mrs Dixon who had been employed by the ambassador. It seemed therefore that little reliance could be placed on Colonel Wilson's view. Edwards was the only other person known to us who might fit the bill. As a servant of the Japanese Embassy he would naturally have had books and papers relating to embassy business and he might well have sought Kamimura's instructions about their retention or destruction. It was decided therefore that Major Cussen and Courtney Young would interview Edwards with a view to obtaining some sort of confirmation from him.

TRICYCLE's questionnaire is now in our possession. It shows quite clearly that in August last the Germans were very anxious to get as full particulars as possible about Pearl Harbor.

I heard later that Edwards had been seen and had denied that he was the author of the conversation with Kamimura. We are therefore no further either on the first conversation or the second.

Arthur Frances Henry Edwards, who worked in the Chinese Customs from 1903 to 1928, had been employed by the Japanese Embassy as an adviser.

18 December

I had a talk with T.A. Robertson and Cyril Mills about the Stella Lonsdale case. Mills is emphatically of the opinion that Stella is a German but it is going to be very difficult to trip her up. She is now pressing to be allowed to return to France. Mills and T.A. Robertson have had a long talk with Claude Dansey who has put all his cards on the table. He said he had never received Buster Milmo's report giving the information about Gaessler. He produced his own traffic which if it had been seen by us some months ago might well have prevented SIS being led up the garden path so long. It was quite clear to T.A. Robertson from its form that Gaessler was under control. Dansey is very anxious that his officers should collaborate closely with ours, but feels that this is not possible under existing regulations. He suggests that we should raise the matter through the Director-General and C. I am quite certain that if we do this it should be done with the concurrence of Valentine Vivian and that he should be kept informed of the contacts which we make. These contacts will be mainly for the purpose of discussion and comparison of notes. There is no doubt we should be of great help to Dansey's people and they might be of help to us. We must, however, keep Section V informed.

I also had a discussion with T.A. Robertson and John Marriott about Christian Hans von Kotze. This man who formerly lived in South Africa has been working for the German secret service in Brazil. He has given us a lot of valuable information about German secret service activities in Brazil and South Africa, partly I think because he dislikes the Nazi regime, and partly because he wishes to get back to his wife and family in South Africa. The Germans now wish him to go back to South Africa. We think it would be a good thing if we could send someone to establish a better liaison with the South Africans and to give them our views on how von Kotze should be handled. This raises once more the question of rapid transport, concerning which I have submitted a memo to the Director-General. It is almost impossible now to carry on our work without rapid transport facilities.

Stewart Menzies told me today that the lost bag at Ankara has been found in a lumber room. The embassy are so naïve as to think that it has not been compromised. Meanwhile a man called Sherrington has evidently handed out certain information regarding an increase of security staff in the embassy, since there is a reflection of this in ISOS. I gather however that Sherrington is being used as a somewhat curious double-cross. He has Hungarian connections. An enquiry has been sent to Ankara with a view to finding out whether the passing on of the information about the security staff was authorised.

I spent the rest of the day going through the Gibraltar leakage case with Dick White. Our conclusion is that in five cases leakage seems to be due to either a cipher break or to a hand-out by an agent but that in one case the evidence definitely points to a hand-out. I went over to see Commander Neville in the evening and arranged with him for Dick to have credentials from the Secretary of the Board empowering him to investigate in the naval office in Gibraltar and ordering that he shall have the SOI placed at his disposal for this purpose. There is no question of sending anyone else with him as we can only get one place on the flying-boat.

The *Barham* case has come up once more. A medium has produced a drowned sailor called Syd who was recognised by several people present at the séance and said he was one of the crew. Edward Hinchley-Cooke and Edward Cussen are once more taking up the trail.

Dick White tells me that we appear to have got into the Italian ISOS through the Rome–Jeddah traffic which was carrying a repeat of the Rome–Helsinki messages. Hugh Trevor Roper must be held to be to some extent responsible as he was very insistent that we should continue to regard Rome–Jeddah as a priority.

I had a talk today with T.A. Robertson about Stella Lonsdale. Everybody has come to the conclusion that she is thoroughly unreliable and untrustworthy and almost certainly a German agent, and everybody is opposed to her being allowed to return to France. J.C. Masterman thinks we should now proceed to direct interrogation of a detailed kind on the evidence obtained. Up to now we have merely been trying to get her to talk. She certainly has, and I am told that some of her conversation is of the filthiest kind.

Kim Philby of Section V has produced details of a number of agents in Gibraltar which have been sent to Colonel Medlam. It seems that the Rock Hotel in Gibraltar, the Hotel Reina Cristina at Algeciras and a hotel in Tangier, are all in the hands of the

Germans. The Reina Cristina is run by a German called Leib who is undoubtedly the central figure in the local German espionage network. The hotel seems to have belonged at one time to Lord Farringdon and is now the property of his grandson, Lieutenant Schreiber, our air attaché at Lisbon. His name was found on Mayorgas of Kleinworts who has been arrested by the FBI recently. There is no reason to think that there is anything wrong with Schreiber. The Villa Leone, which was featured, rather prominently, in the SUNDAE case, is used by Leib for housing his German friends.

I had a discussion afterward with Klop about Vera Eriksson. He is quite ready to have her but would welcome the assistance of one of T.A. Robertson's Field Security Policemen. He does not wish to see Vera until she arrives at his house.

Edward Travis came in to discuss the ZPT telegrams and to give us the original text. He was inclined to agree with Wilson of the Admiralty that it was unlikely that Cipher 'C' had been compromised. Had this been so he thinks there would have been some reflection elsewhere. I took the opportunity of asking him about our own ciphers. He said that he never had very much confidence in Williams at the Foreign Office who is supposed to be looking after our interests. I mentioned this to Charles Butler who is arranging for Malcolm Cumming to get into direct touch with Travis. Travis seemed to think there was too much delay at the Radio Security Service in submitting their material to GC&CS. He was taking steps to get this speeded up.

30 December

DUCK has received a reciphering ticker-tape and a number of cipher messages with the reciphering figures written in underneath. These are of the greatest value to GC&CS.

BALLOON has received a letter with DUFF cleverly concealed under the flap. The GPO failed to detect it.

31 December

Malcolm Frost discussed with me the cases of detection of illicit wireless which came up on six consecutive days and was located as being somewhere in the vicinity of the Russian Embassy. We were out with the vans because we were trying to detect illicit transmission by the Japanese. These signals were only picked up by chance. Subsequent enquiries showed that at least some of them had been picked up by the Radio Security Service Y units but had presumably been discredited because the discriminators were only interested in ISOS and kindred groups. This raises the whole question of the function of RSS which was originally set up in order to detect illicit transmissions from this country.

Victor Rothschild has had a talk with Lord Swinton about the new substance called Lauryl Thio-Cyanite which, if worn in a belt, kills or drives away lice. This new discovery might have a very important bearing on the course of the war owing to the fact that lice are the bearers of typhus and that this disease is prevalent in Russia. The medical authorities are just about to publish the information about this new discovery in some medical journal. This has been prevented.

1942

The first officer of a Spanish ship, the *Aldecoa*, has been known to us for some time from ISOS as a German agent. This ship recently arrived in Pointe Noire in Equitorial Africa and as it went into a prohibited port the captain has been arrested by the Free French. The protests have now been made, one from the Spanish shipping company to their London agents, Messrs Harris & Dixon, and the other by the Spanish ambassador here, asking him to give Harris & Dixon his support in obtaining the immediate release of the captain. We have told the Free French, and the Belgians since the ship has now proceeded to Matadi, that we have strong grounds for suspecting other ship's officers and that they would be well-advised to submit them to a thorough interrogation.

Henry Arnold came to see me about a new Ministry of Aircraft production scheme. There is apparently to be a committee consisting of Walter Linnell, Henry Tizard and Sir Frank Smith which will be responsible for bringing to the notice of the proper authorities various technical developments which require attention from the security point of view. Co-opted on this committee will be a representative of the Air Ministry and the Security Service. In the meantime Arnold has been asked to look into the whole situation in MAP and report. The Director-General does not wish him to be the representative on the committee but for some reason or other MAP do not wish to have Joe Archer. There is obviously a good deal of intrigue going on.

Len Burt tells me that Oreste Pinto has a thoroughly bad record in Special Branch based on enquiries which were made in 1930 when he applied for naturalisation. The report shows that he has been associating with fraudulent company promoting.

Barra has left his safe open and DUCK has discovered two rolls of deciphering which will be brought out and photographed.

An amusing incident was recounted about a Scots Guardsman who escaped from Germany to Russia but had been interned in a concentration camp. It seems that when he told his captors he was from the Scots Guards they thought he said Scotland Yard. He has consequently remained in internment ever since.

5 January

Colonel Stephens has submitted a long report on the Hirsch-Gilinsky case. The general impression is that both of them are crooks of the first water, ready to do anything that will fill their pockets and save their skins. There is at least a certain amount of doubt as to whether they undertook to work for the German secret service merely in order to get out of German clutches with as much of their property as they could save. Details about the Aubain-Poirier scandal are interesting. Baroness von Einem, acting as an agent for Herman Goering, made use of Hirsch to transmit about 4.6m French francs to *Le Temps* and *Figaro*, ostensibly in order that these papers might publish articles favourable to Germany. In actual fact, two million francs went back to Goering and a million to the Baroness von Einem and very little alteration was made to the tone of these papers in a sense favourable to Germany. Hirsch says he reported these facts to Lemoine and Gianvetti of the *Cinquième* and *Deuxième Bureaux* respectively, that neither of these people was allowed to come forward at his trial, which he said was staged as a red-herring by Edouard Daladier in order to distract attention from the fact that Daladier had tipped off Ambassador Abetz to clear out of the country at a time when his arrest was imminent. How far all of this is true is difficult to say. The fact remains that Hirsch was given a sentence of ten years and immediately after the German occupation he was released in order to work with the Sonderdienst. Gilinsky has been singularly uncommunicative but personally I do not feel his case has been examined sufficiently from the point of view of him being a Soviet agent in addition to his past as a purveyor of arms to the Spanish republicans, and I believe a connection with the Soviet Jewel Trust, since it is stated in the depositions that he had visited the Soviet Embassy in Paris and also that his son is now fighting in the Soviet army.

On Saturday I learned that [XXXXXXXXXXX] produced two documents which we had planted on Luis Calvo some two months ago. It is difficult to see why Calvo did not send them to Alcazar de Velasco sooner, unless perhaps he was intending to take them over personally, and owing to the long delay eventually decided to send these by other means.

6 January

I saw de Puey, an SIS man who has just got back from Gibraltar. He says that Nicol Grey, the Assistant Defence Security Officer, is rather worried about security in Gibraltar, particularly about Harry Norton, a Gibraltarian who has made himself indispensable to the Governor in the capacity of secretary. Norton, though regarded as pro-British, is thought to have something of an eye to the future and to relations with his Spanish friends to whom he is inclined to ask the Governor to grant facilities. He is always preaching moderation and appeasement. Recently, in the case of smuggling tobacco, he advised the Governor not to prosecute the representatives of a rich Spanish tobacco merchant, and to deal leniently with members of the police who were involved. Grey thinks that this kind of thing leads to a very lax state of affairs, and that if people think they can smuggle tobacco with impunity they will certainly smuggle other things. Medlam does not seem inclined to stand up to the Governor in matters of this kind.

Victor Rothschild told me that Sir Frank Smith had asked him to look into the security of an important Radio Direction-Finding development. We apparently have a device which reflects anything vertically, and which will give a clear indication when a plane is over any particular town, village or factory. This invention should be of immense importance and it is vitally important to us to devise means (a) to safeguard it in the production stage and (b) to ensure its destruction in the event of a bomber which carries it being brought down over enemy territory.

Dr Goertz has been tried by military tribunal, condemned to death and reprieved. We have not had this officially, but we understand this to be the case. So far the Irish tell us very little. They probably fear that we should use this case as a pretext for pressing the Eire government to forego its neutrality and turn the Germans out. There is fairly conclusive proof that Goertz was working in close conjunction with the IRA.

7 January

Today's *Times* mentions that Admiral Canaris is intriguing with General Marschner for the overthrow of the Nazi regime. The information comes from the *Times* Washington DC correspondent. The matter is of interest since C told me some little time ago that he had reason to think that Canaris might possibly lead an army revolt or at any rate be a party to it. Apart from this there is Krivitsky's information that Canaris at one time was working more for the Russians than the Germans.

[XXXXXXXX] is giving considerable assistance to Basil Fenwick of SIS in building up some sort of organisation in Spain which might be able to function if the country was invaded by the Germans. At present there's nothing. It is said that Ambassador Sam Hoare is a serious obstacle to any SIS development in Spain.

Klop came to see the Director-General today and to talk about Vera Eriksson. He has I think satisfied the Director-General that his plan is a good one and we are now able to proceed.

8 January

We had a Radio Security Service meeting this morning at which the question of Japanese ISOS was again raised. I explained what had happened at Lord Swinton's meeting the previous day and asked for information about the possibilities of covering the Pacific area, and particularly systems which might be concentrated at Bangkok. There was evidence from BJs that stations had been established at Bangkok, Saigon, Hainan and Singora but it seemed likely that there may be a number of outstations which could probably not be picked up in Canada. Ted Maltby explained that he was having considerable difficulty in getting a proper establishment out of the War Office and that it was impossible for him to recruit other staff. I suggested that steps might be taken to get hold of civilians and to make a start with their training at Barnet. Malcolm Frost agreed that this was desirable if such people could be found. Frost suggested that John Marriott's section at the BBC might provide useful material. It was decided to continue with our ISOS priority list and to add to it the ISK Groups. The ISK Groups are apparently in blocks. While certain Groups can be dealt with which are in a particular block it does not mean that Groups in other blocks can be unravelled at the moment. It is however merely a matter of time and the preparation of an index which may take some two months.

I had discussions with Anthony Blunt and Geoffrey Gibbs who are disturbed about TRIPLEX facilities at Whitchurch, and D4 are taking the view that the Security Control Officer's office does not provide sufficient cover.

TRIPLEX was MI5's interception of diplomatic bags and the surreptitious copying of the contents.

Dick Brooman-White came to tell me about the secretary at the Portuguese Embassy who is perturbed at the advance knowledge of Spanish journalists about matters of importance, in particular the journey of the Prime Minister to America. I think this lady may be useful to us.

Ned Reid has tumbled on an extraordinary story through the tracing of bank-notes delivered to the Yokohama Specie Bank. One Parmentier, a KLM pilot, has been paying sums of money to a Miss Steele, now employed in the WAAFs. This girl has access to quite a lot of confidential information. Examination of her account shows that she has paid fifty guineas to an Irish Communist doctor called de Caux. These payments were probably for an abortion. Quite independently it has been ascertained that the Yokohama Specie Bank notes have been paid into the account of Miss Lucy Joad, daughter of Professor Joad, by one A.J. Russell, believed to be of the Group Movement. These sums have been paid in from various offices of Lloyd's Bank. This led us to another account of Miss Lucy Joad at Barclay's Bank, Marble Arch. Miss Joad had been introduced to Barclay's by de Caux and the account was operated by him. It was filled by payments in notes which totalled something like £10,000. De Caux has another account which is being investigated.

9 January

Major Felix Cowgill came to see me yesterday evening accompanied by Ralph Jarvis, a representative of SIS in Lisbon, and I have since had a number of further discussions with them, Kim Philby of SIS and with the Naval Intelligence Division. Jarvis told me that through an agent in the service of Weltzein, a German secret service representative in Lisbon, it has been possible to obtain from Weltzein's index the cards of three British subjects employed by us at Lisbon. They are:

1. A Mr Stillwell, a local business agent for various firms and an honoured member of the British community, whose son Francis is the assistant naval attaché in Lisbon. It is thought that the son may be quite innocent but that the father may be extracting information from him without his knowledge. The son has been recalled to this country to undergo a naval course.
2. A Mrs M. Lawrence, who is No. 4 in the UK Contraband Control Office in Lisbon.
3. A Mr W. Haeburn Little, an Irish artist now employed in our naval shipping office in Lisbon. He has been in close touch with Section V officers and knows a great deal about the SIS organisation in Lisbon.

There have also been obtained the names of two ships' captains, concerning whom it is said we have already received notification. One of them is named Peck or Beck and serves on the *Sylvan Arrow*, a tanker flying the Panamanian flag.

We are at the moment principally concerned with W. Haeburn Little, Lieutenant RNVR, who is the confidential assistant to the NCGC Lisbon, and is proceeding on the yacht *Venus*, due to arrive at Gibraltar from Lisbon at noon on Monday, 12 January. The yacht is going to pick up certain wireless equipment at Gibraltar and return almost immediately to Lisbon.

The card about Little which is alleged to have been taken from Weltzein's index gives certain particulars and the numbers of the German agents who are in touch with him. It also has entered upon it in ink the dates and the amounts of payments which Little has received from Weltzein. The Admiralty do not consider that a photostat copy of this card, obtained through an agent who cannot be produced, would constitute satisfactory evidence for a court-martial unless it could be supported by other testimony. In order therefore to obtain further evidence, the following action is to be taken:

1. The *Venus* is to be delayed on some plausible excuse in Gibraltar so that Little can have the opportunity for forty-eight hours for making contact with somebody in Gibraltar. Instructions will be issued for him to be kept under observation during that period.
2. An attempt is to be made to photograph all the cards and a certain number of the files in Weltzein's office on Tuesday night.
3. Little's premises in Lisbon will be searched during his absence.
4. As there appears to be no plausible excuse for ordering Little to return to England and since if he became suspicious it might be difficult to force him to leave Portuguese territory, it has been thought preferable and opportune to allow him to carry out his normal duty by proceeding on the yacht *Venus* to Gibraltar. He will then be on British territory and can be dealt with as we think fit. It seems particularly desirable that if possible his arrest should not be carried out in Gibraltar, since any action of this kind would be bound to be a matter of common knowledge and might seriously embarrass Dick White in the enquiries in which he is at present engaged. It has therefore been decided to bring him back to this country. I gather that this proposition

presents considerable difficulties but I have pressed the Admiralty very strongly to regard the whole matter as a major operation which has now been going on for several months in Gibraltar and has reached a stage where it is impossible to send a signal to the Flag Officer without grave risk of it being in the hands of the enemy within forty-eight hours, and that therefore it is of paramount importance to avoid any action which might prevent us from bringing our enquiries to a speedy conclusion. The telegram at 2a has therefore been sent to Colonel Medlam through SIS.

5.   If arrest at [XXXXX] is impossible, it is proposed to send a further cable ordering the arrest of Little by the naval authorities and his return to this country under naval escort by the first available means of transport. The Legal Advisers to the Admiralty consider that his arrest by the naval authorities is preferable to that of the civil power which would require invoking Emergency Regulation 18(b)(a). Instructions will be issued that every possible step is to be taken to prevent the arrest becoming known, but it is realised that this may well be impossible. The captain of the yacht *Venus*, unless he turns out to be Little himself, will be informed in strictest confidence and told to provide some suitable excuse to his officers for Little's disappearance. It has been decided that Little should not be interrogated in Gibraltar or informed of the reasons for his arrest.

I saw Kim Philby about the Little case and we drafted a telegram to Tito Medlam and Dick White. I am very anxious if possible to avoid the arrest in Gibraltar as I feel certain that any action of this kind would seriously impede Dick's enquiries. Practically my whole day has been taken up in trying to make arrangements with the Admiralty, who now have agreed to delay the yacht *Venus* until 14 or 15 January when one of HM ships will be in the vicinity of Gibraltar and return to the UK. It is proposed tht Little should be allowed to board the *Venus* in the ordinary way and then be intercepted at sea.

I spoke to the Director-General about TRIPLEX at Whitchurch. He was apparently under the impression that we were proposing to deal with TRIPLEX material with unskilled SCO personnel. I have reassured him on this point and he is quite agreeable to our fixing up anything in the Security Control Officer's office which is plausible. I had a word with Colonel C.H. Burne who will go down with Anthony Blunt on Tuesday in order to work out suitable cover for our operations.

An Eire officer and three other ranks have just been landed in a Walrus biplane at St Eval in Cornwall. It seems that the officer was disgruntled owing to his having been placed under open arrest for drunkenness. The men have stated however that they were asked whether they would like to go for a short turn and they had no idea they were going to be brought to England. There is just a possibility that the officer intended to proceed to France and was forced down in Cornwall owing to lack of petrol. Eire are already getting excited and wish to send over an escort to fetch the officer and men and mechanics to bring back the plane. We are in the meantime proceeding on the lines that the whole party has landed without the permission of the immigration officer.

The Naval Intelligence Division has agreed to the plan by which Little will be taken off the yacht *Venus* by submarine.

I talked with J.C. Masterman and John Marriott about the case of Little and Weltzein. On the assumption that Weltzein was planting his information on us, he might merely wish to cause alarm and despondency in our various offices in Lisbon. It occurred to me that we might think out some similar plan for causing alarm and despondency in the German offices.

13 January

I attended a meeting at the Admiralty with the Assistant Director of Naval Intelligence, Phillip Johns and Carpmael, where an alternative plan was agreed to about Little's arrest. It was decided that he should be warned half an hour before the *Venus* sailed that an urgent telegram had been received telling him to report for special duty at the Admiralty and that since the submarine was leaving immediately for England he should transfer his kit to that vessel. He is to be kept under discreet observation until he is on board the submarine and if he attempts to destroy any papers he will have to be arrested. As soon as he gets on the submarine he will have to be searched by an officer from the Security Service and kept under restraint during the voyage.

14 January

I saw Philip Johns and Len Burt, who is going to provide some skeleton keys for use in Lisbon on the Weltzein index case.

A short time ago we received a report from SIS in which it was stated that the Germans were receiving meteorological reports from Dundalk, Cork and an area between Edinburgh and Newcastle. Enquiries were made through the Radio Security Service and have revealed that GC&CS had been regularly receiving the Nauen meteorological reports which disclose the existence of a German station in the vicinity of Cardiff and another at Blackpool. The various possibilities have had to be explored: (1) are the Germans decoding our meteorological reports? The answer is that their reports differ slightly from ours. (2) Is it possible for the Germans in the light of the reports that they got from places in Europe to be able to report accurately the weather conditions at Cardiff or Blackpool? It seems doubtful whether they can. (3) Have they been making use of the reports of our own agents? The answer here is that the reports of our agents differ slightly and they are not situated in the areas referred to. There are other avenues to explore but at the moment it looks as if we may have an undetected agent at Cardiff and another at Blackpool. If it is so there is clearly a deficiency in the organisation of RSS. As regards Eire it may be significant that the two stations reported are at Dundalk and Cork in the east and south respectively and this was the reason why Joseph Lenihan was sent to get weather reports from Sligo in the west.

The government is having a great deal of trouble with General de Gaulle about St Pierre and Micquelon. It seems that in spite of an undertaking that he would not take any action against these islands without the acquiescence of the

British government, he gave orders to Admiral Muselier that this should be done and failed to inform anybody. He has been taken to task by the Lord President and the Prime Minister has given instructions that he is to be told to evacuate the islands. The Americans are seriously embarrassed by the incident as they do not wish to fall out with Vichy at this stage. It seems that the Monroe Doctrine for some reason or another comes into the picture. De Gaulle is being extremely truculent.

Malta has discovered that the contents of cases which contain machine-gun ammunition and which are supposed to be water-tight, are seriously corroded. A test has been carried out here of ninety of these boxes which come from Woolwich Arsenal. Sixty-eight of them were found to leak when placed in a bowl of water. This means that several mission boxes will now have to be examined.

15 January

I arranged with James Herbertson of the Ministry of Civil Aviation to stop Mrs Stilwell from going to Lisbon over the weekend.

I had a long talk with Tommy Harris and Buster Milmo about the case of Fernando Casabayo, a Spanish republican employed by SO2 who had gone to the Spanish Embassy and supplied them with information about our latest explosive and the methods of the Commandos. Casabayo has been picked up as a deserter. It seems that he has five other accomplices also employed in SO2. This information has reached us through a contact of Ignatius. Ignatius's contact is going to report the facts to Alcazar de Velasco when he visits him in Madrid. It will be interesting to see his reactions. We may put in an *agent provocateur* ostensibly as one of Casabayo's accomplices.

Harris tells me that some individual posing as Alcazar de Velasco's secretary has produced a number of documents in Madrid which purport to give the names of certain individuals acting as Geman spies through Alcazar de Velasco. One of these is Lynch who is said to have received the sum of £3,000. We regard the information with considerable doubt. It has all the appearance of a plant.

John Senter came to see me about a party of Norwegians arriving at Lerwick. They are to load up with nine tons of explosives which they are taking back to Norway. He wanted to obtain sanction for their not being sent to the Royal Victoria Patriotic School. I only hope they are not all German agents.

Superintendent Finney of Special Branch has been on the telephone all day about a man called Reginald Kendall Cook, alias Reginald Gordon Scott, alias George Campbell Scott. This man appears to have a criminal record. When his baggage was searched at his lodgings certain plans and specifications relating to the Whittle engine were found. He appears also to have been employed at one time by the Daimler Company, and also by Rolls-Royce. He is now said to be looking for a ship of the Ellerman Line which sails to the Iberian Peninsula. It is just possible that he has been collecting information which he intended to take away to Spain. He is being looked for and will be arrested when found.

The aero-engine designed by Frank Whittle was Britain's first jet.

I had a talk with Victor Rothschild, Theresa Clay, T.A. Robertson and Roberts about Mrs Ray Johns. It was decided that at a convenient moment Roberts should reveal that he is an agent of the Gestapo who is contacted periodically by a man whose identity he does not know, and that his business here is to check up on the reliability of certain people whom the Germans think might be ready to assist them in time of invasion. We decided that he had better not have any credentials except perhaps a draft on the Swiss Bank Corporation for several hundred pounds. Details of this are to be worked out by Ned Reid.

Some days ago we discovered that the transmitter which had previously been active in Kensington Palace Road was in actual fact operating from the top floor of the Soviet Consulate, Rosary Gardens. We had previously asked the Soviet Embassy whether they were transmitting on the call-signs given but they had given us a denial. We have decided not to register any protest but to listen in for the time being in order to see what happens. So far there has been no answer to the call-signs. The Radio Security Service seems to have failed us rather badly in this case since their monitoring service never reported the signals. It was only because we happened to have found out through having vans out in search of signals from the Japanese Embassy that we knew anything about it.

I was rung up at about 10.30pm by the Night Duty Officer who had received via SIS a telegram from Philip Johns at Lisbon to the effect that Wing Commander Lord Carlow was flying over from Lisbon with the wax impressions of two keys. He wanted us to send down an expert to cut the keys which were to go back by some passenger on the plane leaving on Monday. This operation against Weltzein's office was to take place on Monday night. The keys have been cut at Lisbon but as it was felt that this might not have been done very skilfully it was thought better to have duplicate keys done here. Unfortunately the wax impression of one key has been somewhat damaged and skeleton keys of the Yale type are also required. I got on to Len Burt who is going to do the necessary. The plane should arrive sometime tomorrow afternoon.

Inspector Spooner and an expert key cutter have gone down to Bristol by the 10.30 train this morning. They will be met by the RSLO and taken to the SCO's office. I now hear that the plane from Lisbon is likely to land in Devon owing to fog. I have therefore arranged with the SCO to bring Lord Carlow to Bristol by car. There is a further complication since the plane leaving for Lisbon tomorrow is a freight plane and cannot carry any passengers without the express permission of the Air Ministry. This means that the keys will have to go back in charge of the pilot and his assistant, who are both Dutch. I am trying to arrange to have the keys put in the BOAC bag, since not only would it be difficult to get Air Ministry permission for a passenger to travel but the passenger would require a Portuguese visa which would be quite impossible to obtain by 9am. I spoke to Major Ferguson at 4.15 and explained the position, suggesting that he should telegraph to Lisbon.

The Director-General had a conference with Toby Pilcher and myself about the Stella Lonsdale case. He is anxious to know whether I thought she should be interned, since in view of the trouble there has been about Ben Greene he does not wish to have any more backwash on an 18(b) case. I said that I thought that while it was quite likely that as long as she remained in this country she would not dare to engage in espionage, she was such an adventuress that she might well try and escape to Ireland and get back to France in that way. If we left her at large we should have to keep her under constant observation which would waste a good deal of valuable time and cause immense trouble. SIS were firmly of the opinion that they did not want her back in France where she had probably already done a good deal of harm. Toby put the matter rather well by saying that if she was left at large and she did do anything detrimental to this country we should undoubtedly be blamed for not putting her case forward for internment. Our experience of this woman after endless interrogation, listening to telephone conversations and mike conversations, is that she is quite unequalled as a liar, and that she is either a dupe or an accomplice of the German secret service, more probably an accomplice. The Director-General was anxious that we should let the Home Secretary realise that the Advisory Committee might possibly decide in this woman's favour if she were interned under 19(b). He had this very much in mind owing to the case of Ben Greene who has been released with apologies. One of the principal witnesses, Harald Kurtz, was severely cross-examined by Sir Norman Birkett on his statement made eighteen months ago. On certain points his memory not unnaturally might have been expected to have been at fault and on one particular point he slightly modified his previous view. This seems to have been the occasion for Birkett, without due regard for the whole circumstances of the case and without submitting Ben Greene to cross-examination, to make what can only be described as an onslaught on the unfortunate Kurtz and to tear his evidence to pieces in the technical sense. Toby has little doubt that the Committee were just lying in wait for an MI5 informant and there is no doubt whatever that even if Kurtz's evidence is not accurate in every particular he was certainly present at a treasonable conversation with Greene. One of the points that Birkett completely ignored was the fact that Greene said that he had telephoned to Scotland Yard reporting Kurtz's visit. Scotland Yard had said that no such message had ever been received. Birkett seems to have accepted Greene's denial almost without question. It is thought there has been a good deal of encouragement of Birkett's attitude by Frank Newsam who has already expressed his disapproval of what he calls *agent-procateur* methods in the case of the Reverend Dymock. The whole business of Greene shows only too clearly how hopeless it is to establish any reasonable degree of security under this quasi-legal system by which the prosecution and its witnesses are subjected to severe cross-examination whereas the word of the accused is accepted without question. It was only after the Home Secretary had written his letter of apology that we were called into conference.

I was rung up at 8.30 by Ferguson's secretary who said that a message had been received during the night asking that the keys should not be sent in the BOAC bag but handed to the Dutch pilot who would be told to give them to Ford Anderson of BOAC in Lisbon. This did not seem to be such a good arrangement as the one made the night before, namely to send the keys in the BOAC bag addressed to the embassy, but we complied with the request from the other side. At 10 o'clock however we got a call from the aerodrome to say that the freight plane would not be leaving today owing to fog at Lisbon. It was therefore decided to let the arrangement stand for the following day and I rang Ferguson in order that he might send a wire to Lisbon.

I discussed with the Director-General the case of Joseph Lenihan. He has agreed to this man taking a job and to him being given the sum of £250, £50 to be handed to him now and £200 to be placed in an account and released to him after the war, provided he behaves himself. He is to be warned against going back to Eire and will be told to report his movements. He is not to be allowed to leave the country.

The Director-General has also agreed to our dispensing with the services of the Field Security policeman who was to assist in looking after Vera when she is released. Klop though that this man might spoil the atmosphere.

The double-cross account shows a balance in our favour of between £7–8,000. We have netted about £26,000 odd and spent over £19,000. This figure does not include sums of money taken from spies who have been executed. If they were included the total receipts would be in the neighbourhood of £33,000.

I saw Reg Spooner who had been down to Bristol to arrange about the keys which were to go to Lisbon. The expert he took down appears to have been able to carry out the job satisfactorily.

Victor Rothschild received a call from Lord Swinton this morning asking him what steps he has taken to implement the decision arrived at the meeting of the Security Intelligence Centre on the security of our ships proceeding to Melilla. Victor said quite properly that he was submitting this matter to the Director-General since the proposal involved the running of six men under the Defence Security Officer at Gibraltar and their payment. Swinton then told him that the placing of this matter before the Director-General was just a formality and that he (Swinton) gave him an order to get on with it at once. The Director-General was extremely annoyed and was only persuaded by Victor not to write a pretty stiff letter to Swinton calling his attention to the terms of the written agreement by which the Director-General should be master in his own house.

The Security Intelligence Centre was a short-lived attempt to insert a member of the Security Executive's Secretariat into the Security Service to improve coordination.

I had a talk with Tommy Harris about certain messages relating to our shipping which had come into the possession of Alcazar de Velasco. Copies of these messages had reached us through SIS Madrid. They purported to come from Newcastle, Edinburgh, Liverpool and London, and dealt with shipping matters. They appear to be the type of information that comes from the Spanish Consul. An interesting fact is that these messages, with slightly altered dates, have appeared as Japanese BJs from Madrid to Tokyo, information having been sold to the Japanese by Alcazar de Velasco.

We also discussed the position of Luis Calvo in the light of certain BJs which implicate him very definitely. Alcazar de Velasco has given the Japanese what purported to be the lay-out of his organisation in this country. Most of them are, I think, known to us or actually working for us. Alcazar de Velasco has evidently been trying to blow himself up in the eyes of the Japanese and grossly exaggerating his powers for obtaining information from this country. At the same time his organisation may be slightly more extensive than we know. We decided to allow Luis Calvo to leave by plane tomorrow. He had been held up owing to some mistake about his name being left on the Home Office Black List.

22 January

At the Radio Security Service meeting today we discussed the possibility of there being two or three agents in this country sending meteorological reports, none of whom had been detected by RSS. I also mentioned the possibility of one at Baldock and the case of the Soviet transmissions from the consulate in Rosary Gardens. I asked what could be done to improve the situation and whether if in fact transmissions of this kind were going to stations other than those covered by ISOS, etc there was much hope of picking them up. The answer seemed to be that if the Germans were working to some other network the chances were extremely remote. RSS is doing some discrimination work on the residue of the material which the Y stations and Voluntary Interceptors collect. There is apparently a similar residue from the various systems covering the army, navy and air force Y units. There is, however, no pool where all these residues are sorted out. Kenneth Morton Evans was very strongly of the opinion that some coordination was necessary. Felix Cowgill undertook to make enquiries. For some reason he did not wish anything to be said in the minutes of the RSS Committee.

Dick White and I had a long talk with Felix about the attempted raid on Weltzein's index. It seems there must have been a traitor in the camp. To begin with, there was a slight difficulty about the key but when they managed to get inside they found the International Police waiting for them. An Austrian and his Swiss wife were arrested. It then became necessary to get rid of all the intermediaries to Gibraltar. The SIS contact with the International Police stated that they had been warned by someone in Weltzein's office. Felix thinks that an extra chauffeur who was taken on at the last moment may have been the cause of the trouble.

The Austrian and his wife, both professional photographers engaged by SIS to copy the card index, were released by the International Police on condition they left the country immediately. The entire operation had been masterminded by the Germans who had duped an SIS source, Frank Verscheuren.

23 January

I went over to see C with Dick White in view of the suggestion that John Codrington should go out to Gibraltar to take over a part of SIS's activities from Colonel Medlam. Dick gave a general picture of the situation. C was rather worried at the general set-up and the fact that the Governor obtained most of his advice from Harry Norton and Peter Quennell. I gather that the Political Warfare Executive was sending out Medlicott, presumably to do propaganda in North Africa and Spain. It seems that he will also be joining the general confusion of functions which seems to exist, and that he will almost certainly quarrel with Quennell.

24 January

I have just seen a report about Donaldson's Camp. A prisoner of war who had been taken by the Navy while on a meteorological expedition to Greenland had reported that there was a plot going on in Donaldson's Camp, by a number of prisoners of war who intended to escape. He said also that messages and codes were going in and out of the camp and that he thought that somebody had a wireless transmitter. Certain enquiries were made but with a more or less negative result until occasion was found to examine the belongings of all the inmates. A diagram of a wireless transmitter was discovered and also a valve, a soldering apparatus and other electrical equipment. In addition, a number of prisoners of war seemed to have the names and addresses of certain people in this country from whom presumably they had been told they could obtain assistance in an emergency. Among these names were those of Kuchenmeister and Mrs Roy. I am arranging for the prisoners to be interrogated about these names and for further enquiries to be made. It seems just remotely possible that there may be a basis of a Fifth Column organisation, but the organisation must be old since the names of some of those found have been interned since the beginning of the war.

26 January

Felix Cowgill has put forward the suggestion that Stilwell should be discredited in Lisbon instead of being recalled here by Thorneycrofts. It is thought that if a story is put about that he is in the pay of the Germans he will protest his innocence and may wish to come back to this country to clear himself. He could then be thoroughly interrogated.

27 January

The Director-General has been asked by Desmond Morton to look into certain cables sent by a man called Walter Karig who is in close touch with Senator Knox, to his London agency under C.P. Brook. Karig cables are in code and on one occasion they disclosed information about the Prime Minister's visit to America. It has been decided that subject to Morton's approval Censorship should call for some explanation from C.P. Brook. This would probably react on Karig. If necessary we could bring the matter to the notice of the American Embassy.

There has been a case of sabotage in Gibraltar on board the *Eirn*, an anti-submarine trawler and so far very few facts are available. It seems, however, that it may be desirable to send one of CID officers out to assist in solving cases of this sort. It has also been suggested that we might have a finger-print index which could quite easily be provided since all Spaniards entering the Fortress have passes with their finger-prints on them. If a bomb was found finger-prints might provide a useful check. There has also been a case of sabotage at Lorenco Marques. This place is evidently extremely important since we know from other sources that the Germans are spending £200 a day on cables between Lorenco Marques and Berlin. It seems very desirable that SIS should have some liaison with this place.

FATHER has been asked to indicate the map square in which he carries out his patrols. The answer is being considered.

28 January

Herbert Hart has ascertained that our friend Henderson of the Censorship who was notorious for his pro-German and Pacifist views, has now landed up in the office of Sidney Barnes, Permanent Secretary at the Admiralty. The matter is somewhat delicate as we have already told Barnes to get rid of one of his secretaries who was a thorough-going Communist.

29 January

I saw Sir Alexander Maxwell this afternoon and discussed the case of Vera Eriksson. He said he would arrange for the rescinding of the 12(5)(a) Order and for the issue of an 18(a) Restriction Order. We were to write him a letter giving him the necessary particulars. He would also arrange for the transfer to Aylesbury Prison.

We propose to get Vera Eriksson to Aylesbury Prison on Sunday, and to Klop's on Tuesday.

30 January

Ned Reid has told me that the Midland Bank know of a firm called F.W. Porter & Porter who are apparently Admiralty sub-contractors. They have a most remarkable account from which £1 notes are drawn and are then converted back into Bank of England notes which find their way into Porter's private account. The £1 notes are ostensibly for payment of wages to employees who do not exist. Porter seems to have swindled the Admiralty of some £90,000. We have ascertained that one of his co-directors, named Clare, is at present under arrest for somewhat similar activities. This must have alarmed Porter who has been to the Midland Bank asking for all his cheques. We have informed the Liverpool Police and pending their obtaining a magistrate's warrant we are holding the cheques under 80(a).

I have discussed with J.C. Masterman the drawing up of a memo on the execution of spies and the publicity that should be given to these matters. I am urging (1) that there should be no further publicity except where we consider it desirable and (2) that the execution of spies should be the exception rather than the rule, since we stand to lose much through not having them available for further interrogation.

There is also a report from our military attaché in Stockholm to the effect (1) a loyal Norwegian detective with contacts with German police in Oslo has stated that two Norwegians in London in high positions belong to the Gestapo. They are not military and possess a wireless transmitter thus being in constant touch with Norway. (2) that the Germans were aware three days ahead that British action against Norway about Christmas was intended. Steam is said to have been raised on all trains in the Bergen area. The Germans anticipate the large-scale landing. The two Norwegians in London may possibly be MUTT and JEFF. There may be many explanations of the second part.

31 January

Ned Reid tells me that Porter has committed suicide. He went and asked for the return of his cheques from the bank and was told that they are being held by head office. It was on receipt of this information that he went home and did himself in.

1 February

Vera Eriksson was told by Edward Hinchley-Cooke about her proposed move. She asked what had happened to Drücke and Wälti and was much concerned to hear that they had been executed.

A letter has been intercepted by the Censorship addressed to H. Yamamoto, c/o Tramstrasse 56, Munchsenstein, Switzerland. The letter was dated 12 September 1941 but was only sent from the London WC district on 24 January 1942, the inference being that it had remained in someone's pocket for some time owing to doubts as to the method by which it should be transmitted. The letter says: "Here is the picture you wanted. It is best could do and hope it suits. When you write or wire Tokyo tell my brother keep money for time being as I cannot write him again soon. Tell O. not to worry about me as silly bastards here believe anything and I am well in with them and get good pay. Kind regards to anyone at old firm. Writing in English because K. has promised to get this to you and first wants to see what I say. Cannot use D.B. any more as K. says now inspected. Banzai." signed in pencil "D". We are inclined to think that this is 'Donald'. 'O' may possibly be Oka. 'K' cannot be a Japanese but might conceivably be Eric Kessler of the Swiss Legation. 'DB' is, of course, the diplomatic bag. We are sending a slightly different letter giving a cover address, hoping that we may get a reply and so confirm that identity of D. The picture referred to was a picture postcard of King George V.

4 February

According to an intercepted letter a New York publisher is trying to arrange with Watt, London, for the publication of Major Gribble's book *Diary of a Staff Officer* in German. It is to be printed in Switzerland. Gordon Lennox has got hold of Gribble and will tell him to stop the publication. If the book circulates in Germany there is a possibility that what has been overlooked may come to light.

5 February

The Spanish Consul from Liverpool has deposited some parcels at Liverpool Street Station. We should like to have a look at them but unfortunately there does not seem to be much time. A wild suggestion has been made that a small explosion should take place in Liverpool Street Station's luggage office. A police cordon would then be placed round the office and we should have time to examine the parcels at our leisure. I need hardly say that this suggestion was heavily sat on by me.

6 February

There have been some interesting Prisoner of War reports. Very strange conversations between von Ravenstein and Schmitt, two German generals captured in Libya. Both of them seem to dislike Erwin Rommel intensely. They regard him as an *arriviste* who by pressing his troops to do what is almost impossible hopes to make a name for himself. He had apparently set his heart on taking Tobruk, and incurred very heavy casualties in the attempt. He is evidently a man of iron will and ruthless in getting rid of anybody who does not conform to his ideas, and is in every way an unsympathetic character.

The conversations between Generals von Ravenstein and Schmitt were recorded at special quarters at CSDIC Cairo.

It seems that the Vera Ericksson case is going on well. The lady is doing her best to help though it seems likely that she has not got a very intimate knowledge of the organisation.

SIS now tells us that the chauffeur in the Little case was introduced by a Portuguese employee in our legation who was in touch with Weltzein, who was distrusted. This seems to cause serious doubts to be cast on the original information and is an aspect of the case which should have been made clear to us and the Naval Intelligence Division at the start.

Jack Verlinden, who we have at Camp 020, has said that he reported long ago about Joseph Laureyssens and Alphons Timmerman, whom we discovered on our own, and also about a man called Florent Steiner concerning whom we likewise had no information from SIS. Steiner has been at large about eight months, but we have now picked him up.

Jack Verlinden had denounced Joseph Laureyssens upon their arrival in Wales, and later was to inform on Dr Hilaire Westerlinck, whom he had met with the Abwehr in Lisbon. Florent Steiner had arrived in England in June 1941 but was not traced to Liverpool until eight months later. Under prolonged interrogation he admitted possession of secret ink, and two cover addresses in Lisbon, but he had not contacted the Germans so he was detained until the end of the war.

Both J.C. Masterman and Buster Milmo put in reports about the suggested arrest of Luis Calvo. J.C. is strongly opposed to the whole project as he feels it will seriously embarrass the work of the Twenty Committee owing to Calvo's previous connection with G.W. Milmo on the other hand takes the view that some action is necessary against the Spanish ring being run by Alcazar de Velasco. Personally I do not feel that the arrest of Calvo is going to have very serious repercussions. On balance I am in favour of the arrest. We cannot allow his activities and those of his associates to run on indefinitely. We intend to take Felix George Sturrup in under 18(b), and Onofré Garcia Tirrador and Antonio Castre de la Torre under 12(5a). Pedro Marcos Rinao and Castillo are to be interrogated and searched.

Kim Philby came to see me with a programme for discrediting Alcazar de Velasco by various insinuations. It is desired to give the impression that he has double-crossed the Spaniards.

I had a word with Ferguson about the Little case and explained to him that it was almost impossible to proceed until we got the documents and the assistance of certain people from Lisbon who had the full details of the case.

I had a discussion with Felix Cowgill about Alcazar de Velasco and his liquidation. Felix is strongly in favour of Philby's scheme. I was at first rather opposed to it on the grounds that if our information coming from that quarter was of value it would be better to leave Alcazar in position so that we should learn what steps he was taking to reform the organisation over here after the arrest of Luis Calvo. Felix pointed out however that he had a rather special interest in the matter since Alcazar was also running an organisation in South America. He thought therefore that any steps which would jeopardise Alcazar's position would be of value. I therefore agreed to the course suggested.

Irma Stapleton has got ten years' imprisonment.

I dined with Klop when Vera Eriksson's case was discussed. He has got a number of interesting details, but his picture is not yet complete. He is quite convinced that Vera is doing her best.

11 February

I had another meeting with William Codrington, William Malkin and William Strang. The Foreign Office said that they could not give any guarantee that the embassy would not be allowed to visit Luis Calvo but if they were pressed they would do their best to stall things as long as they could. This point was put to Anthony Eden who agreed. The Foreign Office agreed that Castillo should be searched. The question of Calvo carrying a bag was then discussed. It was agreed that the bag should be taken from him and returned to the Spanish Embassy by the Foreign Office. The Foreign Office would say that they had opened it as it was being carried by a man who had been arrested as a spy. I have discovered that Onofré Garcia is employed by the Cuban Minister and therefore had diplomatic privilege. Unfortunately the Minister is away in Torquay recovering from influenza. It will therefore be necessary to get hold of the secretary who will go to the Foreign Office and telephone for approval of Garcia's arrest and search on the Legation premises. I discussed with the Director-General the possibility of deporting Calvo if he were not confronted with Castillo. It was decided to proceed as arranged and consider this point at a later stage if necessary. I spoke to C and asked him to let us have his approval of the whole Calvo project in writing.

I saw the Director of Military Intelligence today about the Calvo arrest and the views of the Twenty Committee. He did not take a gloomy view about G.W. and seemed quite satisfied about our going ahead.

12 February

I heard that last night Stewart Menzies was worrying about Luis Calvo. He is afraid that in view of the Tangier incident there may be serious repercussions on his own organisation. I therefore went over to see him. He had by that time spoken to Sir Alexander Cadogan and seemed somewhat reassured. I said that I thought that I was right and that as all the plans were made we really ought to go ahead. He agreed, and he told me that SOE were definitely responsible for the Tangier incident. It seemed that in addition to limpets, the *Rescue* had taken over a certain amount of gun cotton and detonators. Owing to the atmospheric conditions the gun cotton ignited and there were disastrous results. Peter Quennell is, however, resigning and SOE have been told that they are to cease all operations for the time being in Spain and Portugal.

I attended the Radio Security Service meeting today but I did not stay for very long and nothing of special importance was discussed.

I had a meeting with Sir Alexander Maxwell about the case of Sam Stewart. He was inclined to agree that it was difficult to get over the evidence of the SNOW traffic which seemed to indicate that Stewart had at one time or another had dealings with the Germans.

The Twenty Committee have held their weekly meeting today, and are rather upstage about the arrest of Luis Calvo. They have passed a resolution asking for directives from the Wireless Board owing to the altered circumstances. I spoke to the Director of Military Intelligence who thinks that the Twenty Committee are taking an exaggerated view of the situation. He wants me to speak to them and calm them down.

13 February

At 8am the Night Duty Officer rang up to say that Luis Calvo had signed a comprehensive statement at 6.45am. He did not reach Camp 020 until 1am. Later I saw the statement which throws the blame on others and tries to imply that Calvo has merely been an unwilling intermediary in various acts of espionage. Calvo states that on several occasions the bag has been used by diplomats and others for the transmission of information from this country which would be of use to the Germans.

I had a meeting with Sir Alexander Cadogan, William Strang, Peter Loxley and William Malkin at which it was agreed not to touch Brugada's bag. An extremely awkward situation would be reached if he refused to give it up and we were forced to take it from him by violence.

In view of Calvo's statement it was agreed that in addition to saying that he had been arrested for espionage carried out under the instructions of Alcazar for the Germans, we should say that we had definite evidence that the diplomatic bag had been used for improper purposes, and request the embassy to carry out an investigation. It was further decided that he might perhaps begin by an examination of the bag of Mr Brugada, which was arriving today.

The Assistant DNI is getting very worried about the Little case. He does not feel that he can keep Little under close arrest for much longer. I explained to him that we had only just got certain of the documents and it was going to be difficult to proceed without the presence of Captain Arthur Benson, the Naval attaché, and Ralph Jarvis of Section V. Certain things had been gradually leaking out which made me rather skeptical about the original information and unless we had an opportunity of getting down to it with the actual people concerned I did not think we could find a solution. I then spoke to Ferguson and impressed upon him the necessity of getting Jarvis over at the earliest possible moment.

I had a discussion with Victor Rothschild, Jack and Theresa Clay about Plan QUASI DORMOUSE. We are trying to find a way of giving Walter Wegener a wavelength on which to transmit, and also a code. We came to the conclusion that Dorothy would probably have to be the intermediary but it is difficult to make the scheme plausible. We considered the possibility of getting the Germans through B1(a) channels to open up from their side but we agreed that before doing anything more it would be desirable if possible to find out the present position with regard to Walter's wireless set. We do not know whether he has yet converted it into a transmitter or whether he is attempting to use it. We have had a van working in the vicinity but he has so far not been picked up.

Dick Brooman-White, Edward Cussen and I had a meeting with General John Lakin to discuss the Marshall group. SOE have apparently paid a lump sum to Marshall who runs a group of Republican Spanish thugs operating in France. They did not appear to be interested in the people Marshall employed but merely in Marshall's information. They sometimes used his organisation to communicate with France via New York. Marshall has apparently complained to SOE that we have arrested a number of his agents including Onofré Garcia. We had told SOE months ago that the Marshall group would probably be compromised but it seems doubtful whether they have done anything about the matter. We are now anxious to know exactly what payments have been made by Marshall to Garcia and on what dates. This is important as we are examining Garcia's account and wish to eliminate all genuine payments. We think it likely that he has been receiving money from the Spaniards since he has obviously been giving them information which he has been obtaining through his contacts with the Free French Forces. Lakin undertook to make enquiries.

Dick Brooman-White has had a talk with Ignatius. José Brugada appears to have had an interesting time in Madrid. He was entertained rather lavishly by Alcazar de Velasco and on the last day was summoned to Alcazar's house ostensibly to discuss press matters. When he got there he found a German car outside, and inside two obvious German officers, calling themselves Gonzalez and Garcia. Alcazar de Velasco was obviously not unacquainted with them both. The position of Collier was discussed with reference to the dangers of implicating an Englishman, and Brugada himself received instruction for future work. Brugada has brought over with him in the bag a number of envelopes for himself and others containing money and a questionnaire relating to army, navy and air matters. Brugada has secret ink for correspondence through the bag and similar facilities are made use of by Barra, who is part of the Alcazar de Velasco organisation.

Ignatius came to the office today and gave us a picture of what was going on in the Spanish Embassy. Everybody is running round in circles. Villaverde is very anxious to avoid a crisis as he thinks that if the ambassador opens Brugada's bag and finds that it contains inflammatory material he will blow up and get both himself and Villaverde recalled. Villaverde is therefore anxious if possible to get the Foreign Office request withdrawn. Our only interest lies in the possibility that the ambassador may vent his rage on Brugada and send him back to Madrid. It is also thought that he will burn the contents of the envelopes. This would be unfortunate.

Dick White and I went over to the Foreign Office to see Frank Roberts with a view to finding some way out. It was suggested that possibly the Foreign Office might modify their request by saying that they were only interested to know whether the bag contained any documents addressed to Luis Calvo. The Foreign Office did not feel that they could go back on what they had said already and they were reluctant to do so, because the accusation that the bag was being improperly used was a useful card in their hands as a set off against the Tangier incident which was causing them a lot of trouble in Madrid. When José Brugada arrived he was asked by Villaverde whether he had anything to tell him. Villaverde repeated this question three times, each time with greater emphasis. Brugada was evasive. He said that he would be seeing Gannon of the Political Intelligence Department who was a great personal friend and who might possibly be able to help about Calvo. He was going down to the country to see Gannon and was anxious if possible to say that Gannon had ascertained that the Foreign Office request only referred to correspondence addressed to Calvo. I said after consultation with the Foreign Office that I did not think he could go as far as this. There would however be no harm in his saying that Gannon, who had nothing to do with the affair, thought on general form that as the authorities had arrested Calvo their request for an examination of the bag might well be due to a belief that it contained letters to Calvo. In fact Brugada never saw Gannon at all and it was therefore still open to the Foreign Office if they were pushed into a corner to deny that Brugada and Gannon had ever met. Ignatius seems to be working for appeasement and we are inclined to think that he has kept certain things back.

16 February

We have had an account from Ignatius of what occurred at the ambassador's house last night. Most of the members of the staff were assembled in the ambassador's room. The minister ceremoniously opened the bag and laid all the packets on a piece of white paper. There were envelopes addressed to Brugada, Barra and others. The minister then addressed the assembly in the following words: "Gentlemen, the Foreign Office have suggested that our diplomatic bag is being improperly used. I shall know how to deal with this matter myself, but for my own satisfaction I should like each of you to open his packet, and if it contains anything of an espionage character I should be glad if you would hand it to me. I should also like to know if your envelopes contain money." Brugada opened his envelopes. One contained £40 for Collier and another £200 odd for G.W. The minister took the money saying that he would refer the matter to Madrid and if it was in order the notes would be returned. Brugada then opened the envelope containing the questionnaire. He read it and then handed it to the minister saying he thought perhaps it might come within the term of improper correspondence. The Minister read the questionnaire, turned round and put it in the fire. Barra was not present at the interview and his envelope therefore remained unopened.

I saw William Strang this morning and gave him an account of what had happened. The embassy has now begun to press for an interview with Luis Calvo, and the Foreign Office seems to think that this will have to be granted sooner or later. I spent the afternoon dictating at home. I dined with Klop who gave us an account of Vera Eriksson, who has gone back to Aylesbury Prison. She has, I think, done her best for us. Klop is submitting a long report. Right at the end of her stay he discovered that she had Jewish blood and that Karl Drücke was also non-Aryan. This accounts for a great deal, particularly the attitude of Bruhns and other officers, who refused to eat with them on their journey to Norway. The whole expedition seems to have been extremely hurried and singularly ill-conceived. No details had been worked out and most parties concerned seemed to think that the plan was doomed to failure. Klop is very definitely of the opinion that Dr Rantzau was just throwing agents into this country in order that he could report to his superiors he had agents in England. This is very much in confirmation of my theory that the matter was not given serious consideration until the Germans reached the Channel ports.

17 February

We propose in future to take a rather strong line with José Brugada and Ignatius. We have got some of Brugada's secret ink, which is in the form of a small piece of cotton wool dipped in Acqua Vitae. We also have his nib. We propose to get if possible the remainder of his secret ink. He will then have to do all his correspondence through us. We do not think that he has told us all he knows, and we intend to exercise pressure unless he comes clean.

Dick Brooman-White has seen Ignatius and told him firmly that we are not satisfied with his behaviour. Ignatius is penitent. The ambassador is said to be extremely grateful to the Foreign Office for their method of handling the case of Luis Calvo.

TRIPLEX obtained last night shows that Barra has sent accurate descriptions to Madrid and specifications of the performance of several of our tanks. It seems almost certain that he has obtained this information by improper means. I have instructed Anthony Blunt to keep his assistant Munoz under close observation and to lay on any other forms of observation that are possible.

The Assistant DNI has been pressing me about the case of Little. The naval officer in charge of him does not think that it is wise to place him under open arrest as he could easily escape from Greenwich at night. I asked Jim Hale to see the officer who has had long conversations with Little. He does not altogether like Little, but is rather inclined to think that he is innocent. I asked Jim to go and talk the matter over with the ADNI in the light of this conversation.

William Strang tells me that the ambassador has informed the Foreign Office that there were no letters to Luis Calvo in Brugada's bag, and no communications of the nature suggested.

18 February

William Strang is pressing me for a date on which Luis Calvo might be seen. I saw the Director of Military Intelligence and Graham about the resolution of the Twenty Committee. The DMI agreed with my view that things had not reached a stage where the Wireless Board could give any useful direction. I went on to see the DNI and obtained an agreement from him. I informed the DMI about Barra, the TRIPLEX reports about tanks, and the fact that Barra was using secret ink. I told him that Blunt would be making enquiries with various MI branches concerned.

19 February

I saw the Home Secretary with Sir Alexander Maxwell and John Morris about the case of Sam Stewart. Morris was inclined to take the view that SNOW on his visit to Antwerp had built up Sam Stewart in the eyes of the Germans and that this was why they had confidence in him. I said that I did not think that this view was justified by a close study of SNOW's traffic. Had the Germans really been relying on SNOW they would have replied by leaving the decision in his hands, on so important a matter as the operating of a radio set from Belfast. I did not think that we were justified in assuming that they would have lightly thrown SNOW, who to them was an important agent, into the arms of somebody about whom they had any serious doubts. Morris was allowed to see the actual traffic but was given strict instructions that on no account was he to communicate this information to the committee or to anybody else. The interview lasted one and a quarter hours at the end of which the Home Secretary said he would like to think the matter over. He would also like Morris to consider the case in the light of the information which had just been made available. It was proposed that a further meeting should be held on Monday.

20 February

A further meeting was held at the Foreign Office at which I was present, between Sir Alexander Cadogan, the Director-General, Sir William Malkin and William Strang. From information that we had received it was clear that the Spanish ambassador was trying to get the Foreign Office to pull his chestnuts out of the fire in the case of Luis Calvo. He had clearly been shocked to find that the allegations by the Foreign Office about the improper use of the bag had been fully justified, but while he would welcome a strong line by the Foreign Office he obviously did not wish to become involved himself in a serious row with the Spanish Foreign Minister, Ramon Serrano Suner. He would therefore protest energetically on behalf of Calvo but would not mind very much if he received a rebuff. The Foreign Office took the view that in this matter they had to deal with Madrid and that the reactions there were more important than the reactions here. They were therefore anxious that Calvo should if possible be interviewed under certain safeguards by a member of the embassy. We said that we would arrange this but we would like to consider whether it would be better to get the interview over at once or to wait another five or six days. Sir William Malkin seemed doubtful about the man's detention under 12(5a), but since he had not got a copy of the order in his archives the other day and had clearly not read the copy obtained, his views did not carry much weight. It was pointed out to him that the order made it quite clear that if the carrying out of the deportation order was in anyway prejudicial to the efficient prosecution of the war, we had a perfect right to keep the alien in detention with-out necessarily preferring any charge.

I had a discussion in the afternoon about Luis Calvo. We thought it would be best to get the interview over and it was subsequently arranged that Calvo should be seen at the Oratory Schools by Vitturo, the second secretary. We undertook to pick him up at the embassy in a car. The meeting would be held on the understanding that only Calvo's personal condition would be discussed. Vitturo at first thought that the presence of a British officer rather implied that there was an imputation against his honour. It was explained to him that this was a mere formality and had no such significance.

21 February

The meeting at the Oratory Schools between Luis Calvo and Vitturo has gone off quite successfully and the undertaking was strictly adhered to.

Cecil Liddell has compiled a memo for the Director of Naval Intelligence which tends to show fairly conclusively that the German legation as such is not actively engaged in espionage although it may be cognisant of what is going on. He argues that Preetz was asked to obtain confirmation about the disposition of troops in Northern Ireland and that this is a matter which could quite easily be carried out by the legation. He also gives proof that Herman Goertz on his own admission was told to keep clear of the legation unless he found that this could not be avoided. On the other hand it is known that the legation has an illicit wireless set communicating with Germany. Messages from Germany are of almost daily occur-rence but the messages to Germany are only very occasional.

Willy Preetz had been arrested three weeks after landing from a U-boat in Dingle Bay.

23 February

I saw T.A. Robertson this morning, who told me that in conversation with Ralph Jarvis the latter had asked him whether any of his agents corresponded with addresses in Madrid. He mentioned that one of theirs had written to Apartado

1099. This immediately raised the question in Jarvis' mind and he there and then rang up Felix Cowgill to ask if he could communicate with Robertson information about a man called Juan Pujol Garcia. This man had been regarded by the assistant naval attaché in Madrid as a double-cross agent. It had been arranged by the Germans that he should be sent to England. In fact he had never gone further than Lisbon, where he was remaining in hiding. He had told the Germans that in addition to himself he had three other agents in England and he had been furnishing them with information which ostensibly came from this country. It seems not unlikely that this accounts for the very wild messages on the ISOS about our shipping, which are described as coming from Felipe's V-Mann, in this country. BALLOON has been asked to confirm some of these messages, which are grossly inaccurate. The folly of this enterprise needs no comment. We are looking for Felipe's V-Mann when his existence may be perfectly well known to Section V. Apart from this it is obviously essential that if anybody is communicating false information about affairs in this country we should know exactly what he is saying. We should also know about the questionnaire that he is receiving from the Germans, which I understand is in the possession of Section V.

I attended a meeting called by the Home Secretary at which Sir Alexander Maxwell and John Morris were present, to discuss the case of Samuel Stewart. Morris had evidently been trying to think up every possible point for the man's defence. He was really acting as counsel for defence. He still stuck to his old arguments, and advanced the following new points:

Was it possible that in 1940 SNOW made an arrangement with the Germans by which they understood that his traffic was under control, and they received information which was reliable though perhaps not exciting? I said that I thought that I could probably prove that this was not true since I was practically certain that the Germans had shown their confidence in SNOW in matters which had acted seriously to their detriment. I would however verify this point. He also thought that as we had had Stewart under observation from April 1940 to the time of his arrest and had discovered nothing, this might very well prove his innocence. I said this did not follow and that when people talked about suspects under observation they were often not aware of the immense difficulties involved. It was for example quite impossible to follow people in the black-out. It was even difficult to follow them in daytime, if they were suspicious. The Samuel Stewart case was a particularly difficult one as he had such very good cover for carrying out his activity. If he had intended to send messages to the Germans he had every opportunity of making use of an employee on one of his ships. Morris brought up another point which rather caught me unawares. He said that he had been told very confidentially by Toby Caulfield that we had had an agent in as secretary for a considerable time, but that she had not been able to discover that Stewart was acting as an agent. I said that I was not au fait with this side of this case. I did recall that action of the kind had been suggested but I could not remember the details. It suddenly occurred to me however that in speaking to Morris Toby made up the secretary to camouflage the mike, and from subsequent enquiries I am quite sure that this was his intention. Since the mike did not function very well I shall now have to tell the Home Office that the secretary was rather deaf and could not therefore perform her task as well as we had hoped. We shall be in serious difficulties if the Advisory Committee asks to see her. Personally I think the best thing to do is to make a clean breast of it to Maxwell and the Home Secretary, and leave John Morris guessing. Morris raised one point which will be rather difficult to get over. He said that Sam Stewart was accused of hostile association but had never been told the name of the individual with whom he was accused of being associated. He asked whether we could put the name to Stewart of the member of the German secret service who had sent the messages. I said that this would present us with a considerable difficulty. First of all, we did not know the name of the agent. We knew the name of the head agent but we did not know whether Stewart was known to him or his subordinates. The only alternative would be to put forward the names of all those representatives of the German secret service who were known to us but this would not be conclusive, as we did not know them all. In any case one would expect Stewart to deny association. I explained that we had already given him the opportunity of mentioning the names of any Germans or suspicious aliens with whom he had made contact. He had not been very helpful in this respect since he had only mentioned three or four whereas he must have been in touch with hundreds. The Home Secretary then asked Morris whether he thought that release under 18(a) would be satisfactory. Morris took the view that Stewart ought either to be released entirely or detained. The matter was left for final decision by the Secretary of State after he had received our answer to the two points raised by Morris. I have asked T.A. Robertson to see Sir Alexander and explain. The Home Secretary was extremely reasonable and patient in exploring every possible avenue. He seemed to be by no means persuaded by Morris's arguments, although he naturally finds the case an extremely difficult one.

4 March

I returned from leave today. While I was away the Luis Calvo case had been giving a certain amount of trouble. From information subsequently received it transpired that at his interview with Vitturo, Calvo had, unobserved by Eric Goodacre, passed a note to Vitturo in which he said that the British authorities had really nothing on him and that the Spaniards should watch Armesto and Pastor. Colonel Stephens was extremely upset with this, since clearly Calvo should have been searched before he went to the meeting and observation should have been kept to see that nothing was passed. At subsequent interrogation Calvo confessed that he had passed a note and told us what was in it. Today he confessed that while in Madrid he went to a certain address where he was questioned by two German officers known as Pablo and Frederico (both ISOS characters) ... These were men originally named by him as Gonzalez and Garcia. They had asked him to work for them in England. He replied that he would do so provided they would let me know what was required. They then proceeded to ask him to provide them by means of messages in secret ink with information about troop and convoy movements etc. Calvo demurred but said that his objections were overruled. He then went on to say that his questionnaire, secret ink etc was coming in the diplomatic bag being brought by José Brugada. He has also given information to the effect that Barra is running the military organisation and controlling the activities of Lugo, Castillo and Pinedo. Brugada and Calvo were to run the civilian side.

We had a meeting with Colin Gubbins and Bill Dunderdale on the case of a woman called *Victoire* who has come over here with an SOE man, Pierre de Vomécourt, codenamed *Lucas*. *Victoire* was apparently connected with a Polish-cum-SIS organisation, under a man called *Walenty*, which had been rounded up by the Germans. *Victoire* was made to work for the Germans according to her own story and in the course of her business she was put on to *Lucas* who runs the SOE organisation there which is of considerable dimensions. *Lucas* who is evidently in love with her, tackled her with this and they concerted a plan by which she should go to England with *Lucas* ostensibly to find out about his activities in this country and report them to the Germans. Both she and *Lucas* intend to go back to occupied France, where they will carry out various coups. They will both then disappear. The whole story is extremely involved and there are considerable difficulties about *Victoire*'s bona-fides. She looks a little like another Stella. We have got to try and get her sorted out. Personally I think that SOE would be extremely ill-advised to let her go back. *Lucas* would also be in very great danger unless he decided to change his identity entirely, and re-establish contact with his organisation by the back door.

Pierre de Vomécourt was one of three brothers based near Limoges who worked for SOE. After the AUTOGIRO circuit was rounded up, de Vomécourt was sent to Colditz, and survived the war. Victoire was Mathilde Carré, a collaborator who had betrayed Roman Garby-Czerniawski, codenamed Walenty, the head of the Polish INTERALLIÉ organisation.

5 March

I attended a meeting at Kinnaird House on the question of British Security Co-ordination in New York and Felix Cowgill made some rather offensive remarks about Victor Rothschild's efforts to get information on the question of sabotage. Although I did not wish to wash dirty linen in public, I was obliged to say that Rothschild's sole interest was to be kept informed of details of any case of sabotage where this could be attributed to enemy action, or where the case was non-proven. Felix wanted the definite cases to be passed through SIS and the non-proven cases to go through the Security Executive, but this was ruled out. He took strong exception to Rothschild's writing to SIS whenever he saw cases of sabotage reported in the papers. I said that Rothschild only did this because he felt that unless he stimulated action nothing was being done. There was in fact a lack of confidence owing to the paucity of information. If we could be satisfied that we were receiving details of any cases of suspected enemy sabotage it would not be necessary for us to be making the enquiries. Ingram Fraser, from Security Co-ordination, was present and obviously felt himself in a very difficult position. He said that he had supplied information of all these cases and he also complained that he received very little information from this country either about sabotage or about the general set-up of German espionage organisation. The Director-General pointed out that all information at our disposal was also at the disposal of SIS and since they were the channel we rather naturally expected that they would keep their own representatives informed. He complained that we got practically no information about the various important cases which had been running in the United States. It seems fairly clear that the information is sent from here to Section V by ourselves and from Security Co-ordination to Section V by New York but that it sticks in the bottle-neck, because Felix is the judge of what concerns New York and London.

Dick White and I went over to see Peter Loxley and Frank Roberts about the Luis Calvo case. A telegram had come from Madrid indicating that the Spanish government was proposing to take reprisals if Calvo was not sent back to Spain. Alcazar de Velasco apparently said that if we could produce a statement in writing by Calvo to the effect that he had been working for the Germans he would be prepared to drop the case. The ambassador, the Duke of Alba, had announced his intention of visiting Sir Alexander Cadogan tomorrow morning and if such a confession could be shown to him the situation would be greatly eased. The Foreign Office proposed to take the line that Calvo was a non-diplomatic Spaniard who had come here to spy on behalf of the Germans, that it could not be said that there was analogy between his case and that of any British consul and that before they embarked on a policy of reprisals they had better consider matters very carefully. It would be explained to the ambassador that in the interests of appeasement the Foreign Office will endeavor to use their influence in order to dissuade the parties concerned from bringing Calvo to trial since if this were done there were to be some extremely awkward revelations of the Spanish Government involving high officials of state, namely Ramon Serrano Suner himself. If he is not prosecuted, Calvo would be held in detention until after the war under 12(5a) of the Aliens Order.

6 March

We have obtained the necessary confession from Luis Calvo, which is merely a repetition of statements that he has already made to the effect that he was working on instructions from two Germans that he had met in Madrid. This has been sent over to the Foreign Office. In the meantime ISOS indicates that the Spaniards are contemplating the arrest of Toby Ellis, our consul in Tangier.

RAINBOW has been told about Gunter Schutz's escape. He has taken the line that as Schutz is an old school friend of his it would be extremely difficult to have to hand him over to the police, should he take refuge in RAINBOW's house. After consultation with the Director-General, it has been decided to give RAINBOW a guarantee that if he gives information leading to Schutz's arrest, Schutz will not be executed but he must understand that if Schutz falls into the hands of police by other means he will have to take his chances. We decided on this course since there is obviously nothing to be gained by executing Schutz. On the contrary, it may be possible to obtain a great deal of useful information from him if he attempts to come to this country which in my view is extremely unlikely.

7 March

DUCK has produced the Duke of Alba's telegram after his interview with the Foreign Office at which he was shown Luis Calvo's confession. Alba states the position to Madrid and tells them that he does not think there is much chance of Calvo being released. While I was away DUCK obtained a copy of an interesting message from Ramon Serrano Suner to Barra asking the latter to find out what the reaction to a peace move would be in this country and to report the facts to the new Turkish Minister here for transmissions to the Germans, presumably via Ankara. It is difficult to see why Barra should not send this information back to Serrano Suner.

I had a talk with Kenneth Younger about the transmission of secret messages by the Free French through the BBC. Apparently the Free French are the only Allied force who are allowed to send these messages unvetted by SIS. I said that before taking this matter up on a higher level I thought we ought to be satisfied that something useful would result. What, in fact, would SIS do if they were informed that a number of messages were being sent over? They could do nothing useful, and in fact the Free French organisation was more or less under their control. Was it therefore worthwhile telling the French virtually that we did not trust them unless we were going to get something out of it? Malcolm Frost's reply to this is that all and sundry turn up at the BBC to send these messages and nobody seems to know who they are. This I think is definitely a point. We should at least know that those who are sending these messages are properly approved by the appropriate department of the Free French forces. Richard Gambier-Parry is by way of taking responsibility for the security of these messages but, as far as I can ascertain, has done nothing about them.

12 March

I attended a meeting with the Director-General at the Cabinet Office. The meeting was called by Findlater Stewart. Those present were C, Sir Horace Wilson, and Archie Boyle. Findlater said that he has from some time past been called upon to give a good deal of confidential information for transmission to the Germans in order to keep certain of our agents in position. He felt considerable responsibility and wanted to be informed about the grade of information which we were getting from our own agents. He did not think that, in the present circumstances, the Twenty Committee was being sufficiently well informed. He went on to state in his opinion there might with advantage be far closer co-operation between the

SIS people who were running agents and the Twenty Committee. We obviously both had a good deal to learn from each other. C agreed that this was so, and said that in future he proposed to put Frank Foley on the Committee in addition to Felix Cowgill. He thought that Foley would probably be of considerable assistance to us. I said that I felt that we also might be of considerable assistance to Foley if we knew more about the SIS traffic with their agents and C also agreed to this point. I stressed very strongly the importance of seeing that all information transmitted to the enemy from British or ostensibly British territory and all information requested by the enemy regarding British territory should go into the pool of the Twenty Committee. If this were not done we were bound to get into difficulties. I quoted the case of the Lisbon agent of SIS who for months had been transmitting information about this country and had even got two ostensible sub-agents. He had received a questionnaire which we had not seen, neither had we seen any of his traffic. The result was that quite possibly we were looking for an agent at this moment who was, in fact, this man at Lisbon and what was worse we were considering the question of discrediting him in the eyes of the enemy who were asking us to check his information. The discussion ranged over a fairly wide field, including the Wireless Board. I said that I did not think that the Wireless Board was fulfilling its proper functions. It had degenerated into a duplication of the Twenty Committee. At best, it dealt with a few ad hoc questions put up to it but it never gave any direction on matters of major policy, one of the purposes for which it was originally set up. Findlater entirely agreed, and we all thought that on matters of deception we should have to go either to Oliver Stanley or to the Chiefs of Staff. Findlater is going to draw up a note on the meeting which will be submitted to us all for further consideration. Our main interest in SOE is when their agents pass under the control of the enemy. In such eventuality we should always like to know. I understand however that arrangements for this had already been made. This was confirmed by Archie Boyle.

I lunched with Sir Nevile Bland and went into the question of vetting. I explained to him the whole procedure and how the mistake had arisen regarding Nancy Parish. He told me that she had tried for a job with SIS and had been turned down. I said that I thought SIS must have applied to the Foreign Office about her since no application had been made here.

While I was at lunch I saw Courtney Young sitting with a Japanese half-caste, whom I suspected to be Donald. It transpired afterwards that Donald had made two rather startling statements. First of all, he had referred to the Stop List at the Censorship and drawn attention to an 'Any Name address' near Tadworth. He said that a girl in the Censorship had brought this to his notice since the address was somewhere near his own. Courtney Young expressed no interest. This is, of course, the address to which we hope Yamamoto will send his reply. A little later in the conversation Donald started to talk about the address of a man named Yamamoto in Switzerland, and drew attention to the fact that these names always got wrongly spelt. This all seemed extremely odd and tends to confirm our view that Donald is the culprit. The probability is that he was throwing a fly over Courtney, who did not rise. We shall now have to see that the lady in Censorship does not go running to Donald if the letter comes from Yamamoto. It may be that there is no girl but that Donald managed to get hold of the Stop List to which I think he would not normally have access. We are going to leave things for the time being and then get Molly, who is now employed in the Swiss Legation, to make some convenient approach. She might say that she had received a message for Donald through the Swiss bag.

13 March

It has been decided that *Victoire* should stay here and *Lucas* should go back under an assumed name.

SIS reports show that a certain number of peace feelers are being put out by the Germans through Switzerland. There have also been vague rumours of approaches by the Germans to the Russians via Sweden.

17 March

Jim Hale talked to me about the Little case. He has now seen the two Portuguese informants from the British Legation, COSTAR and SOSO, and finds a good deal of the evidence conflicting. The story doesn't look good to me and the more I hear of it the more I feel the whole incident has been a plant.

18 March

I had a talk with Courtney Young about the possibility of testing Donald out by putting him in touch with Matsumoto at the Oratory Schools and miking the conversation. The position is more difficult than I thought since Donald does not apparently know Matsumoto and it would therefore be difficult to find a plausible excuse for bringing them together. Courtney Young is going to try and think out some better scheme.

I had a long talk with Len Burt about Gibraltar. He paints an even worse picture than Dick White. There is hardly a soul in Gibraltar whom he has not seen and sized up from the Governor downwards. He says there are six bodies in Gibraltar doing security work but that in spite of this, security is practically non-existent. There is not the slightest doubt in my mind that some drastic cleanup is necessary. The DSO, Colonel Medlam, is disliked and superficial in his work and with few exceptions the same can be said of the remainder of those engaged on intelligence or security work. Dick and I are seriously considering recommending that Tin-Eye Stephens should go out in spite of the loss that he would be to us. A man of presence, drive, and almost ruthlessness is needed. The only other person I can think of is Kenneth Younger, who would do it well but as usual his youthful appearance would be against him.

Felix Cowgill has sent me a note saying that SIS in future should have their own representative at Censorship. He quotes three instances where he alleges there have been serious delays in transmitting Censorship submissions to SIS. The fact is that owing to the caginess of SIS we have never really been able to act as more than a postbox. We have however performed quite a useful function in putting the Censorship material over Roland Bird's sausage machine, which has linked it up with previous specimens. Originally the emphasis was on MI5 but now, owing to the developments at Bermuda, and the fact that America is now in the war, the emphasis is to some extent on Section V. The trouble is that they did not do anything with the material when they got it, and we who are dependent on them for studying counter-espionage probably do not get the results. The examples quoted by Felix are bad ones since most of the delay was in the transmission of the intercept from Bermuda to this country. In one case there was a delay of eight days owing to the fact that the Director-General insisted on seeing the photostats. Most of the submissions are passed on to SIS within twenty-four hours and if they are of the slightest importance they are telephoned immediately. What is really at the bottom of Felix's decision is that we have on a number of occasions been more or less forced to point out that submissions passed to SIS which have been intercepted between the Americans and the Iberian Peninsula have reposed in Christie's tray for a matter of weeks when they were of vital interest to Kim Philby who was sitting in the next room. This leads to prodding on our part which is so resented by Section V. The remedy is that they should perform their duties more efficiently and our *locus standi* is that if they are not efficient we suffer.

19 March

There have been two serious cases of leakage at GC&CS. The Director-General wants to prosecute under the Official Secrets Act but Valentine Vivian and Jim Hale I think rightly take the view that this will only increase the surface and make things worse. One of the culprits is a brilliant young mathematician aged nineteen who divulged the information to his old tutor and other dons.

Derek Tangye tells me that the Home Secretary has sent for the editor of the *Daily Mirror* and told him that unless his paper alters its present somewhat malicious and defeatist tone it will be suppressed. Fleet Street is rather on the warpath and it seems likely that there will be trouble.

21 March

Geoffrey Gibbs tells me that he has made arrangements for dealing with secret ink communications between José Brugada and Angel Alcazar de Velasco which are likely to be conducted through [XXXX].

Brugada will communicate in [XXXX] and as a result of recent experiments it will be dealt with in the following way. A piece of damp paper is pressed on the document containing the secret writing. This is removed and allowed to dry. It is then treated with a very strong re-agent, which will bring it up for a sufficiently long period to allow of its being photographed. The amount of ink removed is infinitesimal and cannot be detected.

23 March

Edward Cussen and Len Burt came to see me about the case of José Estella (RATS). As soon as final approval is received from the Director of Public Prosecutions, Estella is to be extradited and tried here under the Treachery Act. The Home Office will have to be consulted.

A Spaniard, José Estella Key, had been arrested in Gibraltar for sabotage.

25 March

A Prisoner of War report shows that our naval messages are intercepted by the Beobachtungsdienst in Berlin. These are deciphered and put out to the units of the fleet within half an hour.

Victor Rothschild has brought me a scheme by which Jack Bingham is to organise the Fifth Column as an agent of the Gestapo. His various friends and connections naturally look to him to give them a lead. It seems that certain of them already know about the invasion list and if and when the time comes they do not propose to be just where the police can find them. It may therefore be a good thing to get them organised so that we know where to put our fingers on them. A difficulty arises over the Home Office Order since it will be based solely on the information of one informant. They will have to face up to this if we are to go on with the scheme.

26 March

I had a talk with John Marriott and J.C. Masterman about *Victoire*. We have taken over the transmitter in this country and are in direct communication with the Germans, although they think that we think we are in communication with one of our own agents. There is therefore a good opportunity for major deception. If by our questions we express a great interest in some French coastal area they may think we are going to attack it and make preparations accordingly. Our difficulty is to get some sort of direction. We have plans and cover plans but they keep changing place and nobody seems to know from one day to the next what we really are going to do. In consequence we get no directives.

GC&CS is giving us the Algeciras–Madrid traffic which should be an extremely valuable service. It may provide us with the answer to the Gibraltar leakages.

The Director-General has written a letter to Valentine Vivian about Section V not reporting to British Security Co-ordination in New York the leakage of information in Rio de Janeiro about the *Queen Mary*. He thinks that whatever the circumstances and the correctness or incorrectness of the details given, Bill Stephenson should be informed. I think on broad lines that he is right although it might well be argued that Stephenson probably already knows that there is a good deal of German espionage going on in Rio. The facts given in the particular message could all have been obtained from casual observation, except the destination which was correct. The route given was incorrect. The ship has in the meantime got through and after touching at Cape Town arrived safely at Adelaide, with some four thousand American troops on board.

Felix Cowgill came to see me about the Lisbon agent Pujol, codenamed BOVRIL. He gave me no explanation as to why we had not been informed until quite recently about the existence of this agent, his questionnaire and his traffic. Apparently Section V at Lisbon knew about him as long ago as December. Felix in fact had a copy of his traffic which would have to be examined carefully. He then said that as he felt confident that BOVRIL was a reliable agent he proposed to bring him over here for interrogation by Frank Foley and then to send him back to Lisbon. His point was that he did not propose to do this until we gave a guarantee that BOVRIL would be allowed to return. I said that first of all we none of us really knew anything about BOVRIL except in a negative way. Ralph Jarvis had not seen him, and we had the story of the American naval attaché, the questionnaire and what was alleged to be the traffic. BOVRIL had been posing for months as a head agent in England with three sub-agents. It might be that he would be better placed here than in Lisbon. Our interest was a mutual one and I thought that whatever happened we ought to get the man over to England as soon as possible and that we should reserve judgment until we had heard his whole story. Felix was evidently suffering from professional jealousy. He had found this agent through the good offices of the American naval attaché and he did not wish to give him up or to allow us to have access to him even though in all our interests it might be better that he should remain here. Fundamentally his attitude is "I do not see why I should get agents and then have them pinched by you." The whole thing is so narrow and petty that it really makes me furious. I am quite sure that we shall never get this right until we take over Section V.

28 March

Charles Cholmondeley has made an interesting discovery. An ISOS message of 2 March discloses that the Germans were anxious to put over an item of false information about a minefield having been laid between Jersey and Guernsey, from Cherbourg Peninsula to the coast south of it. On 17 March this information was passed from Paris to *Victoire*. This would seem to indicate fairly conclusively that the Germans believe that *Victoire* has not told us that the transmitter of her group in France is under German control. The plan for misleading the Germans about the return of *Lucas* should therefore go through as soon as possible.

John Senter came over to enquire about the possibilities of bringing over a German called Otto Witt with whom SOE are in touch in Stockholm. This man is thought to be a German agent. Francis Aiken-Sneath is interested in him because his name was mentioned the other day by Hans Jäger, one of the German émigrés here. Jäger suggested getting Witt to this country, as he thought he would have useful information. It may be that Jäger also is a German agent. He has certainly lied to Aiken-Sneath about certain letters that he wrote to Witt. He denied having sent him any letters. We are prepared to have Witt over as long as we get a fairly good case for keeping him inside.

29 March

Kim Philby telephoned to me today to say that Hans Ruser had told the Poles in Lisbon that he was prepared to accept our offer to come to this country with his mother provided he could have a guarantee that he would not be interned and would be allowed later to go to America. Although Ruser is probably a time-server of the worst variety I think it may pay us to get him over. I think however he must satisfy us as to his bona-fides and that any guarantee as to his liberty will be on the assumption that we are satisfied that he is working 100% for us.

Hans Ruser was a German journalist in Lisbon, in touch with the Abwehr, who did defect to SIS.

30 March

I discussed with Dick White the case of BOVRIL and we both agreed that we ought to make a stand on the question of running double-cross agents in this country and also on the unreasonable attitude taken up by Felix Cowgill in this particular case.

31 March

I dined with Ned and Evelyn Reid, who had just returned from America, where he had been working both for the Treasury and SOE. He was evidently rather horrified by what he had found. He said that on the thirty-fifth floor of the Rockefeller Building there were a large number of people drawing $800 a month for doing absolutely nothing. He liked Bill Stephenson personally and thought possibly in certain lines he had done a good job of work. On the other hand he thought many of his duties should now be handed over to the American authorities. Stephenson's liaison with Bill Donovan was good and it was bad with the FBI and State Department. There had been a very unfortunate incident with the latter. One of Stephenson's men had spoken in derogatory manner of Birle of the State Department, and had expressed his views unconsciously to an agent of the FBI. The latter arranged for him to repeat the conversation on the telephone and had a record taken of it. It was then passed to Birle and the balloon went up.

Evelyn thinks that SOE in South America should cease and that all work of that kind should be in the hands of the Americans. If we could help them in any way so much the better. The only matter of real importance from our point of view is that

Stephenson's relations with the FBI did not appear to be very good. If, therefore, we contemplated setting up in the United States it would probably be better to do so under our own steam.

(Sir) Evelyn Baring was Guy Liddell's cousin, and a future Governor of Southern Rhodesia, and High Commissioner in South Africa.

I April

Gilbert Lennox tells me that Combined Operations have got our old friend Commander Shoppee, on their staff. He told Lord Mountbatten who asked him to refer the matter to Casa Maury who has been unfortunately chosen as the head of Combined Operations Intelligence. I told Lennox that subject to the Director-General's approval, Casa Maury should be told that Shoppee was extremely indiscreet and rather a heavy drinker.

I saw Major David Keswick of SOE about the *Lucas* case. He is not unnaturally extremely reluctant to spread the surface of this case further than is absolutely necessary, since Lucas is obviously in great danger and the same applies to the whole of his organisation. I said that I would do what I could to keep his name out and to prevent the circulation of the traffic. I discussed this matter afterwards with John Marriot and J.C. Masterman who will explain the position to the Twenty Committee tomorrow. It was rather reassuring to find that SOE are so concerned about the future of their agents. One point in the whole case which puzzled Keswick was the fact that *Lucas* having discovered that *Victoire* had betrayed him should have been at her throat but in actual fact within a very short time he seemed to be her slave. This could not be explained by the evidence of the mike which seemed to show that although *Victoire* was very much in love with him, he was not nearly so enamoured with her.

I went on afterwards to see William Codrington about leakages. I explained to him that it was important for us to know when leakages took place in any of our embassies abroad, particularly if the stolen matter related to this country. It might easily happen that we might be looking elsewhere for such a leakage whereas in fact the answer could be found in Washington DC or Ankara. He saw the point and promised to keep us informed.

2 April

I had a discussion with Felix Cowgill, Jim Hale and Jack Ivens about the Little case. It was decided to forward Jim's report to the Assistant Director of Naval Intelligence with the reservation that it might be subject to modification in the light of certain further enquiries that were being made in Lisbon and any evidence that might be given by Captain Benson on his return. As regards Costa, we were agreed that he should be held under Emergency Regulation 12(5a). Sousa, we thought, should be released from the Royal Victoria Patriotic School as soon as SIS could make arrangements for his welfare. It was recommended that if possible this should be done before Easter. With regard to Stilwell we were all agreed that it was not possible to get him over unless the position was explained to him that he came voluntarily. It was thought better to do nothing until we got further with the case of Little and had seen Captain Benson.

---

7 April

There has been an interesting case of suspected sabotage at Gibraltar. A man went on board one of our trawlers called *Blossom* with a basket of eggs. When he went away several blocks of TNT fused to go off in about half an hour were found under the eggs. The matter was reported to the Spanish police and one man named Sanchez was arrested. ISOS disclosed that a project had failed and that the ISOS character Felipe had been arrested. The eggs were addressed to someone called Henricks in Gibraltar. Three people of this name are being interrogated.

We have just received from Canada a small incendiary bomb said to have been found on board the aeroplane which took General Sikorski to America. The Polish officer who found it said that a similar bomb had ignited under his mattress in the plane but that he had extinguished it by putting it in a refuse bin. He did not report the fact when he arrived at Montreal but mentioned it to the FBI in Washington DC to whom he gave the unexploded bomb. The bomb is exactly similar to those manufactured by SOE. We are inclined to think either that the officer wished to gain kudos for himself by planting and discovering the bomb or that there is some political intrigue against Sikorski. It appears that there is an SOE station near Prestwick whence the aeroplane took off.

---

8 April

I saw Blanshard Stamp and asked him about Fascists. He said that the released members of the British Union of Fascists had been getting together on the question of support for the relatives of other members of the organisation who were interned. Not much money had been forthcoming but the names and addresses of those who were still active supporters of the movement were being brought to light. Stamp had recently seen W.E.D. Allen who has given him the full story of Mussolini's subsidy to the Party. Allen on one occasion went to Rome with Dundas. The subsidy at that time was £5,000 per month. The subsequent scheme for the transmission of the funds through a broadcasting company did not actually materialise. Our information however was correct that a nominal sum would be paid to Radio Rome for so many hours a week. This time would be sold by a British company to various advertising firms and the profits would be placed at the disposal of the BUF. Allen gives the impression of being completely amoral and politically unstable. He might just as well be a Communist as a Fascist or a Conservative. He is now employed in the Royal Air Force and says that he is a whole-hearted supporter of this country since it has given him a lot of good food and drink. He fell out with Sir Oswald Mosley some time ago. The meeting was apparently at his own request. He had been seen some time ago by Francis Aiken-Sneath and Dixon but had not been very forthcoming. He then wrote to say that there was certain information that he would like to give to the authorities. He started by lying and was confronted with one of his intercepts, he then came right off it and told the truth. He knew of the scheme for getting funds from Germany through a broadcasting company but said that for some reason or another this also did not materialise. He alleges that Mosley got some £40,000 for the part he played in arranging for the release of the Rothschild family on the continent in 1937. It is said that the family paid up a large sum of money, part of which was given to Mosley presumably by the Germans and part to the Rexists in Belgium.

10 April

Dick White tells me that the firm of Trauss is owed by one German or Hermann Brucker. Trauss, in Lisbon, are import and export agents, might possibly be responsible for the OSTRO messages which appear on ISOS and give grossly misleading information about shipping movements from here, West Africa and the Middle East. Trauss has an agent here, a Miss Paula Widman, whose husband was a member of the Nazi Party in 1934 and who Ned Reid discovered had been receiving remittances through the Banco Espiritu Santo in Lisbon. She has a stepson in West Africa. We know from the censorship that Paula Widman receives information from Trauss in Lisbon and that he is receiving letters from her. We have however failed to intercept her correspondence to him. Recently there has been a further interesting link-up. Harter of the London Merchant Bank, through which GIRAFFE received payment some time ago, has now gone to reside with Paula Widman. The books of the London Merchant Bank disclose that Trauss was one of their clients. It looks as if we are on to something here.

13 April

The Spanish police appear to have arrested SUNDAE, whether on their own initiative or on account of German pressure is not clear. The police are appearing to be very co-operative but this is difficult to reconcile with the fact that the whole area has been cleared of the civilian population in the vicinity of Algeciras in order to install some new infra-red apparatus which the Germans are using to spot ships coming through the Straits of Gibraltar.

Cuthbert Bowlby, the SIS representative in Cairo, has telegraphed to say that according to a statement by T.A. Robertson, C had a meeting with Findlater Stewart and others and had given an undertaking that the Security Service should be allowed to run agents abroad. When pressed as to his source he said that he had learned this from Findlater's secretary. I cannot quite make out what he is talking about, since no such undertaking has ever been given or asked for. The Director-General has replied to this effect.

We are still awaiting a reply from Felix Cowgill about BOVRIL. I have sent him another letter.

TATE has been ordered to pay MUTT £60 under the MIDAS scheme. It is difficult to draw any really positive conclusions although it might be said that this is once more a vote of confidence in TATE and perhaps in MUTT.

TRICYCLE has received a message through his employers asking him to ginger up BALLOON whose reports are not considered entirely satisfactory. Personally, I should have thought that BALLOON was doing very well.

Len Burt has had a talk with me about our special plans in connection with Barra. He pointed out many difficulties from the police point of view and regards the whole operation as difficult. It looks as if we should have to call it off.

15 April

ISOS shows that a number of arrests in southern Spain must be due to a German desire to prevent doubtfuls from working for the British. It seems also too good to be true that the Spanish police would be working wholeheartedly in our interests. SUNDAE has been taken in principally because the Germans thought he was working more for us than for them.

18 April

Kenneth Younger told me about an agent of Colonel Passy called Jean Pelletier, alias Laroche. There is no doubt that this man is a German agent. He has given away a good many of his colleagues, having been arrested by the Germans and forced to work for them. This he appears to have done somewhat willingly. I am going to take the man over for further interrogation. He has already made something in the nature of a confession.

I saw the security film *Next of Kin* last night. It is extremely well done but unfortunately there is an Irishman who features as a German courier. I am going to try and get this part cut if the film is to be for general circulation.

Buster Milmo talked to me about the case of Jean Pelletier. It seems that this man was instructed to work his way into the wireless section of the *Deuxième Bureau* and if possible to acquire a set for his own use. The French are therefore considering the possibility of using Pelletier as a double-cross.

20 April

A Japanese BJ discloses that our action in connection with Luis Calvo has had a somewhat far-reaching effect. Ramon Serrano Suner had undertaken on behalf of the Japanese to send certain people who would be attached to the embassy at Washington DC and the consulate-general at San Francisco and would be engaged in espionage. The issue of diplomatic passports had been fixed up but unfortunately at that moment the Calvo incident had occurred and Archibald MacLeish, who is head of the Bureau of Facts and Figures in the United States, had made speeches attacking the State Department for its policy of appeasement towards Spain and France. As a result the attitude of the American administration stiffened and they refused the application for the Spaniards on the score that they could not recommend the appointment of more than a fixed number of career diplomats. It seems therefore that the Calvo incident was happily timed to frustrate this plan of Spanish–Japanese collaboration. This was part of the plan that we had in mind when we decided on Calvo's arrest, and had the Foreign Office not insisted on isolating the Calvo incident from its connection with Alcazar de Velasco and Serrano Suner the effect might have been still greater. Serrano Suner apparently shows all telegrams from London and Washington DC to the Japanese. A particularly clear instance of this is in a telegram sent from Madrid to Tokyo on 12 April which is almost a verbatim copy of the message sent from London to Madrid on 10 April.

Cecil Liddell has put up an interesting report on Henry Lundborg or Londborg who has just got himself two years' imprisonment and a fine in Northern Ireland. This man is a British subject who has resided in Belfast all his life. He was travelling as a restaurant car assistant between Dublin and Belfast and when arrested at the frontier three documents were found in his sock, from the Dublin IRA to the IRA in Belfast. One was from Sean Harrington, the IRA's Chief of Staff and two others from Sean McCool, the IRA Adjutant General and acting Director of Intelligence. These were addressed to McNamee, alias Peter Donnelly, the chief representative of the IRA in Northern Ireland, who has since been arrested. Lunborg's work had previously been carried out by a man called Lawlor who was also a restaurant car attendant. The documents were collected at Kingston's Drapery Store in Dublin, which is owed by the Brugha family. The father was shot in the 1916 revolution. He was an Englishman and his real name was Burgess. His family seem to have remained staunchly IRA ever since, and one of his sons has been under detention for some time. The documents were carried by Lunborg to Lawlor who gave them to McNamee. They referred to details about the American forces and to the nature of defence works at power stations and factories. There was nothing to show posivitely that this information was required for the Germans but there is at least a strong inference that this was so.

21 April

A plan to be known as SPIDER has been worked out for the *Arctic* transmitter and Richman Stopford is to go to Iceland to carry it out. The idea is that we shall first report the fleet as moving North from Scapa and report a convoy en route to Murmansk, and the position of the fleet as being somewhere out in the Atlantic west of Iceland. A suitable moment will have to be chosen so that aerial observation does not give away our story. It is hoped in this way to draw the *Tirpitz* out and then put the Home Fleet on her. The chances are one in a million but as we stand to lose nothing the project seems worth the doing if the Commander-in-Chief Home Fleet agrees. Richman Stopford will go to Scapa with Ewen Montagu to discuss matters. In the meantime we hope to prevent Wise from dispatching the crew of the *Arctic* who will be wanted on the spot for purposes of deception. Ronnie Reed is going with Stopford to look into the wireless side.

Anthony Blunt came to see me about the cases of André Grauer and Collon. As regards the former we have practically no starting point. There is first of all the delicacy of the position vis à vis the Soviet government; secondly the difficulty of observation on the Soviet embassy, thirdly the lack of Special Material or BJs. We therefore decided to concentrate on Collon with Special Facilities. Having sized him up we can decide whether we make a direct approach or not.

André Grauer was a suspected Soviet intelligence officer working under diplomatic cover at the embassy in London, having been expelled from Sweden.

Victor Rothschild came to talk to me about the General Sikorski case. I said that I hardly thought it worth while pressing the Air Ministry to get us a seat on the plane for Len Burt to go to Canada and America, until we had made an attempt here to clear up the case through the interrogation of various Poles who have travelled on Sikorski's plane. It was decided to do this through Burt and Stephen Alley.

I went with the Director-General to see Dick Casey who is leaving for the Middle East on Wednesday. He seemed in grand form and as usual was thirsting for knowledge. The Director-General gave him a general picture of our responsibilities and of intelligence in the Middle East. Casey said that arrangements had been made by Dick Ellis to become a member of his staff for the purpose of intelligence liaison with the Americans.

I lunched with Sir Alan Brooke and Lord Tyrell, the former British ambassador to Paris. I was much impressed with the latter's knowledge and understanding of the German set-up and the possibilities of Franco-German collaboration. He said that it was only German stupidity since 1870 which had driven us into a forced alliance with France. When he was ambassador in Paris he had been deeply conscious of the unreality of Anglo-French relations and at the efforts being made by the Committee des Forges to develop relations with Germany. Tyrell had been astounded at the blindness of our own politicians from 1933 onwards. He had had several personal interviews with Chamberlain when he told him frankly what he thought was going to happen. He said that Chamberlain was hopelessly provincial in his outlook and quite incapable of understanding the position. Tyrell was apparently called in the other day to try and settle the dispute between Admiral Muselier and General de Gaulle. He said that on personal grounds he infinitely preferred Muselier but that in the national interests he felt bound to recommend that de Gaulle should be supported. He apparently told them both that in all their quarrels there was one consideration which did not seem to have crossed their minds. That was the future of France. This appears to have almost reduced them both to tears. He of course saw them separately and conveyed his findings to the Prime Minister. When I was coming back with him in a taxi he was loud in his praises of Brooke whom he thought was one of the most likable, most intelligent and most incorruptible of men that he had ever met. He told me that Joe Ball when he took over films at the Ministry of Information tried to get rid of Brooke and from what he said I rather assume that Ball had tried to make something on the side and had come up against Brooke. Tyrell told me it had taken him three months to get rid of Ball but he had eventually achieved his object. Tyrell also expressed very strong views about the control of allied intelligence services and security services by the British. He knew all about the Muselier business and he was quite certain that we should make a strong bid for the control of the foreign services on the grounds that it was in allied interests, that they were operating on British soil and that therefore they must collaborate with the local authorities.

Admiral Wilhelm Canaris, according to ISOS sources, arrived in North Africa on 17 April and has visited Tangier and Tetuan and has also seen his chief representative in Casablanca. His visit to Algeciras has been cancelled and he is proceeding from Tangier direct to Madrid, where he will meet the head of his service there and also Ludovico von Karsthoff, his Lisbon representative. He will have interviews with the High Commissioner of Spanish Morocco, Spanish Minister for War Asensio, and General de Campos of the Spanish General Staff. The Spanish authorities have been facilitating and collaborating wholeheartedly with the German espionage organisation in Spain particularly as regards setting up of elaborate technical devices for maintaining a twenty-four hour watch on British shipping passing through the Straits. There is further evidence to show that they are now withholding the necessary permission for the organisation to start operating. Canaris will presumably take this matter up in Madrid. The head of the German organisation at Algeciras, formerly referred to as Bodegas, has now been identified as Georg Anton Kellar, who lives at the Hotel Cristina and has an associate in the manager, Hans Leeb. He is also associated with Alberto Carve who lives at the hotel and is a former electrical engineer employed in Siemens. A German secret service station has been established at La Linea and is reporting the movements of British aircraft flying from Gibraltar. A German agent in Lisbon is being dispatched to Egypt via Lourenco Marques and he is to use a mixture of lemon-juice and alcohol as secret ink. The Germans are very apprehensive about an invasion of Norway. The Germans have established in Portuguese Guinea an organisation which is manned mainly by Portuguese. Its main duty has been to report on shipping from Freetown and Bathurst, but it may shortly be closed down owing to the inadequacy of its service. There is also a German intelligence organisation in Lourenco Marques which appears to be staffed by Portuguese nationals. Through this organisation the Germans have learned about a large concentration of shipping in the vicinity of Cape Town. The recent activity in South America where the Brazilian authorities have rounded up large numbers of Germans has caused considerable confusion.

Dr Weber has now been found to be Dr Hilaire Anton Westerlinck, a Belgian who first came to our notice in September 1940 when he was known to be working for the Germans in Lisbon and to be persuading Belgian seamen to desert their ships by promising them a safe return to their homes. It appears that he has been for some time past in Belgium but returned recently to Lisbon, intending to proceed to the Belgian Congo. As he could not make the necessary arrangements it was subsequently decided to send him here. He was expected at the latest by 15 April but has not so far arrived.

25 April

Francis Aiken-Sneath came to see me about the case of Otto Witt who has been in touch with our legation in Stockholm. Witt has formerly been connected with Otto Strasser's organisation and at the beginning of the war was in Denmark. He has been putting forward various peace feelers and suggestions for Germany's future after the war. He wants to come here on a temporary Swedish passport and go on to America in order to see Strasser. Our authorities in Sweden are more or less convinced that he is a German agent for the following reasons: he seems to dispose of an unusual amount of money; he has penetrated endless organisations in Sweden and seems to make it his main occupation to find out what he can about secret organisations of the allies, particularly British, Norwegian and Russian. Before going to Sweden he had been in occupied Denmark for over a year. After a few whiskies Witt disclosed to our representative in Sweden that he had made his position with the German authorities secure because he had on arrival in Sweden offered his services to the Gestapo. According to his own story he had not been accepted but this had resulted in exchanges of correspondence between the German authorities in Sweden and in Berlin by which he had successfully cleared his record. He said that he had had an offer to work for the Russians and added that if we did not accept him he would work for them. The question now arises as to whether we should allow him to come here. I am inclined to agree to his coming and I will have him watched for a period and then pull him in. He has a close friend here called Hans Jäger, concerning whom we are doubtful.

26 April

There is an ISOS reference to Luis Calvo which makes it quite clear that he is on the German books as one of their agents.

There has been another leakage case of a man called Anthony Friere Marreco, of the Fleet Air Arm who has been talking very indiscreetly in a pub in Chelsea. One of Max Knight's people put down his statements which have been verified and found to be correct. The man will be brought down for interrogation and possibly court-martialled.

An interesting case is that of Dr Paul Borchardt, a German Jew of Catholic faith. He is an explorer and an authority on the geography of the Libyan desert and during the last war he worked in the Middle East as a German agent under the name of Abdul Hamil Battota. In 1932 he was director of the German Military Geographical School but in the following year he was discharged owing to his Jewish blood. As an ex-officer he received military protection and was allowed to go on teaching unofficially until November 1938 when he was arrested and interned. In April 1939 he was told that he could no longer receive army protection, so he came to England as a refugee from Nazi oppression. Soon after his arrival he offered his services to the Admiralty who declined them. He was vouched for highly by English friends, strongly recommended by the Society of Friends and was in close touch with the Catholic Committee, Bloomsburg House. Altogether his references were excellent. Although he was offered academic employment in the United States he decided to remain here for, so he said, he preferred to put his abilities to the service of this country in some military capacity. On the outbreak of war he called at the War Office and offered to work for us in the Near East. He was quite frank about his past and made a most favourable impression. His offer was again refused. When he appeared before his tribunal he was classed Category 'A'. A month later his case was reconsidered and he was exempted from all restrictions. Finding he could be of no service to us, in December 1939 he obtained an exit permit to travel to the United States where he was to take up a professorship in South Orange, New Jersey. In December 1941 he was arrested in the United States on charges of treasonable conspiracy and espionage. The court found him guilty and three months ago he was sentenced to twenty years' imprisonment. This is the first proved case of a Jewish refugee (who had even been in a concentration camp) who eventually turned out to be an important Nazi agent. Possibly his protested hatred of Nazism was genuine but in time of war his loyalty to Germany and to his military caste became paramount. I am going to take steps to get this story brought to the notice of the Advisory Committee in the Home Office and other interested departments.

27 April

Valentine Vivian rang me to say that the Prime Minister was interested in the Sikorski incident and wanted a report. I have asked Victor Rothschild to supply this.

PEPPERMINT has got £100 pounds from Alcazar de Velasco and a message in secret ink which he submitted. The message contains nothing of importance.

Desmond Morton telephoned about the M&E Construction Company Limited. Peregrine Churchill, the son of Jack Churchill, is managing director and owner of the firm and his brother is employed under the Director of Camouflage in the War Office. Both brothers are worried because we have recommended to the War Office that the firm should not be employed on account of the association of a German, Erica Schofield, with one of the directors, Linfield. They were trying to make out that though Linfield was a director he did not know anything about the secret work which the firm was carrying out. We have said that we are only advisory in these matters and that if the ministry cares to disregard our advice on urgency of production grounds they are at liberty to do so.

I had a long talk with Dick Ellis at the club and he gave me a picture of what had been happening in New York. Apparently BSC very nearly closed down a few months ago. Certain isolationists or anti-British elements both in the government and in the Senate had got together and drafted a Registration Bill which would have forced BSC to submit all their papers, personnel etc to examination by the police. This was due to several causes. J. Edgar Hoover was annoyed because Bill Stephenson had been dealing with Donovan. The senators were annoyed because certain friends of Stephenson's had got to know about the German ramifications of American chemicals, General Motors, Standard Oil, etc and Adolf Birle, an Under-Secretary of State for the State Department, had taken the view that BSC were going far beyond their charter for liaising with the appropriate departments of the government. A copy of the draft of the bill was shown by Stephenson to the embassy in Washington DC and they took the view that it was only directed against organisations under enemy control or influence. Stephenson did not accept this view and told Dick Ellis to go and see Birle in the State Department. Birle was extremely unpleasant, accused BSC of having 3,000 agents in America and bumping people off in Baltimore. He said that this could not tolerated and that BSC would come within the terms of the Registration Bill. Ellis pointed out to him that BSC had been set up by the Presidential decree and had been working in close co-operation with Hoover since their inception. If therefore he would not accept Ellis's statement that the allegations were categorically untrue he could refer the matter to Mr Hoover for investigation. Ellis then went on to point out that BSC were doing a considerable amount of work for the War Department and Navy Department and that as facilities had been accorded to these people to work on British territory, the British government might have to consider whether these activities could continue if BSC were virtually closed down. Ellis then went to Donovan who wrote a letter to the President. The latter decided to veto the bill. Birle, Francis Biddle (the Attorney-General), and Hoover got together and redrafted the bill in a slightly less noxious form. BSC then went to Quinn Tamm of the FBI who told him that a meeting was to be held between Biddle, Birle, Hoover, the War Department and the Navy Department and suggested that Stephenson should be present. After listening to Biddle and Birle who both thought BSC should be reduced to the position of a liaison section with the appropriate government departments, he said that these conditions entirely met with his approval since that was in fact what they had been doing since the beginning of the war. He referred to Mr Hoover for verification and pointed out that he had rendered no less than 3,900 reports to the FBI. Since however the authorities had decided to proceed with the bill he proposed to close down his organisation forthwith and to have no further relations with them. The meeting broke up in confusion. Next day Hoover came down to see Stephenson. Stephenson told Hoover exactly what he thought of him. He said that he had been a party to an intrigue for some considerable time and that had there been any real objection to any of Stephenson's activities it would have been quite simple for Hoover to ring him up and ask him to discuss the position. This he had not done. Stephenson therefore did not propose to have any further dealings with him. Hoover then tried to get Stephenson to agree to pass all his information through the FBI. Stephenson again refused. Eventually Hoover went away rather apologetically and undertook to smooth matters out which he did. The situation is now much better and Hoover has told his subordinates to co-operate wholeheartedly with BSC.

28 April

The Director-General has agreed to our sending expert falconers to the Scilly Isles to see if we can get some of the pigeons said to be passing over the island en route from Eire to the Continent. The item is a rather expensive one and will cost about £200.

29 April

Felix Cowgill has written me a somewhat insulting letter in which he complains about my letter to him regarding BOVRIL and other letters that he has received from B1(a). He says that all these letters seem to be based on some idea that it is our business to control double-cross agents all over the world, and makes a number of other allegations which are completely unfounded.

1 May

Anthony Blunt tells me that he has heard through ORANGE that Sulzer was approached by Schacht before he came to this country regarding peace proposals, but that he refused to make any soundings.

2 May

Major Thornley of SOE came to tell me that his German escapee agent Kuhlner had landed up in Bergen where he had been greeted by the sentry, placed on an aeroplane and sent straight to Berlin. This had been reported by one of C's agents. C was taking the view that this was another dud SOE project. As Thornley pointed out, it might well be a highly successful one. In any case, SOE and ourselves had nothing to lose.

4 May

Jock Whyte came to see me about his cases. He discussed with me the case of John Wilfred Cook to whom he had written an imaginary letter from a foreign seamen who had brought news of the Baroness von der Goltz with whom Cook was formerly in touch. I said I did not think the case was worth pursuing on these lines. Jock said he had further information that Cook had told a fellow employee in his solicitors' office that he had had a letter from a friend in the army who was employed in some office where he had access to plans about an attack on France. I told Jock to find out the atmosphere in which the conversation had taken place. Was Cook conspiratorial about it or was he just making a statement of fact?

Machell told me about a woman called Callachan who had leaked to a friend of his about translation work she was doing on TRIPLEX material.

5 May

Dr Westerlinck, alias Weber, arrived with his wife by air from Lisbon today. He appears to be an agent of the German secret service station at Bremen and is employed by the naval section of the Abwehr. The German secret service officer in Lisbon is Hans Bendixen.

A former ship's doctor, Westerlinck supposedly was en route to the Belgian Congo, but his luggage was found to contain ingredients for secret ink. He confessed that he had been recruited in Antwerp but failed to realise that he had been enticed to Britain by SIS. He and his wife were detained until the end of the war.

The Germans are showing intense interest in Iceland. In addition to the recent arrivals they are planning to obtain the services of a U-boat. Some kind of expedition is evidently being planned in Tromso.

8 May

ISOS shows that TRICYCLE is mistrusted. It may be that it is only due to the fact that the Brazil station of the Abwehr has been raided. The Germans may think that TRICYCLE has thereby been compromised since he was formerly in Brazil.

Frank Foley is now to deal almost exclusively with double-cross agents and will be a member of the Twenty Committee. This should ease the position as between Felix Cowgill and B1(a).

Richman Stopford has sent a rather agitated telegram from Iceland. It appears that Wise, the Defence Security Officer, with the assistance of a couple of Americans, has rough-handled the crew of the *Arctic*. The GOC has sent Wise home with a recommendation that he should be tried by court-martial.

Desmond Morton is trying to find a way out of the M&E tangle. He wants us to tell Churchill to sack Linfield. I have told him that this is entirely a matter for Churchill. We can no more order a firm to sack one of their employees than we can place a ban on a firm's employment by a Ministry.

David Boyle came to see me about the Callachan case. I suggested to him that he should not prosecute but merely interrogate. I also told him about his secretary Miss Matthews who appears to be living with Querios of the Portuguese Legation.

I saw today certain correspondence which throws an interesting light on the origin of ISOS. On 26 September 1939 T.A. Robertson wrote to Valentine Vivian forwarding the original of a message intercepted on the previous night from XGP which was believed to be in the Stuttgart area. He said that from the procedure and method of sending we were inclined to think it might be the same station that was working to SNOW, call-sign OEA, particularly as we knew that Stuttgart was one of the areas where the Germans had established a station for foreign correspondence. T.A. Robertson suggested that the message should be passed to GC&CS and intimated that we should like to know the result. On 3 October 1939 Vivian replied to the effect that GC&CS had stated that they could do nothing as regards breaking the messages which were returned. They expressed the view that they were Russian telegrams sent from Shanghai. It was not thought that they were German. After this rebuff E.W. Gill, Hugh Trevor Roper and others in the Radio Security Service decided to try their hand at breaking the messages and eventually succeeded. They were, of course, German, and part of the ISOS network. It was from SNOW's messages that the form of ISOS was learned and efforts were then made to pick up others of a similar kind. Gradually the network developed until it covered an area from Kirkness to Ankara, and later on North and South America.

We now learn that Hans Marschner, alias Schutz, was re-arrested in Brugh's house in Dublin. He was in possession of code messages which he had sent and received from Germany. This would seem to imply a secret wireless method of communication from Eire or communication by boat to Lisbon. It is believed that Marschner was also connected with a man named McGuinness who was in touch with Joseph Lenihan in Dublin before the latter gave himself up in Northern Ireland. McGuinness, who has a boat at Cork with a wireless set, has been in touch with Masgeik, the manager of the steel works, an ex-Siemens man. Both McGuinness and Masgeik have been arrested. This information comes from SIS sources and needs confirmation.

The LAND SPIDER, Ib Riis, established contact with the Germans on 5 May and has exchanged traffic daily since that date. His control station is in Hamburg but difficulty is being experienced in intercepting replies owing to fact that the frequency used is difficult to pick up in this country.

General Wavell is putting over a big deception plan. He has evidently arranged for a lot of dispatches to be left in a derelict car somewhere in Burma. These contain a lot of misleading information about reinforcements in the air and on land. He has sent an agitated telegram to the War Office in a cipher which he thinks may well be broken. Even the officials in the War Office have not been told.

I had a discussion with J.C. Masterman, John Marriott and Ian Wilson about SWEET WILLIAM, who not has been playing straight. He appears to have sent over traffic which had not been approved. This was discovered through TRIPLEX sources. It was agreed that he should be liquidated. He cannot however be interned as the evidence cannot be produced, neither have we any power to sack him from the Spanish embassy. My suggestion is that we should interrogate him, tell him that we think he has been double-crossing on account of certain information that we have received through an agent in Madrid and that we can therefore no longer employ him. We should then ask him to sign a statement to the effect that he is no longer in our employ and make it clear to him that in future he cannot communicate any information to the Spaniards without being guilty of treachery.

12 May

I had a long conversation with Desmond Morton about M&E. Morton feels that an impasse has been reached since while we point out to the War Office that we are only advisory, they say that they cannot ignore our advice. In other words, they take what we say as an order. Morton raised one point which is perhaps a good one. He said that if we minuted War Office files, our so-called advice obviously carried ministerial authority. In giving the advice, Harry Allen is acting as Director of C and D Divisions, rather than as the Deputy DMI (Security). We should therefore write a letter to the War Office which would be placed in the file. War Office departments therefore would then have greater freedom of action since they would only be receiving a letter from an outside department. Morton wants us to write him a letter indicating that he could tell Churchill that if he gets rid of Linfield we should raise no further objection. I said that we should find it extremely difficult to do anything of the kind, since we had no power to order firms to dismiss their employees.

14 May

Edward Cussen discussed with me the case of Mrs Callachan which is complicated by the fact that she is going to have a baby. She is to be interrogated and reprimanded. Her services will be retained until she has her baby. She will not be asked to return.

I had a talk with T.A. Robertson and Dick White about the running of double-cross agents in time of invasion. I said that it was desirable to work out some plan with Home Forces. A number of agents might be dropped with wireless sets and it would be necessary to co-ordinate their deception with that of our own network. For this purpose closer contact with GHQ Home Forces would be necessary.

The prosecution of Wise, our DSO in Iceland, has been dropped. There was an allegation that he had ill-treated certain prisoners who had been taken off the *Arctic*. There was no doubt that he had been faced with an extremely difficult problem and that it was vital to ascertain which members of the crew were in fact German agents, and to get the full story. This he succeeded in doing. On his return here he has married Jack Curry's secretary.

The German organisation in Lisbon is sending to this country within the next few weeks an agent who is to work as a mechanic in an aircraft factory here and is to communicate by secret ink letters. He will arrive here by aeroplane. He is an agent of the naval section of the German secret service in Lisbon and is controlled by Hans Bendixen.

Unreliable information said to come from an agent in England is being passed by Madrid to Berlin. It appears to come from Alcazar de Velasco's organization, six of such agents are known to us by designation though not by name and only one of them to our knowledge has passed information which would be considered even remotely true.

15 May

Francis Aiken-Sneath has seen Leonard Ingrams about Otto Witt. Aiken-Sneath is doubtful about Witt but we both thought that he might possibly be made some use of if he was allowed to follow his own line of putting out on a special transmitter propaganda which would cause disruption in army circles. I suggested that he should be put on an island where he could be controlled and where he would be powerless to send any information of any value. His propaganda should be made to appear independent of the British government.

16 May

Lieutenant Park of SOE came to see me about the case of the Frenchman Gourand, alias Lee, who is married to Miss Davies of the Home Office. Lee is said to have been very indiscreet, although as an SOE officer he has done extremely valuable and dangerous work. The trouble is that by his indiscretions he is likely to give away his comrades. I had already drawn SOE's attention to other indiscretions which had come to my notice from entirely independent sources. I suggested that rather than court martial him they should interrogate him very severely and impress upon him that it was not only his life at stake but many of his colleagues. They should then place him on his honour to state the names of all those to whom he had talked. These people should then be interviewed and told to keep their mouths shut. Park thinks this might be the best way out of the difficulty. He will let us know if he wants our assistance.

Francis Aiken-Sneath tells me that some very clear sounds of tapping have been heard going on in Otto Witt's room and it is suspected that he may be tampering with his new wireless receiving set which we have given him. It is of a kind which can be easily converted and we are anxious to test him out.

18 May

Francis Aiken-Sneath tells me today that his informant took Otto Witt out last night to Kempinski's. Aiken-Sneath's informant took with him his rather attractive mistress and altogether the evening appears to have gone with a swing. Witt, who had refused to drink with Aiken-Sneath, started with beer, went on with Chianti and then took two whiskies and sodas with ginger ale, which he described as "das ist ja blos limonade". By this time he was talking rather loudly in German, and had already informed the girl that he knew Reinhard Heydrich and had worked for the SA and SS. He was removed from Kempinski's in a taxi and taken back to his rooms and finally put to bed. At his rooms he became even more indiscreet and intimated that he was too clever for the British, that they would never get him as he would take poison. He was also heard to remark "den Sneath werde ich verkillen". Next morning he rang up our informant in a great state and wanted to know what he had said the night before. Had he talked about his past? He was reassured by the informant saying that he was so tight himself that he really did not know what had been said. He did, however, think that there had been some mention of Witt meeting Heydrich. Witt immediately said he had never met Heydrich but he did once meet a man who came from Heydrich. The informant then said that in any case it was of no consequence.

José Estella, the rock scorpion who gave information about the movements of shipping to the Germans, has been condemned to death at the Old Bailey.

As regards Operation SPIDER, COBWEB who is the LAND SPIDER, established contact on 5 May 1942 and has exchanged traffic daily since that date. His control station is in Hamburg. The date of the operation of Plan SPIDER has had to be retarded since the convoy on which the plan was based is not sailing as early as we expected.

The question of employing Dr Westerlinck on double-cross work is being considered. His codes are very ingenious. One of them is based on syllables. The message begins from the first word that is crossed out. Two one-syllabled words followed by a three syllabled word is 113 and this denotes a certain letter of the alphabet.

19 May

There have been several indications recently that Dr Hans Ruser, who had been connected with German espionage work in Portugal at least since 1937, is now in disfavour with the German authorities. Recently there has been a suggestion that he was preparing to break away altogether from his German associates and attempt to seek refuge in this country. Subsequent to this information it has come to notice that the head of the German secret service in Portugal is making attempts to have Ruser called up for military service although his age group had not yet been reached.

Len Burt, Jim Skardon and Edward Cussen came to see me about the Admiralty case of the discovery of part of a letter accusing certain members of the War Registry of selling information. By a comparison of handwriting with existing records Skardon identifies the man as one Doran who had formerly been employed in the registry and had a grievance. Burt and Skardon went down to see him and approached him on the lines that they were investigating on behalf of the Admiralty certain troubles that had been going on in the registry. They thought that Doran would be able to help them. He fell for this quite easily and told them that drink was one of the main troubles, and that Oswald and others (whom he had mentioned in his letter) were the principal offenders. He was then shown the letter but denied at first that he had written it. Burt took the line that he had doubtless done it from patriotic motives but perhaps it might have been better if he had approached his senior officer. Doran eventually admitted that he had written the letter and also another one which had been sent in anonymously. My view is that the case should go to the Director of Public Prosecutions. In the meantime, we have almost completed arrangements for putting someone into the War Registry with the concurrence of its head. Now that the culprit has been identified, I do not think that we can concern ourselves further since we should be laying ourselves open to accusation that we were employing Gestapo methods on the Civil Service. Further, the head of the registry could only conclude that our informant was coming in to criticise his management. He would therefore be certain to spike the informant's guns. Cussen is going to put this view to the Assistant Director of Naval Intelligence who is very keen that we should continue our enquiries.

I attended a meeting at the Foreign Office with Sir Alexander Cadogan in the chair. C, Valentine Vivian, Sir David Scott, Oswald, Brian Roberts and Jim Hale were also present. It was extremely satisfactory in that the principle on which exchange of prisoners should be carried out in future was laid down. It was agreed that exchange should only take place where it was in the interests of the national war effort. Spies should as far as possible be exchanged for spies and those with specialised knowledge for British subjects who were in an analogous category. The Germans had made demands for a number of Persians because they were obviously contemplating operations in the Middle East and found it extremely difficult to find people with suitable knowledge to act as agents. It was therefore decided to refuse to send back any known agents who had formerly been operating in Persia. We would begin by having an exchange of diplomats and Major Richard Stevens' name would be included on our side since he was a Third Secretary who had been abducted *ultra vires* from neutral territory. It was probable that the Germans would refuse to send him back but a beginning had to be made at some stage and if his name was omitted we should by default be branding him as a spy. As regards the remainder, the Germans would be told that they could name other individuals for return to take the place of those who were being held. This is very satisfactory, as it puts the whole matter on a better basis.

Scott spoke to me afterwards, and expressed himself very strongly about the previous attempts to handle this matter purely on personal and humanitarian lines.

20 May

Otto Witt's case is developing in an interesting way. At about 10.30 last night some very curious sounds were coming from his flat. He had his wireless set working and we gained the impression that he was trying to pick up morse signals. It is possible that he may have been trying to transmit but this is by no means certain.

We propose to let him go on in the hope that we may get to the bottom of this very interesting case.

<hr>

23 May

I had a talk with Buster Milmo and T.A. Robertson on the possibilities of getting a double-cross agent over here who had a certain knowledge of wireless. In this way we thought we might be able to get more up to date on German wireless procedure, etc. A number of lessons have been learned through Jean Pelletier, who says that the Germans have found out quite easily how to get on to our agents. The trouble is twofold. First of all, SIS control both their and SOE agents from Whaddon Hall, and secondly they have a number of agents working to one station on the continent. Agents also have a very obvious call-sign which identifies them as belonging to a certain group. If one of their men, whose call sign is XYZ, is moving about on the continent, his itinerary is quite easily to be traced by the Germans. Equally it is a fairly easy matter for the Germans to concentrate on Whaddon and find out what our other stations are. It happens occasionally that they are communicating with one of their stations abroad when they have to break off after a little ham chat and switch on to the other caller. The Germans being aware of this twiddle the knobs until they get the other station. In Morton Evans' view it would be possible to work out the SIS layout and procedure in a matter of a few hours. The only real answer would seem to be to decentralise and have a separate operator and apparatus for each agent. The fact that SIS control both SOE's and their own transmitters in this manner probably accounts for the crossing of the lines in the Victoire case. Incidentally, apropos of the Victoire case, it seems that Lucas and at least two other of his assistants have been rounded up. It seems that the Germans have made a very close study of the form of Whaddon operators and can recognise them very easily. Their Direction-Finding apparatus is considered to be extremely good and accurate. They must think that ours is very bad in view of the fact that TATE and company have got away with it for so long.

<hr>

28 May

I rang up Bill Stephenson's office. Stephenson was away but John Pepper came down to the hotel and took me up to 630 Fifth Avenue, where the SIS and SOE offices are situated on the 35th and 36th floors. I saw Stephenson later in the day and was introduced to Freckles Wren and others. I spent the next few days talking with Wren and looking at various files. Wren has in his section Gavin Young, a Canadian who is more or less new to the game, Ronnie Sinclair, Mrs Silverston (Sylvanus Vivian's daughter), Mrs Montagu, the wife of Ewen Montagu of the Naval Intelligence Division, and one other lady whose name I forget. Bain of the RCMP who has a seat in the downtown office is by way of effecting liaison with the FBI and with the RCMP, but his work seems to be concerned more with security matters than with counter espionage. It was quite clear to me that Wren was very much in the dark about what we were all trying to do and what we knew about the German intelligence services, and that this made his position vis-à-vis the FBI very difficult. He got questions of one kind or another from home but he was rarely told what was behind them.

2 June

I visited the downtown office. Connop Guthrie, who is more or less head of this office, was away. Nelson, his second in command, was in charge. Nelson is an extremely likable fellow but strikes one as being somewhat of an intellectual. He belongs to the publishing family, but has for some years been running a farm in Wyoming. He gave me the general lay-out of the office. Bates is in charge of the Consular Security officers in the United States and Karri-Davis of those in South America. Formerly the office had had a good deal to do with the security of armaments being manufactured by the British while they were in transit to the port of embarkation. This work had now been transferred to the American authorities and the personnel had been transferred to Washington DC where they were doing work for the Australian Purchasing Commission. There had also been a Fire Protection Squad who had been engaged in looking after goods awaiting shipment. This squad had also been disbanded and the work handed over to the FBI. Liaison with the FBI, the state police and the RCMP were in the hands of Bain. I had a talk with Karri-Davies. He was very keen to get any material from us on the question of sabotage, particularly material which he could transmit to the Consular Security Officers. He said that anything we could tell them about German methods would be invaluable. He had seen the X-ray photographs and diagrams of infernal machines.

Communist activities are handled by Jean-Paul Evans, although it would seem that this should be an appropriate job under Wren who would pass the information to Section V and so to ourselves. The subject has up to now been handled by the Security Division probably on account of labour disturbances, which affected the production and transit of armaments after manufacture for the UK. Evans struck me as being intelligent and conscientious. He is making quite a study of the subject and getting hold of some quite useful material both through his liaison with the Americans and Canadians, through Censorship and through the press. He clearly needed guidance and I did my best to impress upon him that information which illustrated the control and policing of the Comintern was of greater interest than strike disturbances due solely to economic causes. We were particularly interested in directives from Moscow, methods of communication, funds, etc since America was one of the few places where data was available for comparison with that received at home.

Babette Gross, Willi Munzenberg's mistress, is apparently now in Mexico and a certain amount of her correspondence has been intercepted. Other correspondence which Evans thought would interest us was that passing between Apartado 8620, Mexico, which I gather is the Central Catalan Syndicate to one Carlos Pi-Sunner, 22 Wendover Court, Finchley Rd, NW2.

If Evans wishes to make enquiries in South America he passes them through Section 3 of the town office. For matters in North America he relies upon his liaison with the FBI and others. He had been much interested in the report on the Shop Stewards Movement in this country, a copy of which he had given to the FBI who were also deeply impressed. He said it would be of great assistance to him to receive any memoranda of this kind or any reports on Communist activities here with which he could bargain with his opposite numbers. Even if the reports cannot be passed on, he would be very glad to have them himself as they would assist him considerably in his work. As regards Communist literature I said that we should be glad to receive any papers or periodicals which contained articles denoting some new feature of the movement, and that we should be grateful if he would, when forwarding them, arrange that they be suitably marked. He undertook to let us have any information about the formation of any new Communist or pseduo-Communist organisation.

Downtown is responsible for the vetting of personnel employed by the Purchasing Commission and other British missions and also for the vetting of the personnel of allied forces recruited in the Western Hemisphere.

I had a talk with Kenneth Maidment, the Radio Security Service representative at the uptown office. He told me that there had recently been a conference known as the Wilkinson Conference at which certain vague principles had been laid down on the subject of monitoring and cryptography. Monitoring must be done by the Federal Communications Committee, army and navy including Coastguard, cryptography there only being done by the army, navy and FBI. No very definite decision was arrived at about distribution except that all deciphered material was to go to the State Department. In the matter of cryptography there is a complete barrier between the services and the FBI. The personnel employed by the FBI is not of a very high grade and they have no experience. They are, however, trying to build up a huge organisation. The navy refuses to give them the benefit of any of their experience. They are therefore trying to crack the Japanese cipher, which is already dealt with by the navy. Our policy in the past has been to keep in touch with all organisations on the understanding that we do not pass anything from one to the other. The FBI is apparently setting up some organisation on the Pacific coast both for monitoring and deciphering. No diplomatic traffic is apparently sent to British Security Co-ordination from England. Bill Stephenson, it is believed, got a certain amount of Japanese BJs from the Americans. Maidment said that as far as he knew there was no illicit traffic from the Argentine to Europe but there was of course cable communication which was used freely by the Germans. He thought that there was a cable which formerly ran to Gibraltar and then to North Africa but that it had been cut at Gibraltar. Unfortunately, SIS were extremely weak in the Argentine and up to a week or so ago they had no one. It was obviously highly desirable that somebody should be got into the post office at Buenos Aires in order to collect all diplomatic cables to Europe, particularly since it is the policy of the FBI to get South American states to close down all illicit wireless.

---

3 June

I went to Washington on the night train and saw Quinn Tamm, who is Hoover's second in command. I was accompanied by Walter Bell who is the liaison man with the FBI in Washington. Bell was formerly in Passport Control New York and has long experience of America. I talked mainly generalities with Tamm. He sits in an enormous room with an enormous desk in front of him and is surrounded by telephones, microphones etc. A large map of America on the wall is covered with pins and bits of cotton which are by way of demonstrating the activities of the FBI. The Americans seem to have a mania for diagrams, many of which I fear are quite meaningless if not misleading. I was shown a map of the United States. Superimposed on this were two talc covers. On one of them covers the areas where enemy aliens were concentrated were painted in colour, and on the other the big industrial centres. It was thought remarkable that the alien population should correspond almost exactly with the industrial centres. I was told that the Chiefs of Staff had been much impressed. Personally, I was unable to understand why any significance should be attached to the identity of location. I came to the conclusion that all this vast *mise-en-scène* was not so much to impress the visitor as to impress the gentleman who occupied the room of his own importance. He might perhaps lack confidence without all these stimulants. He told me about all his difficulties in dealing with the internment question, etc. The numbers of enemy aliens interned were on the whole small. I think only roughly between 2 and 3,000 Germans, a similar number of Italians, perhaps 4,000 Japanese. The Japanese have been pushed back from the Pacific coast and are to some extent being employed in large camps. They are able, therefore, to move about within limits. There is nothing in the way of legislation equivalent to our 12(5a) of the Aliens Order or 18(b) of the Defence Regulations. The only way of getting an American citizen of German origin interned is to proceed by de-naturalisation. This is extremely cumbersome and only successful if concrete evidence could be obtained. Without any prompting Tamm said that he had been amazed that there had been no act of sabotage committed in the United States which could be definitely traced to enemy agency and that all the cases of German espionage which had come to their notice has been of an extremely crude variety. So crude were they that he wondered very much whether they had not been faked to pull the wool over the eyes of the FBI. I told him that our experience had been very similar and that the same doubts had arisen in our minds. We were however fairly satisfied that the Germans had not got an extensive organisation in Britain and that such cases as had come to our notice were genuine cases. The German machine was well conceived and well planned but it seemed to vary very much in efficieny when it came to action.

I went on to see C.H. 'Kit' Carson, a young and very keen officer who is responsible for espionage activities in South America. He told me that Albrecht

Engels was under interrogation and that Werner Nicolaus, who was undoubtedly MAX of Mexico City, had recently been deported to the United States. A difficulty had arisen about deportees from South America. The State Department had given an undertaking to the South American states to send them back to Europe in exchange for the nationals of the countries from which they came. The FBI was anxious to hold all those who were connected with the German intelligence service, and was in conflict with the State Department about this matter. They hoped that we should be able to do something through the British Embassy to strengthen the FBI's hand. The Spanish Consul-General in the United States was under grave suspicion. Information had been received that he was using the diplomatic bag for improper purposes and recently he had had his bag opened under his own eyes. Unfortunately nothing was found. The incident however passed off without protest. The FBI is very perturbed about the sinkings in the Caribbean and says there is no doubt that the Germans have extremely accurate information about the movement of ships, and wonders how this information is conveyed to submarines, which seem to know in the greatest detail the name of ship, captain, and all about the cargo. I imagine they get this information wirelessed back and it then goes to the submarines by ZPT but I could not of course tell the Americans about this.

4 June

I saw Mickey Ladd of the FBI and was again accompanied by Walter Bell. Ladd is a Middle Westerner and a sticky personality. He is virtually in charge of all the practical side of espionage activities. I handed over to him details of a number of cases which we had had in the UK, also data about secret ink and certain codes. He seemed pleased with this information, but it soon transpired that he had a strong suspicion that we had been holding up on him in the past, and he mentioned the incident of the bombing of Tokyo. We had made a suggestion that the José Mosquera transmitter should be used for intimating to the Germans that Tokyo would be bombed. The idea was to try and draw off planes and aircraft carriers from Burma and the Indian Ocean. By a pure coincidence Tokyo was bombed three days later. Ladd wondered first of all how we knew about this, whether there had been any leakage, and was disinclined to believe us when we said we had no prior knowledge of the matter. We then asked him, if this information was false, we had indicated that we would prefer that it went over from the Mosquera transmitter rather than the one used by TRICYCLE. We explained that TRICYCLE was at the moment in a rather delicate position. Ladd was not very inclined to accept this information particularly as we had told him that we only put across information that was true. In this case we had no knowledge of the fact that the information was true. He thought therefore that we were trying to pass off a piece of dud information on Mosquera which would have jeopardised his position. We pointed out that the message was so worded as to leave José Mosquera plenty of loopholes, since it had not been worded in definite terms. Ladd then went on to complain that he was asked to make enquiries without being told the reason. I entirely agreed with him that this was undesirable and that in future we should do our best to give him the fullest possible background. I explained to him that we did not wish to pry into American affairs but that we were anxious to exchange information on the broadest possible basis particularly with regard to the procedure of Germans agents and data relating to German intelligence organisations and personnel. Ladd told me that as far as he knew no DUFF was going from the United States. He also said that he had no cases of espionage by Italians. The case of TRICYCLE was discussed. Ladd complained that he had not yet received BALLOON's traffic which had been promised. I said that it was on its way and that we should keep him fully informed in future. We in return should be interested to see the Mosquera traffic. I referred to the case of Keller and Stahlder, the two individuals who had come from Gibraltar with plans and photographs and had been arrested in the United States and asked whether we might be given facilities for interviewing these men. Ladd promised to do what he could.

Codenamed MINARET, José Mosequera was an SIS double agent in Buenos Aires.

I then went to see R.P. Kramer and Harry Kimball, two of Ladd's subordinates. Kramer told me afterwards that he was of pure German descent and that his grandfather was in the Kaiser's bodyguard. There is no doubt however that he is 100% American in sympathy. I explained to them both the workings of the Twenty Committee and the double-cross agent system. They were enthusiastic, particularly Kimball who was very quick to see all the implications, and the necessity for getting the co-operation of the service departments. They intended to put the idea to higher authority. They said that a careful search of Nicolaus's belongings had revealed microfilms contained in the toe of his boot. These films were of the latest American submarine escape device. Nicolaus did not know at the moment that this had been found. The FBI were particularly pleased as they thought it would strengthen their hand in dealing with the State Department in the matter of detention of enemy aliens from South America who had been connected with the German intelligence system.

I lunched with Assistant Commissioner Bruce, who is the RCMP liaison officer with the FBI. I asked him to tell me quite frankly what the FBI thought about us. He said "If you really want to know, they think you are too cagey and that you are holding up on them." I told him that I thought that in many ways they were quite right and one of my preoccupations would be to get things loosened up. He said that he wholly trusted the FBI and that they had always given Commissioner Stuart Wood the fullest co-operation. I gather that Bruce is allowed to see the FBI files. I asked him how the suggestion that we also should have a representative in the FBI would be likely to be received. He said that it was difficult to say but that he thought such a suggestion might quite possibly be acceptable. He emphasised that the FBI particularly disliked being asked to make enquiries without being given full facts. Bruce was very anxious that I should treat what he had told me as strictly confidential and that I should make no use of his name.

In the afternoon I rang up John Maude and I subsequently went out to see him at the embassy. He told me the whole story of his career in America. He seemed to think that he had been badly treated and he had quite made up his mind to come back to England. Stratton had suggested to him that he might like to take over the DSO's job in British Honduras, but he was evidently sick of the whole business and anxious to get back. He said that anybody could do the job of looking after the security of missions and that he could not go on drawing a large salary for what really was a very small job. Personally, I think that he has had rather a raw deal. He fell foul of Ingram Fraser, which is not surprising, and somehow incurred the displeasure of Bill Stephenson, and therefore never had a chance of dealing with enquiries which affected our office. I do not think he got on very well with Stratton or with Dick Ellis, who are departmentally quite different people. John seemed to think that he went down very well with the Americans and that he had done a good job as far as he had been allowed. Other people, however, seem to regard him rather as superficial and rather a joke. He is going back without any stink but is I think clearly a disappointed man.

[XXXXXXXX] and I dined with Kit Carson of the FBI. We had a long discussion about our work and methods. Carson was very understanding and very keen to learn. He would very much like to pay us a visit.

5 June

I lunched with Bill Donovan and Barty Bouverie. I gave Donovan a general view of our experiences here. He told me that he now had a mandate from the Chiefs of Staff to start up an organisation covering the activities of SIS, SOE, PWE and ourselves in Europe, the Middle East and Far East. He wanted to know whether in his outstations he should make one person head of all four organisations or whether they should communicate separately to headquarters in Washington DC. I said that from our experience I was quite certain that he ought to place the four departments under one head, otherwise they would undoubtedly get across each other's tracks and the work of one might well be damaging to the others. This had been our experience, but it seems impossible under present circumstances to get any change. If he had the opportunity of building from the bottom he would be well-advised to consolidate his organisations in the outstations. Donovan is a very likable personality and was apparently a great figure in the last war, when he got the equivalent of the Victoria Cross as commander of a battalion on the Western Front. I am told that his great trouble is that he has no first class Chief of Staff to keep him on the proper organisational rails. He is full of ideas but bad at organisation.

I went back to New York on the 4 o'clock train and dined with Edwin Herbert at the Plaza. He told me that he was still struggling to get the South America mails brought up for censorship to Trinidad or Bermuda. It had however been agreed provisionally that they should at any rate go to San Juan in Costa Rica where they would be examined by American censorship with representatives of our censorship alongside. This was not wholly satisfactory but it was better than nothing and certainly closes the existing gap. He had apparently had a very successful meeting with the combined Chiefs of Staff to whom he had shown several DUFFs indicating leakage of information about the movements of American warships in the Canal Zone. They were all very intrigued and they clearly saw the urgency for getting something done. Herbert certainly is very good at putting over his points.

---

6 June

I lunched with Ingram Fraser. He does not appear to have any clearly defined job in the office and I cannot find anyone who has a really good word for him. He was, I believe, at one time employed in SOE and it is probably therefore that from the organisation he drifted into British Security Co-ordination. He and John Pepper seem to be running a certain number of agents who they employed before America came into the war. An undertaking was given some time ago by Bill Stephenson to J. Edgar Hoover that he would no longer employ agents in his area. These agents were therefore handed over to Donovan. Donovan has however asked Fraser and Pepper to continue to run them and let him have the information. They are certain to be found out before very long and the damage will be considerable, since Hoover hates Donovan's guts. I was told that Fraser had been running a mistress in Washington DC who was supposed to be acting as an agent on the Finns. She was getting $500 a month for her flat and $500 for her services, all paid out of office funds. Stephenson heard about this and had it stopped. Another unsavoury incident was when Fraser and Pepper bought sterling on the black market which they spent on their visit to this country. On return they claimed their expenses at the full rates.

I dined with William Guthrie and Stratton. Guthrie strikes me as being something of a bluffer but energetic or probably up to a point energetic. He is certainly a go-getter. I am certain, however, that his first consideration is the aggrandisement of Guthrie and possibly a peerage. We discussed his recent visit with Stratton to Newfoundland and Canada on the question of security. They said that in both places security in so far as ports were concerned is practically non-existent. They complained rather bitterly about Stuart Wood. They had eventually succeeded in getting a ruling from the Cabinet in Ottawa that the port security organisation should be set up under the RCMP with military and naval personnel. We were to send out two or three people to train various sections. There are also to be security points along the frontier and at the airports. Stratton seemed to think that two hundred men would be sufficient but in conversations that I had subsequently with Wood he seemed to think that the job could not possibly be done efficiently with less than eight hundred men. Stratton is clearly a great supporter of Guthrie and would like to see him as a successor to Lord Swinton. I should say that Guthrie was somewhat similar in type to Swinton but not so able. He is certainly ambitious and unscrupulous.

A wartime Section V officer, William Guthrie was later Professor of Ancient Philosophy and Public Orator at Cambridge University.

In the afternoon I saw Tibbett who works with Le Foregeais of the downtown office in vetting personnel of allied services recruited in the western hemisphere. I gave Tibbett Theo Turner's memo on the white card system, asked him to consider it and discuss it with me on my return from Canada. I left by the night train with Freckles Wren, for Ottawa.

Wren and I called on Colonel Murray, who is GSOI to the Canadian Director of Military Intelligence, in order to discuss SPRINGBOK's traffic. It had been suggested that both he and TRICYCLE should put over certain figures about the training of aircraft personnel which had been mentioned at the inter-allied conference at Ottawa. These figures had been approved by the Joint Intelligence Committee in Washington DC, the Air Ministry in London, and the Americans, but apparently the Canadian officer who had just taken over Air Intelligence, and was quite unacquainted with double-cross procedures, was extremely apprehensive and shocked at the idea of supplying the enemy with such important information. I pointed out that although the information was interesting I thought it would be more likely to depress the enemy than anything else.

I went with Walter Bell by the night train to Toronto. SPRINGBOK came to our hotel and we had a long conversation with him about his position. He had made carious attempts to establish contact with the South, but these had not been entirely successful. He had however carried on considerable correspondence in code with Sao Paulo. He was also trying to get into touch with Buenos Aires by letter in order to acquaint Berlin of his position. I had a long discussion with him about the Abwehr training he had had. He had been three months with Abteilung II and eight months with Abteilung III. A number of interesting facts emerged which I subsequently recorded in the form of a report. Perhaps the most interesting facts related to Frank Ryan who had been working with von Branderstein in Abteilung II. Ryan was apparently assisting the formation of Casement Brigade. SPRINGBOK did not know his name but he did know that he had taken part in the Spanish Civil War and had been interned by the Falangists and was subsequently released at the request of the Germans. In Abteilung III SPRINGBOK had served under Major Lieber, who had frequently visited this country before the war, staying at a boarding house in Southhampton. He had generally been accompanied by Miss Schraeder. At the time of Munich he was going round the Isle of Wight in a pleasure boat. He noted the movements of British ships and reported them to Berlin. He had also been responsible for recruiting of a Scot who had been in communication with Berlin prior to the war by wireless. SPRINGBOK thought that the

Scot was a Scottish Nationalist. It is just possible that he may be confusing this man with SNOW, but I rather doubt it, since SNOW did not communicate as far as we know before the war, nor was Berlin his control station. SPRINGBOK had received instruction in secret inks, microphotography, etc. He had seen the DUFF machine, and had given us a drawing and description of its working.

SPRINGBOK is a mine of information and one could probably go on talking to him for a month and still obtain from him further facts. The one confusing point in his story is his statement that Abteilung III was not concerned with counter-espionage. He bases this solely on his own experience and the instructions he received when working for III Luft. He said that he was told to report on sites for aerodromes and on existing aerodromes and that he received special instructions and that if he obtained any counter-espionage information he was to report back but not to investigate. There is probably some explanation though what it is I cannot imagine.

I spent the evening with Tommy Drew-Brook, who is Wren's representative in Canada. He is more or less in charge of SPRINGBOK. I was very impressed by his keenness. He is certainly out to do everything he possibly can to help and is taking immense trouble to provide SPRINGBOK with the necessary business cover.

SPRINGBOK was Hans von Kotze, a German aristocrat married to an Englishwoman, who had emigrated to South Africa in 1929 to work as a fur buyer and miner. Soon after the outbreak of war, hoping to avoid internment as an enemy alien, he had moved to Portuguese East Africa but had been expelled. In a further attempt to avoid internment he had taken a passage to Europe but had been captured by a French ship and detained in Morocco until July 1940. When he was finally released he was offered the option of serving in the Wehrmacht or working for the Abwehr, and he had chosen the latter. In June 1941 he had been dispatched to Brazil to join the Albrecht Engels organisation under commercial cover as a buyer in the leather trade, but what he really wanted to do was re-establish contact with his wife, who had been interned in South Africa, and their children. When finally in March 1942 he was ordered to move to South Africa he wrote to the British Consulate in Sao Paulo and offered his services to SIS. In exchange for a British passport after the war, some money and the opportunity to be reunited with his wife without being arrested he supplied a wealth of information about the Abwehr's network in Brazil, its members and codes, and he was resettled in Canada.

10 June

I saw Stuart Wood again. He told me that he had had no case of sabotage and no case of espionage since the beginning of the war. He was amazed but not complacent. He realised that he had an enormous area to cover and that he was under-staffed and that his force was not very well-equipped for counter-espionage work. I suggested to him that his best insurance against penetration would be the establishment of four or five first-class double-cross agents, and that he should regard SPRINGBOK as a beginning. He seemed pleased with the idea but I doubt whether he had much notion of how to set about the problem. His subordinates whom I saw are Assistant Commissioner Tate, an oldish man who is just about to retire, and Drysdale, also oldish and over-worked. Neither of them seemed to welcome the idea of any direct assistance from an officer of the Security Service. Wood however was quite open-minded. He felt however that anybody going out would very shortly be out of date. I suggested that it might be more profitable to have someone in New York who could pay him constant visits. I rather think that Tate and Drysdale have been somewhat upset by the visit of Guthrie and Stratton who must have given the impression that they do not think very much of the RCMP. This is apparently the view of the services but I think it is somewhat exaggerated. The RCMP are very well equipped to deal with Communism but not very well equipped to deal with counter-espionage. They are essentially a police force employing police methods. There is not a great deal of imagination and there seems to be little inclination to take the offensive. They give me the impression of using their pre-war machinery of informants' notes and reports and hope that their existing network will throw up any spies who happen to be around. It may well be therefore that they are more penetrated than they imagine. They have a large enemy alien population very few of whom have been interned. At the outbreak of war they only interned twenty-three Japanese. They have since taken in about a hundred. They only have a few hundred Germans and Italians under lock and key. I discussed the question of the Portuguese ship which had called at Halifax in Newfoundland, *Alvarel Martens Homen*, the master of which is Carlo Maria Tomaz Texeira. It had been reported from home that this ship had already deposited two wireless sets in Newfoundland and was in the guise of a vessel controlling a fishing fleet, but actually reporting on the movements of our shipping. The boat had been examined at Halifax and found to contain a fairly powerful wireless set. It had subsequently proceeded to Newfoundland where the crew had been allowed to land. There was however no force there which could keep track of their movements. I asked about the Spaniards and I was told that there was a Consulate-General in Montreal with a right to communicate in cipher with Madrid and Washington DC and also to send dispatches by bag. There was also a Consulate in Vancouver which was looking after the interests of the Japanese and which had a fully-fledged Japanese assistant. The consul in Montreal was a man called Schwarz who comes from a Rhenish family which fought for Napoleon in Spain. The Vice-Consul is one Iturradde and may be a relation of the man here who is suspect. The Montreal one is a member of the Falange. In Montreal there is also a Japanese assistant who is a dual national. I ascertained later that Ramon Serrano Suner's son is also employed at Montreal and that the Spanish Consul at Panama, Bernard, was to be reinforced by a new Spanish arrival from Madrid.

I saw Stratton and Oliver Strachey in their little house on the outskirts of Ottawa. Strachey, I gather, is coming home shortly. I told them both about SPRINGBOK, whose traffic they are trying to monitor and also about the Abwehr station at Stahnsdorf where SPRINGBOK was trained. Stratton was interested to learn that Dublin was included in the Abwehr network.

I saw Colonel Murray again. He was very worried about the RCMP whom he considered to be dilatory in their methods and lacking in energy. I think, however, that a good deal of his apprehension is similar to that which we experienced here from the military in the early days of the war. I do not think the RCMP are as bad as he paints them, although their methods may be orthodox and old-fashioned. I explained to him the Spanish situation and told him that I was proposing to see External Affairs. I thought this was a good idea. He told me that in the meantime he had been able to get approval from the Cabinet of External Affairs authorising SPRINGBOK 's traffic. The Chiefs of Staff had delegated to him and his naval and air colleagues the necessary powers for approving any messages submitted.

I talked to Captains Brand and Little of the Canadian Naval Intelligence Division about Texeira. It seemed to me that if this man was doing any harm he would be communicating either with submarines or with Germany. What steps could the navy take to monitor his traffic? Did they know whether he sends any signals at all? Little confessed that they had no notion, and that it might be difficult to pick up. The best he could do would be to detail two or three Voluntary Interceptors in Newfoundland, but he did not think they would be able to do any very effective work. The difficulty about dealing with Texeira was that London has deprecated any drastic action on account of refuelling services which the Royal Navy got in the Cape Verde Islands. This puts a very different light on the whole position.

As I was going out of the navy building I passed Lord Mountbatten who was under a battery of press cameras. I lunched with Stuart Wood and Anderson of the Department of Justice at the RCMP training centre. Afterwards, we were shown all over the buildings and were given a display by the police dogs. After lunch I saw Stone of External Affairs and talked to him a good deal about the Spanish situation, and he arranged for me to see Norman Robertson, the Under-Secretary of State on the following day.

I had a long talk with Norman Robertson of External Affairs when he told me that the policy as regards Japanese was to evacuate them as far as possible from the Pacific coast. This included Canadian citizens of Japanese origin. I gave him all the information I could about the Spanish situation and impressed upon him its importance. He said that he would speak to the Commissioner and I hope that this may result in an intensification of the enquiries that are already on foot. Robertson, I should think, is able though rather the Foreign Office type, who would do anything rather than risk any diplomatic unpleasantness. I had a final word with Wood and also with Assistant Commissioner Bruce who had come up from Washington DC. I told Wood again that I was certain that his best insurance against penetration was a development of the double-cross system and that he might well get the FBI to collaborate with him in this matter. Possible they could find a few suitable people whom they could introduce into the Germans' network and send up to Canada. Bruce is going to talk to them about this. I returned to New York by the night train.

13 June

I lunched with Walter Bell and Hamish Mitchell, the SIS man who is working in conjunction with the Censorship at Bermuda. Mitchell is a tremendous enthusiast and a confirmed believer in amalgamation of SIS and the Security Service, with dual representation through the Caribbean. He says the present system is ridiculous and wastes time and energy. He was full of complaints about London and its lack of understanding. He struck me as being a very live wire. He obviously did not think very much of Piggott. He liked him personally, but fully realised that Piggott was not much of an intelligence officer. The real problem both at Bermuda and Trinidad is the transit traffic both in mail and personnel. The security of the island is a very minor matter. A man holding Piggott's position really ought to be a fully-trained B Division officer, whereas in fact he never even saw a soul in B before he left. His only experience was as a Security Control Officer.

15 June

I dined with Harford Hyde and his wife. She was formerly employed on TRIPLEX work in London then at Bermuda and now in the New York Office where she has a little laboratory. She and her female assistant are apparently quite efficient at their job. They gave a course of instruction to the FBI whose methods in these matters are somewhat crude.

16 June

I had a talk with Edward Coffey who is the FBI representative in charge of crypt-analysis, laboratory work, cameras and technical appliances. He had seen the code 111/333 which had been in the possession of Dr Westerlinck. He said that it appeared in a book entitled *Elementary Crypto-Analysis* by Helen Fouche Gaines, published by the American Photographic Publishing Company of Boston in October 1939. He showed me a copy of this book which contained a number of other codes. We are taking steps to obtain copies for circulation to censorship points and other people who may be interested. It seems likely that if the Germans have been using this book they may be employing some of the other codes it contains.

I saw Quinn Tamm who took me in to J. Edgar Hoover, who is obviously the prima donna type. He was very cordial and held forth at great length about his organisation and his difficulties. I gave him some picture of our experiences in England whenever he showed signs of drawing breath, which was not often. It was obviously no good discussing with him such matters as double-cross agents. His mind is working more on political relations with other departments. Before I left Tamm I made an appointment to discuss five points, on which I hope we can reach agreement. I afterwards saw Kramer and dined with him, Harry Kimball and Edward Coffey. We had a very cheery evening. Kimball told me that he had already got going on on the double-cross Committee idea and that the sanction had been obtained. Kimball is bursting with keenness and longing to come over to England. I think they all feel that Mickey Ladd is rather a stumbling-block to better collaboration and it may be that it would be more profitable if we could get him over to England. If he once could be convinced of our sincerity I think things would go better.

17 June

Walter Bell and I went down to the FBI school which is about twenty miles from Washington DC in the State of Virginia. I listened to one of the lectures on office procedure. The course is quite a good one but it seems to be purely a police course. I do not think that there were any lectures on the German intelligence system, probably because nobody in the FBI really knows anything about it.

We dined with Richard Coit, a pleasant individual who, according to Walter Bell, has done good work. He apparently goes down very well with the Americans. There are stories about his activities in the last war when he was said to be connected with Thornley Gibson in some sort of peace move in Switzerland. I gather from Bill Stephenson, however, that there is nothing in this and that Coit explained it all before he was taken on. He had a letter from the Under-Secretary of State exonerating him from all blame. He appears to be pretty well off since he receives no salary from British Security Co-ordination. His real name is Wetzler. He was formerly in Schwab & Snelling who have a very unsavoury reputation in the City. Financially he may have been a bit shady in the past but I should say that he was now solely concerned with assisting the allied cause to the best of his ability.

19 June

I lunched with Hamish Mitchell, Charles Watson and Wilfred Hill-Wood. Watson is in charge of censorship at Bermuda and Hill-Wood is doing censorship work in New York under Des Graz. They mentioned the case of correspondence intercepted in Liverpool passing between Mexico and Stockholm. This correspondence had a distribution of five but New York was not included. All present were strongly in favour of some form of amalgamation between SIS and the Security Service in the Caribbean, if not elsewhere. I wrote a long letter to the Director-General and one to Dick White which I sent by Stratton, who is leaving tomorrow for the UK.

3 July

Walter Bell and I saw George McSwayne at the FBI headquarters in New York. We had intended to see Percy Foxworth but he was tied up with the generals trying to make arrangements for a court-martial of the nine saboteurs who had just been arrested. Apparently the two parties, one at Long Island and the other in Florida, were operating independently although they each knew of the others' existence. They deposited their material on shore and after burying it went to reconnoitre or to make contact with certain people who were thought likely to be sympathetic. Six of these people have also been arrested. The eight spies were caught on their return to collect their explosives. The whole project has been in preparation since last April. There is a great deal of confusion about the court-martial procedure to be adopted since no case of the kind involving the death penalty has been known since the days of Abraham Lincoln.

George McSwayne talked a certain amount about the lack of powers in dealing with citizens. Two of the saboteurs were Americans of German origin and they might claim the right to be tried in the civil courts. The problem of interning American citizens is equally a difficult one. There was nothing equivalent to our 18(b) and it was therefore necessary to proceed by de-naturalisation. This is a cumbersome business and a good deal of convincing evidence is required. Captain Drexler, who featured prominently in the 1938 espionage case, was an American citizen and formerly Marine Superintendent of the Hamburg–Amerika Line, but since he was a citizen he could not be interned even though he was taking a lively interest in German internees in Canada. Attempts were being made to get him de-naturalised, but McSwayne was not hopeful.

4 July

I saw TRICYCLE in company with George McSwayne and Freckles Wren. He seemed to be rather full of complaints as regards his treatment since he arrived in America. It was quite embarrassing for me as he was so full of praise for the way he had been handled in England. He maintained since he arrived in America his case had never been given careful consideration. He had been obliged to spend a good deal of money because otherwise the Germans could not have expected him to move in the circles in which he was to collect information. Had they wished him to do otherwise they should have arranged a suitable cover. He was now in financial difficulties and the Americans were refusing to support him. He said he was quite ready to live on a modest scale but it was up to the Americans to think out some suitable cover. There is no doubt I think that TRICYCLE has been living pretty well and that in anticipation of financial support from Germany he has run himself heavily into debt. I do think however that he has been seriously mishandled. In order to meet his immediate needs Freckles Wren paid him $2,000. I doubt however whether he will get anything out of the Americans. Wren offered to pay half the liabilities which run into something like $15,000. I asked TRICYCLE about his visit to Lisbon and he said that nothing much occurred outside what he had already reported. The principal incident was the arrival of the General Staff officer who had to consider Plan MIDAS. He explained that in order to get to Rio de Janeiro he arranged that he should be given a diplomatic mission by his government. This enabled him to carry a bag and to deliver certain information which had been approved for transmission to the Germans. He saw the military attaché and naval attaché, and was eventually passed over to Albrecht

Engels, since arrested. He then made an arrangement by which he could communicate from New York to Rio through a Brazilian captain. This arrangement subsequently broke down owing to the declaration of war by the United States. TRICYCLE received roughly $9,000 in Rio.

Later Wren and I went on to see Percy Foxworth with whom we discussed the position of TRICYCLE. I gave Foxworth our views about the double-cross agent system and impressed upon him that it was impossible to run a man like TRICYCLE the way they were doing. We had found it necessary to have as many as eight or nine people who devoted themselves entirely to double-cross work. Foxworth implied that it was impossible for his organisation to detail so many men for this work. He did not seem to comprehend the importance of it. He was thinking all the time in terms of a balance sheet. TRICYCLE had been there for so many months, he had cost the FBI so much, and had given the enemy certain good if not vital information. All this was on the debit side but there was nothing on the credit side. I tried to explain to Foxworth that there was a great deal on the credit side. He had had a man who for six to eight months had been in the confidence of the enemy and who was therefore something in the nature of an insurance against penetration. If he could reach a stage where he had the majority of the German agents in the United States under his control, his problem in dealing with counter-espionage would be largely solved. Having heard that Foxworth was by far and away the ablest and most intelligent representative of the FBI, I was a little disappointed by the interview. He struck me as being singularly narrow in his outlook. It may have been that he was too harassed by the sabotage case to enter into serious conversation on the question of double agents. He had just returned from a long visit to South America. He said that his policy there was to get all the illicit wireless stations closed down. I rather gathered that he had been responsible for closing the station at Valparaiso. His idea was that by getting Chilean and Argentinian authorities to take action public feeling would be aroused against Germany and that ultimately both these countries would be driven off their neutrality. If there were any chance of his being successful in this regard the price might be worth paying, otherwise he was obviously doing himself and us harm since he would drive communications into other channels which it might be difficult to discern.

Foxworth gave me a promise to send full details about the sabotage case as soon as the trial was completed. Matters are being so rushed that it seemed doubtful whether they would ever get the full story.

5 July

I had a talk with Pat Bayly, the Canadian professor who is charge of Bill Stephenson's communications. He showed me his adaptation of the Telecrypton which is a tape punched with holes in such a way as to put any message into a one-time table. This is then transmitted and comes out at the other end. This is used for communication both with Ottawa and Washington DC. Some adaptation is being suggesting for communication with Europe. Bayly is very worried by the restrictions being placed upon a frank talk with the Americans on the subject of ISOS. He said that our present reluctance to tell then what we were doing was creating a very uncomfortable atmosphere. Kenneth Maidment had recently received a list of the stations that we were monitoring with strict instructions that they were for his information only. Bayly on his own initiative has passed these to the Americans in strict confidence. If he were challenged he was quite ready to stand the racket and had the support of Stephenson. I told him that on my return I was going to propose firstly that he should be given a mandate from the Security Service and secondly that Cyril Mills should go on in order to assist [XXXX] in working double agents. He entirely agreed with these proposals. He asked me to let him know if we had any records in England of Richard Coit, since it had been suggested to him that Coit had a bad history dating from the last war. He explained to me that Coit had told him before being taken on that he had been accused of having been connected with some peace move in 1916 but he produced a letter from the then Under-Secretary of State for Foreign Affairs, exonerating him from all blame. At the time in question he was in Switzerland. I promised to look up the records and let him know.

7 July

[XXXX] and I paid a visit to Superintendent H. Royal-Gagnon, the head of the RCMP in Montreal. We discussed with him the question of action against the Spanish Consulate in Montreal. He said that the telephone so far revealed nothing of interest. I gather however that he was going to try and insert a mike and also to get an agent inside. He talked a lot about the French Canadians. He seemed to think that question of conscription had been badly handled. It was largely a political issue which had been running since the Boer War. He thought there would be no difficulty in getting French Canadians to enlist voluntarily if they were allowed to have their own battalion officers. There was no necessity to put them into the same division or even to brigade them but the English Canadians did not really understand the habits and customs of the French Canadians and provided they had their own officers all would be well. He explained that the French Canadians were interested in the French language and culture of the 17th century but that they had no interest in France or Frenchmen of today. They were 100% Canadian. They were increasing rapidly compared with the English-speaking population. Royal-Gagnon struck me as being a very fine fellow, and I should imagine that he would probably be Commissioner before he is finished. I gather that he comes next but one on the list. We discussed the Kleczynsky case. I said that we were quite convinced that the whole incident of the bomb being placed in Sikorski's plane was phoney. Royal-Gagnon entirely agreed. The officer on the case had come definitely to this conclusion after his interview with the Polish ambassador in Washington DC. Obviously there had been an attempt to hush the whole thing up.

Upon his return to London Liddell's diary was updated with events that had occurred in his absence. These entries are indicated by left-aligned dates (1 June to 8 July).

1 June

One Leon Jude, a Belgian, who came here in March from Canada as a pilot, and was supposed to have been vetted over there, was denounced by FATHER as an agent of the Germans, trained by the same man who trained FATHER. He was interrogated by the Belgians and confessed that this was so, but that he had not intended to work for the Germans once he got there. He is to be sent to Camp 020 at Ham.

Price, the Portuguese aircraft technician who was said to be one of Weltzein's people, has now been discovered to have been provoked by an *agent provocateur* in the pay of SIS into saying he would work for the Germans. He is coming here on the *Inaki* and will go to the RVPS.

Otto Witt wishes to move into another flat as he suspects that his present one is miked.

2 June

A cover address from the Valparaiso service was put on the intercept list, as a result of which a letter was seen going from a firm in Switzerland to a firm in the City written in the same style as the "Joe K." letters. Only a photostat copy was taken and the letter was allowed to go on, but a further letter, going from London to Switzerland, has now been intercepted written in the same style, on which certain brown marks were found which are being tested for DUFF. Although the second letter was written after the first must have been received, it is not in any way a reply to the first, which it does not even mention. It does however deal with the subject of coffee, as did the first.

3 June

Jens Palsson, the wireless operator on the *Arctic*, arrived at Camp 020 on 31 May 1942. It has now been definitely established that Magnusson and Dalberg are innocent and their release will take place in the near future.

Regarding the case of Van Ackere and Bruely, it is the opinion of all concerned that Van Ackere's trip to this country was connived at, if not actually instigated by the Germans, and that the Germans were behind the message which he brought with him. The real issue is whether the two are guilty parties or innocent dupes.

A Belgian repesentative of Frigidaire, Eugene Van Ackere was released without charge after five months of interrogation.

4 June

Richard Gambier-Parry attended today's Radio Security Service meeting, and has undertaken (1) to intervene diplomatically with Edward Travis in order to secure that better attention is paid to Group VIII, and (2) to represent to the Y Committee, of which he is a member, that RSS should have a representative on the Inter-Services

Wireless Board and that closer liaison in general should take place between RSS and the Interception Services. He further reported as an "off the record" confidence that it was proposed to set up a meteorological station in Spitzbergen and that he thought it possible that RSS might avail themselves of this position to attempt to intercept the northern Norwegian services. Again, "off the record" he informed the meeting that Edward Travis was on the warpath about general search. It appeared likely that he would get RSS to take over general search for all the other services. Gambier-Parry seemed not to be in favour of this but Dick White said that it was highly logical and that he was in a position to demand equipment from other Y services in exchange for covering their responsibilities in this respect.

Van der Willik is going. There is further suspicion against Acworth owing to a report by Roberts that he may be an agent for his uncle and Captain Rogers. The Director-General has agreed to some research into his activites. [XXXXXXXX], Max Knight, Victor Rothschild and Roberts are the only people in on this matter.

The Irish reported that when Luke Jr. was arrested and searched, a piece of paper was found on him containing the names of T.A. Robertson and John Marriott, the address Room 055 and the War Office telephone number with our extension, and a note to get in touch with them in any emergency. He had not told us before that he had this on him, and it is a bit of luck that the Germans did not get hold of it when he visited the legation in Dublin. He is being questioned by John Mair in Glasgow on this point.

5 June

Klop says that the Czechs have got hold of a story that reprisals were going to be taken for the death of Reinhard Heydrich by an attempt on the life of Eduard Benes. The Czechs were anxious that special steps should be taken to guard him.

The back numbers of ISBA have now arrived. Thirty-five of them refer to IVAN or his sub-agents and contain information which B1(a) certainly ought to have received. Eleven refer to an agent called MAX who is a Czech agent not an SIS one, and there is therefore no excuse for including them in ISBA. One of them was of considerable operational importance as it referred to possible targets on the French coast for Commando raids.

C rang up to draw our attention to recent Special Material which seemed to indicate that Leonard Plugge MP has been instrumental in supplying the Egyptian ambassador with some means of direct communication with Cairo. C seemed anxious that Richard Gambier-Parry should be brought into the matter. Dick White had a discussion with Alex Kellar and Hughes and it was arranged with Malcolm Frost over the phone that a conference should be held at Barnet tomorrow to which Gambier-Parry should be invited. C was informed that we were taking necessary action.

6 June

The ISOS character ARMANDO has been identified as Dr Cunha a Costa, a relative of President Salazar of Portugal. He has been arrested at Bathurst and the Foreign Office agreed to this action on condition that concrete evidence of his guilt has been produced. Unfortunately a search has revealed no such evidence in any form although it is made perfectly clear on ISOS.

8 June

Information has been received from two quarters that there is a German spy in the Southampton area. One source is the Poles, who give a call sign EOT or EOT 4, with changing frequencies and changing times of transmission. The other source is an informant in contact with the German intelligence service, who gives a circumstantial account of an agent being dropped in the Liverpool area in April 1942, named Chollier, who is now living with a Miss Betty Cumming at an address in Southampton. This may turn out to be identical with SWEET WILLIAM. The Radio Security Service once intercepted a transmission with a call-sign EOT. (Later B1(a) stated that there was no connection with SWEET WILLIAM.)

Klop and Christopher Harmer have seen a Frenchman named *Adam* and a Pole named *Maurice*, members of the *Walenti* organisation, whose stories throw further doubt on *Victoire*.

9 June

It was decided to intern *Victoire*.

Mathilde Carré (Victoire) was returned to France and tried for collaboration in 1949. She was condemned to death, reprieved, and finally released from prison in 1954.

Otto Witt was sent to Camp 020 today. Plura, Federn and Hans Jäger were interrogated and searched. They all spoke in favour of Witt.

11 June

Kenneth Morton Evans attended the 12 o'clock meeting today and the possible use by German agents of VHF was discussed. Morton Evans considered that it was improbable that any VHF sets were being used by long-term agents as the technique was so new that sets as they were manufactured were almost certain to be sent to the forces for operational use. VHF was still in the stage where it was a matter for radio engineers and not for intelligence.

A letter has been intercepted on the Spanish embassy check, written by someone in the Aylesbury district asking if they can provide him with a means of earning £100. He states that his unit is shortly going abroad. Jim Skardon is trying to trace the writer. Permission has been asked to impose checks on the Swedish and Portuguese legations so that any similar letters can be picked up. The writer in this case suggested the insertion of an advertisement in the *Daily Telegraph* as a reply.

12 June

The Poles have a large organisation in Scandanavia through which they obtain information from the Japanese, known for the purpose as EGGS. This material appears on TRIPLEX and the information is graded according to the size of the EGG.

Ned Reid has done a critique of the Camp 020 interrogations and reports on Leopold Hirsch and Oscar Gilinsky which throw considerable doubt on the value of any of these interrogations. He has torn many of the statements made by these men to pieces and has shown them to be much smaller fry in the financial world then we had been led to believe. The inaccuracies in their statements which he has been able to prove naturally throw doubt on everything else they have said.

Gilinsky and Hirsch were transferred to Huntercombe and remained in captivity for four years before being released.

13 June

The case of the arrest of ARMANDO, Dr Cunha a Costa, at Bathurst has shown plainly how fatal it is for SIS representatives not to work in collaboration with our representatives who know routine procedures. The SIS representative at Bathurst, in an attempt to keep the arrival and search of ARMANDO secret, failed to inform the airport of the arrival of the plane, so that instead of a routine search which would not pinpoint ARMANDO, the wretched man was dragged off to a customs hut, stripped and his belongings gone through with a toothcomb, while the rest of the passengers waited impatiently for this "suspect" to be dealt with. The incident was cabled to the Censorship Officer by the head of the local censorship unit, who complained that he had not been informed in time of the arrival of the plane to get his censorship machinery into action. The Censorship Officer has cabled to the Governor asking him to investigate the incident. The whole affair has thus been dragged into the full blaze of publicity. This is all the more unfortunate as nothing was found on ARMANDO, who by the terms of the arrangement with the Foreign Office had to be allowed to continue his journey. However, he can hardly claim to work as a secret agent for the Germans on British territory in future.

16 June

The Czech double agent MAX, who is shown on ISBA to have betrayed us to the Germans, is to be brought back to this country if possible. The present suggestion is that he should be delivered over to the Czechs for court-martial and further interrogation.

The Royal Victoria Patriotic School has turned up a spy in the person of a Dutchman called Johannes Dronkers. This man arrived in England nearly a month ago in company with a half-caste and another man, who like himself was an employee of the Posts & Telegraph. Dronkers was interrogated by a Dutch intelligence officer who by his knowledge of certain associates and contacts was able to prove that Dronkers had a brother-in-law who was a well-known Quisling called Klaever. Dronkers eventually confessed that he was Karel van Dongen, an ISOS character known to us for some time. His cover address is the same as that of FATHER and Meissteuffen, and was brought over in the pages of a dictionary. He also tried to get a broadcast message of his arrival sent in the name of Karel.

24 June

Stilwell is on his way over from Lisbon with his lawyer. An Order is being made out for his detention on arrival and Jim Hale will interrogate him.

It is becoming apparent that the latest cover story for German agents arriving here is that they have been indulging in black market activities and are making their getaway before they are caught.

29 June

A Spanish-trained German agent named Juan Lecube has been taken off a boat at Tobago where he was en route for Panama and Colombo. He is to be sent to England as soon as possible.

Identified by ISOS as a German spy, Lecube was found to be carrying secret ink formulae and several known cover-addresses. Nevertheless he resisted his interrogators at Camp 020 and was moved from Huntercombe to Dartmoor in December 1944 before being released in August 1945.

Stilwell has arrived, and Jim Hale and Herbert Hart are at Brixton Prison interviewing him.

Duff Cooper toured Royal Victoria Patriotic School on Saturday.

The appeals of José Estella and Alphons Timmerman have been refused.

One of the German wireless expeditions in the desert, known as the Schildkroete Expedition, was captured at Bir Hakim and is now in Cairo, complete with wireless sets and codes.

The results of the Stilwell interrogation go to confirm our view that these people were decoys of Weltzein's meant to engage the energies of the SIS people in Lisbon with false scents and clues. If nothing further emerges from cross-examination tomorrow, Stilwell will be released.

1 July

Victoire is being sent to Aylesbury Prison this afternoon in company with My Ericson, Stella Lonsdale, and Mrs Mathilde Krafft.

3 July

SIS has received a cable to say that all records have now been moved from Cairo to Jerusalem. No information as to whether Raymund Maunsell and his staff have gone too.

4 July

Joseph Lenihan has been caught trying to get out of the country by joining the crew of a fishing-boat leaving Fleetwood, Hampshire, to fish off the coast of Donegal.

8 July

ISOS shows there is a plan to sabotage the SS *Hartington* at Las Palmas by means of a bomb fixed to the hull by a diver. The ship is to sail tomorrow. We have done all SIS will let us to warn the authorities.

13 July

I saw both the Director of Military Intelligence and C about the Wireless Board meeting which was to take place on Wednesday. T.A. Robertson wished to put forward a suggestion that MI5 officers on the Twenty Committee should devote their whole time to this work since it seemed that the double-cross network which for a variety of reasons appeared to be on a firmer ground than it had ever been, was not being made full use of. The DMI did not seem to be very enthusiastic since he envisaged that they would go to the operations branches and knowledge of the whole system would spread. He thought it was preferable that John Bevan, the successor to Oliver Stanley, should be brought on to the Wireless Board and should be made acquainted with the work of the Twenty Committee.

I had a long talk with C, and gave him my impressions of America. He asked me my views about the new organisation to be known as DOCE (Directorate of Counter-Espionage). I said that I had not really had time to consider the matter, which involved a reinforcement of Section V with certain personnel from B Division under Dick White. Felix Cowgill and Dick were to be assistant directors and Valentine Vivian a director with dual responsibility to C and the Director-General. The idea of a joint section had apparently been accepted by the D-G at a meeting with Lord Swinton before the latter left for West Africa.

I gave C my views about the attitude of the FBI. I said that the main trouble was the dearth of information about what was going on in Europe and the feeling among the Americans that we did not trust them. I did not put forward the suggestion that Bill Stephenson should be given a mandate from the Security Service.

14 July

Majors W. Field-Robinson and R.H. Thornley of SOE came to see me, firstly about Harald Kurtz, whom they want to send to Switzerland in the capacity of a legation official. I said that although I had thought that he was thoroughly trustworthy I should rather hesitate on security grounds to recommend to the Foreign Office that he be employed within the legation where he would be bound to have access to a good deal of information. He still had relations in Germany and pressure might be brought to bear on him. I doubted whether he was a very strong character. It was eventually decided to sent Kurtz to South America and to try Edward Bloomfield for the post in Switzerland.

Thornley was anxious to know about Otto Witt. I got down Francis Aiken-Sneath who explained the position. Aiken-Sneath, contrary to the view held by Camp 020, believes that Witt, though anti-Hitler, is a National Socialist and a German agent. There is, however, no satisfactory proof.

15 July

I attended Dick White's Wednesday meeting and later I had an hour's interview with Duff Cooper. I gave him an outline of B Division and a brief history of our activities since the period preceding the war. I also told him of my experiences in America. He was not very responsive, but I dare say he was feeling somewhat bewildered. I got the impression that he imagined himself in the position of a Secretary of State running a department but without any papers or red boxes which would show him what the department was doing. He was anxious to see as many members of the Security Service as possible, in order that he might become better acquainted with our work.

18 July

I lunched with Brooksbank, the security man at British Security Co-ordination in New York, Air Commodore Lousy Paine, who is going with Evelyn Baring to look into SIS matters in South America, Oliver Hoare, who is also I think an SIS man, and the Director-General.

Jacques de Guélis of SOE and John Senter came to see me about the case of a man called Dufour who was held by the French as a Vichy agent but had escaped. The Free French had asked us to look for him and he had been traced to the house of Andrée Borrel, his mistress, who is to proceed on a very secret mission for SOE in a few days time. SOE was afraid that if Dufour was handed back to the French, the story of Borrel's visit might be extracted from him. Our point of view is that we jeopardise our relations with the French *Deuxième Bureau* if we try and conceal

Dufour's whereabouts which are probably already known to the French, since they have suggested that we should keep a watch on Mademoiselle Borrel. It was agreed that we should temporise with the French and that in the meantime SOE should ascertain whether Borrel had said anything to Dufour about her mission.

Andrée Borrel is apparently a woman of great courage, and the only female parachutist that SOE has at the moment.

Andrée Borrel parachuted into France near Paris in September 1941 to act as a courier for the PHYSICIAN network, but was arrested in June 1942 and was executed at Natzweiler concentration camp in July 1944.

20 July

Jacques de Guélis and John Senter called again. They have found out that nothing had been said by Borrel to Dufour. It was finally agreed to tell the French that for a special reason we wished to retain Dufour for a few weeks before handing him back. This would cover the period of Borrel's visit.

Dufour later sued General de Gaulle and his intelligence chief, André Dewavrin, alias Colonel Passy, for false imprisonment and alleged that he had been tortured. He won £3,000 in compensation.

Kleczynski, formerly referred to as Placzynski, which is not his name, has confessed, but we are not entirely satisfied with his confession. He says that the incendiary bomb was given to him in the course of a visit to an SOE establishment. He wanted it to use in an emergency if he had to make a forced landing, in enemy territory. He had put it in his gas mask and thinking that it was likely to go off he had gone along to the lavatory at the tail of the plane. He had invented the story about finding it because he thought that otherwise he might get into trouble. Sharkovitch, of the Polish *Deuxième Bureau*, is by no means satisfied with this explanation.

21 July

Evelyn Baring came in the afternoon. He was just off to South America. He seemed rather diffident about his job and was entirely without instructions as to how he was to proceed when he arrived in Buenos Aires. He had of course business contacts of his own but no other starting points. I suggested to him that he should attempt first of all to get a suitable introduction to someone in the police who was concerned with counter-espionage matters. Dick White and I also gave him a number of other hints. I saw the Director of Military Intelligence about certain information which Anthony Blunt wishes to pass to [XXXXXX XXXXXX] the Brazilian [XXXX]. There had been a certain amount of difficulty with the appropriate section of military intelligence which was not very well acquainted with our methods. The DMI agreed to let the information go.

I attended Dick White's meeting at which I presided for the first time. We discussed the case of Rogeiro de Menezes, a Portuguese ISOS character who has taken up a minor post in the Portuguese legation. He is an agent of the Sicherheitsdienst. We have got another agent in the legation who is watching him and we are keeping him under observation outside.

The famous Directorate of Counter-Espionage meeting took place today. Present were the Director-General, C, David Boyle, Felix Cowgill, Jasper Harker, Dick White and myself. Dick Butler took notes. SIS took the line that it was impossible for Section V to move up from the country and that the location should therefore be St Albans. I argued that we had been faced with the difficulty of having our registry in the country but that everything was now running smoothly and that we had not suffered in consequence. Felix said that all the telegrams came into St Albans and that advance copies are available to other sections in Broadway, if they were concerned. From 10 o'clock onwards he was in communication with these sections in order to decide who was to take the action. He did not see how it was possible to perform this function in London. I said that I thought it was possible he might find it much easier since files could be joined up to the telegrams and sent up to London with only an hour's delay on the present procedure. If they were required at Broadway they would already have travelled 7/8ths of the way and he would be readily available for discussion. Felix made one rather fantastic claim that 80% of the agents caught were due to SIS information. It was subsequently shown by Buster Milmo that SIS had been responsible for the capture of sixteen agents out of eighty-seven, that only in one case has a capture been attributable to an SIS agent, and in nine of the cases for which SIS had been given credit, the original information had been derived from ISOS. Further, that in five of the sixteen cases SIS had made contact abroad with persons anxious to double-cross the Germans and that in one of the sixteen we had discovered that a woman employed by SIS was in fact double-crossing them with the enemy. Out of the grand total of eighty-seven, twenty of the agents have ISOS to thank for their captivity. Unfortunately we were not in a position to produce these figures at the time. It was quite clear that Felix had set his face against any move of his organisation from Glenalmond. C maintained that Section V was so concerned with other departments that it was impossible to separate the work that they did for the Security Service. I finally said that I thought that the whole scheme must stand or fall on the question of location. It was essential for us to be in London and unless Section V were housed with us in the same building nothing would be achieved. C then tabled a plan for a directorate to be known as ACE (Axis Counter-Espionage) which would have a dual responsibility to C and the Director-General. Vivian was to be the head of it, and to remain Security Advisor while Felix and Dick were to be assistant directors. As we had had no opportunity to study this document it was decided to postpone the discussion. David Boyle, however, suggested that Dick and Geoffrey Gibbs and possibly Reg Horrocks should visit Glenalmond in order to satisfy themselves about the question of the move. I think David Boyle, seeing that Felix Cowgill was obviously obstructing, thought that this might pave the way to a settlement, and to the explosion of what is largely a myth, I am sure. This suggestion was accepted.

24 July

I had a talk with John Marriott about the possible use of Leon Jude and Grobben as double agents. Jude is the Belgian who came here from Canada and joined the Belgian Air Force. He knew FATHER and had been approached in Belgium by Hacke. Although he knew FATHER had also been approached by Hacke, he never reported the fact. We therefore came to the conclusion that he could not be allowed to leave this country, and would probably have to remain in internment for the duration. I had thought that possibly he might have gone back to Canada as a double-cross. Grobben is a reliable seaman who might have been employed if his case had not been bungled by the navy at Gibraltar. His mission was to go to America and then come back to England. He had been recruited at Genoa or Rotterdam. The navy had pursued him from Gibraltar and picked him off a trawler in mid-ocean. This fact would therefore be known to all the crew and reported back.

25 July

Allan of the GPO came to see me about certain United Sattes diplomatic correspondence which was clearly being opened. This fact had been detected by special examiners, owing to the crude way in which the work was being done. I thought at first it might be one of the B2 agents, but this proved not to be the case. Allan is inclined to suspect somebody in the Post Office.

1 August

Ernesto Simoes, the ISOS character, has arrived at the Royal Victoria Patriotic School. It is intended that he should join the Percival aircraft factory at Luton. The Royal Victoria Patriotic School were not told about him, in order to test the examiners. They reported that they were not satisfied with his story. At this stage they were let into the secret. Simoes will be kept under observation at the factory for a time in order to see if he makes any contacts. We are also anxious to find out his cover address, and a strict censorship has therefore been laid on.

SPRINGBOK has mentioned a man named Rudolfo Buente, a cork merchant of Seville whom he had met at the Abwehr headquarters in Berlin and was connected with Abteilung II. It seems quite likely that he may have been a party to the attempted sabotage.

2 August

There has been a long OSTRO message about the Middle East giving our dispo-sitions in detail. The service is 90% accurate and denotes a serious leakage.

Jones' organisation has put up quite a good performance during the last six months. Over three hundred agents were recruited, and out of this number twelve are possible double agents, two have been taken on by the German intelligence and are reflected in ISOS and one has £70 out of the Japanese in Lisbon with a promise of £150 a month and instructions to recruit a regular courier.

There has been a long telegram from Raymund Maunsell about the arrest of two German agents, Johannes Eppler and Peter Sanstede. Count Almassy started on an Abwehr Kommando expedition to southern Egypt in May last with the intention of dropping two agents at Assiut with wireless sets. This information which was obtained originally on ISOS, is confirmed by the capture of two I Heer members of the Abwehr. Almassy unfortunately escaped. The agents Eppler and Sanstede are both members of the Abwehr. Jenkins had been looking for them until the end of July when he discovered that two mysterious strangers were in touch with an Austrian employed at the Swedish Legation in Cairo. These two were arrested on 25 July and were found to be Eppler and Sanstede. Twenty other local residents were arrested at the same time. Eppler is an Arabic speaker and has been resident in Egypt. The Austrian employee of the Swedish Legation had to be kidnapped. Up to now there have been fifty arrests in con-nection with this case, twenty-four of whom have subsequently been released. Eppler and Sanstede are proving communicative and providing useful informa-tion. Maunsell says that Stellmacher, an escapee from Zbv. 800, is on his way from Turkey to Egypt.

3 August

Rogeiro de Menezes has sent a letter to his sister by TRIPLEX. The letter shows signs of secret ink under violet ray.

4 August

There are indications that the Sicherheitsdienst are proposing to kidnap [XXXXXXXXXXXXXXXX] who is regarded by them as a [XXXXXXX] traitor, owing to his attempt to escape from Lisbon to England.

The eight saboteurs who landed by submarine on the coast of the United States in June were, according to ISOS, trained and dispatched from Northern France. They spent some time in Paris shortly before their departure.

It has now been established that [XXXXXXXX] FRITZCHEN the British agent being trained by the Germans at Nantes for a parachute drop over this country is going under the name of Chapman. He does not appear to be identical with Chapman of SOE, who was captured some time ago.

The ink on Rogeiro de Menezes' letter cannot be brought up. An impression has been taken and further experiments are being made.

I lunched with Sir Phillip Vickery. He told me that George Hill, the SOE man in Moscow, had had a curious approach on the subject of two Russian agents who had been operating in Afghanistan. They had been kicked out and the Russians were seeking our assistance. In fact we knew all about these agents. They had been working for Subhas Bhose who wanted them to facilitate his journey to see Stalin in Moscow. Later, however, he decided that he liked Hitler better. The agents, who received quite a lot of money from Germany, helped him as far as possible and then reported the facts to Stalin. Subsequently they had fallen foul of the Afghanistan authorities. This is the first indication that the Russians desire any form of co-operation on intelligence lines. It followed a formal request by our minister in Kuibishev to notify us of any attempt by Subhas Bhose who was then in Berlin to get back to India, but whether there is anything to connect the two incidents is not certain.

5 August

McCullen, the Member of Parliament for Western Argyle, an old friend of the Director-General, called to see me today about the leakage of information at Inverary. He said that indiscretions of officers in the area were appalling. He proposed to see Duff Cooper and Desmond Morton.

Jasper Harker has seen William Codrington about the leakage of information connected with the Prime Minister's visit to Moscow. It seems that the Prime Minister had a telephone conversation with President Roosevelt before leaving.

Francis Aiken-Sneath came to see me about Aron and Ritter, who both need looking into. Ritter was formerly German assistant military attaché in Paris and was brought over here with his mistress Althius from Switzerland at the beginning of the war. He had been one of Sir Robert Vansittart's informants, but as many of these were notoriously unreliable it is not altogether impossible that Ritter was double-crossing him. I told Aiken-Sneath that I thought we should make a real effort to sift the case to the bottom and that the first step would be to obtain copies of all the reports that he had written to Vansittart. We should then review these in the light of subsequent events.

I went over to see William Codrington about the Prime Minister's leakage. He seemed to think that he was in charge of the whole case and that he should call upon us to clear up certain points which were not within his jurisdiction. I told him it was difficult for us to operate unless we knew the full facts of the case. Did he know exactly what the Prime Minister had said to President Roosevelt in his telephone conversation? He said that he did not but that he had been assured by one of the secretaries at Downing Street that no details were disclosed. I said that either the Prime Minister had intimated to the President that he was going to Moscow or the conversation should not have taken place. He might have said nothing which would have aroused the suspicion of the ordinary telephonist but he might just have said something which would disclose his movements to the informed listener. This coupled with a certain amount of signals intelligence, such as telegrams going in Chef de Mission cipher from here to Moscow, Middle East, or Washington DC would be quite sufficient. It was obvious that at this time, if the Prime Minister was moving he would probably be going either to the Middle East or Moscow. I asked Codrington to let me have a copy of his report.

6 August

There is a considerable stir in the Irish world owing to twenty-nine priests and three nuns having been stripped at the port. The action had apparently been taken in accordance with the rule that anyone coming from enemy territory should be thoroughly searched. The priests and nuns had come from Rome. Joe Walsh and John Dulanty appear to be in arms. Desmond Orr has not made things better by severely cross-examining some of these priests at Room 055, and asking them if they were loyal to this country, etc. He is within his rights, but the incident is unfortunate.

7 August

I have been asked to review the work of the Press Section and I have been through Derek Tangye's reports. He seems to cover the ground required by most of the sections but he is spending a good deal of money. We must I think have a Press Section, but I am bound to say that I should feel better if someone else were running it. Tangye has nothing to offer the press except drinks, lunches and dinners. It must therefore be accepted that in terms of a balance sheet we cannot really get value for money. We could of course employ somebody of a better type but I doubt whether he would take the trouble to get the information which we required and which can only be picked up in places like the bar at the Savoy Hotel.

8 August

The Twenty Committee has devised a plan known as ASSASSIN. The transmitter which we got some time ago on the *Arctic* and which we intended to use for strategic deception in bringing out the *Tirpitz* is now blown. We therefore intend to use the Iceland transmitter to inform the Germans that the *Arctic* was given away through the indiscretions of Tome, the Danish Consul in Vigo, who was in fact responsible for the whole expedition. It is hoped that this will throw a spanner in the works in Spain.

11 August

The traffic of enemy agents to the western hemisphere is growing, according to ISOS. The case of Hans Ruser has now reached a further stage. Lisbon has told Berlin that Ruser has come into the open and informed the Dienststelle that he can no longer collaborate with the Abwehr. This decision had followed a meeting of important Spanish and German officials in Madrid. The Dienststelle had agreed to accept his decision but could only do so if he were released from his military obligations. Ruser agreed to go to Berlin and arrangements have been made to take him into safe custody as soon as he arrives.

FRITZCHEN is to carry a captured British wireless set.

Information has been received from the Admiralty that when a U-boat was recently sunk in the Mediterranean, the crew and one alleged Lebanese were picked up. The latter stated he left Mersem for Beirut with a small sailing craft which fell in with a northerly gale and after the twentieth day he was rescued unconscious by a U-boat, apparently the sole survivor. He had in his possession $3,500 and £450 also some small amounts of Turkish and Egyptian currency.

The Belgian spy called Franciscus Winter has been caught by the Royal Victoria Patriotic School unaided. They were suspicious about his story and eventually broke him down. He has now confessed. He was not carrying secret ink but was to purchase his materials at a chemist shop. It seems that owing to the publication of details in the case of Alphons Timmerman the Germans have now realised that the carrying of secret ink material even though disguised as medicine, is likely to be highly compromising. They are therefore being forced back on to simpler methods.

The Director-General has written a letter to William Codrington about the Prime Minister leakage, asking for the fullest possible details and pointing out that matters of this sort come within his jurisdiction. It is impossible for him to conduct enquiries unless he knows the full facts and Codrington in any case has no powers. The D-G has also written to the Cabinet Secretary, Sir Edward Bridges.

Raymund Maunsell writes that the SOE representative in Palestine has just been sacked for arming the Haganah. The Haganah is the secret military organisation of the Zionist movement. They were formed to deal with the Arabs, but I suppose that SOE imagine that they can be effectively used against the Germans.

A man called Oliver Green was arrested in May for forging petrol coupons. When his premises were searched it was found that he had a dark-room, and an exposed film of military intelligence documents. These documents related to information that we had obtained regarding the German military machine, its weapons etc. Green has been interrogated by Hugh Shillito in prison. At first he contended that this was a film which had been sold to him as unexposed and which he had subsequently found was used. He denied ever taking the photographs himself. Enquiries with local chemists shops had shown that this statement was probably untrue and on the face of it it seemed extremely unlikely. Green finally admitted that he was a Soviet agent. He then said that he had been recruited in Spain and asked to spy against the Fascists. He consented to do this but the suggestion was not followed up. Instead he was taken to a hotel where he met a man whom he took to be Russian. This man asked him if he was prepared to do espionage work in England for the Soviet Union. When Green accepted he was given £40 in dollar bills and told to find his way back to this country. He was told where and when he would be contacted after arrival. For the first twelve months after his arrival in England he was not called upon to do anything. After another year he was again approached and told to take a flat, to construct a dark room and buy a Leica camera. Early in 1939 he began what he described as his organisational work which apparently consisted of building up agents and contacts. When this machinery was eventually completed before the outbreak of war he was told to collect political information, that is to say representative opinions of every class of English society. After the fall of France two new considerations became important (a) it was possible that England might be invaded successfully in which case the organisation would be used for collecting military information about the German army (b) it was thought that a Fascist government might arise in England which would declare war on the Soviet Union. The main interest in his whole story is perhaps his statement that between five and six months before the German attack on Russia he had instructions to turn over his organisation to the collection from British sources of information concerning German armaments and troop concentrations. His main source of information appears to have been intelligence summaries. He said that of course he would pass on anything regarding British armaments which seemed of interest but that the Russians' prior interest was in German not English military information. Most of his agents worked for ideological reasons since those who worked for money were considered unreliable. Enquiries are being made about various names and addresses found in his notebook. It is remarkable that the whole set up of this organisation is exactly similar to the one in the Miss X case. Green is, of course, a Communist and has been known to us for some considerable time. In 1938 Max Knight reported that he was employed in certain highly secret work the nature of which was not then apparent. He has got fifteen months' imprisonment for forging coupons and now tells us that he did so in order that he could use his car to make contact with his agents. Ideologically, he is a curious character, and not altogether unlikeable.

12 August

Len Burt has told me about his visit with Edward Cussen to see the Prime Minister's Swedish cook, who had clearly told a friend that the Prime Minister went on a journey. William Codrington and Anthony Bevir of the Prime Minister's office were both present and interfered to such a degree that both Burt and Cussen had to register a protest. They neither of them have the slightest experience in these matters and should keep out. They made Burt's task extremely difficult but he was eventually successful in getting at the true facts. Codrington has previously talked to the cook very foolishly as a result of which she had blabbed to her contact and her contact to someone else and the whole ground was fouled. I am rather glad in a way as it will teach Codrington a lesson in the future.

13 August

MUTT and JEFF have prepared a new sabotage act. Home Forces have passed a plan to make a fire at a camp near Barton Mills in Suffolk. This operation is being carried out in conjunction with SOE.

PEPPERMINT is being summoned back to Madrid in September.

Lucas, who was connected with the *Victoire* case, is said to have been captured and sent to Berlin for interrogation.

SWEET WILLIAM has terminated his employment at the Spanish Embassy and has signed an undertaking that he will have no further contact with any member of the Spanish Embassy or colony in England.

14 August

John Senter came to see me and brought with him an interesting document which had been extracted from the kit of one of the Russian parachutists sent over here who was to be dropped in Europe. These people had come over by arrangement between George Hill of SOE in Moscow and the NKVD. It is a remarkable fact that Hill who formerly spied for us in Russia and wrote a book about it, was acceptable to the Soviet authorities. The people sent over here appear to us to be of a pretty low mentality and our efforts to get them dropped have on the whole been somewhat disastrous. An aeroplane carrying two had to return owing to bad weather conditions and crashed on landing. All the occupants were killed. Another one was destined for Vienna which under any conditions was an extremely hazardous flight. One of our best wing-commanders insisted on doing the job himself and has never been heard of again. The document which Senter left with me contained the following addresses with which the agents were evidently to make contact: Madame Marie Jeanne Compere, 56 Charles Quint, Ganshoren. The agent was to say that he was sent by Jacques and knew the son Pierre Gaston, who was at one time in Spain. Another address was Otten, 112 Avenue Laura, Berchen. The agent was to call himself Delstranche and give greetings from Irene. The third address was that of Marcelle Lerory, 1 rue de l'Aurore, Brussels. This woman may be identical with a Marcelle Leboy mentioned in *Inprecorr* as attending some Communist meeting in 1936 in connection with the Spanish Civil War. The fourth address was that of Stig Lindal, Bondegarten 60, Stockholm. The sender of a letter could give any name in writing to this address and should congratulate Lindal in French on his birthday. Senter told me that Novikoff at the Soviet embassy is Ivan Maisky's master and Stalin's personal representative. There is also here a Colonel Chichayev who is in charge of the parachutists. He has got it into his head that General John Lakin is head of the Secret Service and arranged a luncheon party with him at Claridge's. As they could not get a private room there, they lunched alone in the middle of the ballroom.

15 August

Nash came in to see me. He is one of our Security Control Officers and is to go as Security Officer to the Bahamas. I doubt whether the Duke of Windsor will like the look of him. Nice fellow but not very exciting.

Jack Curry has got an idea that we should endeavour through T.A. Robertson's organisation and other channels to embroil the Sicherheitsdienst with the Abwehr.

There are of course already signs that the two organisations have their differences from time to time.

Len Burt spoke to me about Antrim's case. He thinks there should be a prosecution of Mrs Broad in whose possession has been found a large number of compromising documents, some referring to private affairs and others to military matters. These documents are the property of the Earl of Antrim and Lady Diana Bridgeman.

Edward Cussen is seeing Duff Cooper on the Prime Minister leakage. The Director-General has written a criticism of William Codrington's note on certain lines which I have suggested. There is still much that is not clear.

There has been an unfortunate incident in connection with the case of Erland Echlin, the Canadian journalist interned under Emergency Regulation 18(b). Klop had reported that he was in regular receipt of £38 a month from the German Embassy in 1937 or 1938, and in putting forward the case we had said that this was confirmed by the examination of Echlin's passbook. We had intercepted a letter from the bank showing an entry which looked like £80. In fact, '80' was the number of the cheque which was for the sum of £3 odd. The Advisory Committee examined the passbook and found no entry and they wanted to know on what our information was based. As the Advisory Committee are only too ready to pick holes in our cases, I thought it advisable to try and get Noakes, who knew Cockburn and explain to him how the mistake arose. Cockburn seemed to be satisfied and friendly but he is going to recommend release. This is I think a bad case, since only within the last week we have obtained definite information that even Freddie Kuh of UPI thinks that Echlin's case is not worth his support. Echlin is still an admirer of Hitler.

Derek Tangye says that Gordon West of *Inside Information* wishes to put in a paragraph about the Prime Minister leakage. He wants to say that the whole question is occupying serious attention of the authorities and to ask all those who heard about the Prime Minister's visit prior to 1 August to write to the *Daily Sketch*. Tangye has told him that we have no objection to his saying that the matter was the subject of enquiry but that we did not wish anything said about 1 August. The *Daily Sketch* is complying with our wishes.

I took the weekly meeting. There have been certain difficulties about getting Simoes' employment at the aircraft factory at Luton. Everybody seems to be highly suspicious about having an alien which is to say the least a good sign. These difficulties we have overcome. I told the meeting that we were considering MI5's duties in the event of a Second Front. Victor Rothschild thought it was particularly necessary that something should be done about sabotage since ISOS shows quite clearly that the Germans intend to leave saboteurs behind. Another letter from Rogeiro de Menezes has been seen. It has been decided to let it go on after taking an impression and to attempt to get a sample of ink from his lodgings. There is no doubt that secret writing is being used but unfortunately we cannot bring it up. It shows up very sketchily under ultra-violet ray but it is not responsive to any request.

Jim Hale has succeeded in breaking down Duncan Scott-Ford who confessed that he was known to the Germans as RUTHERFORD. On his last voyage from this country he was interrogated on the basis of ISOS with other members of the crew. He volunteered the information that he had been approached by the Germans who had said that he had told them nothing. On this occasion he was again interrogated and admitted that he had told the Germans about certain ships and also given them other information. He was stupid enough to carry on him documents giving full details of the course of the convoy and it was his intention to hand this document over to the Germans on his next visit to Lisbon. For some reason or other he thought that the worst that could happen to him would be internment. He little knows that there is a clear case against him under the Treachery Act, based on his own statement and on the documents found in his possession. He has talked vaguely about other people being connected with the same game and is clearly extremely conceited. His hobby seems to be women. He was contacted in Lisbon by the Germans at some café and got into the hands of prostitutes who were obviously being paid by the German intelligence service to pick up recruits.

20 August

I saw Jim Hale about Duncan Scott-Ford, to decide whether Edward Cussen or the local police should take the usual statement. It was eventually decided that this matter should be left to the local police who seemed to have Scott-Ford well in hand.

Special Material indicated that the Pasha may be transmitting from Luppitt over the weekend. Malcolm Frost has rung up to say that Richard Gambier-Parry, plastered with red tabs, is proposing to go down to Luppitt in a Packhard car to see that all machinery is in working order. This will, of course, blow the whole gaff. I spoke to C, as a result of which it seems that Gambier-Parry will make a somewhat less spectacular entrance into Luppitt, a village where anything unusual is immediately the subject of gossip.

I dined with the Director-General, Duff Cooper, Lord Selborne, David Keswick, I think of SOE, and Sir William Wiseman. The latter just arrived here from the United States and conversation was of a general kind. Wiseman seemed to take quite sound views about America. He was obviously fully au fait with all Bill Stephenson's work and difficulties. He said that the Americans were making a frightful bungle of their business relations with South America. Instead of buying up the enemy business in a quiet and unobtrusive way they were taking over firms and plastering the place with the stars and stripes. This was doing them a good deal of harm. Wiseman did not think that we were running any risk of losing our business connections in South America after the war. He thought we would be welcomed back.

FATHER took part in the Dieppe raid on 18 August. As far as we know he is all right. The operation seems to have been somewhat costly but doubtless valuable experience has been gained.

MUTT and JEFF are to carry out an act of sabotage which is being carefully planned in conjunction with SOE.

21 August

We have just had a teleprinter message from SIS to say that Walter Bell, Clarence Hince, and Harry Kimball are arriving here "at the invitation of MI5". We have been asked to make the necessary arrangements for their reception. I do not quite understand what this means, unless it is the result of a general invitation which I gave when I was in Washington DC. In any case we shall be very pleased to see them.

22 August

I had an interview with the Manchester Police on the case of Duncan Scott-Ford, who has been brought down to Brixton Prison. We had a full statement under caution. It had been thought possible that we might perhaps send back a double agent on Scott-Ford's boat with the copies of *Jane's Fighting Ships* and *Jane's Aircraft* which Scott-Ford had been asked to procure. Ultimately it was decided to take no action on these lines but to try and find out what the reactions were in Lisbon to Scott-Ford's removal.

23 August

Geoffrey Gibbs tells me that Malcolm Muggeridge, SIS's man at Lourenco Marques, has done an extremely good job of work. The real menace there is Campini, the Italian Consul, who is communicating regularly the movements of ships to his government. He is now trying to get a wireless set with which to communicate direct to Tokyo. One of his principal agents was a Greek named Serafamides. An agent of Muggeridge succeeded in getting this man onto his ship on the grounds that they were both engaged in a plot to help German submarines. The skipper then placed Serafamides in irons and handed him over to the police in Durban. We are trying to get this man back to England as he may form the basis of a case against Campini. If he confesses, we might induce the Foreign Office to press the Portuguese government to close down the Italian Consulate or to declare Campini *persona non grata*. A telegram has been sent to Webster in this sense.

25 August

Harry Kimball of the FBI came to see me and told me that before leaving America he had spent two hours with J. Edgar Hoover and Quinn Tamm, and was given a mandate to discuss the affairs of his department with me and to explain Mr Hoover's grievances. The real cause of the trouble is this. When the Americans came into the war Bill Stephenson handed over all the agents that he had been running with the connivance of the American authorities to Bill Donovan instead of to Hoover in whose area they were operating. Worse than this, he had been running some of these agents since the outbreak of war on Donovan's behalf. Kimball said that the FBI knew all about this. In particular, he mentioned an agent who had been trying to get information from the Spanish Embassy in Washington. This agent reported regularly to the FBI and told them exactly what British Security Co-ordination wanted. Mr Hoover could not understand why this sort of thing still went on. If Stephenson wanted to know anything about what was going on in the Spanish Embassy he had only to ask.

FATHER has got back from Dieppe unscathed.

TRICYCLE has told the Germans that he is trying to make arrangements for a journey to Lisbon and London. The Germans still appear to be trying to pay him through the medium of a "venereal disease investigator without hair".

GELATINE has at least heard from the Germans and has been given a questionnaire.

The WEASEL has received a communication from the Germans. He has told them that he cannot go to the Congo.

DRAGONFLY is protesting loudly about not receiving money. He has been given further promises that he will receive a remittance via Switzerland.

RAINBOW has worked himself into quite a good position and can give valuable production figures. It is proposed to use him for deception.

Plan NUISANCE has been devised for attacking the German intelligence service and diverting their energies into unproductive channels.

Admiral Wilhelm Canaris is paying one of his periodical visits to the Iberian Peninsula. The German intelligence service in Lisbon is preparing to send to England a Belgian agent said to have been in England for a long time and to be now working as a purser on an English ship. His assignments, secret ink, cover address and money have all been arranged. We are trying to identify this man who is known to the Germans as THORN.

The Second Officer on the Irish SS *Kyle Clar* has been reporting to the German intelligence service in Lisbon on convoys. The agent FRITZCHEN who is being trained in Nantes is to be provided with two identity cards, one for an Englishman and one for an Irishman resident in England. It is thought that this latter will be of use to him as he is of military age. Ration cards and other papers are also being provided. There is no evidence from ISOS that the Dieppe raid was anticipated by the Germans. The German intelligence service in Sofia has reported that the British intend to bring an attack in Africa on 10 September.

27 August

Denys Page of GC&CS mentioned a proposal of giving ISOS to the Americans, and that a man called Solomon Kullback and two naval representatives had recently been given the whole run of GC&CS, including MSS and ISOS.

Bourne and Harry Allen came to see me about a letter from the American Embassy, which had obviously been tampered with before it reached the GPO. This had been discovered by the special examiners. It was decided to give the Americans photographs of these letters informing them that our attention had been drawn to the flaps by a sorter. Subsequent enquiries had shown that other mails from the American embassy had been tampered with in a similar way. It seemed likely that either Coe was carrying out an internal censorship somewhat inefficiently or that some ill-disposed person inside the embassy was opening the mails.

I saw Harry Kimball again and he gave me an account of Pearl Harbor. It seems that four or five days before the attack a telegraphic or telephonic message had been picked up going from Honolulu to Tokyo in a very simple flower code which gave the exact disposition of all American ships in the harbour. The local authorities were fully aware of this but did not apparently take any precautions. On the night before the attack there was a huge party on the *Pennsylvania* to which a great many officers from other ships had been invited. Everybody got extremely tight by the time the party broke up at 5am. At 7am they had a rude awakening. The aircraft carrier *Lexington*, which was some way out, never even knew there had been an attack, and not one plane got off the deck.

28 August

I lunched with Roger Fulford. He seemed to think that this office had taken a biased view about the Communists and had neglected the Fascists. In this he appears to have struck a sympathetic chord in Welles of the Security Executive. I told him that he was wrong, or at any rate misinformed as to the difficulties of the situation. If he was contending that the vetting of Communists by C Division for special employment was not always very intelligently done, I was in entire agreement. He had to realise however that 50,000 people per week were being vetted by this office and that if this was all thrown on the investigating sections they would have a serious grievance. This meant that vetting was to some extent rule of thumb and unintelligent. This was regrettable and in many instances got us into serious trouble. Apart from this I thought that we had taken a very reasonable line about the Communists. As regards the Fascists, the movement was comparatively young. It had been taken in hand several years before the war, and our enquiries might have been considerably helped if we had been given some encouragement by the Home Office. For years Jack Curry wanted to get a Home Office intercept warrant on the British Union of Fascists headquarters and on Sir Oswald Mosley but could not get the necessary authority.

Duncan Scott-Ford has told us that one Henderson on the *Finland* is suspect. It was decided to let our agent on board the *Finland* work this out rather than approach the captain.

Klop rang up to say that perhaps the answer to the bombing of Nuremburg last night might be the bombing of Oxford. I spoke to the Director-General who decided to warn the country office. Jasper Harker rang up later to say that nothing had been said to the chief constable as it was thought that might go off the deep end but that possibly I might say a word to Harold Scott. I tried to get Scott but he was away. I also tried to get Colonel Alan MacIver but he did not ring me back. Finally, I spoke to the Duty Officer at the Ministry of Home Security. I told him at least three times that we had no specific information whatsoever but merely a hunch on the basis of Baedeker raids, that the answer to Nuremburg might be Oxford. We had accordingly warned our own people but not the chief constable as we thought he might regard the matter as interference or possibly work himself into a state of pathological excitement.

I lunched with Brook Wilkinson, after seeing an American film depicting a spy-ring in Britain. The Chiefs of Staff, or what they described as the 'Inner Intelligence Council', were shown as being hopelessly inept, and *The Voice of Terror* was broadcasting and foretelling acts of sabotage which were taking place all over the country. Finally, Sherlock Holmes and Dr Watson were called in to put things right. I said that on the whole I should be against this being shown though it was argued that the presence of Sherlock Holmes would stamp it in the minds of the British public as being pure invention. I doubted whether any but a small section of the public would know very much about Sherlock Holmes. The impression on their minds would be that the Chiefs of Staff were hopelessly inept and that it needed an amateur detective to come in and put them right. Apart from that, it would give a similar idea to the American forces whom we were trying to educate against spy psychosis. There are plenty of people in this country who are quite ready to say that the whole of our staff is bad, as indeed a good deal of it may be, without their being given any further encouragement. Brook Wilkinson said that he would refer the film to Lord Tyrrell and if the matter was still under dispute he would ask me to come up again. It seemed fairly clear that the film had been produced for the American public in order to make them spy-conscious, and not wishing to depict their own Chiefs of Staff as inept they fobbed this view off on the British.

Charles Medhurst has written a letter to the Director-General complaining that a Captain Liddell rang up the Ministry of Information last Saturday to say that MI5 had information that Oxford was going to be bombed. As a result, the police had been warned and all the Fire Service, ARP, etc called out. Medhurst said if we had any information it should have been passed to him. I rang up Medhurst and explained the circumstances. He seemed satisfied. Evidently the Chief Constable at Oxford, as we expected, lost his head.

I had a talk with Ronnie Haylor about SIS agents at the Royal Victoria Patriotic School. The arrangement is that all the accredited agents should pass through RVPS. SIS resent that that those who pass through were questioned about their work. Haylor's point of view is that it is impossible to examine these people from the security angle unless the whole of their activities and contacts are discussed. I am inclined to agree, particularly since we have had two cases of agents coming through who have really been double-crossing us or the French. I refer to the cases of Robert Petin and Jean Pelletier.

Pelletier remained at Camp 020 until August 1945 when he was deported to France where he was convicted of treason and sentenced to life imprisonment.

2 September

I took the Wednesday meeting. Manso Barros, the wireless operator on one of the Enrique trawlers, has been examined at Camp 020 and has confessed that he was working for the Germans. The company is backed by German money. It seems certain that the masters were cognisant of what was going on. These trawlers were pulled in by the navy, owing to their suspicious movements in the rear of a convoy. The Spaniards are protesting.

Rogeiro de Menezes appears to be reporting on anti-aircraft defences but we are still unable to get up his ink properly.

Duncan Scott-Ford has given the names of others in his racket. We are not at all sure, however, that he is speaking the truth.

Herbert Hart has told me about another cod-fishing ship called the *Gil Eannes*. This is a Portuguese vessel which, according to ISOS, seems to be signalling the movements of our ships from the port of St John. The difficulty is to know what action to take as no one in Newfoundland can speak Portuguese. At the best we shall find a wireless set which is somewhat out of the ordinary. It may, however, be held that such a set is necessary in order to keep in contact with other bodies in the fishing fleet. The navy do not wish to offend the Portuguese as they are given certain oiling facilities in the Azores.

FRITZCHEN who is being trailed at Nantes is to be given means of transmitting intelligence supplementary to his wireless set. One possible method suggested is the use of newspaper advertisements. He is to land at some suitable open space near London.

3 September

I had a meeting with Richman Stopford, Paul Matthews and Joe Stephenson about the Pair Fishing Company which employs Spanish fishermen and runs boats from Milford Haven which fish off the coast of Eire. Sometimes the boats put into Eire ports and the whole set up seems to be extremely undesirable. We recommended certain action but the navy refused to support us. It is now proposed that we should get agents on board these boats.

Clarence Hince came to see me. He had seen quite a lot of Grogan, from whom he had gained valuable information. In the course of conversation he mentioned a method employed by the Americans in interrogating prisoners particularly criminals of the gangster type. He mentioned a case where two men had been apprehended for murder. They had used a car which had subsequently been found. The FBI has published a detailed description of this car and also details of the crime. Certain particulars of the car had however been omitted form the press article. They gave the prisoners the papers and when they had read them they were taken away, and the prisoners were asked to give a description of the car they had read about. They were then in a position of not knowing exactly what information they had got from the papers and what they knew from personal observation. In this particular case they committed a major blunder by describing some detail of the inside of the car which had not been mentioned in the papers. They were unable to explain how they knew about it. This is known as the method of supplied information. I rather doubt whether it is applicable to spy cases but it might be on occasions.

Hince said that he would like to have a talk with our pigeon expert about two-way pigeons. The Americans thought that the Japanese had been using pigeons of this type. It is apparently quite possible to train a pigeon to fly out to a ship and then come back to its loft.

4 September

Dick White has seen the Foreign Office about Manso Barros and the Spanish ambassador is to be told that the Foreign Office is satisfied that this man was communicating with the enemy regarding movements of convoys. They did not at the moment propose to show the ambassador any documents. I am personally very much opposed to this as I feel that if we continue to show confessions to the Spaniards as in the case of Luis Calvo, an awkward precedent would be created. If in future cases we fail to get a confession the Spaniards would press for release. Ramon Serrano Suner has been sacked. We hope to get some reaction about this when PEPPERMINT goes to Madrid.

I had a further meeting about the Pasha with Malcolm Frost, Alex Kellar and Anthony Blunt, when methods of further investigation were discussed.

5 September

On the occasion of the Dieppe raid two complete sets of operational orders and intelligence supplied by ourselves and SIS about the area were left on the beach. These were picked up by a retiring party and brought home. It seems however that another copy was left behind. After the raid we gave out that the enterprise had been satisfactory and that we had learned many lessons. The Germans in their broadcast replied that the lessons were nothing to those they had learned from the documents which we had so kindly left behind. There is a complete copy missing and there is no doubt from the details given that this fell into the hands of the Germans. The copy belongs to one of the Canadian brigades. The matter has been brought to the notice of the Chief of the Imperial General Staff who proposes to have someone on the mat. There was no earthly reason as far as anyone knows why the order should have been taken across the channel at all.

7 September

At the Press Meeting Derek Tangye reported that Ivan Maisky was giving mildly pessimistic accounts of Churchill's visit to *The Times*, and trying to dictate a pessimistic version to the *Daily Herald* and other papers. It was decided to inform the Foreign Office.

Ned Reid tells me that he had been informed by one of the London banks that the sum of £750 pounds was sent by the Spanish ambassador in Ankara to Chaman Lal, the well-known Indian. This money was to have gone through a bank in Switzerland but Ankara apparently did not realise that the transaction could only finally be carried out through London. I believe that Chaman Lal does represent some Spanish paper but this would not account for the money being remitted from Ankara. Ned also tells me that one Gillearo has sent money from Gibraltar to six Indians.

9 September

Buster Milmo mentioned that Sobhy Hanna who had been caught at Dar-es-Salaam, had now arrived at Camp 020. He had in his possession a wireless receiving set which had a concealed transmitter. This had escaped the notice of controls and was only discovered on close examination here. Hanna has stated that he was on a political mission for the Germans in Egypt.

Hanna was detailed until August 1945 and then deported to Egypt.

Stewart Menzies rang me up about an RSS leakage. We had been asked to say what the Turkish Ambassador was doing on 2 and 3 September, but unfortunately our informant was away at the time and it was difficult to know how to proceed unless we knew a bit more about what the whole trouble was about. It seemed that a Turkish BJ disclosed that the Ambassador had been informed about certain information which had appeared in MSS and had telegraphed this information to Ankara, the result being a blaze in the press. Matters had not been improved by the Generals Alexander and Montgomery blowing the information to Wendell Wilkie, who had passed the tidings round in Ankara and elsewhere. Stewart is going to get a list of people who were in the know and their contacts. We on our side will get a list of the ambassador's contacts and see whether there is anybody common to both lists.

Pan has arrived from Lisbon to clear up the case of the Czech counter-espionage man Alexander. Colonel Pan appears to believe in Alexander implicitly. Our evidence that Alexander is double-crossing the Czechs is based on ISOS and in our view is incontrovertible. There is no doubt that Alexander procured a wireless set from SIS which he sent out ostensibly to one of the Czech stations in Paris. In actual fact this set is under control. He has also doubled crossed us in the case of Hans Ruser. We now have to convince Pan and cover up the ISOS. In our view Pan should not be allowed to return to Lisbon until Alexander reaches this country.

Sloane and Bartik are very worried about this case and our own opposition to their General Frantisek Moravec.

J.C. Masterman came to talk to me about MULLET, who has just returned from Lisbon where he has been in contact with Dr Koessler. MULLET met Koessler on a previous occasion when the latter engaged in peace talk. On this occasion Koessler came much more out into the open. He said that he was interested in a military coup d'etat. Some of the generals were opposed to Hitler. They would be ready to revolt at an appropriate moment and Admiral Wilhelm Canaris, to whom he was working was wavering. It was necessary to convince him by facts that we were in a really strong position, and that Germany was as good as beaten in the long run. This may of course be merely an attempt to obtain information. It rather reminds me of the Sigismund Best and Richard Stevens case at Venlo. J.C. Masterman is inclined to think that Dr Koessler is genuine.

MULLET was a British businessman named Fanto with interests in Belgium.

Dick White is getting rather desperate about Section V. He says that Tim Milne is now ill with blood-poisoning and that Kim Philby has got to go to Lisbon and clear up some mess or other. Further, SIS is sending out more people from Section V to West Africa. Glenalmond will therefore be in a worse pie than usual. I said that there was a limit to the extent to which he could be used as a recruiting ground for SIS. We had very serious obligations for our own which we were not fulfilling in West Africa at the moment. We were likely to have other obligations if a Second Front was opened. I thought that so far from giving men away we ought to be building up in the regions and in the ports, since the regions particularly had the right kind of experience of Defence Security Officer work. Dick thought that possibly total amalgamation would be the solution. I said I should be in favour of this if the amalgamated body came under the Director-General. It would be wrong in my view to start a separate organisation, but admittedly this might be better than nothing. Dick does not seem to see the importance of the relations between counter-espionage and security. He thinks there is a division between the two, whereas there should be no division between ourselves and Section V. I feel there should not be a division between either.

There may be something to be done on the lines that he suggests, if I were to see Duff Cooper but organisationally I still think such a move would be unsound. There is no doubt that an impasse has been reached in what is really a very serious problem.

13 September

The Americans are leaving early tomorrow morning. Walter Bell is staying on for a few days and also Bill Stephenson. After lunch we had a short talk, and Stephenson told Hince and Kimball that he had heard they were under the impression that he had been holding up stuff in New York. They both denied this but said that quite clearly information passing through New York had not been reaching ourselves. They expressed satisfaction with their position here and hoped that things would now move more smoothly. I saw Stephenson for a moment afterwards. He told me that he had several hours with Duff Cooper who, I gather, is in favour of Stephenson holding a mandate for the Security Service. There is apparently to be a meeting tomorrow on the subject. This ought to work if Stephenson refrains from carrying out operations on his own in J. Edgar Hoover's territory. I rather doubt however whether he will. At any rate, it will be a step forward and if the situation is still unsatisfactory we shall have to press for our own separate representation in America. Stephenson is going to see the Director-General tomorrow and wants to have a private talk with me outside the office.

14 September

Dick White spent the morning closeted with the Czechs and Colonel Pan, who has been brought back here from Lisbon to discuss the position of Alexander, who is undoubtedly working for the Germans. Although Pan himself is believed to be reliable, he is an unpleasant blustering personality. He left the meeting disconcerted and annoyed. This may be due largely to a matter of pride. It was eventually decided that Pan should send a message to Alexander intimating that his presence was urgently required here in order to discuss certain matters connected with the Second Front.

The Royal Victoria Patriotic School reports two spies, Dykstra and Grootveld, who arrived in a party of twelve Dutch escapees. Pieter Schipper, who is already in Camp 020 and who gave us valuable information, has recognised these people as German agents from Ymuiden. Grootveld appears to have communicated with one of the ISOS trawlers which has recently been operating in Skategatt.

Ned Raid has been investigating the bank account of Paul Fidrmuc. He opened an account at the Chase National Bank here in 1923 which was closed in 1939 and transferred to the Chase Bank in New York. He is a prominent German agent working in the Iberian Peninsula. Ned has also discovered that certain Bank of England notes of high denomination which were obtained at the beginning of the war by Albert de Bary of Amsterdam, passed through the hands of Prince Paul of Serbia. Other notes in this series have already been traced as having been in the possession of Alcazar de Velasco and Gunther Schutz, the German agent under arrest in Eire.

15 September

I had a meeting at Broadway with C, Claude Dansey, Valentine Vivian and Ronnie Haylor on the subject of interrogation of SIS agents at the Royal Victoria Patriotic School. Dansey was all smiles and said that he would always be only too glad to let us have access even to his accredited agents, provided somebody from his Production Sections was present. It was agreed that we would not demand the right to interrogate accredited agents, but as regards the others they should go through the RVPS and be interrogated in the presence of a Production officer with similar treatment to be accorded to allied agents, and that Haylor should have the opportunity of establishing direct contact with Production officers. SIS undertook to let us know when their accredited agents came through and where and when we could see them. While I do not trust Dansey, I do think we may ultimately break down the prejudices of some of his Production officers if we can get into direct touch with them. So far, we have always been prevented from doing this owing to the rigidity of our liaison with Section V, whom Dansey dislikes even more than ourselves.

C told me that he has just seen Colonel Frantisek Moravec, head of the Czech intelligence service. He had told him that he was profoundly dissatisfied, not only with the Czech organisation in Lisbon, but also in Constantinople. He told him however that he had decided that Colonel Pan should not be allowed to return to Lisbon at any rate until the Alexander question had been settled. Moravec said that whether Alexander returned or not he had quite made up his mind to dispense with his services. He was ultimately satisfied with the evidence against him which we had put forward. C further told him that it had been decided to send a message to Alexander in Paris, written by airmail, since this would give the impression to Alexander that the message had not been drafted by the British intelligence.

Alias Wilhelm Gessman, Jean Alexander was an Austrian working ostensibly for the Czechs in Lisbon but suspected of being a German double agent.

On 31 August 1942 Special Material shows that an Englishman has informed the Chinese ambassador's secretary that Mme.? is starting a deep-breathing class and wanted to know if the ambassador would like to join it.

Secretary: Deep breeding?
Englishman: No, deep breathing.
Secretary: Please spell that last word.

Another extremely reliable report has been obtained by the Germans from Egypt about the disposition of troops, stores etc. It comes from the OSTRO organisation. Rochman Stopford is making strenuous efforts here to establish a line of communication which we feel must be on the air routes via West Africa.

16 September

Roger Fulford rang me up about Derek Tangye's relations with Claud Cockburn. I told him that Jasper Harker was handling this matter and I thought it might be a good thing to have an early conversation.

17 September

T.A. Robertson and I went over to congratulate the Director of Naval Intelligence on his promotion to Vice-Admiral and to give him one of the Pogo Bank of England notes and a clock fuse. Rather, I fear, with my tongue in my cheek, I thanked him for all the help that he had given to us in connection with the work of the Twenty Committee. He seemed pleased and said that he was deeply touched. The £5 note is to be framed and a note put on the back to the effect, at his request, that it was presented to him on his promotion.

I lunched with Derek Tangye and Douglas Hyde, the news editor of the *Evening Standard*. Hyde explained his difficulties about making enquiries as to what was known generally in press circles about future operations. He said that it was perfectly simple to obtain this information through a confidential contact, and I rather gather that he had in fact done so. He did however admit to me that he had known nothing of the attack on Madagascar. He said that the security arrangements for that operation must have been particularly good. When I mentioned this subsequently to Gilbert Lennox he said that the cover in an operation of that kind was naturally extremely good since troops had been going round the Cape to Suez for a month. A few more or less did not make much difference. I asked Hyde about D-Notices and he told me that at least ten people in the office would know about them before they were restricted for distribution to those who would have to know. He suggested that possibly the Lobby Correspondents' Committee would be a better medium since in that case only two people would have to know before distribution was made to the necessary staff. Apparently the Lobby Committee are extremely cagey. Hyde said that he had considerable difficulty in getting information about their proceedings even from his own representative.

18 September

I lunched with Jack Curry who told me that he had received an unsolicited visit from a representative of GC&CS who was in search of information about the Abwehr. He had heard that Curry knew something about the subject and as he could not get anything out of Felix Cowgill, he had decided to take evasive-action. Curry showed him a part of the proofs of his work on the Abwehr.

The GC&CS man said that that kind of information would be invaluable to him. It would make the difference of spending ten minutes on some problem instead of the whole day. He started to discuss the *Imber*, from which a bomb had been removed at Gibraltar. There were certain parts of ISOS relating to this incident which he had great difficulty in elucidating. Curry took him up to see Victor

Rothschild, who showed him the actual bomb and explained to him the exact meaning of certain parts of the messages. He said that all that kind of information was invaluable and asked if we could let him know any other particulars. In the ordinary way I should have felt inclined to put the full facts to C or Valentine Vivian but honestly in the present atmosphere I do not feel that we should get anywhere. I should merely be told that the countenancing of irregularities of this sort was disloyal and disastrous and the wretched fellow from GC&CS who is sweating his guts out to do a decent job of work, would still be left to languish from Abwehr-starvation.

I had a talk with J.C. Masterman and T.A. Robertson about the MULLET case. It is very difficult to assess the genuineness or otherwise of [XXXXXXXXX]. Personally, I think he is working for a combination of motives. He wants to carry on his business which is quite profitable. He realises that he cannot do this unless he is allowed to move about. He will not be allowed to move about unless he renders some service. He has therefore got an assignment from the Abwehr. Whether however this involves the obtaining of information about our strength and dispositions on espionage lines or for the purpose of stimulating the military clique, and Admiral Canaris in particular, against the Nazi government is uncertain. We are going to submit the whole case to Bill Cavendish-Bentinck in order to decide whether it should be handled on a high political plane or purely as an espionage case.

20 September

Lieutenant Bedford, formerly the Security Control Officer in the Faroes, came to see me. He painted a rather gloomy picture of Larsen, our Defence Security Officer. As far as I can make out, all that Larsen does is to censor the telegrams which go out. He is a heavy drinker and whenever a ship comes in there is always some difficulty in finding him. The general form is to ring up four prostitutes and he is generally to be found with one of them. Bedford said that Larsen is quite a decent fellow but he thinks that it is unfair to leave a man too long in the Faroes. There are twenty-five ports from which sea-going fishing boats go out and these are situated in different islands. From fifty to a hundred of these boats are involved. The Faroese police, who number twelve, are generally useless and unreliable. The Norwegian official representatives are quarrelling with the representatives of the Danish government and there is no really reliable person with whom to make contact. Bedford suspects Ihlen, a Norwegian escapee who is secretary to the Norwegian consulate and has considerable fishing interests. He arrived penniless in the islands and is now quite wealthy. It is estimated that his bill for drink alone must come to something like £50 a month. One interesting fact emerged: Ihlen is in the habit of making a careful study of all foreign broadcasts. This he admits freely to all his friends. It may be therefore that he listens carefully to the KMD broadcasts which are supposed to denote the movements of submarines. Ihlen was apparently at one time in trouble with the Norwegian government about his accounts. I am proposing (a) to recommend the removal of Larsen and (b) some enquiry with the Norwegians about Ihlen. We shall then have to consider what we shall do in the Faroes.

In the evening I went down to Tring with Victor Rothschild and Duff Cooper. He talked to me about Axis Counter-Espionage. He said that he had only taken a cursory glance at the papers. He thought the Director-General's letters were admirable and that our complaints were really justifiable. He evidently did not think much of C's replies. He said that clearly all three organisations should be under one head and in one office, but that this was an ideal which could not be realised in present circumstances. The only thing to do therefore was to make the machine work as smoothly as possible by minor adjustments. He thought that it would be difficult to uproot Glenalmond and that therefore we should make a gesture by sending people down there. In return for this we should get adequate guarantees from them that in future we should get all we wanted and as rapidly as possible. I said that I was absolutely certain that operating from the country only led to stagnation. I was convinced that Glenalmond could move not only without dislocation but with considerable advantage to itself and that a good many of the workers there were similarly convinced. I thought that the *via media* which we had suggested would be a good step since nobody would relinquish any of their present responsibilities, but things would be speeded up and friction avoided. I do not think that communication would necessarily present any great difficulties since lines that we were now using to Glenalmond would be available for them to use for communicating with their registry etc. As regards their scramblers they could bring them with them. Duff said that it was only his first impression but that he meant to study the papers very closely before giving a final opinion. I told him about my visit to SIS when I saw C and Valentine Vivian about our direct communication to America. He said "Oh, I understood that all that had been settled, and you can take it from me that it has been." I said that I was quite certain that this was not C's view. While he agreed that we should communicate direct with Bill Stephenson on matters affecting the Caribbean, he did not agree that we should communicate direct on matters affecting us in North America. Duff implied that he intended to fight this point and more or less intimated that we should carry on on the assumption that we were authorised to communicate direct. This won't do, of course, and we shall have to get it settled.

Duff Cooper also talked about the black market. He seemed to think that it was wrong for the Security Service to take part in investigations of this kind, and evidently thought that we were dealing solely with the grocer who gave overweight to his customers. When we explained to him however that our only interest was that some other departments did not abuse our machinery and so jeopardise our counter-espionage enquiries and that we only imposed checks in cases of big deals involving sums such as £500 and bigger, he took a different view. He evidently did not know that the black market was operating on such a large scale. I agree in principle that it might get us into difficulties if we were associated with black market enquiries but I think that the limited action which we are taking is fully justified. Victor is going to try and arrange a meeting between Duff and Charles Teggert. I think Duff was feeling rather bad about this question since Lady Diana Cooper is threatened with a prosecution for having accepted free gratis a sack of stale bread from the baker which she was intending to give to her pigs.

Duff has a tremendous feeling about the superiority of the British race and about our system of government. He is entirely die-hard on questions such as education for the poorer classes and the old school tie. He thinks the old school tie is one of the finest institutions that we have got and that widespread education is a mistake. His argument is that people in this country have far more freedom and better conditions than in any other country in the world and that therefore there is much to be said for the existing regime. Duff also referred to the decision of the Cabinet to go to the assistance of Greece. He said that he weighed this matter up very carefully and that he had voted in favour of the action taken. His reason was that we should have lost a great deal in the eyes of the Americans if we had refused to go to the assistance of a nation which had fought so gallantly. He maintained that whatever we had done we should not have been able to go on to Tripoli, owing to lack of equipment and transport difficulties. He did think however that had we not assisted Greece we might have prevented the Germans from landing south of Benghazi.

After the collapse of France, the Prime Minister said to Duff "The end is very near, but there will be no surrender. We shall go down fighting." At this moment we were of course at our lowest ebb, without any Home Guard, and with 30,000 troops returned from Dunkirk totally unarmed.

23 September

Jasper Harker, Max Knight, Roger Fulford, Derek Tangye and I considered the case of Claud Cockburn, who had approached Tangye and wanted him, Douglas Hyde, and Wilfred Roberts MP to form a small committee to assist Cockburn in running *The Week*. The policy of *The Week* was to get inside information about government scandal. Tangye, Hyde and Roberts were to follow certain clues that he would give them and also supply him with as much information as possible. Roberts was not very sanguine about the part he could play. He said that he did not think it would be possible to get much out the civil servants, and indeed many of them might not know what was going on. We decided that in approaching Tangye, Cockburn must have a fair idea that he might well be connected with the Security Service. On the other hand, he probably felt that he was a person discontented with the general conduct of the war and therefore probably ready to assist in exposing the deficiencies of government departments. It was decided that, as far as possible, Tangye should use Hyde as a screen. It would be difficult for him to go very far since we could not possibly supply information without the knowledge of the departments concerned. There was a danger that if Tangye was ultimately found out or retired from the party Cockburn might try and expose him in the *Daily Worker*. This would be extremely damaging to ourselves. On the other hand, we thought that the party should go on for the moment as it was valuable to us to know exactly what Cockburn was up to. We formed the impression that under cover of pep movements he was really seeking inside information and having compromised Tangye he would probably try to blackmail him.

I took the weekly meeting, and we are expecting another agent here, who goes by the name of Georgie. It is just possible that he may be FRITSCHEN. He is a saboteur, and there is also a possibility of a Belgian named Johannes Huysmanns coming here, his destination at the moment being uncertain. There is another agent on the Shetland Islands, and it seems likely that Prynne is acting under instructions of SOE in Lisbon.

EGGS had got in alongside Ernesto Simoes. The latter's room has been searched but without result. EGGS' view is that Simoes is not a very high-class agent. We are still unable to get Rogeiro de Menezes' ink and we now consider the question of extracting the next letter and subjecting it to major tests.

Richard Coit came to see me. He had just come over on a fast convoy and was horrified that both the customs officer and the immigration officer at Belfast were tight when they came on board and tighter when they finally landed. He thought that some order should be issued that immigration officers and customs officers should not take drinks on board. The fact is that they have a drink with the captain of every ship in the convoy. I said I thought this should be a matter for Duff Cooper to take up with the Treasury and the Home Office. I would mention it to him next time I saw him. Coit, I gather, has come back to this country for good.

I saw Patrick Reilly in the afternoon about the Zionist intercepts. I said that I thought that the military should have been consulted but that as it had now been decided to close down the station this might not be necessary. I thought that we should have a complete set of these messages which could be studied by Alex Kellar who is responsible for Palestine. I also said that I could not see that there would be any harm in either Victor Rothschild or Herbert Hart seeing the message if Kellar thought fit. They had been of considerable assistance to him on Zionist matters. Rothschild was violently anti-Zionist and as far as I knew Hart is too. There was also the question of informing Raymund Maunsell. There has been a great deal of fuss about these telegrams, which Robinson of the Dominions Office and, I gather, also the Secretary of State did not wish to be shown to us. They have consequently been piling up. We should never have known the true situation unless the matter had been raised on the Radio Security Service Committee. Denys Page pointed out that RSS and GC&CS were dealing with this material and the Committee were asked to give them priority although they had no information about their contents. I have now got to tell the Committee that the Colonial Office was interested in these telegrams but have now decided that the station should be closed down, if it can be located by the RSS unit in Egypt. In the meantime the decoding of these telegrams is to go on. The interception would if possible be transferred to some Y unit.

Richman Stopford had made a careful analysis of the OSTRO messages as a result of which he had come to the conclusion that they are being carried probably by BOAC pilots on the west coast routes. We have decided therefore to check at Bathurst for a period of two to three weeks. We propose to inform the head of the Civil Aviation Department of the Air Ministry, the Director of Military Intelligence, the Assistant Chief of the Air Staff (Intelligence), the Governor of Gambia via the Colonial Office, and Maurice Haigh-Wood. I think that we should also inform Raymund Maunsell whose enquiries he states have reached a delicate stage. It may be that our action will jeopardise these enquiries and before moving we should have his approval.

I talked to the Director-General about Malcolm Frost and his proposal to take over the mobile units. I found great difficulty in convincing him that this was necessary. He kept on saying that as there was no evidence of any illicit transmission from this country he did not think there was any need to worry. I tried to point out that we relied upon the mobile units for the final round-up of any wireless spy. We were at this moment expecting FRITZCHEN and the prospects of locating him through wireless interception were not particularly bright. If he transmitted three times a week for about ten minutes or quarter of an hour at a time we might reasonably expect to pick him up in due course. We should then have an area of some sixty miles in which to operate the mobile units. These units were not however particularly satisfactory since unless we happened to be fairly near at the time of transmission and searching on the direct frequency we should not pick up the transmission. If the man only came up occasionally on the call sign and changed his frequency and time it was on the whole improbable that we should pick him up at all. The technical tool was not therefore a particularly efficient one. If we were called upon to operate on the Second Front we should find ourselves singularly ill-equipped. The Director-General's only suggestion was to get hold of Kenneth Morton Evans and somebody from the Post Office, exactly why the Post Office I do not know, and have a conference. I told him that it would be difficult to consult Morton Evans without bringing in Ted Maltby since the proposal was to take over certain units which were at present under Maltby's command. The Director-General did not seem to think that this mattered. Nothing can be done till he returns from leave, when I shall hope to get the whole question straightened out in his mind.

24 September

I attended a meeting of the Wireless Board at which all members were present and in addition Colonel Bevan and T.A. Robertson. C read our various notes which I imagine must have been prepared by Felix Cowgill. They were designed to show that we were not solely responsible for the double agent organisation, which is working to the Twenty Committee and the Wireless Board. The argument was not very clear to me nor to anybody else. I said that the present network really started with SNOW and was developed through the arrival of parachutists and others, some recruited here and some abroad. We originally conceived the purpose of this organisation to be insurance against penetration; deception was a subsidiary advantage gained as well as general intelligence about the enemy's intentions and organisation. I felt however that I ought to say that if we at any time were directed by the Wireless

Board to put information through our channels which would jeopardise this network, the Director-General would reserve to himself the right to refuse. In the same manner he felt that in the case of the Luis Calvo arrest he was the final arbiter. This did not mean of course that he would not give every possible consideration to the views of any department concerned. C said that he also would put his foot down if certain action by the Twenty Committee did not meet with his approval. It was not clear however what would happen if C's interests and our own were in conflict. It was pointed out that the Twenty Committee had no charter but it was agreed by all that as things had worked smoothly and everyone's interests had been reconciled without friction it was better to leave well alone. C had based his intervention in this matter on some phrases in the DMI's circular letter to members of the Wireless Board turning down the DNI's proposal that John Bevan should become chairman of the Twenty Committee. The meeting then considered certain suggestions by Ewen Montagu that there was not sufficient intelligence deception as distinct from strategical deception. He instanced the case of a query about some factory. In proceeding to this factory the agent was forced to pass certain aerodromes etc. The Air Ministry had refused to allow him to report on these aerodromes because they were new fighter aerodromes. Montagu thought that this was foolish since the aerodromes had probably already been located by the enemy and if it was desired not to emphasise the fact that they were fighter aerodromes, some form of implied deception could be put over to mislead the enemy. The same applied to army and naval matters. It was generally agreed that this should be done in future. T.A. Robertson asked that those who approve the traffic should have periodical meetings. He thought this would give greater unity to the methods employed. This was also agreed.

After the meeting Stewart Menzies showed me a copy of a BJ from Madrid to Tokyo disclosing a long report by PEPPERMINT to his masters. This report embodies a good deal of the information which we gave to PEPPERMINT but it also deals with other matters. There is no reason to suspect any disloyalty on PEPPERMINT's part. In fact, he seems to have done pretty well. The other facts mentioned may be in answer to certain questions which were put to him by his masters or may have been invented by Angel Alcazar de Velasco.

I had a discussion with the Director-General about our obligations on the Second Front. He said that he would take this matter up on his return. He told me that during his absence he wished me to talk to Duff Cooper about (a) OSTRO and (b) direct representation in America. He thought I should tell Duff Cooper what Valentine Vivian had told me about Bill Stephenson, namely that SIS thought that if we had direct representation Stephenson would try and play one party off against the other. I told the Director-General that in my view SIS would be considerably strengthened in their dealings with Stephenson if we had direct representation since he, the D-G, would be much more likely to drop heavily upon Stephenson than SIS, who seem to be afraid of him. I told the Director-General that they had considered his replacement by Denham, but had ultimately come to the conclusion that he was so well dug-in with Bill Donovan and President Roosevelt that there would be a major upheaval if he were removed.

I went over this afternoon to see C and Sir Edward Bridges about PEPPERMINT. Bridges was mainly worried about MacCarthy who is quoted as one of PEPPERMINT 's informants. MacCarthy is employed in the War Cabinet offices and he resides in the same house as PEPPERMINT who knows him and, I think, regards him as being mildly indiscreet. I explained that the statement attributed to MacCarthy had not necessarily emanated from him. PEPPERMINT might have been using him as a peg in which to hang the information. Bridges, however, wished to get rid of MacCarthy in any case, as he was inefficicent. I asked him to postpone any action that he could for two or three weeks, which he agreed to do.

C talked to me about an ISOS message indicating that General Henri Giraud was to be approached by a V-Mann. He said that he was dropping a man over tonight to warn Giraud. He also told me that Giraud was thoroughly on our side and that 75% of the army at least were with us. He had recently dropped an anti-tank gun in order that the French could adapt their armoured vehicles to take these guns as soon as the second front opened. The man who took the gun over said that the landing-place was floodlit to a degree that was almost unbelievable. C had sub-sequently had a message to say that the gun had been received intact, and that the operation had been entirely successful. It is to be hoped that he is not being dou-ble-crossed. Slesser, late of the *Deuxième Bureau*, is in command of a battalion and was ready a short time ago to take Nantes. We were prepared to meet him. The French are getting to a stage where it may be rather difficult to hold them. As regards North Africa, the Americans have been making all sorts of approaches but it is not known yet for certain what opposition there is likely to be. On the whole it is considered unlikely that the French Navy will put up much of a show since they well realise that it can only lead to the bombing of Toulon. C is rather worried about certain members of the *Deuxième Bureau* who had recently been sacked. They were formerly working with us. Colonel Louis Rivet is no longer head of the *Bureau,* but is working very much behind the scenes.

The Radio Security Service has once more blotted its copybook. It was co-operat-ing with ourselves in a special exercise run by GOC Northern Command. The problem was to detect an illicit transmitter of our own which was being run by Swann and also another which was to have been provided by the Royal Signals. At the last moment the Royal Signals failed to produce a transmitter or to inform Elmes or Sclater. Elmes had strict instructions not to make an arrest without prior reference to one of our officers. Our own transmitter had been located by intelli-gence means and not by the mobile units. Elmes started to work on what he believed was the transmitter provided by the Royal Signals. Unfortunately, how-ever, he got on to the transmitter being used by the umpire controlling the operation. This transmitter was located at Jesmond and Elmes who I believe got some indication from Peter Hope that the second transmitter would be in this area, put two and two together. Elmes then observed an army wireless vehicle hearing umpire marks, in which were two operators wearing single white arm-bands instead of two white arm-bands, the official marking. He leaped to the conclusion that this must be the agent's transmitter. He then effected the arrest of the operators in collaboration with the police. The operators protesting violently that they were official umpires, were taken to police headquarters where they were detained. It subsequently transpired that they were those working under the direction of the Chief Umpire controlling the exercise and that owing to the breakdown in the umpire's communications which resulted, the exercise came to an abrupt and early conclusion. The GOC, General Brooman-White and his staff, were not unnaturally extremely annoyed. They were loudly demanding blood, but were stalled by being referred to the Director of Military Intelligence. It is to be hoped that in future RSS will be able to catch the spy and not the umpire.

Gilbert Lennox came to see me about the prosecution of Colonel Daubeny for revealing information about Operation TORCH. The Chief of Staff now wants to postpone the prosecution till after the operation as they feel that it will give away our order of battle to a number of unauthorised persons even though the proceedings are held *in camera*. There has been a further incident in connection with TORCH. A case of maps which had been sent to Lord Swinton en route for the port of departure has been opened and resealed. The officer in charge of the party is suspected. It is suggested that Edward Hinchley-Cooke and Len Burt after getting the full facts should investigate. The difficulty in these matters is to avoid spreading the leakage through emphasising its importance.

28 September

I had a meeting Dick White, Richman Stopford and Herbert Hart about action in connection with OSTRO. We sent off a more explicit telegram to Raymund Maunsell explaining to him our reasons for thinking that we are more likely to be successful in Bathurst than in the Sudan. We decided that action in the Sudan would take place ten days after the first search at Bathurst. In order to set the wheels in motion I went to see Charles Medhurst to get his help with Civil Aviation. He told me that he had seen the Vice Chief of the Air Staff who approved of our action, and he, Medhurst, would have a talk with William Hildred of Civil Aviation, and tell him that he had to be prepared for a good many protests owing to the searching of aircraft and possible delays. Medhurst suggested that it might be possible to make some arrangements for other planes to take on the passengers after they had been searched.

If ISOS only produces a fiftieth part it should be included in the calculations of the General Staff.

Ivan Maisky is still propaganding here about a Second Front. There is a certain irony in the present situation. Russia with the utmost cynicism signed the Russo-German pact and thereby precipitated a world war, doubtless on the assumption that the British Empire and Germany would fight themselves to a standstill when

Russia would come down like a vulture and pick up the pieces. It is now Russia and Germany that are fighting themselves into a state of exhaustion while we are to a certain degree enjoying a welcome respite. This situation must be a source of considerable irritation to old Joe, although in advocating a Second Front he fails to recognise that we are already fighting a war in the Middle East, in the Atlantic and by aerial bombardment of Germany, not to speak of supplying war materials to Russia and other theatres of war.

I dined with Barty Pleydell-Bouverie and I asked him a good deal about British Security Co-ordination. He confirmed all my stories about agents employed in the embassies in Washington DC which had caused so much trouble between BSC and the FBI. I asked him how far Stephenson's removal would have caused an upheaval. He said that Bill Donovan would probably have protested but he did not think it would have gone much further than that. He does not think Donovan's influence in the White House was particularly strong.

30 September

I had a slight dust-up with Jasper Harker on the question of Night Duty Officers and I said I thought there ought to be some uniform procedure throughout the office. I was quite ready to withdraw the privileges from certain officers in B Division provided people like Abbott did night-duty. Harker evidently does not wish to deal with this.

I took the weekly meeting. Herbert Hart said that there had been a large number of inaccurate reports from the Paul Fidrmuc (OSTRO) source reaching the Germans this week, dealing with the alleged arrival of British troops in India, the "launching" of the *Hood* and *Anson*, both of which have been in commission for some time, etc.

We have heard that FRITZCHEN is to leave on some date prior to 9 October.
Bamford of the Delhi Intelligence Bureau came to see me about Peter Fleming, who is returning to this country from India. He is responsible to General Archie Wavell for deception work but it seems, however, that his channels to the enemy are slow and complex. I should say that what he required was a good double-cross agent in touch with Kabul where all the Axis countries are represented. The Delhi Intelligence Bureau should be able to provide such an agent. Bamford is going to see Fleming and John Bevan on this matter.

I saw Cuthbert Bowlby who has just returned from the Middle East. I had hoped that he might be able to tell us something about OSTRO and the investigations being carried out on this subject in Egypt but unfortunately he seemed to know very little. He is of course concerned with the offensive side of espionage. I gather that he leaves most of the defensive work entirely to Rodney Dennys. Equally, Bowlby seemed to be somewhat ignorant about MAX and MORITZ.

MAX and MORITZ were suspected double agents run by the Soviets whose wireless traffic to Sofia had intrigued and baffled RSS.

APPENDIX I

MI5 organisation

Director-General	Sir David Petrie
Deputy D-G	Jasper Harker
Legal Adviser	Jim Hale
Operations	Gilbert Lennox
A Division	Charles Butler
	Malcolm Cumming
	Reg Horrocks
B Division	Guy Liddell
	Dick White
	Malcolm Frost
B1(a)	T.A. Robertson
Special Agents	
B1(b)	Herbert Hart
Special Research	
B1(c)	Victor Rothschild
Sabotage	
B1(d)	Ronnie Haylor
RVPS	
B1(e)	Robin Stephens
Camp 020	
B1(f)	Courtney Young
Japanese Espionage	
B1(g)	Dick Brooman-White
Spanish Espionage	
B1(h)	Cecil Liddell
Ireland	
B1(k)	Mr Machell
Leakages	

B2 Agents	Richman Stopford
B3 Communications	Malcolm Frost
B3 (a) Censorship	Malcolm Frost
B3(b) Illicit Wireless	F.A. Sclater
B3(c) Light Signalling	Fl-Lt. Walker
B4 Country Sections	Jock Whyte
B4(a) Espionage	Jock Whyte
B4(b) Industrial Espionage	Mr Craufurd
B5 Investigations	Len Burt
B6 Watchers	Harry Hunter
PS Press Section	Derek Tangye
C Division Examination of Credentials	Harry Allen Major Bacon
D Division Travel Control	Harry Allen Colonel Norman
E Division Alien Control	Theo Turner Kenneth Younger
F Division Subversion	Roger Hollis Blanshard Stamp
F1 Military Security	Colonel Alexander
F2 Left-Wing	Roger Hollis

F2(a) Communist Party	David Clarke
F2(b) Comintern	
F2(c) Russian Intelligence	Mr Pilkington
F3 Ring Wing	Francis Aiken-Sneath
F4 Pacifists	Roger Fulford

APPENDIX II

Mode of arrival of German agents

A Illegal arrivals i.e. by other than recognised and approved channels

1 Surreptitious arrivals
  (a) *by rowing boat ex-trawler towed across the Channel by minesweeper*
      1   Meier, Carl   03.09.40   Dymchurch, Kent
      2   van den Kieboom, Charles
      3   Waldberg, Carl   03.09.40   Lydd on Sea, Kent
      4   Pons, Sjoerd
  (b) *Parachute*
      1   SUMMER   06.09.40   Denton, Northants
      2   TATE   19.09.40   Willingham, Cambs
      3   GANDER   03.10.40   Wellingborough, Northants
      4   Ter Braak, Jan   02.10.40   Haversham, Bucks
      5   Jakobs, Josef   31.01.40   Ramsey, Hunts
      6   Richter, Karel   12.05.41   London Colney, Herts
  (c) *Rubber boat ex-seaplane*
      1   Walti, Werner   30.09.40   south of Moray Firth
      2   de Deeker, François
      3   Eriksson, Vera
      4   Lund   25.10.40
      5   Joost
      6   Edwardsen
      7   MUTT   47.04.41
      8   JEFF
2 Refugee parties from Norway
  (a) MV *Volga*
      Hansson   06.03.41   Shetland
      Oien
      4 innocent passengers

   (b) MV *Taanevik*
        Hansen   27.04.41 Wick
        Torgersen
        Strandmoen
        Hansen
   (c) MV *Hernie*
        Wallem   06.07.41 Shetland
        2 innocent Norwegians
   (d) MV *Hornfjell*
        Saetrang   13.09.41 Iceland
        7 others

3 Other illegal arrivals
   (a) *La Part Bien*   Jonassen 23.09.40 Plymouth
        de Lee
        Libot
   (b) *Josephine*   Robles   12.11.40 Fishguard
        Hecheveria
        Pazos
        Evertsen
        Krag
        Vandam
        Martinez
        Jezequel

B Legal arrival

1 By air from Lisbon
   1   GIRAFFE   28.09.40
   2   DOOLITTLE   11.10.40
   3   TRICYCLE   10.12.40
   4   Gerth Van Wijk   05.04.41

2 By ship from Lisbon
   1   FATHER   20.06.41
   2   CARELESS   15.07.41
   3   THE SNARK   04.07.41

3 Seamen
   1   De Jaegar   04.10.40
   2   Laureyssens   06.12.40
   3   Timmerman   01.09.41

C Agents sent to Ireland

The following agents all landed or descended surreptitiously:

   (a) *by rowing boat ex-trawler*

1	Obed, Henry	July 1940
2	Tributh, Herbert	July 1940
3	Gartmer	July 1940

   (b) *by parachute*

1	Goertz, Herman	May 1940
2	Marschner, Hans	March 1941
3	Lenihan, Joseph	July 1941

   (c) *Rubber boat ex-U-boat*

1	Preetz, Willi	June 1940
2	Anderson	June 1940

D Captured on the high seas

   (a) *Vesli Kare*

Hoel	18.8.40	King Oscar's Fjord
Giaever		
Hannestad		
Coll, Axel		

   (b) *Freese*

Finckenstein	Jan Mayen Island
Hansen	
5 others	

Compiled by Helenus Milmo, 25.11.1941 B1(b)

INDEX